CELTIC POLITICS

Politics in Scotland, Ireland, and Wales

Kurt W. Jefferson

University Press of America,® Inc.
Lanham · Boulder · New York · Toronto · Plymouth, UK

4501 Forbes Boulevard
Suite 200
Lanham, Maryland 20706
UPA Acquisitions Department (301) 459-3366

Estover Road
Plymouth PL6 7PY
United Kingdom

Printed in the United States of America
British Library Cataloging in Publication Information Available

Library of Congress Control Number: 2011927686
ISBN: 978-0-7618-5580-4 (paperback : alk. paper)
eISBN: 978-0-7618-5581-1

™ The paper used in this publication meets the minimum requirements of American National Standard for Information Sciences—Permanence of Paper for Printed Library Materials, ANSI Z39.48-1992

Contents

Preface

Writing this book was a true labor of enjoyment. I began studying British history as an undergraduate at Western Illinois University (WIU) in Macomb, Illinois, USA in 1986. I took an upper-level course on the history of England from pre-history to 1688 with Dr. Thomas Watkins. Dr. Watkins was an expert in Roman history and Roman Britain (55 BC to 450 AD). His erudition, acumen, and enthusiasm for British history rubbed off on me. I also remember classmates in that history class missing a class period because they had gone to see a wildly popular Irish rock band, U-2, on the other side of our state in Champaign, Illinois. They came back to class humming the haunting song, "Sunday, Bloody Sunday" and, ironically, over twenty years on the meaning of that song is discussed at length in this book. A semester (a few months) later, I wrote a paper (as a senior majoring in political science) in an American foreign policy course taught by an excellent political scientist, Dr. William Anderson, at WIU. The paper was a United States foreign policy memorandum on how to handle the Ulster problem. This too stoked my interest in Britain and the Celtic regions of the United Kingdom (UK). When I went off to graduate school I knew I wanted to study British politics. That is exactly what I did. My great-grandfather emigrated from Scotland to the United States (and Ellis Island) in 1893. I had heard much about my Scottish heritage from my grandfather and my mother as a child. The fact that my mother's family was named "Wallace" also spurred much interest given the long ties to Scotland (and even Northern Ireland) that name connotes (think "Braveheart!")

When I went to the United Kingdom for the first time in 1990, I truly found myself becoming more interested in British politics and history. I went to the House of Commons. I traveled throughout England and Scotland. I had a good experience. I went back in 1992 and did fieldwork for my dissertation on the Scottish National Party (SNP). It was an interesting process interviewing SNP activists and leaders. Little did I know that a small, nationalist party would by the time this book was ready to go to press (15 years later) be in control of Scotland's devolved government. I actually interviewed several current SNP cabinet officials when they were right out of college and just getting started in politics! They were a wide-eyed bunch: idealistic and grateful to talk to anyone who would listen to their ideas for Scotland! After starting my full-time career as a college professor in which I teach about Britain and the European Union (EU) as well as international politics, I continued to study Britain, but not in as much depth as I had in graduate school and while writing my dissertation. My interests moved on to other topics in comparative and international politics. However, I made another trip to the UK in 2003. That trip got me interested in writing this book. I had continued to write on Scotland and compare it to newly developing small regions and states in the EU (namely, Slovenia). But, that trip allowed me to see how much the UK had changed since 1992 and my last trip to Scotland and England. The rise of the Labour Party in power under Tony Blair after 1997 transformed the UK into a different state constitutionally as devolution took place in 1999 in Scotland and Wales. It also occurred in 1998 in Northern Ireland. So, much was changing and it all was manifesting how important the Celtic regions and nations were to political developments in the UK. Also, the role of the EU (which was the European Community when I began studying it in the late 1980s) was much enhanced and affecting the plight of Scots, Welsh, and Irish. As a result, I decided to write a book on "Celtic Politics." I had some knowledge of Irish politics in the south and north of the Emerald Isle. But, it was largely via a British lens. So, I sought to incorporate much about the Republic of Ireland and its development historically as well as the Northern Irish statelet too. I found all of this fascinating and clearly in the historical development of the Celtic areas of Britain and Ireland one sees the shadow of the English and their influence in all things (this influence goes back to 1166 in Ireland).

My goal in writing this book has not been to take sides in any historical or contemporary debates about the rights and plight of the Celts in British or Irish national life. As an American, I hope I bring some objectivity to the table in describing politics and history in an area that gets little academic play in England and the United States—that is, Celtic politics. My father always told me, "One should write to inform, rather than impress." I hope I have kept to that aphorism. Thus, creating a loose model of Celtic politics seems like an important goal and as a heuristic for students of British, Irish, and European politics and history this seems like something that will help them make sense of these regions and people that are developing in a transformational age (as I allude to in the concluding chapter). Political scientists try to create models or theories (as we fashion them) to help us organize and understand facts. These models will help us generalize about empirical data and information that we use in our investigations. I think in this sense, and with this spirit in mind, I have tried to add to the discussion in the study of comparative politics, British politics, Irish politics, and EU politics. The need for more discussion and analysis of Celtic politics (or politics in Scotland, Ireland, and Wales) in various governing contexts—whether national, sub-national, regional or global—is relevant to the newly evolving Celtic politics model. I hope this textbook is a welcome, refreshing, and new perspective for students in many disciplines (not just political science and history) as I have tried to purposely make it interdisciplinary.

I would like to thank several individuals for their support and encouragement in writing this book. First, I thank my parents, Bob and Sally Jefferson for their love and support. They both read the manuscript and my father (the former Dean of the Gordon Ford College of Business at Western Kentucky and Professor Emeritus of Marketing) helped me write the instructor's manual. My mother was a longtime lecturer in business communication at WIU and Illinois State University. I thank Richard Allen of the University of Sunderland, Sam Goodfellow of Westminster College, Paul Ward of the University of Huddersfield, and Robert Tyler, Visiting Fulbright-Robertson Professor of History at Westminster College (2009-10) for reading parts of the manuscript. This is a better work of scholarship because of their criticisms and insights. I thank Lawrence Black of Durham University and Rob Havers and Bill Young of Westminster College for their encouragement in writing the textbook, each of them gave me helpful comments in numerous discussions about British and Irish society, culture, history, and politics. I thank my PhD adviser David M. Wood, Professor Emeritus of Political Science at the University of Missouri–Columbia, for introducing, instructing, and guiding me into the professional field of British and EU politics. His wisdom and knowledge were outstanding and he was great to work with. I also thank him for his willingness to review the manuscript and make comments on it. I also thank then-dean (now president) Barney Forsythe of Westminster College and the Council of Chairs for financing parts of the book given their issuing of a summer research grant to me in 2006. I also want to thank my colleague Dale Ley, graphics specialist at Westminster College, for his outstanding work in creating the book's layout. Without his hard work and help, this project could not have been completed. I thank my nephew, Jason Gilbert, who spent several days with me in Fulton, Missouri (in the summer of 2010) indexing the book. He did an excellent job. I thank my wife, Lori, for her love and willingness to put up with me during the book writing phase. I thank her and my daughter Nikki for proofreading. And, last, I thank my children, Kelly, Megan, and Nicole, for their patience in accepting their father who, at times, became obsessed with the Celts and their politics and history. Megan heard more than once that her name was a Welsh one. Kelly was told that her name was Irish for "Brave," and Nikki smiled and yawned each time I gave them (or myself) a lecture on Tony Blair, William Wallace, Bertie Ahern, Owain Glyn dŵr or Winston Churchill. For these things, this book is dedicated to them. I accept responsibility for any errors of fact or interpretation. The model and the discussion herein remain my own.

Kurt W. Jefferson
Fulton, Missouri, USA
Winter 2011

CHAPTER ONE

Introduction

Celtic Politics as a Unit of Study

This book will take the reader down a path that is not trod normally in the study of British or European politics. It will focus exclusively on the politics and political and institutional evolution of the Celtic people of the United Kingdom (UK) and Ireland. A few books exist on this topic. Some specialized studies in political science and history exist on the nations of *the Celtic fringe* in British politics. However, a decent comprehensive treatment of national political life in the Celtic regions of the British Isles is difficult to find. What's more, virtually no comparative textbooks are found on the politics of the Celtic fringe and its relationship to developments in an integrating European context. Given the profound importance of Britons and their political evolution historically (aside from the *Anglo-Saxons* and, eventually, English political development), this book will look at the three major Celtic regions: Scotland, Ireland, and Wales, in that order (without respect to importance or normative or emotive causation, but rather size/population and territory—largest to smallest). Other smaller Celtic groups, such as the Cornish in Southwestern England, the Manx on the Isle of Man in the Irish Sea, or the historical Picts in Scotland or Bretons in France, will not factor as much into this work due to the consequences of time and space. However, that is not to say that other non-Anglo-Saxon groups are not important to the English-centered political settlement in the United Kingdom since the reign of Alfred the Great in the ninth century. Certainly, the entanglements of the French nobility and the English nobility, especially after 1066 and the Norman invasion have left historically an indelible mark on the institutions of government in Britain. The Celtic fringe has taken on increased salience in the political life of the UK in the last two centuries and it continued to play an important role in British and European politics at the dawn of the twenty-first century.

After the Second World War, as seen in concert with the rise of nationalism in Scotland, Wales, Quebec, Catalonia, the Basque region of Spain, and other contexts globally, the Celtic peoples have watched their fortunes change dramatically as pieces in the patchwork quilt of British politics. What were once considered backwards and minor nations geo-politically for landed elites in the long span of Anglo-Saxon governance in Britain became major regions of political, social, and economic development. Not only for political reasons, as was the case in Scotland as it was a bastion of Conservative Party support in the 1950s and swung to the Labour Party in the 1960s and became the permanent base of support and solidity for the party in its run up to regaining power after 18 years in the wilderness in 1997, but for social, cultural, and economic reasons, did the Celtic people move toward the realization of a new politics in the second half of the twentieth century. However, much of their "new" politics were rooted in ancient discussions and conflicts tied to time-honored concepts such as home rule, sovereignty, and political liberty.

Can we say that the politics of the Celtic fringe warrants status as a separate unit of study within British politics, European politics, and political science as well? This question will be addressed in greater detail in both the current and last chapters. However, with the awkward, yet salient seemingly contradictory trends of nationalism on one level clashing with supranationalism on another level (both in Europe and globally—from Basques in Spain and France to Quebecois in Quebec to the Hindu nationalist Bhataryia Janata Party in India, for example), the Celtic regions of Britain can be analyzed for their distinct ethnic, cultural, political, economic, and regional importance. They can also be viewed within a broader conceptualization in international relations as part of a Europe of regions that will continue to play an important role in the evolution of the European Union (EU). We will discuss the Celtic fringe and its relationship to multi-level governance and the EU in the last chapter as well. With these conceptualizations, Scotland, the Irish Republic, Northern Ireland, and Wales all play a role in events changing the landscape of not only Britain, but also Europe. These regions have seen centripetal forces push them to new levels of political institutionalization and their roles as independent units of analysis, apart from the UK, have changed the empirical understanding of these regions and nations. The normative discussion about these nations and their "countries" has been altered as well. Hence, although the Republic of Ireland is a bona fide nation-state, the other nations of the Celtic fringe under analysis in this book (Scots, Northern Irish, and Welsh) may be on their way toward representation as full-fledged nation-states at some point in their development in the twenty-first century. Although purely speculative, this statement may not be as farfetched as one might have thought in the 1960s and 1970s. Whether each of these nations should eventually possess and govern independent sovereign nation-states is another question altogether.

Indeed, the heightened importance of the Celtic regions of the UK by the 1970s led students of British politics to change their Anglo-centric approach to the study of politics from expressed "English" institutions and Anglo-Saxon norms and mores to the inchoate discussion of a multi-ethnic or multi-national Britain replete with special histories, stories, cultures, institutions, and so on. This change was difficult for many given the fact that British politics was essentially conceptualized as an English phenomenon and the study of British politics was best done by studying the electorate in its relatively straightforward and dichotomous manner. For years the British electorate was known for its "homogeneity and simplicity" (Kellas 1989). The electorate was divided by socioeconomic factors rather than regional dissimilarities. The two party arrangement strengthened the dichotomous nature of the vote along working class and middle class lines; hence third parties, i.e. minor parties predicated upon nationalist or regional themes, did not fare as well at the polls. In 1970, the two major parties got all but 14 seats in the House of Commons. This changed in 1974. In studying the British electorate, scholars generalized about the social, economic, and political characteristics of the entire state. "England" and "English politics" were seen as synonymous with British (i.e. English, Scottish, Welsh, and Irish) politics and society. Political scientist Richard Rose's standard text on British government, *Politics in England* (1965), is an example of this homogenous portrayal. Historians Clayton and David Roberts's *A History of England* (1980) was a main text in British history (for American students), and it too depicted an Anglo-centric approach to the study of a multi-national state (Roberts and Roberts 1980; Rose 1965). Although both of these works were popular among students of British politics and history, they evince the transformation of the study of how students of Britain and its politics have thought about the increased importance the Celtic fringe displayed in the last decades of the twentieth century.

Another interesting issue that arises in the study of politics in Scotland, Ireland, and Wales is that much of what is written on the Celtic fringe is written from these areas. Few commentators outside the Celtic parts of Britain and Ireland are found in the literature in political science and other disciplines. This insularity has tended to obscure and leave a perception that national politics in the regions of the UK and Ireland are not as important as politics in England or British politics in general. The Celtic fringe provides an intriguing context to look at both British and European politics in the twenty-first century. It also provides a vibrant context for issues confronting other parts of the globe as well.

Chapter Two will provide an overview of Scottish, Irish, and Welsh history. The remainder of the book will then focus on the context and the politics in those Celtic areas as distinct phenomena, but undoubtedly connected by ethnicity, politics, and culture (language, sports, religion, etc.). The latter will be discussed in Chapter Six. The concluding chapter (Chapter Seven) will look at speculative issues related to the Celtic nations and their transforming politics in the twenty-first century. Questions related to internationalizing and globalizing forces (such as the EU), structural change politically, and psychological change will be addressed. We will also ask if a distinctive "Celtic politics" is apparent vis-à-vis the English political model that has dominated the British mainland for centuries. This appears to be a highly subjective question, laden with normative assumptions. But, it may have some empirical merit. Remember, political scientists are interested in applying the theory to the facts and seeing if those facts help explain the theoretical assumptions. We will try to answer that question in the final chapter. The story of the Celtic nations under discussion here (Scots, Irish, and Welsh) is a profoundly important one for both historical and contemporaneous reasons. The distinct politics of these peoples should be understood ipso facto and also in the larger context of UK politics. Few have attempted to bring the consolidated empirical discussion of these people to print in order to explain not only normative political considerations, but also outcomes and potential solutions to the issues and politics that confront these regions of Great

Britain and Ireland. Although the author may evince some biases in his work, any analysis will attempt hopefully to look at various points of view and allow readers to make up their own minds as to the future of the unitary political state in Britain, the importance of Celtic fringe in British and Irish political life, the future of the Celtic nations in European politics, and the ways to best interpret politics and history within Celtic as well as English contexts.

The Study of British Politics

The study of the British *political system* has for years been synonymous with "English" politics. In attempting to understand and analyze the political, social, and economic development of the UK, political scientists tended to overemphasize the role of England and downplay the role of the Celtic nations in British national life. A classic example of this asymmetrical Anglo-centric approach was Rose's *Politics in England* (as seen above). Rose's work is systematic and authoritative. It was written at a time when the systems theory propounded by political scientist David Easton was being used to analyze the variables that helped students understand holistically how government functioned and reacted to various types of causality. However, Rose engaged in a time-honored approach to the study of British politics, that held fast in the late twentieth century, by overly generalizing about the variables found in English politics and society as he applied them to the entire UK. Rose also mentioned, as others did before him, that England provided the appropriate context to understand mature, bloodless, civilized democratic development at its best. Although, Anglo-Saxon politics did indeed provide the democracies of the global North and South with appropriate models of democratization in terms of political processes, the assertion is dubious given the examples one can give to question the time-honored civility and linear progress that is connoted in the assertion. For example, the question of Ireland in British politics (as we shall see below) led to much bloodshed in the twentieth century both in the north and in the south of that land. Excessive institutionalization has also been a perennial problem for political scientists trying to understand British politics. Although the structure and function of the British House of Commons is important, several works focus more on the machinations of the UK legislature at the expense of the particularisms in other parts of the realm. Political scientist Samuel H. Beer's work *The British Political System* (1958) and his famous *British Politics in the Collectivist Age* (1965) are two solid studies of British legislative, executive, and party politics, but again, they emphasize the function and process and less the substance of issues that may affect historically the Celtic Fringe (Beer 1958 and 1965). Thus, the student of political science has been given the impression that all one needs to know is found in English society and politics and the ideological and intellectual currents in England will tell us what is happening in the various corners of Britain. Beer wrote *Britain Against Itself* (1982) as a kind of reflection on the end of the two-party consensus in English politics. In fairness to him, he does deal with the politics of culture and political culture (both concepts will be addressed below in Chapter Six), but his argument that deference in the British political culture ends in the 1960s due to various socio-cultural variables such as the Beatles or the Rolling Stones, does not help explain the alienation that mounts in the Celtic Fringe by the late 1960s and early 1970s (Beer 1982). Again the Anglo-centric focus does not help political scientists in explaining all aspects of British politics insofar as they relate to political culture.

Many political scientists have tried to explain British politics through a lens of modernization and economic and political development. Political scientists Gabriel A. Almond and G. Bingham Powell applied a developmental approach in *comparative politics*. Their typology for understanding developing and developed nation-states has been applied to British politics. Essentially Rose's work did this as well. But, the modernization of the British system is a topic political scientists and historians have studied much since the 1960s. Again, to look at the categories of a state's capabilities (which include extractive, regulative, distributive, symbolic, responsive, and domestic and international) one may find a different set of empirical outcomes in the Celtic areas of the UK and Ireland than England.

Applying Almond and Powell's Typology on Capabilities of Political Systems: England, Scotland, Wales, and Ireland

In 1966, Almond and Powell wrote the seminal *Comparative Politics: A Developmental Approach* (Almond and Powell 1966). The book reflected the interest in American political science with a behavioral approach to understanding empirically how nation-states evolved in both Western industrialized and non-Western developing contexts. In using a conceptual approach that would yield more analytical fruit and less description, Almond and Powell hoped that development studies would bring the discipline a greater understanding of the nuances of politics in terms of the capacities and capabilities of political systems. Instead of just describing how politics worked, actually looking at cause and effects, as well as how stable political systems were was emphasized. It captured a whole generation of political scientists in the discipline's sub-field of comparative politics. Certainly, Almond and Powell's typology is not flawless. It is somewhat subjective in terms of criteria, reflects a certain amount of ethnocentrism, and may lead to circular reasoning in understanding causes and effects within systems (for example, authoritarian or democratic political systems perform the way they do because they are authoritarian or democratic). Still, one way to demonstrate differences between the English political system and Celtic political environments is to empirically test them against the assumptions of a model like the development approach of Almond and Powell.

	England	Scotland	Wales	Ireland
Extractive	Light manufacturing, labor, services, agriculture	Coal, oil, agriculture, fishing, services	Agriculture, fishing, services	Agriculture, fishing, services, light manufacturing
Regulative	Common law system	Scots law system (civil or codified law system)	Common law system	Irish legal system (mix of Common law and European continental law)
Distributive	Ancient customs and class distinctions, had elitist educational system (change began in 1960s)	Educational system (more egalitarian, yet sectarian at primary and secondary levels), clan-based politics historically	Customs inherited from English after 1283	Education, role of church in honors and recognition, egalitarian traditions
Symbolic	National symbols of monarchy, military, Union of 1707 flag—Union Jack, St. George's Cross, Anglican Church	Scottish saltire and lion rampant flags, the Kirk, Tartans of Clans, Scottish Crown Jewels, Stone of Scone	Ancient Welsh monarchies, Welsh language and culture, Welsh Dragon flag	The Irish tricolor, symbols of parliamentary democracy (Dail, Taoseich)
Responsive	Constitutional monarchy—how flexible is the constitution?	The Scottish Parliament after 1999 in Edinburgh	Welsh Assembly after 1999 in Cardiff	The Dail after 1922 in Dublin
Domestic & International	A new image on global stage—decentralizing (federalizing?) UK	A newly evolving Scottish nation in both the UK and the EU	A newly evolving Welsh region in the UK and the EU	A post-British Commonwealth (after 1949), Irish Republic that evolves within the EU after 1981

Table 1.1 Almond and Powell's Typology of Political System Performance as Applied to England and the Celtic Nations (Scotland, Ireland, and Wales)

For Almond and Powell, the extractive capabilities, which draw on materials and human resources from domestic and international contexts such as economic resources (commodities—raw materials, foodstuffs, labor, minerals, etc), are a key component of any political system. England may have different extractive capabilities such as greater services, agricultural outputs, greater numbers in the workforce, and various types of light manufacturing. Scots and Welsh may emphasize different extractive capabilities like natural resources such as coal, aluminum, and other heavy industries found historically on the Celtic fringe. North Sea oil for Scots and fishing for both Welsh and Scots may be seen as a vital extractive variable in their national lives. Second, Almond and Powell use regulative capabilities that include controlling the behavior of individuals and groups through law enforcement and other measures. England may see one type of law based on Anglo-Saxon common law whereas Scots may see Scots law and other domestic constraints factoring into regulating social behavior in Scotland. Also, economic constraints such as fiscal policies, the House of Commons and the Scottish Parliament may take separate approaches to stimulating economic activity in England and Scotland respectively. Third, distributive capabilities are an important component of the developmental model. To what extent is the distribution of values important in Celtic and Anlgo-Saxon cultures and societies? How are services, goods, honors, and opportunities handed out? Does the state or the private sector play a role in these calculations and to what extent? Scots and Welsh may be more statist than English. A social democratic tenor politically seems to be more in tune with Scottish and Welsh political cultures than a more conservative, yet laissez-faire, class-based English culture. Fourth, symbolic capabilities differentiate the two contexts—England and the Celtic fringe. How fluid is symbolic flow from domestic to global contexts? Do Scottish and Welsh symbols offset UK or English symbols? What does the use of the *Scottish Saltire* (Cross of St. Andrews) or the lion rampant flags mean versus the Union Jack or St. George's Cross? Is the symbolic capability of each region in the UK and Ireland hampered or helped by an increase in national symbols in the Celtic fringe that challenge English symbols or UK ones? Scots and Welsh have plenty of symbols that help underscore national identity. The English do so as well and their national consciousness is growing with more English willing to identify with distinctly English symbols (the national soccer squad in international competitions, various cultural and literary icons, etc.) Can these symbols interact without the rise of virulent nationalism? Fifth, responsive capabilities tie to relationships between inputs and outputs. It is a holistic assumption that looks at whether governments in parts of the UK will attempt to suppress or liberate these forces. How flexible are the levers of power in Scotland, Wales, and England? Can Scots have political institutions in both Edinburgh and London and still maintain both Scottish and British identity and loyalty? Empirically this may be challenged, but it may also be verified via experience, and also increased multi-level governance (factoring the role of the EU in Britain's domestic and international politics) may actually allow the Celtic nations to have more flexible responsive capabilities than the Westminster government in London. Finally, domestic and international capabilities are the sum of the parts of all of the previous five developmental capabilities. Can the system function and maintain systemic stability given the pressures on each layer of capabilities? This becomes a question of institutionalization to a certain extent (which will be addressed in Chapter Five). But, we do see a pattern of distinctly Celtic capabilities that are somewhat exclusive of English capabilities in the Westminster political system. Hence, this model may allow for separate regional and national development of politics within and outside the scope of British national politics. Of course, the EU context also challenges the assumptions of an Anglo-centric political system in the lives of Celts on the periphery in British politics, since the Celtic fringe may evolve as a separate region in Europe without having complete political autonomy or sovereignty in a formalized sense (even if devolved structures persist).

Is There A Distinct "Celtic" Model of Politics?

In political science, the interest in finding appropriate conceptual models or theories to explain facts is important. Unlike historians, political scientists are trying to find ways in which generalizations about socio-political phenomena may be made and applied. Historians shy away from broad-gauged generalizations. They prefer to let the facts drive theory. Political scientists often times do the opposite. Creating broad gauged theories or mid-range theories to help explain the facts or empirical pieces of information that fit into the context of the scientific inquiry is important. The political scientist believes that to build on theory (or models) helps the discipline (and future political scientists) begin to explain why politics occur the way it does in various contexts.

In the Celtic nations of Britain and Ireland, the question is rarely asked if these people have a distinct type of politics that may be different from the models they have inherited from the English. Over centuries of interaction between Anglo-Saxons and Celts (given customs, mores, and political and social systems), can we say that Scots, Irish, and Welsh have a different political system, not just structurally, but in other ways too? Although highly normative in its assumptions, perhaps some generalizations can be made regarding a distinctive Celtic *model* of politics. Here are some assumptions that can be posited in a model of Celtic politics:

1) Language and Race: Most Scots, Irish, and Welsh will tell you that they are a different nationality from English. Whether this distinction is based on language (which is what the original distinction for Celtic peoples was made on, or based on race is usually up to the individual). Although highly subjective and somewhat normative when it comes to race (and also language when it is a dialect of English), this characteristic holds importance for political identification for peoples of the Celtic fringe (the descendants of ancient Britons—as opposed to Anglo-Saxons).

2) Territory: Identifiable territorial claims make defending a nation's identity much easier both socially and politically. The sense of political legitimacy Celts get from their territorial ties is seen in the historical importance of land in the struggles for national self-determination in Ireland and Scotland in particular. Ireland provides a curious problem given its partition, so a brand of Northern Irish nationalism has caused divisions within the national continuity of the Irish in their national politics after partition in 1921. At any rate, as in deciding the characteristics of a nation, territory may be one variable in our model that allows us to see commonalities among peoples' experiences as national minorities and majorities on the Celtic fringe.

3) Political Culture: The attitudes, values, and orientations that shape a people and their views toward government are important as a variable in any model of national politics. In the case of Celtic politics, to make a distinction between Anglo-Saxon or English political culture versus Celtic political culture (as found in Scotland, Ireland or Wales) may be difficult, but the recent Celtic fringe con-

texts sees distinctly national issues (such as separate legal systems, the role of religion in the society, national symbols and culture, and separate political institutions with different voting systems based on proportional representation—i.e. PR—or modes of operation all vis-à-vis England) suggest that the Celts have some different mores and patterns that make political life unique from England. Of course, using England as a kind of dependent variable may not be the best example since not only can these systems be judged on their own merits, but also in relation to a regionalizing and globalizing EU as well.

4) Social Democracy: Britain has had a social democratic ethos in many ways since the Second World War given Labour's rise to power as the second party of British politics in the twentieth century. However, continued class-based politics (which were lessening in the 1990s and early twenty-first century) and ancient customs and institutions (such as the House of Lords), continue to evince a political divide between Britain and European democracies. The Scots, Irish, and Welsh appear to be somewhat more interested in European-style social democracy (broad-gauged welfare states with high amounts of health coverage and education for all). State capitalism is a feature of these systems and the state's role in the economy is a general assumption that most make. The use of PR in Ireland and Scotland's devolved parliament is another European component of these systems. Hence, the Irish and Scottish political contexts may be closer to a Scandinavian model of politics and we might see this model with its focus on environmental and post-materialist issues (including health, education, and egalitarian participatory democracy) come to the fore in the years ahead. Wales's centuries long relationship with England does perhaps limit this assumption's explanatory capability somewhat. As many in Wales may be more tied to English-oriented solutions to Welsh issues.

5) Economics: The Celtic regions of Britain and Ireland have historically been less industrialized (with some exceptions such as Belfast, Cardiff, and Glasgow), but the common economic linkages include agriculture, fishing, services (especially education and finance), and some light manufacturing in electronics (both have gained currency with EU support in Ireland and Scotland—neo-Silicon Valley-type manufacturing and software development). Also, perhaps the main up-and-coming staple of these economies is increased tourism (as is the case in most of Europe). A distinct Celtic identity politically and socially may lead to more visitors and immigrants moving into these regions.

6) Religion: Finally, the role of Christianity in its various forms in these regions is very important for both national identification (political culture) purposes and for attempting to find solutions to, or creating, problems (as is the case in Northern Ireland). For the Irish, Roman Catholicism is the chief religion. For Scots and Northern Irish, Protestantism (under the Presbyterian model for most in both nations) is the norm (although a significant minority in Northern Ireland is Catholic). For example, Welsh Methodism left a Liberal imprint on the nation, Calvinism left a dour, austere stamp on both Scots and Protestant Ulster-persons, and Catholicism left the Irish Catholics in the north and south parts of the Emerald Isle independent and with much antipathy toward British or Protestant colonialism. For the Welsh, historical nonconformity (in the face of Anglican pressure) has held true, but most (around 80%) tend to be Methodists

(founded by the Englishman John Wesley in the eighteenth century—one of his first stops was southern Wales and the coal pits to convert the Welsh to a then-evangelical brand of Christianity). Religion is a key component of national identity in the Celtic fringe and it does have historical relevance for politics both structurally and ideologically.

Conceptual Limitations: The Celtic Fringe as Region

Regions are a major component of global politics. They also factor into European and British politics. Regionalism can be conceptualized in a number of different ways. Comparativists in political science and historians tend to view regionalism in an inductive manner. That is, the importance of the region under investigation is viewed based on the characteristics of that region (for example, its linguistic, cultural, political, social traditions, and so forth and how they relate to the identity of individuals within that region). In the political science subfield of international relations, regionalism is conceptualized in more of a deductive manner when investigating a grouping of states that have aligned for either economic, social or political reasons or a combination of these regions. Regionalism is important for students of the EU and the Celtic fringe because it has returned as a dominant unit of analysis and a major analytical framework (i.e. the region) in helping us understand what regions do today and how they interact with various supranational organizations and dominant states.

The Celtic fringe has been conceptualized as a region within the UK. In our present discussion, the Celtic fringe will be seen both in the comparative politics sense and in the international relations sense. We will look at separate cases, Scotland, Ireland, and Wales, and see how and why these Celtic nations have evolved politically. We will also look at the Celtic nations as a grouping of nations into one region and look at how it relates to Britain and the EU. Furthermore, we will even look at intra-regional issues such as the rise of a distinct Northern Irish identity and politics in Ulster and how that has divided both states in Ireland, and also removed Ulster from social, political, and economic linkages with England since "the troubles" began in 1969. The Celtic fringe is a flashy descriptor for the linguistic and ethnic periphery of the British Isles. The Celtic fringe as a region has its analytical limitations as well. It can be a bit too amorphous to describe Celtic politics given the cultural differences and nuances found in each Celtic nation. The term is also too general to describe the status of governance in each Celtic area as Scotland and Wales share similar experiences in recent years and the Irish do not. However, in a broader sense, the role of regionalism in British and Irish politics appears to be increasingly salient since the Celtic nations can be studied as important minorities in a regionalizing and growing EU and the role of ethnicity, language, and culture appears to be increasing, paradoxically, as centralization in Brussels is occurring at greater speed. Despite the salience of regionalism as a helpful conceptual model for understanding Celtic politics, nationalism continued to be a significant concept and mode of politics for these regions as the twenty-first century appeared.

What is a Nation?

The *nation* is a concept that essentially ties a group of people with certain characteristics (such as race, religion, language, economic development patterns, attitudes about politics, and common territory). The nation can be an empirical (based on observation) concept or a somewhat subjective one. As seen in the case of Israeli Jews, the concept of nation can entail endless debate and it can become overly political. Is national identity an objective fact—such as blood relations? Is it a state of mind? Is it tied primarily to geo-politics (i.e. territory and claims related to land)? In the cases of the Celtic fringe, this concept is simultaneously empirical and subjective. Celts have longstanding relationships to territory and language (including regional dialects or a differing brand of English or different languages altogether). These characteristics can be verified and factor into both political and cultural discussions related to the "Celticness" of the non-Anglo-Saxon peoples of the British Isles. The subjective part can be tied to ethnic identity, historical claims (that may be revised to fit the particular Celtic people's political culture and outlook on politics, and the use of cultural symbols for national identification—such as wearing kilts in Scotland, Ireland, and Wales, the latter which has only recently, in the twentieth century, seen a rise in since it seems the logical Celtic thing to do in distancing oneself from the English and drawing closer to your linguistic and ethnic kinspersons in Ireland and Scotland). Race is a confounding issue since, as in many countries, it is a tricky component of national identity in a post-modern, industrialized society where ethnic and cultural amalgamation have occurred. The Scots have ancient Irish, Pict, Viking, Norman, Anglo-Saxon, and Danish currents in their clan histories. Racially the indigenous Scots, as are other descendents from ancient Britons and Anglo-Saxons (or English), are an amalgamation of several races all from the European continent. Yet, Scots, and Celts in general, can be classified as a distinct ethnic identity. Thus, to talk about the descendents of ancient Britons as Celts conjures up several questions about ethnic homogeneity and using ethnicity as a way of getting at national identification. Another confusing element in figuring out the Celts' ethnic identities is the fact that the Celts, as will be seen below, were a people who used language as a more salient ethnic identifier than race. So, language, even into the twentieth century and the reemergence of ancient languages such as Welsh or Gaelic, takes on important social and political overtones in the quest for Celtic national identity and a separate Celtic politics. The Celtic nation is a diffuse, yet distinctive grouping of peoples. Despite major differences, common patterns of political development, socialization, and experiences with dominant English governance helped solidify their experiences. What's more, in the twentieth century, common political developments helped distinguish these nations as separate people (vis-à-vis the English) and make them particular candidates for self-determination politically, greater analysis academically, and increased inclusion into a growing panoply of European nations in a regional, yet globalizing EU.

Nationalism: From Conceptual Confusion to Clarity

The study of *nationalism* takes on important meaning in the study of the Celtic regions of the UK and Ireland. Nationalism is a phenomenon that has the capacity to cause immense frustration to political scientists, historians, sociologists, and politicians. The actual concept may be defined as the feeling individuals have for their nation and the active pursuit of forwarding that nation's goals and agenda through political and other means. The concept of patriotism is another variant of nationalism, but it usually manifests in populations in overtly social and cultural ways, but more muted politically in that the deep pride people feel for their country (nation-state) may not lead to overt nationalism that then demands political action (either via democratic channels or by force). The concepts of nation and state are linked. Hence, the nation has an important impact on the state and vice versa. In Britain, the nations of Britain (both in the ethno-cultural sense and in the regional sense) have impacted significantly the development of the state in the last 200 years. The opposite is true as well. The state, Great Britain and Northern Ireland, has affected national development (regional evolution) over the years. Thus the two concepts, nation and state, are intertwined and often used synonymously.

Nationalism is a key concept in understanding both the historical forces that allowed the ancient Britons and Anglo-Saxons to fragment and coalesce. Although it is not an ancient concept, it largely evolved as a salient descriptor after the French Revolution of 1789. However, it did manifest in Scotland due to the events of 1707 (see Chapter Two). Nationalism developed more steam by the revolutions of 1848 on the European continent. Those rebellions against time-honored hereditary, conservative, and reactionary monarchies have been called the "Springtime of Nations" (Johnson 2002). The kind of nationalism (liberal nationalism) seen in 1848 was the forerunner of and laid the groundwork for the ethno-nationalism of the twentieth century that gave rise to the increase in national identity and action on the Celtic fringe. Britain was largely bypassed when the militant revolutionary fervor hit Europe in the mid-nineteenth century (save the staunched minor rebellion in Ireland—see Chapter Two). Thus, nationalism took root as proponents of Irish Home Rule inveighed at Westminster and others on the Celtic fringe begin to make claims of self-determination by the late twentieth century, such as some Scots and Welsh. Another interesting phenomenon was the rise in militant Irish nationalism in Northern Ireland among the Catholic minority in the 1960s and 1970s, more as a civil rights movement. The response was a strident Ulster nationalism that has almost become ipso facto a kind of Northern Irish nationalism that has less in common with both Southern Irish republican and English traditions as it is a mixture of symbolic Protestant militancy (Orangemen), calls for continued separation from the southern part of Ireland, and an isolation of Ulster from both Irish and British socio-political contexts. This is one example of how nationalism can spin out of control and lead to unexpected or unintended consequences. What began as a kind of British loyalty in the capacity of nationalism ended up as a strain of nationalism that is now seen as unique to both Ireland and Britain—a kind of Northern Irish nationalism: heavy on religion and political autonomy, yet light on historical linkages to either Ireland's other 26 counties or the rest of the UK. Yet, the Northern Irish are still Irish and thus a part of Celtic politics.

Conceptually, nationalism is a problem for students of British and Irish politics because it is a difficult concept to place in a theoretical context. Various approaches to the study of comparative politics, such as the developmental approach (as seen above), which includes political modernization, the study of political culture and socialization, structural-functionalism and political systems analysis, do not yield themselves very well to dealing with nationalism. Nationalism becomes an outlier statistically and empirically in many contexts, especially in the study of West European politics after 1945. Of course, nationalism as in the form of *national socialism* in Germany (1933–45) or *fascism* in Italy (1922–44) and the regimes that foisted those brands of fascism on their people gave rise to the study of nationalism in great detail in political science in the 1940s and 1950s. The 1950s saw the beginning of decolonization in Africa and Asia and a whole new discussion and literature developed in political science to explain this "New Nationalism," to use political scientist John G. Stoessinger's phrase (Stoessinger 1993).

The study of *political theory* (i.e. political philosophy) helps us get at nationalism a bit better, but political theory can muddle the waters somewhat because it attempts to make normative assumptions that when tested can end with normative claims, thus creating a type of circular logic (for example, the nation has a certain destiny, thus the nation's destiny may be thus and such because it is a special nation with certain claims). That being said, nationalism is both an empirical and normative concept. For political scientists and historians, this may be one reason why it is difficult empirically to classify and study. Another problem with the study of nationalism is that it is usually seen as but one small variable in a larger model of politics when in reality it can be and should be studied as an end in itself. That is, it should be the dependent variable in the hypothetical calculation in which other independent variables are assessed as to their relationship and effect on the dependent variable (i.e. nationalist phenomena under study). Thus, instead of only writing about the history of nationalism or the conceptual nuances of nationalism, nationalism can become the foundation of theoretical claims and models that allow political scientists to build on existing theory. Then meaningful generalizations and hypotheses can be postulated and these approaches can help students order the facts about not only nationalist phenomena and movements, but also about regions and states where nationalism is occurring.

In our case, this book posits a model of Celtic politics as a heuristic device (learning tool) for students to help conceptualize the separateness and innate value of politics on the Celtic fringe. Celtic politics is a distinct phenomenon with several characteristics (as seen above). It can be studied empirically and the same can be done with its nationalist components. Thus, the book's logic allows the student to look at Scotland, Ireland, and Wales as not only distinct political systems in and of themselves, but also as subsets of a broader Celtic and pan-European context. What's more, understanding these nations and regions as part of the historical legacy of the British Isles is not only underscored, but enhanced in a way that few approaches to the study of British politics via a more Anglo-Saxon structural model allowed in the twentieth century in political science.

Who are the "Celts?"

The term "Celtic" is an historical one that conjures up several types of descriptions. Although the term can be confusing, the *Celts* are the ancestors of the modern indigenous people situated in the peripheral regions of the UK. Historically, the term "Celt" referred primarily to peoples known for their language. Celts were and continue to be classified primarily based on their languages. Some have assigned racial or cultural overtones to the term, but technically it was the languages brought by early Britons who met the Romans when they arrived in 55 BC. The Celts came to the British Isles around 600 BC. They arrived from Europe and their culture was a derivative of the continental Celtic one that got its name from a village called La Tène located on a lake, Neuchâtel, in Switzerland. Moreover, other groups that invaded Britain from the continent over a period of roughly 600–700 years just prior to the Roman takeover spoke Celtic languages. Celts come from the Greek word *keltoi* which means "strangers." These continental European people, who hailed from the central parts of Europe, were described as such by the ancient Greeks as far back as 1000 BC. The term "Celts" was not used to describe peoples who lived in northwest Europe in what is now Britain. Nor were the languages of the Celts implied in the Greeks' use of the descriptive term for Celts. New scholarship on the Celts calls into questions the Lake Tène origins of the Celts and suggests that Britons have been in Ireland and Britain longer than most histories state and that most of the Celts came from the Iberian peninsula and made their way north through France to Ireland then into what is modern-day Britain.

Box 1.1: The Celtic Race (Part I): The Prince of Wales vs. Eric Liddell, 1924

The 1981 Oscar-winning British movie, "Chariots of Fire," is known for its tale of the boldness of the human spirit against the odds. It is a masterpiece of cinematography encapsulating the paradoxes of national identity and loyalty in the United Kingdom. The movie features the true story of Harold Abrahams, a Jewish Englishman, who went to Cambridge and eventually found a place as a sprinter on the 1924 British Olympic team that went to Paris for the summer games. He is contrasted with the devout Scottish Presbyterian and eventual Christian martyr, Eric Liddell who, at the time, is the most famous runner north of the English border. Both win gold and do so for different reasons: Abrahams for England and to challenge stereotypes about Jews; Liddell for God and the Scottish nation. In the movie, an interesting sequence occurs when David, the Prince of Wales (who twelve years later would ascend the throne of Britain as Edward VIII, and then ignominiously abdicate within 12 months), as head of the British Olympic committee, attempts to talk Liddell out of refusing to run a race on the Sabbath. Despite, the obvious religious overtones (secular English versus devout Scots), the issue of race comes up when the Prince of Wales says, "Mr. Liddell, you're a child of your race [(Scottish)], as am I [(Anglo-Saxon)]. We share a common heritage, a common bond, a common loyalty." Thus, the Prince of Wales exhorted Liddell to put king and country first over personal religious (and oblique national) convictions and, that despite racial and religious differences, similarities should be emphasized. This raises a deeper question about loyalties and identities of Celtic and Anglo-Saxon peoples. In terms of ethnicity, are the Scots from north Britain a different race from the English in the south? This question has been debated often in academic, political, and cultural circles. If a racial difference exists, how is it examined, verified, etc? Hasn't years of intermarriage among Britons caused racial differences to blur? Even at that point in 1924? Thus, the distinction is an important one, and certainly one that is tenable, but where does the identification stop? Are there separate Celtic races (Scots, Irish, Cornish, Manx, and Welsh)? Perhaps, looking at linguistic differences and dialects is a good place to start since this is how the original Celtic peoples differentiated among themselves. However, the debate will linger as to whether the Prince of Wales's race or Liddell's race were, and still are to this day, distinctly separate and mutually exclusive nations in the purely ethnic sense.

The Celts developed and used currency, carried iron from the continent, set up religious rituals, had kingdoms, developed bronze articles for everyday use, and created artwork. The original Celtic Britons built forts, held religious ceremonies, farmed, and exported various types of things to the continent (for example, leather, iron, and grain). Their influence was felt in various parts of what is modern-day England from Yorkshire in the north to Somerset in the south. The Celts were known for their specialized priesthood, the Druids, and their warrior class. Although pagan spiritually, the Druids carried out other functions and held such professions as judges, teachers, and physicians. The Celtic nobility had a penchant for art and unique designs were part of the culture. After the Roman invasion, Celtic art began to die out and remained less fettered in the remote land of Ireland. The Romans tended to mistrust the Celts in what is modern-day Scotland. In 122 AD, the Roman emperor Hadrian toured Britain and began the construction of the wall that was to serve as a defensive fortification in keeping the Picts and other northern Celts out of the territory that is modern-day England. In 367, Roman Britain was invaded by Picts from the north, Scots from Ireland, and Saxons from Gaul. The latter group attacked the east coast of modern-day England. The overlord in charge of Roman Britain was killed, and *Hadrian's Wall* was damaged, but the Roman army restored order. By the early fifth century, Romans were gone, back to the continent fighting various barbarians in Gaul. Celtic tribes thus controlled Britain for a very short period, perhaps a couple of decades. However, by 449 the Angles and Saxons invaded eventually forcing the Celts to remote parts of the British Isles. The *Picts* were found in the far north, in the Highlands of modern-day Scotland. It is believed that they arrived in concert with a general group of Celts coming from the continent around 600 BC. Scholars believe they may have been Scythian in origin. The Scythians may have been the progenitors of the ancient Russians.

The Britons, another Celtic tribe, controlled the Clyde area (from Glasgow) to Cumbria (northwest England). Celts were also driven by the Anglo-Saxons into Wales in the East on the Irish Sea and Cornwall, in the southwest corner of modern-day England. Of course, Celts found their way to Ireland and it was from this outpost that the Scots would eventually come to the mainland of Britain. The *Scots*, which means "pirates," were a bellicose Celtic race from the north of Ireland. They had actually started settling in mainland Britain in the second and third centuries as they left Ireland and moved into northern areas of modern-day Scotland. The Scots ancient homeland was the Kingdom of Dalriada, found in western Scotland and the islands there. The Scots spoke a different Celtic language from the Picts and their relationship was one of conflict. The Picts, were called Picti by the Romans (or "painted people") for their proclivity toward painting their faces and wearing tattoos. The Scots continued to see their allegiance as one to the *Gaels* in Ireland, but over several centuries the fighting between the two Celtic peoples ebbed and the area began to change as intermarriage and outside threats eventually saw the Scots become the dominant tribe in the region.

Box 1.2: The Celtic Race (Part II): Is it in the DNA?

Although political science majors and other social science and humanities majors might not find modern science as fascinating as biology or natural science students, the idea that a bona fide Celtic race exists is interesting and provocative. Of course, any discussion in a globalizing, post-World War II world conjures up images of Hitlerism and evil racial experiments and a discussion of eugenics. However, the salience of the politics of ethnonationalism in the late twentieth and early twenty-first century and how they affect the global order is relevant to the evolution of the politics of the Celtic fringe. Although scholars and scientists have conjectured for centuries about racial predispositions throughout the United Kingdom, Ireland, and Europe, medical science has found empirical links to racial characteristics and certain genetic predispositions toward both good (biologically healthy) and bad (disease) attributes. Dr. Sohan Hayreh, one of the world's top ophthalmologists (those physicians who specialize in diseases and problems of the human eye) who, after leaving the United Kingdom, researched and practiced at the University of Iowa, found in studying patients in Scotland and England some interesting and important issues related to the eye. He found that a condition known as "pseudo-exfoliation of the lens" existed in greater quantities in those of Scandinavian or north European background rather than those found in south England (or those of Anglo-Saxon ethnic background). This condition can eventually lead to the eye disease, glaucoma. Dr. Hayreh, an Indian Sikh, who worked for 3½ years at the University of Edinburgh found a much higher incidence of the condition there among Scots than in London (where he worked for nine years). His explanation for the condition is genetic and he argues that the intermarriage of north European and Scandinavian people (going back over 1000 years) has much to do with the condition. Thus, those with this condition will have dilated pupils and be at a much greater risk for glaucoma. This greater eye pressure can eventually cause glaucoma. Dr. Hayreh cannot explain why Scots, Dutch, and other north Europeans and those who come from these races are at a greater risk to have pseudo-exfoliation of the lens, but the empirical evidence in terms of causation is fairly clear: ethnic background does seem to make a difference. Thus, one's Celtic roots may be more than linguistic as has often been the most important identifier for Celts. The question then becomes: Just how much does the Scottish ethnicity factor into the genetic makeup of Scots? Or is pseudo-exfoliation of the lens tied more to Scandinavian races that have come to Scotland over time and passed a stronger genetic link off to a weaker Celtic one? The debate will continue, but certainly, the ethnic card does play an important role not only in politics for Celts and all ethnicities, but science and medicine as well.

The Irish descended from Celts who made their way to *Éire* as part of a broader Celtic migration from Europe. Eventually, the Celts in Ireland had their own kingdoms, local mores and folkways, and language which became the modern form of Irish Gaelic. The people of Éire developed different customs and ways compared to the inhabitants of Albion (ancient Celtic Britain, what is now England) and Alba (the ancient Celtic region that is now the modern-day Scottish highlands), the home of the Picts. History tells us that the inhabitants of Albion were in much greater contact with Celtic tribes on the continent than their Celtic neighbors in Éire. However, as stated above, the Scots developed out of the Irish Gaels. The term "Gaels" was derived from the term used by the Romans (Galli) which ties to the tribes of Gaul referring to Gallic as opposed to Celtic as a descriptor of these peoples in general. Historically, Celts referred to themselves as Gaels, but the term "Celtic" was used by scholars to differentiate Celts from Gallic people. The latter today are identified with the ancient inhabitants of France. In reality, both were somewhat mixed at times as the Romans saw them as barbarian peoples.

The *Welsh* may be Britain's oldest Celtic nation. Their origins predate historical record and the Neolithic civilization came to Wales in 2000 BC from the Mediterranean area. These people have been called Iberian (from today's modern day Iberian peninsula housing Spain and Portugal). Some came from France, Brittany or Spain and some went to Ireland. Looking for land and food for their animals, they also looked for minerals as well. The Neolithic people settled on flat land and did not have as much interest in the mountainous areas of Wales. Five hundred years later, more people from the continent were coming to Wales and their use of bronze and heavy tools came with them. By 800 BC, as seen above, the Bronze Age people were speaking a language that was prehistoric and not discernible to the modern anthropologist or archaeologist, unless it is similar to the Basque language found among that particular people of northern Spain and southwestern France. As the Iron Age emerged around 600 BC, the Celts brought with them from the continent (mainly modern predominantly Germanic areas from the Rhine to the Danube) an Indo-European language which had two strains: Goidelic (known in modern parlance as Gaelic) and Brythonic (British). These two strains fused to make what eventually is today known as the Welsh language. Like other Celts, the Welsh were a fearsome people who used weaponry to good use and formed tribal groupings based on a monarchical-type system with a social hierarchy. They were pagan and kept the religious traditions of the Druids brought from Gaul. Anglesey in northern Wales was an important pagan center for the Celts prior to their conversion to Christianity. Like all the Celts in Britain, the ancient Britons of Wales were confronted with the Romans after 55 BC. It was not until 60 AD that the Druids were finally subdued, despite the fact that several tribes in the hills of Wales were only controlled in part militarily. Wales was fully taken by Romans in 80 AD. It stayed under Roman authority for 300 years.

Box 1.3: King Arthur's Celtic Roots

The story of King Arthur and the Knights of the Roundtable is an ancient story that has roots in Celtic Britain. Most are familiar with the story of the young boy Arthur who pulls the sword (Excalibur) from the stone and the mercurial wizard, Merlin, sends him on his way to lead the mythical Knights of the Roundtable into battle and establish Camelot with Queen Guinevere. Of course, how much of this is really true? Some scholars believe that a real King Arthur existed somewhere in Wales and that he was modeled on a Sarmatian knight who fought for the Romans in Roman Britain around 400 AD. The 2004 movie, "King Arthur," (starring Clive Owen and Kiera Knightly) follows this line of thinking closely. It also shows the egalitarian ethos of the Arthur and his knights as they sit at the Roundtable! Interestingly, Britain is replete with many historical icons and objects that attempt to underscore the veracity and historicity of the Arthurian legend. Some believe that the real King Arthur is buried in the ground on Mount Snowdonia (Wales's highest point). This is where it is believed that Arthur battled his wayward nephew Mordred. It is also on this mountain where a red dragon and a white dragon fought below ground symbolizing the conflict between the Celts (the red dragon) and the Saxons (the white dragon). Of course, the red dragon later became the Welsh national symbol and is found on its national flag today. A Celtic king, Gwrtheryn (Vortigern), who fought the Saxons was constantly troubled by the dragons when they would arise from their slumber and attack each other inside the storied north Wales mountain according to legend and myth. The Roundtable of Arthurian lore is said to have existed and the one at Winchester in southern England [see the table pictured here] is a medieval recreation of the famous table. Some Britons believe that Arthur is buried at Glastonbury in England. It does appear that an Arthur did battle Saxons (invading from across the North Sea) either up north in what is now Scotland or somewhere in Wales or England. Interestingly, the 2004 movie appears on the surface to venerate the British (or Celtic) Arthur versus the hated Saxons (who are depicted as hunnish characters). But, in reality, this may be Hollywood's latest version of demonizing the English as Arthur is pictured as a Celtic warlord and in conjunction with the Celtic Picts (*Piciti* or "painted people") of the north they battle the forerunners of the English, the Saxons. Some historians and literature experts argue that an Arthur did defeat the Saxons on behalf of the Romans and this is where the interesting and well-done 2004 movie got its theme. Nevertheless, whether Arthur is real or not, his Celtic roots are part of the culture that continues to paint the Celts in a battle against the warring English (or Saxons) and some would argue that this difficult relationship existed into the modern era.

Celtic Politics as a Unit of Study

Celtic politics is a model of politics that allows us to analyze the Celtic fringe in the political life of Great Britain and Ireland in more detail. It is a much needed corrective to the standard academic approach to both British and Irish politics. It is both an analytical approach to conceptualizing and understanding the Scots, Irish, and Welsh, as well as their inter-connected political contexts and systems. It is also a normative and descriptive heuristic that allows for both an historical and cultural understanding of the tongues and races found in ancient Britain and Ireland that continue to carry on, albeit in a far different form, today. It is a mutually exclusive, yet broader *unit of analysis* and scientific investigation. Politics in twenty-first century Britain and Ireland have seen a rise in ethno-nationalism after 1945. The latter decades of the twentieth century saw much change regarding the status of the Celtic nations both in terms of institutional changes, transformations of the political culture, and a geo-political alteration caused by both globalizing and pan-European forces that saw a shrinkage of political, economic, and social activity via the EU and other global forces. However, it actually increased the importance of nationalist particularisms (ethnic, linguistic, and cultural) as phenomena that had to be dealt with, and the Celtic fringe is one area that saw its fortunes change in terms of political salience. Thus, this book will help students of British and European politics understand the complexities, peculiarities, and significance of this important region and set of identifiable nations in Britain and Ireland (Éire) off the coast of northwest Europe.

CHAPTER TWO

History of the Celtic Fringe

Geography

The Celtic fringe in British politics made up the periphery of the United Kingdom of Great Britain and Ireland after 1801. The regions of Scotland, Ireland, and Wales were distinct regions within the British state. Of course, Ireland is a separate island to the west of mainland Britain and after 1921, the Irish Free State moved toward independence. At the same time, a divided island evolved as the Six Counties of the north, Ulster or Northern Ireland, remained part of the British state. Scotland has just over five million people and is roughly the size of South Carolina. Ireland has 4.1 million citizens and the entire island (including the Six Counties) is about the size of West Virginia. Northern Ireland has 1.7 million inhabitants. Wales has 2.9 million people and is equal in size to Massachusetts. The British mainland is about the length of the state of California. Aside from Scotland and Wales, the Isle of Man in the Irish Sea to the west of northern England and due south of southwest Scotland and the far southwestern corner of England, Cornwall, are both historical Celtic homelands. If the entire Emerald Isle is included then the Celtic parts of the British Isles and Ireland make up roughly 58% of the land versus 42% for England. Thus, the historical territory of the Celts is significant vis-à-vis the English landmass after 450 AD and the advent of the Anglo-Saxon era in English and Celtic political history.

Nobility to Nationalism

During the years of Norman ascendancy after 1066, Anglo-Saxon England was gone, but Scotland was governed by centralized authority in the monarchies of Malcom III Canmore and his son David I. The former ruled from 1058–93 and the latter from 1124–53. Malcolm assuaged diplomatically the Vikings in the north and agreed to a settlement with the Normans in 1072. Under David, Norman families from England and Flemish and other European families began to settle and intermarry with Celts in Scotland. This began the transformation of the Scottish social and political context at the onset of the Middle Ages.

Replicating other forms of monarchical conquest, the Normans put into effect relatively strict lines of baronial authority in the politico-economic system in England and Scotland. Royal patronage by the Norman kings led to land grants to loyal subjects. In Scotland, the indigenous elite evolved into feudal nobility which owned land in both Scotland and England. Thus, loyalty to the king was stressed as a political relationship between families rather than races, regions, or states (a non-existent concept in Middle Ages Britain). The Middle Ages evinced a different type of nationalism that was not predicated upon ethnicity or political identity as was seen after 1789 on the continent. Nations in the Middle Ages were not the groupings of people based on ethnicity, religion, language, and culture that arose in the nineteenth century in Europe, but rather representatives of landed elites in large or politically salient monarchies, such as the Holy Roman Empire or kingdoms in Hungary, Bohemia or Poland. These realms were not modern states as we know them, but decentralized alliances which were confederal in nature. Nobles were reliant on kings for support and vice versa, but suspicion often dictated the terms of these relationships. Nations got their identity from small coteries of landed elites—the nobles who had territory and rank. Thus, the modern concepts of nation and nationalism were yet to come and Scotland (as well as other nations in the British Isles) would not see modern political nationalism until the early eighteenth century at the time of union with England in 1707. This was the context that William Wallace found himself in by the end of the thirteenth century in Scotland.

Scotland: Wallace and Bruce

William Wallace arrived on the scene in Scottish history in a relatively unassuming way. He was from a family from the Scottish Lowlands. His family was not part of the Anglo-Scottish nobility. His father did own land, but he was more of a middle class crofter (farmer). The Wallaces had been vassals under the stewards of the kings of Scotland (soon to be clan Stewart—one of the most influential families in Scottish history). The Wallaces may have come to Scotland from Wales from the Welsh Marches (where the Normans had given both Welsh and English nobles land along both sides of the Welsh border after 1066). The Wallaces may have arrived with Walter Fitz-Alan, King David I of Scotland's steward.

Box 2.1: Wallace and Bruce: Scotland's National Heroes

William Wallace and Robert Bruce came from very different backgrounds. Wallace was from a family of lowland Scots in the Ayrshire region in western Scotland. Bruce was from a family of Scots nobility that had worked with the English since the time of the Normans coming to Scotland. Wallace was an out of place "nationalist" for the times; Bruce a devoted noble. However, both men's fates would converge between 1295 and Wallace's death in 1305. Wallace would lead Scotland to its greatest triumph over the English at Stirling Bridge in 1297. He would submit himself to the Scottish nobles and attempt to lead Scotland to independence from English political domination. Bruce would play his cards closely to his vest and would not fully support Wallace until he realized that Edward I wanted complete control of Scotland as a vassal state. With Bruce backing away from supporting the Guardian of Scotland (Wallace) at Falkirk in 1298, due to arguments about the Scottish monarchy's succession, the Scots were forced to retreat and Wallace was eventually hunted down and taken to London and executed. It was not until 1314 that the Scottish Wars of Independence were finally settled and Bruce picking up where Wallace had left off was able to defeat the English near Stirling (ironically, not far from where Wallace had had his greatest success in 1297). Two men and two divergent destinies shaped the future of Scotland as a separate kingdom in relation to its larger neighbor to the south.

Wallace's love of liberty may have been prompted by his father (Malcolm) who, tradition has it, refused to pay homage to the English king, Edward I (*Longshanks*). For his defiance, Malcolm Wallace is thought to have been murdered by an English soldier in 1296. Evidently, Wallace could converse in Gaelic and read and write in French, Latin and the Scots dialect (his native tongue). He was relatively well-educated in science and history. Most have stated that Wallace was a tall man with a domineering presence. Certainly, his leadership in battle hinged on both physical dexterity and innate charisma. In doing the military bidding for the Scottish nobility, Wallace rallied the supporters of the Scottish nation (its political and economic elites), and pulled off an amazing victory in spite of tremendously poor odds. Like today, Scotland was one-tenth the size of England. With a much larger force to his credit, Edward I had the advantage at *Stirling Bridge*. However, Wallace's tactics and vision would foretell other important moments in Celtic political history (such as the challenges by Welshman Owain Glyn dŵr—Owen Glendower to the English—or Irishman Michael Collins to English authority in the fifteenth and twentieth centuries respectively). Using guerrilla maneuvers and the terrain to his fullest advantage, Wallace and the Scots defeated the English on September 11, 1297. The victory established Wallace as Scotland's greatest national hero. He and his army immediately marched south into England and plundered the north of that nation and the Scottish nobles were quick to make him guardian of Scotland, and an indigenous Scottish knighthood came with it. Unfortunately for Sir William, his fortunes turned sour and on July 22, 1298 a better prepared English army met the Scots at Falkirk near the Firth of Forth and with the withdrawal of much of the nobles' support, the Scots were defeated. Although involved seriously in Scottish political matters, Wallace appears to have gone to France, took men with him, might have fought an English army in France, and was probably received by the French king. Having fought the English at every point, Wallace was finally captured as public enemy number one in 1305, tried in London, and executed. Unlike the story in the heralded 1995 Oscar-winning film, "Braveheart," starring Mel Gibson as Wallace, *Robert the Bruce* did not fight with Wallace's army, nor did Bruce support Wallace's attempt to free utterly Scotland from the English yoke. Bruce, an opportunist in the quintessentially medieval baronial elite mode, sought the Scottish kingship at all costs (he would be called a Machiavellian today!) He was so interested in replacing the Balliol line on Scotland's throne that he physically killed John Comyn, his cousin and challenger for the Scottish crown, with his own hands (stabbing him) and left him to die in the church in

Dumfries. Comyn had been supported by Longshanks. However, with Edward I's death the next year, Bruce had a small respite. Bruce's willingness to kill, in a church of all places, got him excommunicated by Rome, but most of the nobles overlooked the slight. By 1309, Bruce was king of Scotland (having been enthroned at Scone—site of the coronations of the ancient kings of Scotland), got support from France, called a parliament of nobles at St. Andrews to formalize relations with France (known by the seventeenth century as the "Auld Alliance" which countered England geo-politically), had support of numerous clans, and was supported by the Scottish church, despite excommunication. With increased armed conflict, Edward II of England sent troops to Scotland. At *Bannockburn*, near Stirling, the Scots under Bruce met the English. On June 23, 1314, 12,000 Scotsmen dispatched a 20,000-man English army. The victory, a greater win than Stirling Bridge, allowed Bruce to rule resolutely for 15 more years. By 1323, Edward II and Bruce agreed to a general recognition, in spite of Edward's hesitance at full acceptance of Bruce's kingship.

What do the roles of Wallace and Bruce tell us about politics in the late Middle Ages and early medieval era in Scotland? First, both had independence as a goal, but for different reasons. Wallace was genuinely interested in seeing Scotland free of English domination. In the geo-political sense, Wallace's anti-Englishness would symbolically mirror nationalistic feelings found 650–700 years later in Scotland in the twentieth century as groups like the National Party of Scotland (NPS) formed in 1928 in a democratizing context of the United Kingdom (UK). Second, Bruce, unlike Wallace, saw independence as a means to an end in establishing his personal authority over a feudal Scotland. Thus, he could become a Scottish monarch fashioned along the lines of the English monarchy (Bruce was only half-Scottish on his mother's side, whereas Wallace was 100% Celt). Of course, Bruce's rationale was not unusual in the wild and wooly context of medieval Scotland. Bruce's nationalism, as Scots might recollect today, was not of the modern sort. Neither was Wallace's, but the ramifications of Wallace's actions are probably more significant in 1638, 1707, and other important years in Scottish history—for purely nationalistic reasons, although, 1314 is the most important date in Scottish history militarily. Third, the Scotland of Wallace and Bruce was still decidedly disadvantaged in terms of population and manpower (400,000 people) vis-à-vis England (four million or so) at the time. This made political and military affairs difficult. The system of governance, as stated above, was a convoluted web of decentralized feudal politics with baronial intrigue and awkward diplomatic settlements replete with marriage for overtly political (both internal and geo-political) reasons. The Scottish culture with its Celtic bellicosity and ingenuity, as well as the Scandinavian influences from 300 years of Viking invasions, was foreign in many ways to the evolving systemic organization and rationality of the Anglo-Normans, who had inherited Anglo-Saxon mores and folkways as an underlay to the legal-political system (with its great hallmark of common law) that was seemingly more administratively cohesive, yet rigid politically than the looser Scottish kingdom. Finally, Scots got a glimpse of the historical asymmetry in their relationship with England and how it influenced passions by the advent of the medieval era. This was a replication of earlier Roman and Anglo-Saxon thrusts into Celtic lands north of England, but the extent to which a stable, or acceptable to both sides, political and social settlement could be found was one that waited until the Scottish monarchy eventually merged with England's royal family in 1603. Even then, the conflict between the Scots and English continued to ebb and flow.

The British Civil War: Effects on Scotland

The British Civil War had a profound impact north of the border in Scotland for many reasons. The Scottish Stewarts had ascended to the English throne in 1603 when *James the VI of Scotland* became James I of England. Thus, the two monarchies were united and the political fortunes of each kingdom were joined. James had been baptized a Catholic, his mother Mary Queen of Scots wish, and his coronation as Scottish king, after she was deposed as queen, occurred at Stirling in 1567 when he was only seven months old. The country was so divided between Protestants and Catholics that many nobles refused to attend the ceremony. After coming of age (19), James took the reigns of Scottish power in 1585 and ruled Scotland as regent from that time until his death as James I of England in 1625. His absentee reign from 1603 was as much a result of the changing nature of politics in England and Scotland, as it was his new responsibility of governing the enhanced kingdom to the south. From the onset James clashed with the English parliament. Thus, his rule in Scotland which most historians characterize as relatively good and stable was conversely poor and unstable in England. His unwillingness to emulate Elizabeth I in putting seasoned politicos around him in dealing with the legislature undermined his authority. Hence, the rise of parliament in England would take a turn that would not revert back to earlier days in Anglo-Saxon England, prior to 1215, when the monarch ruled as absolute dictator. When authority passed to James's son, Charles I in March 1625, the English monarchy was overspending, engaged in typical sycophantic social and political developments that hurt its image and efficacy, and the English parliament had lost respect for the Stewart dynasty. It was this volatile context that saw the Scots and English lock horns, as the English were turning on each other during the pre-Civil War era. In 1629, Charles prorogued the English parliament and governed without it until 1640. The religious dimension of the volatile socio-political context in England and Scotland was important. The Scottish Reformation led by John Knox in the middle of the sixteenth century was now coming full flower. In 1637, Charles made the mistake of attempting to impose Anglican ritual and liturgy on the Scots. The people rioted on High Street in Edinburgh, home of the Kirk's most famous church, St. Giles Cathedral, and the rebellion spread throughout Scotland. The Scottish parliament and the Scottish Privy Council had not been informed about Charles's decision. An economic component also became important. Because of an attempt in 1625 by the king and the English parliament to get back lands lost in the Scottish Reformation, which increased taxes, merchants joined ministers and landed elites in Scotland to voice their disgust with Charles. In 1638, Scots by the thousands signed the national covenant in defending the rights of the Scottish parliament and the Kirk in order to determine their own religious policies. In the same year, the Scottish Presbyterians, in their General Assembly, abolished the bishop posts in the Kirk which infuriated Charles. He was more flexible on liturgy, but on his personal ecclesiastical authority, which he felt was undermined when the Scots tried to knock out his own appointees as overseers of church activity in Scotland, he was more rigid. In 1639, Charles sent an army north to deal with the wayward Scots. This resulted in the *Bishops' Wars* of 1639–40. The first battle, near Kelso, Scotland, saw the English withdraw fearing the Scots would overrun them. In fact, the Scots under the Earl of Leven (Alexander Leslie) had fooled the larger English army into thinking they had a superior force. It was the first Scottish victory over the English in over 325 years since Bannockburn. Charles was then forced to sign the *Treaty of Berwick*, which humiliated the monarch and compelled him to recall the English parliament. Even worse, was the next battle on August 28, 1640 where the Scots beat the English at Newburn, close to Newcastle, England. The English withdrew and the Scots gained more autonomy.

Box 2.2: Stone of Scone

Scone was the ancient sight of the Scottish Kings. Since Kenneth MacAlpin brought Picts and Scots together to form the Scottish kingdom around 850 AD, the kings of Scotland had been crowned there. Today, Scone is a short drive (five miles) north from Perth and northeast of Stirling. The Stone of Destiny had been used in ancient Scottish monarchical ritual. In 1297, Edward I (Longshanks) took the stone back with him to London and placed it in Westminster Abbey where it stayed for nearly 700 years. It symbolized the joining of Scots and English, with the former as essentially vassals to the latter. On Christmas Day 1950, a small group of militant nationalist students from Scotland stole the stone from Westminster Abbey in London and took it back to Scotland. Michael Collins, the founder of the Irish Republican Army, had contemplated doing the same some 30 years earlier. However, the "Stone of Scone," as it was also called was returned to the coronation throne in time for the funeral of King George VI in 1952 and Queen Elizabeth II to be crowned in 1953. The Scots finally got their wish in 1996 when the Conservative government decided to appease pro-devolution sentiment and returned the stone to Edinburgh to the castle where it is displayed today. In 1990, the author saw the stone at Westminster Abbey and returning to the same site in 2003 saw that no stone sat under the English coronation chair after centuries of symbolic linkage between the two nations.

By 1642, *the British Civil Wars* (a.k.a. *the English Civil War*) had begun. Its parties included the parliamentary-supported Roundheads (Puritans) and the monarchy-supported Cavaliers (defenders of the king). It was not until the rise of the New Model Army under the leadership of the landed member of the English parliament, *Oliver Cromwell*, that the fortunes of the English nation would change. It had a profound effect on Scotland as the parliamentary army gained territory and control of most areas of England. However, it was not until the Scottish parliament agreed to send its army south to work with Cromwell's men that the English parliamentary army moved toward ultimate victory in the war. As the English parliament began to lay the groundwork for a genuine English republic, the parts of the Celtic fringe rebelled sensing the monarchy and the realm were coming unglued. Also, the Scots, who watched their nobles fragmenting and aligning with the two sides, saw their parliament and Church call for a march into England to stop Charles. Others like the Earl of Montrose, who supported Charles, had good success in Scotland, particularly in the Highlands, but he and his men were defeated by the Scots at Philiphaugh as the Scottish army was returning from the Battle of Naseby. Parliament's armies stanched the revolt in the southern parts of England and Wales. In July 1647, Cromwell marched north and put down his erstwhile allies, the Scots, who had an army of 21,000. Cromwell's troops numbered 8000. The Scots had openly asked the dauphin, Charles II, to pledge the covenant; which he did. Cromwell begged the Scottish Parliament to end its relationship with the Stewarts, but it was not to be. Once beyond the Pennine Mountains, at Dunbar, the English destroyed the Scots and the Civil War was over. Charles I was then executed by the English parliament after a trial for treason on January 30, 1649. The English under Cromwell governed in Scotland for nine years. Cromwell allowed the Scots to practice their Presbyterianism and the Scots sent 30 men to the Commonwealth parliament in London. The Scottish parliament was prorogued until the Restoration and the ascension of Charles II to the joint English and Scottish throne.

In the wake of Restoration and the return of Charles II (the Scottish Stewart) to the English throne, the English parliament sought more power vis-à-vis the monarchy. With the succession of Charles's son James II (James VII of Scotland) to the British throne in 1685 all seemed bright given the fact that James's coffers were full, the English Church was subservient, the army successful, and parliament and opposition muted. In 1688, a small group of disaffected elites in England alarmed at the thought of increased Roman Catholic influence in the practices and theology of the Anglican religion, as well as James's unwillingness to brook opposition in the House of Commons, sent a letter to William, Prince of Orange of the Netherlands, to come to England to assume the throne. Meeting no resistance, William arrived and was greeted by an army in disarray. Many welcomed him with open arms. James fled, was captured, and brought back to London. But, William allowed him to escape to France. The historical settlement known as the Glorious Revolution in England was the crowning achievement of English constitutional democracy with William handed a Bill of Rights by the parliament and forced to sign off on it. Lockeian liberal political theory had its first victory as the people exercised their rights which would become a hallmark of Anglo-Saxon democracy. North of the English border in Scotland, a similar phenomenon was playing out with the Scottish parliament over whether to recognize James VII (James II of England who had been deposed) and his claims to the throne or William of Holland.

1707: Union and Its Discontents

A Scottish parliament met in March 1689 to consider the rightful accession to the British throne. In April, the parliament voted to prevent James VII from retaining the crown. The parliamentarians went on to pass one of Scotland's most famous covenants, *the Claim of Right*, as well as the Articles of Grievances. These resolutions established four important political limitations on the monarchy's power: 1) parliament's consent was needed for taxation; 2) parliament had the right to meet often and debate openly; 3) the monarch could not override laws; and 4) the Episcopalian church format was unacceptable to the Scots (Fry and Fry 1995). These constitutional measures would be the foundation for abolishing the "English" Church administration in Scotland and the refounding of the Church of Scotland in the form it is in today. Despite some differences, William generally agreed to the terms presented by the parliament. This settlement also paved the way for union with England by 1707.

Box 2.3: Scottish Covenanting Tradition

Covenant movements in Scotland are of historical importance. A "covenant" or binding agreement in Western legal terms is a bit of a stretch in the Scottish cases, but rather the covenants of Scottish history are political documents and statements that show the anger of a minority people against either an absolutist monarch or asymmetrical political arrangement. Scots have issued covenants at various times in their history from the famous Declaration of Arbroath in 1320, which was similar to the English barons' declaration at Runnymeade in 1215, to the Claims of Right in 1689 and 1988. Like the English nobles calling on King John for more political say and control of their feudalistic affairs in compelling the king to sign the Magna Carta, the Scots have simply tried to change the existing state of affairs, usually in regard to the rights of elites, church and state, and local unitary institutions ran from London. Of the various covenanting events (1320, 1638, 1689, 1842, 1949, 1988), the National Covenant of 1638 just prior to the English Civil War seems to be the most salient historically. Over 100 years ago, American president Woodrow Wilson, himself descended from Scotch-Irish Ulstermen and a Presbyterian (and a founder of the modern discipline of political science), would lecture his classes at Princeton and use 1638 and the people's signing of the covenant in the solemn and stern environs of Grayfriars Church yard in Edinburgh (the Kirk's most famous church located on the Royal Mile—the long, famous street in the capital that fits the mood of Scots politically with its gray cobblestone streets and granite and cement gray buildings, many of which date back to the sixteenth century) as a seminal event in the history of liberty and democracy for Britons and Americans. Scots took a stand for liberty that would reverberate to other shores, most notably America in 1776, and began the long march toward democracy.

Prior to union, Scotland's economy had problems. In the late 1690s, the largely agrarian Scottish economy had faltered as crop failures resulted in dire straits. Hunger, poverty, and disease came; as a result, one-quarter of the population perished (just over one million people) by century's end. Making matters worse, England's war with Scotland's historical ally, France, caused the French to attack Scottish merchant ships coming out of Scottish ports in the North Sea to prevent them from trading with European towns. England then imposed the Navigation Acts which said that only English ships could import produce and goods from the British Isles. Scots were preempted from carrying goods back to Scotland. In 1701, the Westminster parliament in London passed the Act of Settlement which allowed William's sister-in-law, Princess Anne Stewart, daughter of James VII of Scotland to assume the throne after William's death. The law also stated that a Protestant must assume the British throne. The Scots were unhappy because they were not advised of the law's substance. Princess Anne was seemingly acceptable to most (as a Stewart), but Anne's heir was to be the German princess, Sophie. This was unacceptable to Scots. Anne ascended the throne in 1701. She had hoped for union between England and Scotland. As a result, she appointed a committee to look into union and in 1703 Scottish elections returned a parliament where division set in. The legislature was split almost in thirds with just over one-third in favor of union, one-third against (Jacobites), and just under one-third uncommitted. By July 1706, a 31-member commission met in London to negotiate union. Issues of trade and economics were paramount. Most of the Scottish nobility, with their ancient ties to English aristocratic politics, were more interested as a collective in lining their pockets than looking at the issue of union from a nationalist perspective. England thus made certain guarantees to Scotland. The Kirk would remain unfettered. The Scottish parliament would come to an end. The German Hanovers would assume the UK crown after Anne's death (they were still on the throne as German Windsors at the dawn of the twenty-first century). Scots would get seats in the House of Commons in London in a newly created "Great Britain." England's currency would be the norm and Scotland's privy council would stay (it was stopped within months of union). On January 16, 1707, the *Treaty of Union* was passed by the Scottish parliament in Edinburgh. It was to go into effect on May 1.

Box 2.4: 1707 Union with England

The most important date in modern Scottish history is 1707. It was during this year that the Scots aligned with the English and fused political systems, although the Scottish and English Crowns had been connected since 1603 and the end of the Tudor dynasty and the rise of the Stewarts. At that time, James VI of Scotland became James I of England and the Catholic-leaning Stewarts took control of the British monarchy. At the time of Union, 100 years later, the Scots were to keep their parliament in Edinburgh and also certain trade rights that had been denied to them after the Scottish Claim of Right in 1689 and the English Bill of Rights placed on William and Mary in the same year. However, within a few years of union, the Scots parliament was shutdown, the English political establishment in control, and Scots were once again subjects to an Anglo-centered political setup. For the most part, the Act of Union held constant until the late twentieth century when devolution was voted on twice and eventually won for Scots in 1997. The question became: how much longer will the Union hold? For most Scots some self-government was better than none at all.

Most histories tend to focus on the reciprocal nature of the union at its onset. That Scots got improved economic fortunes and partnership with London. However, criticism immediately broke loose. Less than one-fourth of Scots wanted union. No referendum had been offered. A very small number of Scots could vote at the time. Anger manifested in political protest and violence. The Duke of Queensberry was attacked with stones while riding in his carriage. Many unionist parliamentarians in Scotland were accosted and verbally abused. The Jacobites were incensed seeing the union as an asymmetrical taxing arrangement in England's favor. By 1715, the *Jacobites* rose in order to defend the Stewarts's claims to the throne. They were defeated then and in 1745 at the bloody battle of Culloden Moor (see Box 2.5). Scotland's political elites had tied their future to England (a country they had battled 13 times in warfare over the centuries) and its constitution. The British constitution as it affected Scotland would not be altered until the referendum on devolution in September 1997 almost 300 years later.

Box 2.5: Jacobites and Bonnie Prince Charlie

The Jacobites were a radical group in the Tory party that tried to prevent the further succession of Hanoverian British monarchs. They had hoped to put a Scottish Stewart back on the throne upon Queen Anne's death in 1714. The Jacobites were strong in Scotland and supported James VII (or would be James II of England) and his son (James VIII—would be James III of England, who in Latin was called Jacobus) and their claims to the crown. After Anne's death, the resulting settlement kept the House of Hanover in power and the Jacobites rebelled under the leadership of James VIII. The revolt was a failure as were subsequent uprisings in 1715 and 1719. The third uprising was better planned and supported by France. It was led by James VIII's son, "Bonnie Prince Charlie," and the lowlands were occupied by the Jacobites and they managed to invade England. However, most Scots in the lowlands did not support the Jacobites, religion factored into the division, and they were repelled by the British troops. The Battle of Culloden was the end of any Jacobite power in 1746 as Scottish lords, led by the Campbells, wiped out the Jacobites and the British government forcibly reorganized Highland life and society to punish the rebels who were largely from the region.

Ireland: Brian Boru to 1801

The Norwegian Vikings first invaded Ireland in 795 AD off of Dublin's coast at Lambay Island. *The Vikings* ransacked settlements and churches. The Irish themselves had done the same at times to the latter, but eventually Vikings intermarried with Celts and began to build towns into the ninth century. After their experiences battling the Anglo-Saxons across the Irish Sea in what is now England, the Vikings brought vestiges of local government to Ireland something the Celts had not tried. The Vikings were largely successful because they found the land and indigenous Irish kingdoms in disarray. Of the four major kingdoms (Connacht, Leinster, Munster, and Ulster) no political links between them could be found. The concept of alliance was a foreign one. Even the Irish sub-monarchies were disorganized. The Vikings undercut several monarchies, but one, the Dàl Cais kingdom, a small one on the river Shannon in County Clare, was to rise to prominence. After its king, Mathghamain, was killed in 976, his brother *Brian Boru* would become arguably the most famous Irish king in history. He ruled from 976 to 1014. Brian defeated the Vikings at Limerick which neutralized Viking power in Ireland and allowed the Celts to subjugate them. He avenged the murder of his brother and took over the entire kingdom of Munster. After battling other Vikings and Irish kings, Brian finally agreed to the division of Ireland with Màel Sechnaill II, the Uí Néill high king who ruled from Tara. In 1002, Máel Sechnaill turned over the high king post bloodlessly to Brian after diplomatic maneuvering. Eventually, Brian went north and recognized the Irish Church and was dubbed the emperor of the Irish people. His last name, Bóroime (Boru), translates to "taker of tributes." Hence, several kings had paid him homage. In April 1014, the Vikings attacked Leinster and the battle, at Clanlaf near Dublin, was a savage one in which Boru and his son, Murchad, were killed. At 72 to 87 years of age, depending on the history, Boru died, but his fellow Gaels prevailed. The Vikings further conquest of Ireland ended, although they had established settlements and influence in several Irish towns (major cities today) such as Dublin, Cork, and Limerick. For the first time, a Celtic king had come close to unifying all of Irleand. But, the island fragmented politically after Boru's death. The political division of Ireland would continue as a main theme in Irish politics into the twenty-first century.

Over 100 years later, the English influence in Ireland began when on August 1, 1166 (100 years since the Norman invasion of England), the king of Leinster, Diarmait Mac Murchada sailed across the Irish Sea with his daughter to Bristol, England to offer her hand in marriage, but to also gain political support from *Henry II*, the English king. In France, he caught up with Henry. Henry offered him support knowing vassalage could be gotten if Diarmait had the right support. Diarmait returned to Bristol and queried Scots, English, Welsh, and Normans in his pursuit of defeating his enemies in Ireland. With Henry's permission, Diarmait married off his daughter to the Earl of Pembroke, the Norman Richard Fitzgilbert de Clare (a.k.a. *Strongbow*). Strongbow's relatives from South Wales helped and the next move was to head back to Ireland. Diarmait took several mercenaries with him, ahead of his newfound Norman comrades in arms. In the Fall of 1167, he sailed back to Ireland. He and his mercenary army and Norman supporters sacked several towns and took back the Leinster kingdom. Strongbow arrived on August 23, 1167 with 1200 men at Waterford (against Henry II's judgment) and the Anglo-Normans were in Ireland for good. It would not be until 1922 that the English would leave, at least the southern part of Ireland.

Box 2.6: Beyond the Pale

We have all heard the phrase in modern English, "That's beyond the pale!" Meaning that something is so far out of the norm or someone has gone too far in his or her actions or argumentation. The phrase is often used in hyperbolic terms today. The concept comes from Ireland where under the medieval English (originally from Wales) Tudor dynasty the Pale was the area to which English rule extended. The Pale was oftentimes a fixed earth boundary outside a region or city, like Dublin. Beyond the Pale the English government had authority, but could not guarantee its citizens and lords security. Beyond the Pale were the indigenous Celts who were seen as heathen and barbarians by the civilized English. What's more, many of the indigenous people were themselves products of Norman-Irish ancestry going back to the earlier Anglo-Norman conquest of Ireland after 1166.

Unlike England, the Normans had more difficulty in taking Ireland. Irish nobility simply went into the hills and wooded areas when the Normans attempted to expropriate their land. Smaller Irish chieftains took their livestock with them into the villages and dales. Thus, the Irish normally went to the hills and mountains and the Normans stayed in the low areas. The Irish, a rough-hewn Celtic lot, lived outdoors in open air camps, tended cattle in the fields, and their kings sat at feasts with commoners much to the shock and dismay of the Normans (who were more class-conscious). Thus, we see the egalitarianism and communal strain in Irish politics versus the class-oriented aspects of English politics that carry down through the ages from William's overthrow of the Anglo-Saxons. Also, the Normans could never fully put the Irish underfoot like the English. Much like the Picts under the Romans in Scotland, the Irish kings were so numerous and formed various groupings that when some were knocked out by the Normans new Irish dynasties appeared. Indigenous Irish nobility (Celts) were large given the prevalence of polygamy and less than rigid marriage conventions. One king, Pilib Mág Uidhir had 20 sons by eight women and 54 grandsons.

The start of the fourteenth century saw the Irish and Scots come together to challenge English overlordship in their countries. The Scots under Robert the Bruce had success at Bannockburn in 1314 and routed the English army. Bruce's brother, Edward, was invited to Ireland by the king of Ulster, Domnall O'Neill, and in May 1315 Edward landed with 6000 soldiers close to Larne. The Plantagenet vassal, Richard de Burgo, the "Red" earl of Ulster, was disavowed and was defeated by Edward by the end of June. Edward moved south to Meath and took Leinster as Norman vassals refused to confront him because they did not work together. Also, the Irish rebelled against the overlords when they saw a fellow Celt, Edward, marching in. Bruce might have taken large chunks of Ireland and a pan-Gaelic alliance between Scots (originally Irish Celts who had gone to Scotland—Alba at the time) and Irish might have been able to challenge Anglo-Norman hegemony, but he returned north to Ulster. In 1317, he returned to Scotland, then came back to Ireland with his brother Robert, the Scottish king, and he proceeded to march unimpeded through much of Ireland taking land, forcing submission and homage, and the payment of the tribute by Norman vassals. The indigenous Irish were not happy with the Scots' actions in Ireland. Edward returned to Ulster and Robert returned to Scotland. The Scottish army under the Bruces had been kept out of Dublin, but Ireland was ransacked and what had been a source of solid revenue for the Norman kings of England became a major problem. In the Fall of 1318 after Edward was crowned king of Ireland, he met an army under the Norman John de Bermingham. In the battle at Faughart, Edward was killed and the Scots defeated. Thus the division between Normans and Irish and the problems of a weak government for the Irish led to difficulties controlling the society. Eventually, the Plantagenets had forced Ireland to adhere to English laws and customs and in 1460, Edward Poynings proclaimed that the English king's writ could not be usurped in Ireland.

As *Henry VII*, the Welshman who would prevail in the English War of the Roses by 1485 and ascend the English throne, came to power, Ireland increasingly became an important colony for the English crown. Ireland's status within the British Isles would not functionally change for over 425 years, until 1922.

The British Civil Wars and Ireland

Under the *Tudors*, Ireland began to become ensconced in the English socio-economic and political landscape. Elizabeth I's policy of sending greater numbers of English landlords to colonize the island was relatively entrenched over a half century later when the Puritan army arrived in late 1649 under Oliver Cromwell. Although Ireland was very much a foreign land inhabited by foreign people with foreign customs, Cromwell was sent to Ireland by the Rump parliament of 1648–53 to quell the political discord in that land. With a divided Irish social milieu, the Cavalier supporters of the dauphin, Charles II, had hoped to continue the rebellion among the Irish that had supposedly ended with cessation agreements in 1643 and 1645. The Irish had rebelled originally in 1641 when they saw Charles I losing control of parliament. The king had dispatched troops to put the uprising down. Of course, one of the main sticking points between the king and the parliament was the payment of monies to the crown to fund the military venture in Ireland. After the execution of Charles I on January 30, 1649, the leaders and troops loyal to the Stewarts, as well as various Irish "confederates," began rebelling against the new parliamentary-led government in England. It was in this muddy context that Cromwell brought the *New Model Army* (NMA) to Ireland.

Cromwell and his forces landed near Dublin in mid-August 1649. He arrived with 35 ships. Two days after he got to Ireland, his aide Henry Ireton joined him with 77 ships. After a speech to Dubliners, who largely supported the English Puritan cause, Cromwell marched north to the town (called by the English) of Tredagh—known today as *Drogheda*. The Irish had called it *Droched Atha*, "the bridge and the ford." Cromwell proceeded to march on Drogheda with 8000 foot soldiers and 4000 soldiers on horseback. The resisting Cavalier army led by the Earl of Ormonde and Sir Arthur Aston only had 2000 troops. They dug into the entrenched walled city for the battle which came on September 11, 1649 at 5:00 PM when the NMA began its siege. Once through the walls, Cromwell's men destroyed the rebellious Anglo-Irish army and killed 1000 civilians as well. Some 3000 total were killed in the battle. Next at *Wexford*, Cromwell's army employed another vicious siege that yielded similar results to those of Drogheda. Ormonde had 500 soldiers and 100 in the cavalry to defend the city. Aside from severe military casualties to the Cavalier army in revolt against the parliament's army, 1500 civilians were killed as well. The sword had delivered a broadside to the parliamentary opposition and the Irish were subjugated by the English once again.

For the most part, the nationalistic implications of these battles in Ireland were muted since the battles were spurred by intra-English politics: the Cromwell's NMA fighting on behalf of the parliament against Ormonde's army, a vestige of the failing monarchy's defense. What's more, the religious overtones were clear given Cromwell's devout evangelical Protestant viewpoints and his relentless rhetoric and actions aimed at punishing fellow Christians, who he viewed as heretics—the Catholic clergy and their fellow Irish citizens, who were loyal to Rome. Thus, the longstanding colonial animosity toward the English continued to take on both national and increasingly religious dimensions after Cromwell returned to England in 1650 after nine months in Ireland. Within three years, he would be Lord Protector and assume military governance over the British Isles.

Ireland's Union with England

When Union with England came on January 1, 1801, Ireland had had its own parliament for 500 years. It was not until 1782 that a kind of empowered quasi-Home Rule was accorded and up to that point England's interests were enforced by landed Protestant elites. Catholics had no say in the local legislature. The French Revolution of 1789 affected the Irish context greatly. By the time of Henry Grattan's actions (he had led the charge for a more independent parliament in Dublin) in the 1780s, Ireland had grown in population, its economy was taking off, and it was forging its own identity apart from England. This progress was not reflected politically as Protestants still controlled the independent legislature, despite the Protestant Grattan's attempts to enfranchise the majority Catholics. Nationalism began to stir and one Protestant attorney, Theobald Wolfe Tone, called for an independent Ireland. He was more radical than Grattan. Wolfe Tone called for a union of Christians (both Protestants and Catholics) to expel the English. His goals of interfaith harmony were shattered, however, as an overwhelming majority of Presbyterians in Belfast in the 1780s were assiduously anti-Catholic. By the mid-1790s, Protestants and Catholics were killing each other in Ulster, a harbinger of things to come less than 200 years later. By

1793, Britain was at war with France, and some Irish, including Wolfe Tone, saw a chance for Ireland to be free of England. Wolfe Tone also attempted to empower Catholics. The British parliament passed a law allowing Catholics to carry guns, participate in jury trials, hold officer ranks in the military, and get degrees at Trinity College in Dublin. However, the parliament did not allow Catholics seats in the London-based legislature.

With revolutionary intrigue seeping in from the continent and the French at war with the British, rebellion broke out in Ireland and in 1798 some 50,000 were killed. In August of that year, the French sent war ships to Killala bay in County Mayo and the French leader, General Humbert, hoisted *le drapeau du vert* with the words "Erin go brach," meaning "Ireland forever!" The French had hoped the Irish would revolt as the Americans had twenty years earlier. The British general, Lord Cornwallis (of American Revolutionary War fame), was dispatched to the Emerald Isle with 20,000 troops and the French backed down when the Irish could not be compelled to mount a revolt alongside their erstwhile continental allies. At this time, the British prime minister, William Pitt, decided that the only way to deal with the Irish was to formally annex them into the British fold as had been done to the Scots nearly a century before. The close debate over union in parliament was furious and heated for two years. Both pro and con sides won formal votes in the House of Commons. Votes were bought, traded, and sold and the future foreign secretary, Lord Castlereagh, helped maneuver a successful union vote for Pitt. The House of Commons voted 138 to 96 on January 15, 1800 for union. With 50,000 English soldiers in Ireland and an Irish parliament that had problems reforming itself, the Act of Union was given the royal imprimatur on August 1, 1800. When union went into effect on January 1, 1801, the Irish parliament that had stood for five centuries was disbanded, the Irish got 100 seats in the House of Commons in London, and they also got 28 peerages and four bishop seats in the House of Lords. The Irish legal and judicial system stayed the same. The *Church of Ireland* fused with the Church of England. In practice, not much changed from the previous 600 years of English control of Ireland.

Wales: Resistance and Absorption

1283, 1485, and 1536: England Consolidates Its Hold on Wales

After 1066, Wales saw its fortunes dovetail with England's. As its larger neighbor to the east continued to encroach on it, the Welsh king Llywelyn II had by 1277 a kingdom with autonomy and a developing economy. However, England's military incursion into Wales in 1277 forced Llywelyn to capitulate to Longshanks in 1283. From this point, Edward I wanted to focus on gaining the Welsh elite's loyalty and in 1301 he created the title of "Prince of Wales" for his son and heir to the English throne, Edward, who had been born at *Caernarfon* in northern Wales in 1284. The first investiture was actually held at Lincoln, England and the future Edward II was given all the territory of what had been the

Welsh kingdom. The ceremony continued to be replicated nearly 700 years on when in 1969 Queen Elizabeth II invested her eldest son, Charles, as Prince of Wales. That ceremony was held at Caernarfon castle in Wales and televised globally. Longshanks successfully incorporated the Welsh nobility into the English-dominated state. He also recruited Welshmen to serve as ground troops in its battles with Scots and continental European states. In taking on Wallace and the Scots at Falkirk in 1298, of the 12,500 infantrymen, 10,500 were Welsh and one-third of the horses used were from Powys in north-central Wales. The English had learned early how to divide and conquer among subjugated people, a lesson they would apply with much success in expanding their empire into the eighteenth and nineteenth centuries.

Box 2.7: *Owain Glyn Dŵr* (Owen Glendower)

Glyn Dŵr was born in 1354. Like William Wallace in Scotland nearly a century earlier, Glyn Dŵr rose to lead a revolt against the English over lordship in Wales. Unlike Wallace, Glyn Dŵr was from the Anglo-Welsh elite. Like Wallace, he was used by the indigenous nobility in Wales to challenge the English monarch's authority. His role became mythic as poems were written of him by the 1380s and his prophetic calling to become the second Cadwaladr (the first Cadwaladr was the son of Cerdwallon and by the late 600s AD lost the kingdom for the Britons—Celts—to the Anglo-Saxons). In September 1400, Glyn Dŵr challenged England's Henry IV. Glyn Dŵr's uprising was primarily a nationalist one. Taking advantage of the chaos in Welsh feudal politics after Henry IV had removed Richard II from the English throne, Glyn Dŵr's fellow rebels named him the Prince of Wales and he spent several years fighting the English. After 1408, he resorted to guerrilla warfare in Wales to challenge the English authorities. Glyn Dŵr also created an indigenous Welsh parliament, the last to sit prior to 1999 when the devolved assembly opened in Cardiff, in 1404 at Machynlleth in north-central Wales. He also summoned one the following year north of there in Harlech on Tremadog Bay. Like Wallace, he was on the run much of his rebellion; although, unlike the Scottish hero, he was never caught. According to most historians, Glyn Dŵr died in September 1415 in Herefordshire at the home of his daughter. His legacy is one of baronial intrigue, not unusual for the medieval period in Europe. However, the other Celtic peoples have their own nationalist heroes in their memories (such as Wallace and Bruce in Scotland and Boru and Collins in Ireland). The Welsh have few mythical heroes historically (due to years of English absorption), and as the twentieth century wore on Glyn Dŵr's legacy began to play a greater role in the history and politics of modern Welsh nationalism and identity.

For 400 years, the *Welsh Marches* were a major geo-political part of Anglo-Welsh relationship. The Marches were the lands that fell on both sides of the Welsh and English boundary that had both territorial and political significance for the Anglo-Welsh nobility. This nobility consisted of indigenous Welsh elites, Anglo-Norman nobles, and the clergy in Wales. Under the Plantagenets, beginning in 1100, the Marches became important. The Norman centralization of authority began to extend into the areas of the Marches and the Welsh nobility was affected. But at first, "Marcher Lords," as they were called, did not recognize

English law, but rather Welsh law, including separate Welsh courts for territory and other rights for Welsh nobles that did not apply to English nobles in Wales. The Welsh elites had greater powers than what the English feudal elites would get under the Normans in Ireland. Some have argued that the indigenous Welsh Marcher Lords had greater power than the ancient Welsh kings in what was prior to 1066 a fragmented, patchwork quilt of Celtic fiefdoms and kingdoms in Wales (somewhat similar to Ireland, but still affected by the Anglo-Norman incursions of that era). Confusing the political dynamics even more was the fact that Normans had put English barons in control of parts of Wales alongside the indigenous Welsh elites. Over the centuries, many in the Welsh nobility were utterly Anglicized eventually moving to areas on the border of Wales in England such as Herefordshire and Shropshire (two regions that today still reflect major Welsh currents culturally in terms of place names, food, landed interests, etc). Many Welsh families, especially the landed gentry, would eventually become "English" nobles losing completely their Welsh identities in physically moving their families farther east into England and even to London.

This entanglement of Welsh and English fortunes would affect the eventual political settlement of Wales itself when in 1485, the Welshman Henry Tudor, descended from an ancient Welsh ruling family—the *Tewdwrs*, which took up the cause of the Lancaster family in battling the Yorks for the English crown in the fabled "War of the Roses." In 1485, after the battle of Bosworth, Henry Tudor, became England's Henry VII after defeating the forces defending the monarchy of the Yorkist, Richard III. Both families had direct political and military ties to Wales and ancient Welsh genealogy. Once the Tudors were on the throne, the way toward further Anglo-Welsh integration was paved and under Henry VII's son, *Henry VIII*, the *Act of Union* was proclaimed.

In February 1536, Henry VIII centralized greater authority in English hands by putting all of Wales under the control of the Welsh aristocracy. Under common law, individual administrators, reeves of the shire (sheriffs), had controlled local government on behalf of the king for centuries during and after the Anglo-Saxon era (c. 450–1066). This policy remained until localized councils in the British counties were introduced in 1889. Within weeks of this edict, Henry enforced law that was passed by the English parliament which became known as the Act of Union. Not to be confused with its namesake in 1707 in Scotland or 1801 in Ireland, it was passed without any Welsh participation in its deliberation or content. The act said that the union already existed (thus creating a fait accompli). It was conceptualized as a further political tool used for integrating parts of Wales controlled by Edward I in 1284 and so the continued administrative annexation of Wales by England began over 200 years before was legitimated by Wales's neighbors in London. Also, the end of the legal separateness of Wales and England was the crowning achievement for Henry as he sought to end what little was left of Wales's legal and political autonomy after 1283. Hence, London's laws and the common law were now supreme in all parts of Wales. The English language would slowly take control in Wales, but this would be contested at various points in Welsh history after 1536. The Welsh got some seats in the Westminster parliament. And in a pattern to be replicated historically, the Council of Wales was created for the King's administrative oversight in the 13 counties of Wales (as well as four English counties). Welsh courts were set up (the Great Sessions) and they lasted into the nineteenth century. Like Ireland, Wales was subjugated and transformed over several centuries. Although unlike Ireland, the Welsh absorbed English currents in general, rather than resisting them until the early to middle part of the twentieth century. And even then, much of southern Wales and the large urban capital, Cardiff, were so thoroughly Anglicized that Welsh political culture had become divided on cultural, linguistic, and other matters.

Nationalism and Politics: The Arrival of National Identity in Scotland

Movement toward home rule began in Scotland and Wales in the 1880s. Home rule, or devolution as it is also known, is the transference of political power to a subsidiary institution in order to allow that body the authority to exercise executive and legislative control over the affairs of a distinct region. This semi-autonomous arrangement allows for a sharing of power between the central government and the devolved government. This type of relationship is similar to the type of government adhered to in the United States between the national government and the state governments.

In 1891 the Scottish Home Rule Association was created to push for a new Scottish Office in London. The Scottish National Party (SNP) has been colored with a separatist hue since its inception. Home rule in Scotland gained favor during the Victorian era. Between 1889 and 1920 the House of Commons voted several times on Scottish home rule. On every occasion except 1889 a majority of Scots MPs voted for self-government for Scotland. The alienation of home rule supporters and the actions of the established political parties led to the creation of the first nationalist party in Scotland. In 1928 a member of the Independent Labour Party (ILP), John MacCormick, founded the NPS.

Prior to World War I, the Liberal Party was supposed to push a program of devolution through parliament for nationalists in Scotland. This, however, failed to take place due to the Liberals' decline in power. After the First World War, the Labour Party began to support the home rule movement in Scotland. Prior to that, the Scottish Trades Union Congress forwarded a resolution favoring home rule to British Prime Minister *David Lloyd George*. He, in turn, supported devolution for Scotland. However, Labour's support of home rule attenuated because of the political ramifications of home rule; i.e., a successful devolution bill meant a loss of potential votes. With the Liberal Party no longer a political threat to it, Labour was still relatively weak politically. Until 1945, Labour was only able to govern as a minority government or in coalition with other parties. Nevertheless, by the 1920s, Labour leaders realized the potential of Scotland as a political force. The election of 1924 exemplified Labour's growing support in Scotland. It gained 41.1% of the vote compared to 32.9% in England. This, coupled with increasing nationalism led to Labour's advocacy of administrative, rather than legislative, devolution.

Box 2.8: David Lloyd George (*Dafydd Lloyd George*)

Born in England to Welsh parents, David Lloyd George became arguably the most prominent Welshman of the twentieth century. As a solicitor in Llanystumdwy, Lloyd George came onto the Welsh and UK political scene right at the end of Gladstonian era (April 1890 as an MP for Caernarfon in northern Wales). By the turn of the century, he was firmly ensconced in local Liberal Party politics in Wales and starting to make an impact throughout the kingdom. Lloyd George was a bit of a paradoxical figure (as politicians oftentimes are). He was a staunch Liberal with unionist proclivities, but favored Home Rule for Wales and led the nationalist extragovernmental movement—*Cymru Fydd* (Wales to Be)—early in his career. He was born in urban Merseyside in northeast England, but served politically mainly in rural areas of northern Wales. He advocated ideas that went down well with the budding socialist movements of his day (including the growing federation of Labour parties throughout the UK), but still represented the liberal ideals of individualism and capitalist free trade; he agitated for Home Rule for Wales and delivered Irish Home Rule at the point of the UK gun, but he first held a constituency at Caernarfon (where the invidious English king, Edward I, had proclaimed his son the Prince of Wales in 1301) and he brought about the investiture ceremony for the Prince of Wales in Caernarfon where the event is still held (the last one in 1969). Still, Lloyd George was the first Welshperson to come from the working classes to rise all the way to the British cabinet. In a few short years, he went from president of the Board of Trade in 1905 to Chancellor of the Exchequer in 1908 (the number two post in modern British politics). He was the first Welshman since 1855 to sit in the British cabinet. He was responsible for pensions for the elderly in 1908, a "People's Budget" in 1909 which taxed the wealthy (which was rejected by the Lords which ultimately led to that body's reform in 1911), and he created a national insurance program for Britons to fall back on in times of unemployment and illness—similar to Franklin Delano Roosevelt's Social Security Act of 1935 in Depression-wrought America. Once war came in August 1914, Lloyd George was in support and he steadily climbed from minister of munitions in May 1915 to war minister in July 1916 to prime minister in December 1916. Lloyd George was reelected in a war coalition with the Tories in December 1918. In spite of victory in Europe in the "Great War," as Britons call World War I, troubles at home, which included Ireland, led to the end of Liberal hegemony in Wales and Scotland and its fabled role in UK politics. In 1922, Lloyd George was out and the Tories in under Stanley Baldwin. One year later, Scotsman Ramsay MacDonald and Labour were in a minority government and the Liberals would see their peak with the Lloyd George era (as government leader) at an end. By 1929, he was the "Father of the House"—the longest serving member at Westminster. He stayed in politics until 1945 when he was given a peerage and died shortly thereafter. Still, he is the only Welshperson to serve as UK prime minister in British history.

Though it was not firm in its support for Scottish devolution, the Conservative Party fluctuated on the issue because of the dilemma in Northern Ireland and factionalism on the issue within the party during the second decade of the twentieth century. After a Speaker's Conference on devolution in 1919, some Conservatives supported home rule for two reasons: First, Scottish Tories believed that the culture of Scotland was important and a degree of devolution was needed to keep the state from becoming too Anglicized. Second, it was felt that some type of regional government would enable Scotland to control some of its own political affairs. However, these ideas, one cultural and the other overtly political, fell by the wayside after 1922. Between the World Wars, the nationalist movement in Scotland was a minor issue in British politics. Though its prospects were exciting to many, nationalism was politically impotent due to the proportionately low numbers in the British populace that it affected.

Scotland from the 1920s to Devolution

The year 1928 saw the start of the NPS and the slow, but steady political and electoral growth of nationalism in Scotland. Although unspectacular in the 1920s and 1930s, nationalism grew out of a cultural heart (as nationalism did even more so in Wales in the twentieth century), but by 1967 and the victory of the SNP's Mrs. Winnie Ewing at Glasgow Hamilton in a by-election, nationalism was becoming a political force to be reckoned with. The SNP's heart and soul was manifested in one person—Billy Wolfe. Wolfe, a businessman, was an old time nationalist who had fought a by-election at West Lothian in 1962 and got an astounding 23% of the vote. He became the party's chair in 1969. Although communalistic, Wolfe was a genuine nationalist calling for independence for Scotland and England out of Scotland. He was cut from the traditionalist nationalist vein like his colleague, and third SNP MP, Donald Stewart, who held the Western Isles for 17 years (1970–87) for the party, who when asked if he was a leftwing or rightwing nationalist said that asking him that question was like asking him if he favored "the Cavaliers or the Roundheads!"

Nationalism began to break through in the late 1960s and early 1970s as the Labour Party in Scotland accepted devolution in principle, a 180 degree turn from its previous opposition to it and the 1974 Westminster elections sent shockwaves as the SNP got 21.9% and 30.4% of the vote and took seven and 11 seats respectively in the February and October elections. The government then moved forward on devolution plans after these elections. Premier Harold Wilson, Labour's longtime leader since the 1960s, served from 1974-76 and then Welshman James Callaghan replaced him and served until 1979. The struggle in the Labour Party over Home Rule continued to grow and the 1979 referendums in Scotland and Wales were examples of Labour's muddled policy.

Prior to the 1979 referendum on devolution for Scotland, Labour created a Scotland Act (which failed in its first manifestation in the House of Commons in 1977, but passed in 1978) that called for home rule in the region, but it had to be accepted by over 50% of those voting and 40% of *all* Scottish voters had to show up to vote at the polls. The vote passed with 51.6% voting "yes" and 48.4% voting "no." But, only 32.8% of the total electorate voted "yes" and the referendum was nullified since it did not meet the 40% threshold spelled out by law. Thus, devolution failed to materialize and the waiting began as three angry SNP MPs, withdrew their support from the minority Labour government and it collapsed. That brought a general election in May 1979 that ushered in 18 years of Tory centralization, although, Conservatives argued that executive devolution under the secretary of state for Scotland's post was more efficient and less costly in the long run than a whole new layer of government in Edinburgh. Even the Tories were tartanized returning the venerable Stone of Destiny to Edinburgh Castle in 1996 to mollify Scottish sentiment. It did not seem to work as Labour swept to power in the UK and promptly went about altering the British constitution. Among many changes, including independence for the Bank of England, reform for the House of Lords, a new mayor for London, and home rule for Ulster, devolution in Scotland and Wales would be tried again. This time no bill would be drawn up until the referendums were completed. On September 11, 1997 Scots voted 74.3% for a new parliament and 60.2% for localized fiscal powers for the new body. Blair said no turnout requirement (like the invidious 40% rule) would be necessary and ironically overall turnout was lower in 1997 than 1979. Thus, Scotland had a legislature for the first time in 290 years.

It was not until 1999 that the new Scottish parliament was up and running (more will be said about the parliament, its powers, and elections to it in Chapter Five). In the court of public opinion it was a very important moment symbolically for Scotland. Yet, problems persisted. The position of first minister was tenuous as the first first minister, Donald Dewar (also Blair's Secretary of State for Scotland) died in the Fall of 2000 of a brain hemorrhage and the nation mourned. He had done much to bring about devolution in Scotland. His successor Henry McLeish was seen as London's man in running Holyrood and this offended many Scots (this same scenario would bedevil the Welsh as well—Celts appear to not like being told what to do!?) He lasted a year and resigned under pressure due to an ethics charge. He was replaced by Jack McConnell, a lesser known, yet popular Labour leader tied less to Blair's team and more to Scots Labour. McConnell would have much more success, despite the minority government Labour would lead in Edinburgh. Since the parliament was elected on proportional grounds, Labour entered a pact with the Liberal Democrats and this kind of consensus building appeared to help start the parliament in the right direction. According to political scientist Colin Pilkington, consensual politics among the parties developed on many issues and give and take took precedence over overt ideology since no party had a majority (Pilkington 2002).

Problems did evolve especially the negative public relations due to certain leaders, like McLeish battling ethics issues, the lack of policy direction (seen in Wales as well), the exorbitant budget overruns in building the new Holyrood parliament building in Edinburgh, and the lack of accountability as seen in the Fall of 1999 when the parliament tried to be the first legislature in the UK to end a ban on the promotion of homosexuality. The media, Roman Catholic church, and others got public opinion moving against the ban (given more traditional views on religion and sex in Celtic areas) and despite an largescale public opposition, the parliament abolished the ban anyway. This led the parliament to come under attack from media outlets, especially the top daily newspaper in Scotland, *The Scotsman* of Edinburgh, and others who saw the parliament as essentially a boondoggle. Yet, the movement toward increased local governance and Scottish solutions to Scottish problems continued to march forward as the second round of elections were held in 2003.

Ireland: Charles Parnell and the Rise of the Home Rule Movement

The year 1848 saw revolutions all over Europe. This *"Springtime of Nations"* saw the advent of liberal nationalism on the continent from Vienna to Berlin to Paris. The two areas where historians notice a lack of liberal impulses are Russia and Britain. Yet, the British Isles did see some revolutionary fervor when the Young Ireland movement attempted to imitate the continental rebellions. These idealistic nationalists called for a free Irish state free from British control. The leaders were Protestants and largely Ulstermen from the old Irish aristocracy. They tried to align with the Chartists in England who had called for social, economic, and political reform including greater suffrage for the working classes. Despite incendiary pamphleteering, public meetings calling for independence, and martial-style marching and drill instruction in the streets, the stillborn revolt was quelled by the police. The July 1848 revolt's leaders were not liquidated, but sent into permanent exile in Australia. In this context of discontent, continued emigration (over one million to the United States) and a final potato famine led the Irish toward greater animosity with the colonial overlord—England.

Out of this context arose the fabled *Fenian Brotherhood* which was a cell-based, militant nationalist organization. It was named after Fianna, the men who had followed the Celt and Irish hero Fionn Mac Cumhaill. The Fenians were radical wanting the complete removal of the British. They were not interested in piecemeal or gradualist change politically. They even kept the cells secret from each other so as not to give away their membership or allow the authorities to catch on to their whereabouts. The IRA and other groups would mimic this modus operandi in the twentieth century. By 1865, 200,000 had joined and some American Civil War veterans came on board after having served in Irish-American brigades. Some 40,000 had weapons and many were British soldiers. A failed putsch in Ireland led to the execution of four leaders in 1867. The next year the Liberals got control of the House of Commons when Prime Minister *William Ewart Gladstone* successfully told the British public about Catholic grievances in Ireland. Of Ireland's 5¾ million about 4½ million were Roman Catholic. Only 700,000 were Protestant. In 1869, the Church of Ireland (based on the Protestant Anglican model) was disestablished. The UK state took over all land, churches, and property. No church was to receive priority over another. The next order of business was the Irish Land Act which gave tenants more rights vis-à-vis land owners. As in property issues in capitalist demo-cracies, land rights and tenure were a stormy issue in Ireland. Issues related to land rights, payouts, and evictions still proved acrimonious in the backwards, agrarian region of the UK. The ancient Anglo-Irish squirearchy continued to prevail. The Irish began calling for their own parliament.

Box 2.9: Boycott

After the Land Act of 1870 was passed by the House of Commons in London, the Irish resented the confiscation of lands by the Anglo-Irish elites. Charles Parnell told his constituents and others that the Irish needed to stand up to the acts of their fellow citizens by isolating them. When Captain Charles Boycott could not get any folk to help him harvest the fields on his Mayo plantation, due to Parnell's blanket request, he called down 50 people from Ulster to help him with his fieldwork. Seven thousand British troops came to provide protection (more than 1/6 of the British army in Ireland)! When Boycott then went to Dublin he could not get a hotel room because the hotels refused to give him one. He left Ireland as a result and thus the infamous unconventional political action—the boycott—was born.

The origins of the modern Irish *Home Rule* movement drew its roots from what we might think today are somewhat strange origins. In 1870, Issac Butt, a lawyer and MP from Ireland, got Fenians, Protestants, and Catholic Liberal Party stalwarts together to create the Home Government Association. By 1873, it was now taken over by the Home Rule League. It appealed to Irish all over the island. In 1874, 59 members were elected to the House of Commons. It was not until the next year that *Charles Stewart Parnell* was sent to the Commons from County Meath north of Dublin. A Protestant from an Anglo-Irish aristocratic background, he provided the charismatic flair that the Irishmen in the UK legislature needed to affect government policies. Upon entering parliament at 29, Parnell took some time to get adjusted. However, he joined with another home ruler, J.C. Biggar, to use delaying and filibustering tactics to hold up the UK's legislative business. He was seemingly in contempt of the ancient house and its procedures. Eventually, the militant Fenians called for the support of a constitutional solution to the Irish national question. The disparate groups that made up the landscape of Irish politics started to coalesce around Parnell and the Home Rule movement. Militants, constitutionalists, Protestant Ulstermen, and Irish Catholics, all were coming together to call for devolution in Ireland. Economically, things started looking better in Ireland in the early 1870s, but by decade's end the economy started to sputter and many were left with nothing. The Tories (under Disraeli) and their one nation policy were jettisoned by the electorate in 1880 and Gladstone and the Liberals returned to power. Parnell and 60 other Home Rulers came back to London. In 1886, the British premier, Gladstone, attempted to accommodate the Parnellites. But, the Lords refused to allow home rule. The Irish were angered at the Land Act of 1870 and other socio-economic factors led to a near revolt. The House of Commons applied draconian measures to keep the peace, such as suspending habeus corpus via the Coercion Acts. Like the Scottish revolt over the Poll Tax nearly 100 years later, Parnell (as had some Labour and SNP MPs in 1989) tried to preempt the bills by parliamentary filibustering and delay. By early 1881, the Coercion Acts were passed. Despite escalating tensions, and problems with land controls, Parnell had to deal with segmentation in the nationalist movement—from radical separatists to constitutionalists. Parnell was then arrested for violating the Land Act in October 1881. He was to sit in jail for six months. While in jail, the top official in Ireland and his deputy were murdered by militants of the Irish Republican Brotherhood. Saddened, Parnell offered to resign but Gladstone would have none of it. In London, Parnell denounced the terrorism. Distancing himself from extremist sentiment, Parnell saw his Home Rule party take nearly every seat in Ireland in 1885.

Box 2.10: Charles Parnell

Charles Stewart Parnell was the Anglo-Irish Protestant son of an American mother who demonstrably hated the English. Parnell hailed from County Meath in Ireland, near Dublin, and sought election to the House of Commons as a member of the Home Rule Party. In 1870, he led the Home Rulers to London where they engaged in thorn-in-the-side parliamentary tactics aimed at thwarting governmental business. This sort of thing was not done in gentlemanly Victorian England. Until the major parties would recognize the movement for Irish Home Rule, Parnell was not to be satisfied. Fortunately for Parnell, the prime minister, the Liberal Party leader William Gladstone, was sympathetic to the claims of Irish Home Rulers. He worked with Parnell and his party to bring about an equitable settlement on land, food, and political matters. However, the Tories and other unionists were not in favor of undercutting the Anglo-Irish gentry in the country. Parnell's downfall came when it was discovered he had been having a longtime affair with the wife of one of his party's parliamentary members. Refusing to step aside as leader, various Liberal Party members, outraged at the immorality of his adulterous relationship, threatened to withdraw support from Gladstone on Home Rule. Parnell was eventually defeated as leader as his party lost support in Ireland. He died at the age of 45 trying to counter Irish unionists' arguments in a last ditch effort to save his political career and his cause.

Northern Ireland: Loyalists and Union with Great Britain

The problem between Protestants and Catholics in Ireland was an age old one. Henry VIII put the Anglo-Irish landed elites on plantations throughout Ireland. The English had first come to Ireland in the Middle Ages on the heels of the Norman lords. The Irish Church was somewhat different form the continental Catholic church with married bishops and paying as much attention to Gaelic tradition as Rome's rules. Henry wanted political and social homogeneity among his subjects, but was not willing to pay for forcible uniformity via the military route. Guerrilla warfare and face-to-face conflict broke out between the landed gentry and the poorer indigenous Irish. Religion played a role as spats over which form of Christianity would be embraced by the Irish people occurred. *Elizabeth I* wanted a more tolerant Protestantism. Given the Catholic world's animus toward her legitimacy, she did not engage many of the continental states in battle. But, she wanted to make sure Ireland was conquered and under the English boot. Ulster resisted for political reasons. By 1585, the Irish had agreed to the end of chieftainships and replacing those with peerages based on the English model. After Elizabeth died, the Plantation Act of 1609, moved the indigenous Irish off their land and both English and Scottish settlers were brought in to work, own, and cultivate 500,000 acres of plantations. This was the point that many Irish look back at when decrying the start of the Protestant dominance of Ireland and Ulster in particular. Just under a century later, in 1690, William of Orange, the king of England, won the *Battle of Boyne* in Ireland in which the former king, James II, was forced into exile in France and Protestant control was solidified. This came in the wake of the Roundhead march through Ireland which ended in a settlement act that called for the Protestantization of Ireland by not only displacing Catholics, but attempting to eventually absorb them into evangelical and Protestant ways. In a sense, the Catholic problem would take care of itself through assimilation and natural retrenchment. This would be the context that served as the foundation for the animosity between Catholics and Protestants in the strict sectarian violence of the twentieth century in Northern Ireland.

The treaty of December 1921 that created the Irish Free State as a dominion in the British Empire was somewhat equivocal about the status of Ulster. Of course, Protestants in the north, mainly descendants of Scotch-Irish settlers from the early seventeenth century, remained inexorably loyal to the London government. American president, the Scottish Presbyterian, Woodrow Wilson's family came from Ulster, descended from the Scotch-Irish settlers. The civil war that ensued in 1922 lasted for over a year. Some 4000 perished in intra-Irish bloodshed. In six counties in the north, Protestants outnumbered Catholics. The Cumann na nGaedheal government of W. T. Cosgrave thought the six counties would eventually be whittled to four when a boundary commission was drawn up and the Free State would absorb the Protestant province. In 1924, a boundary commission looked at Ulster, but its recommendations were leaked to journalists and nothing came of the commission's findings. Thus, the partition of Éire had occurred and over a half century diplomatic, political, and unconventional maneuvering in Dublin and Belfast led to tension, varying interpretations of the regions' relationship, and even de facto recognition by the 1960s. The Republican government in the south had put the de jure stipulation in its 1937 constitution that the six northern counties were part of Éire. Much like *Ostpolitik* between West and East Germans in the late 1960s under Social Democratic foreign minister Willy Brandt in the Grand Coalition government in West Germany, the attempt to work through the troubled relationship between Northern Ireland's prime minister, *Terence O'Neill*, and Éire's Taoiseach (prime minister in the Irish Gaelic), Seán Lemass materialized in 1965. This was a secretive, old style diplomacy that (Lemass's widow said later) was about the reintegration of the two Irelands. The assertion was denied emphatically by O'Neill.

After 1922, the Northern Irish state evolved into a devolved regional government with various domestic powers. The major difference with the Republican state in the south was in the way the political forces were developing and affecting the region's evolution. Where the Irish Free State was developing into a predominant party state with somewhat of an authoritarian political culture due to the conservative social base in Ireland, Ulster was equally conservative and authoritarian, but it became highly segmented along religious lines. Thus, Éire saw its political culture change somewhat due to the creation of a moderately pluralistic party system and Ulster saw unionist parties and groups gain a monopoly on a fractured political context where sectarian values outweighed economic and overtly social and class values. The moderation of Prime Minister O'Neill in the 1950s and early 1960s brought some changes to the political forefront in Ulster politics.

Wales: The Development of the Nationalist Cause

From 1536 to the early twentieth century, Wales was absorbed into the English-dominated political system that would become by 1707 the UK. A discourse on political nationalism began in Wales in the 1880s. Yet, this nationalism was more of a cultural nationalism. It was not by chance that increased political agitation over Ireland's future caused Gladstone's Liberal government to deal directly with home rule and this undoubtedly had an impact on the direction of Welsh politics and nationalism. Over a century earlier, the Welsh spiritual revival had brought evangelical Christianity to the fields and coalmines of *Cymru.* It was a genuinely Welsh religious awakening as *Methodism* came to Wales and the Englishmen George Whitefield and *John Wesley* were instrumental in bringing born-again Christianity to the Welsh. However, indigenous Welsh preachers were the spearheads, not Wesley and Whitefield, of the spiritual transformation after 1750. Also, a distinct Welsh tenor to the revival saw Calvinist beliefs (predestination) mix with free-will Methodism, and it was preached and conveyed in the Welsh language. Whitefield advocated more along the Calvinist lines. The Wesleyan doctrine with its emphasis on justification by faith alone was secondary. But, Methodism developed with a unique Welsh hue, unlike its English cousin. For the Welsh nation, these theological currents were important. By the early twentieth century, the Liberals, under Lloyd George, passed in the House of Commons a Nonconformity bill for Wales in 1920 that ended the Anglican Church's monopoly as spiritual arbiter of the Welsh and the government gave no denomination priority over any other. This answered the religious question for the Welsh as the overwhelming majority, which were *Methodistiaid* ("Methodists" in Welsh), believed the nation's religious calling and political identity needed defense in the face of Anglo-Saxon Anglicanism. Like Scotland and

Ireland, religion played a major symbolic role in making Welsh national identity distinctive in the UK.

Box 2.11: Welsh Methodism

The advent of Welsh nonconformity in religious matters was largely a product of the post-Civil War (1660–88) period in Britain. At the Restoration, Anglicans siding with the English monarchy sought to purge Puritans from the Church. During this period, the state sought to centralize the Anglican Church's hold on Christianity and although nonconformists continued to worship, many Baptists, Calvinists (modern-day Presbyterians), and Quakers left England and Wales for America. The latter group was systematically persecuted by the state in its attempt to shut the Friends Church down. By the start of the eighteenth century, most Friends from Wales's central region had gone to support William Penn in America. Nonconformity continued and it eventually became a symbol of cultural and political distinction and exclusivity vis-à-vis England by the early twentieth century and in 1920 the UK premier David Lloyd George, himself a Welsh non-conformist who had grown up attending chapel in the Disciples of Christ denomination, got a bill of nonconformity for Wales passed at Westminster. This ended the monopoly of the Church of England in Wales and was a major victory for nationalists and non-Anglican Christians.

Despite nonconformity, the major impulse in Welsh religious life that continues to impact twenty-first century Wales was the great *Methodistiaid* ("Methodist" in Welsh) revival of the eighteenth century. Methodism was the product of two unassuming brothers, Englishmen John and Charles Wesley, who while studying at Lincoln College, Oxford, wanted a deeper spiritual walk with God. They founded a group of fellow Christians who were known for their systematic and "methodical" ways and above all else, seriousness about the Gospels of Christ. The great revival in Wales is thought to have started in 1735 in southern Wales. Started by Anglican ministers and laypersons, there were ties with John Wesley and fellow Englishman George Whitefield, a Methodist evangelist. Both preached in Wales, but the Welsh revival, according to Welsh historian John Davies, was more of an internal spiritual revolution than externally prompted by the latter's powerful ministries (Davies 1991). By 1750, only about 8000 had joined the Methodists efforts to expand the (at-the-time) evangelical form of Christianity in Wales. It wasn't until the end of the eighteenth century that Methodism took off in Wales as it began to reach many in the north. Methodism was a new, vibrant Christian experience with spontaneous worship and hymn singing in large meetings. It appealed to the young and was free of the staid formalism of Anglicanism. Theologically, it had both Calvinist strains (which most Welsh adopted—akin to the Scot's Presbyterianism) and the more free-will Arminianism of Wesley and English Methodism (which most American Methodists would claim today as their heritage). Like all spiritual movements it had mixed theological currents and various arguments did occur. It was known for its call for a personal acceptance of Christ, strict and holy living, and the importance of education, which was becoming a Welsh tradition, as literacy increased in Wales in the eighteenth century. The Welsh Methodists tried to keep from making themselves into denomi-nations. Rather, they hoped to influence and coalesce into the Anglican Church instead of being seen as nonconformists. The revival eventually waned by the early nineteenth century, but it left a profound impact on Welsh culture that was not appreciated at the time. By the early twentieth century, its symbolic appeal, despite declining church attendance, gave ammunition to Welsh politicians and nationalists who liked to distance Wales from England. With Methodism as one of the region's top churches, the church founded by Englishman Wesley that had eschewed nonconformity initially, was itself part of the vanguard of nonconformity thus making it synonymous with Welsh cultural and national life.

The Rise of Nationalism and Devolutionary Sentiment in Modern Wales

In Wales, the Liberal party's strident defense of nonconformity by the First World War dovetailed with its gradual, yet increasing, advocacy of home rule. Two personalities were most prominent in the late nineteenth and early twentieth centuries in Welsh politics: Scotsman Gladstone and Welshman Lloyd George. Gladstone would become prime minister four times (1868, 1880, 1885, and 1892). The major issue of this era was the Irish Question in British politics. Although a devout Anglican adherent and loyal subject to the monarchy, Gladstone had some sympathy for his fellow Celts across the Irish Sea. Gladstone had been successful at disestablishing the Church of Ireland (the Anglican equivalent) in 1869. Only 12% of the Irish attended that Protestant church since an overwhelming majority of the Irish was Catholic. This encouraged Irish nationalists. But, his attempt to devolve power to the Irish did not work. The Liberal Party divided among Home Rulers and unionists. The 1885 election had kept the Liberals under Gladstone in power and they had a majority of 86—the same number of Irish Nationalists under Parnell also supported Gladstone on home rule. The Home Rule bill for Ireland was voted on in the Spring of 1886 and due to a split in the Liberal Party the bill was defeated 343–313. Seen as a vote of no confidence, Gladstone's government collapsed and an election was called and the Tories were returned. The election of 1886 saw Wales tilt the pro-devolution direction. More Gladstonian Liberals (27) were sent to Westminster than Liberal unionists (only one). Many seemed to empathize with their fellow Celts from Ireland, although the Liberal unionists in Wales felt the whole Irish Question postponed action on Welsh issues. Of course, the Irish Question dominated British politics for nearly 20 years under the Liberals from 1868-86. Certainly, its resolution 30 years later would take on a far more bloodier form.

In Wales, devolution was a pet project of Liberals, as it had been the UK party's bailiwick. But, the Tories were staunchly opposed and the historical social overlay and regional variations in Wales itself made devolution a more complex issue given the fact that Wales was so thoroughly assimilated into the English socio-political landscape. Although no vote on Welsh devolution occurred under Gladstone, a vote on disestablishment in Wales occurred in March 1886 and it lost by 12 votes at Westminster. Gladstone himself abstained during the vote. After that vote, Liberal unionists died out in Wales. The Gladstonian faction continued to gain strength in Wales, although it began to decline in England. Thus, the Liberals were increasingly a party of the Celtic fringe much like the Labour party from 1959–1997 prior to New Labour's triumph under Tony Blair.

Although Home Rule was not successful for Wales until 1999, just over one hundred years earlier in 1895, Liberals and Scottish devolution advocates in the House of Commons had voted in favor of "Home Rule All Round" in principle. No permanent institutions came as a result, but by 1914, home rule was law in the UK as it pertained to Ireland. However, Irish Home Rule was scuttled by resistance in Ulster and the eventual solution came when the UK premier Lloyd George sat with Sinn Féin's de Valera and spoke their ancient Hibernian dialects to each other at No. 10 Downing Street in 1920 in an attempt to staunch the bleeding in Ireland ravaged by the Black and Tans and IRA terror. Thus, the old Celtic Home Ruler-turned-unionist prime minister helped the Irish move one step closer toward independence while Wales remained part of the Anglo-Saxon-led UK. Despite these events that unionists thought compromised the political integrity of the UK, Lloyd George did deliver disestablishment for Wales in 1920 which enabled nonconformity and the chapel culture (which he was a part of as a member of the Disciples of Christ denomination and had attended their chapels growing up) to become legitimate in the eyes of the state. The bitterness of Anglo-centered solutions to religious and social matters started to tip the other direction. But not fast enough for nationalists who began to call for Welsh solutions to Welsh issues via Welsh institutions by the late 1920s when Wales' first nationalist political party, Plaid Genedlaethol Cymru, came onto the scene.

Wales in the Late Twentieth Century and Devolution by 1999

Wales began to see political change and rumblings in the 1920s when *Plaid Genedlaethol Cymru* (the National Party of Wales) was formed. Its founder, Dr. Saunders Lewis, was more into reviving the Welsh language and thus Plaid Cymru (PC) agitated for cultural and literary nationalism. The PC was dormant electorally for years until 1966 when it won its first seat in the House of Commons with Dr. Gwynfor Evans winning a by-election. Nationalism in Wales was a bit bipolar. It would move along content to make inroads in the culture, and then overt political nationalism would burst on the scene as it did at Penyberth in 1936 or just prior to the installation of the Prince of Wales in 1969. The rise of the Labour Party in Wales mirrored the rise of Labour in Scotland, but in nationalist terms, both were Celticized and began to play the home rule card like the Liberals, had at times on the Celtic fringe in the late nineteenth century. Interestingly, Labour was challenged by PC in the north and west nationalist and Welsh language regions of Wales, while the south and east (Anglicized Wales) became Labour strongholds. This was like and unlike Scotland which saw the SNP grow in rural Highland areas like the PC in rural Wales, but the SNP began beating largely Tory candidates in the rural areas (not Labour or Liberals) by 1974. Tories had had some success in east Wales and PC had challenged both Labour and Liberals in the north and western parts of Wales, but the 1974 outcome for the SNP in both Westminster elections was never even close to replicated by PC until devolution occurred in 1999 in Welsh Assembly elections.

The 1979 Welsh referendum was a colossal failure given the swift and decisive vote against devolution. The outcome was so bad for the Labour government that the "no's" took the day with an 80% to 20% vote. The hopes of nationalists were dashed and came to a resounding thud. Years of English absorption were not going to change many people's minds against the Welsh linkage with England at Westminster. The 1997 referendum occurred a week after the successful and historical Scottish vote for self-government. According to political scientist Colin Pilkington, apathy affected the Welsh electorate with only 50% participating. All parties, save the Conservatives, supported Home Rule—a much more limited legislature than what was to be erected north of England's border in Edinburgh. As election night progressed the population centers of the south and east appeared to have carried a "no" vote, but the last remaining constituency, Carmarthen in the southwest led the "yes" camp to victory as 65% in that region voted for the assembly. Thus, a new Welsh Assembly was created by only 6/100 of a percent (50.3% to 49.7%) just over 6,700 (essentially a small town) separated the two. Pilkington states that the no's and the yes's were evenly divided according to patterns first established in the thirteenth century with the area of eastern and southern Wales (the Marches and "Little England") voting "no" due to Anglicization and the west and north areas which had been annexed by Edward I (Longshanks) voting "yes" (Pilkington 2002)As will be seen in chapter four, the Welsh Assembly was initially fraught with numerous problems. Its leadership issues were severe. Like Scotland, a battle within the Welsh Labour Party which got a plurality of the votes and seats in it ensued and the rift over London's man versus Wales's man widened. After scandals and votes of no confidence, the Welsh Labourite Rhodri Morgan ended up in the saddle as first minister and after a Lab-Lib pact, Labour governed as a minority party from 2003 to 2007 and in mid-2007 invited the Plaid into the coalition government in Wales. For the first time in their history the Welsh Nationalists were governing Wales. The Welsh Assembly had a tenuous legitimacy as its executive often used emergency procedures to bypass normal legislative channels on secondary legislation. Bills would be promulgated by something akin to executive fiat and bypass the committee structure altogether. This led to concerns about the legislative functioning of the body in general and the same kind of criticism of the EU and the Council of Ministers historically began to be leveled at Cardiff and talk of a "democratic deficit" surfaced. Certainly, the new legislature was learning to cope with public opinion and the vicissitudes of politics writ small at the devolved level.

Conclusion

The histories of the Celtic nations of the UK are fascinating and rich in their political, social, cultural, and economic importance. To gain a firm understanding of Celtic politics and a growing Celtic political identity in the UK, Ireland, and Europe, students must grasp the differences between the Celtic peoples and the English and among the Celtic peoples themselves. The salience of important Celtic political actors from Wallace to Glyn dŵr and Gladstone to de Valera enables us to look at key players in the long span of history on the Celtic fringe. The Celts have long struggled to find their identity and figure out appropriate nationalist responses to the Anglo-Saxon dominated polities of the Great Britain and Ireland historically. Years of British absorption have allowed for different responses among the Celts. In Ireland, the Irish resisted English overlordship. The Scots fought the English and maintained independence for several hundred years, then joined forces with the English, and now appear to be losing their ties somewhat to their southern neighbors. The Welsh were conquered in 1283 and as a smaller Celtic group were thoroughly absorbed by the English and still seem to favor closer ties to England than the Scots and certainly Irish (with the exception of the overwhelming majority of Protestants and loyalists in Ulster). Thus, Celtic politics is complex, varied, yet some consonant currents can be found and the process of moving toward home rule by the twentieth century was started with the Irish and ended up by century's end enveloping the Scots and Welsh.

Suggestions for Further Reading and Research:

Boyce, D. G. *The Irish Question and British Politics, 1868-1996*, 2nd ed. New York: St. Martin's Press, 1996.

Coogan, Tim Pat. *Ireland in the 20th Century*, pbk ed. New York: Palgrave, 2006.

Davies, John. *A History of Wales*. London: Penguin, 1994. Originally published in Welsh as *Hanes Cymru* in 1991.

Fry, Peter, and Fiona Somerset Fry. *A History of Scotland*, rpr. New York: Barnes & Noble Books, 1995.

Fry, Peter, and Fiona Somerset Fry. *A History of Ireland*, rpr. New York: Barnes & Noble Books, 1993.

MacLean, Fitzroy. *Scotland: A Concise History*. London: Thames and Hudson, 1993.

Roberts, Clayton, and David Roberts. *A History of England: Prehistory to 1714, vol. 1, 2d ed.* Englewood Cliffs, NJ: Prentice-Hall, 1985.

CHAPTER THREE

The Rise of Home Rule and Independence on the Celtic Fringe

Home Rule as a Model of Political Change and Transition

Ireland

Home Rule came to Ireland after a protracted battle in the British House of Commons and on the ground by Irish nationalists and British police and paramilitaries. As seen earlier, the Liberal Party under its Scottish premier William Ewart Gladstone had favored devolution for the Emerald Isle, but the two attempts at Home Rule failed. The 1886 bill, though destined for defeat in the Tory-dominated House of Lords, lost on a Second Reading in the Commons 343–313. The Liberals had split their vote and Gladstone then resigned and called new elections. The 1893 Home Rule bill was brought by Gladstone under a minority government after his party had split on Home Rule. The bill passed in the Commons but was quashed by the House of Lords. After Gladstone's last attempt, British politics were to be dominated by the Conservative and Unionist forces until the Liberals returned to power in 1906. Although the Liberal ranks were divided on Home Rule, the gradual, piecemeal mode was adopted by the party so the volatile issue was kept on the backburner until just after the constitutional battle of 1909–11. The Liberals under Herbert Henry Asquith tried to end the Lord's veto in Britain's ancient upper house. Also, complicating matters was the 1910 election that left the party of Irish Nationalists sitting on the fulcrum of power in the Commons (similar to Scottish Nationalists within the Labour-led minority coalition in 1979) as they controlled the votes necessary for the Liberals to govern Britain. The Celtic nations played important roles in British politics, especially on Home Rule, in the twentieth century. In this passionate environment, Home Rule burst back on the scene after 1910.

The 1914–22 period in British political history is an amazingly caustic and complex era. With the Parliament Act of 1911, the Lords veto ended, but legislation that was opposed by the Lords had to pass the Commons in three parliamentary sessions in succession without change to go into effect. This allowed opposition to any legislation, including Home Rule bills, to mount due to the complexity of the issue and the legislative process. In this context, so famously described in George Dangerfield's epic *The Strange Death of Liberal England* (1935), the UK political system was in a quandary by 1914 (Dangerfield 1980). Given the support for union by Tories, and the intractable opposition by the party's leader Andrew Bonar-Law, to seeing Ireland leave the Empire, loyalists in Ulster clamored for political support and guns for what they saw as a coming civil war. What's more, the army's refusal to fight loyalists in Ulster—known as the Curragh Mutiny—in March 1914, meant the government was losing its grip on the situation. The only thing that kept civil war from occurring was the outbreak of the Great War (WWI) in late June 1914 in Sarajevo. As it usually did in the British Isles, war brought a modicum of unity to the fractured constitutional setup. Ireland had caused the fault line as the first Celtic nation to attempt to move out from under England's political orbit. However, the war brought a truce between nationalists and unionists in England and Ireland as John Redmond, the nationalist Irish leader in the Commons, called for his party to support war. As a result, the Irish nationalists and Ulster loyalists were on their way to the continent and other parts of the globe to defend king and crown against the Central powers (Germany, Austria-Hungary, and the Ottoman Turks).

Despite this broad unity in UK political life, a minority in the Irish nationalist camp did not believe fighting and dying for England in an English imperial war was justified. So in April 1916, the radical nationalists (who had broken with moderates like Redmond), launched an incendiary assault on the imperial institutions of Dublin. This was largely a group connected to the Irish Republican Brotherhood (that included men affiliated with the general Irish cultural movement) which tried to seize power, but due to poor organization and alienation of the people themselves (since sections of Dublin were flattened) the rebellion failed and many of its leaders were executed. Amid the Great War, the 1916 *Easter Rising* was important because the next year the government tried to discuss the issue of Home Rule in the form of an Irish Convention, but nothing came of it. By 1918, and war's end, Sinn Féin (Ourselves Alone), was rising as a radical new player in Irish politics. As a minority within a minority of nationalists, its leadership, purpose, drive, and relentlessness would eventually force the British to talk by 1921. However, the road to devolution and eventual independence would go through many ups and downs for Irish separatists. In December 1918, Sinn Fein got 73 seats in the House of Commons and refused to sit. Instead, it chose to create a new republican parliament (the Dáil) housed in Dublin in order to challenge the London government. The Welshman and Liberal Party leader David Lloyd George had come to power in December 1916. By the end of 1918 he headed a coalition government that was dominated by Conservatives. Lloyd George, although a believer in Home Rule, was also a strong proponent of geo-political unity in the UK. In 1919, Sinn Fein began a war against Britain. Under the charismatic *Michael Collins*, the IRB and Irish Volunteers were now becoming the new paramilitary force, the Irish Republican Army (IRA). The IRA's guerrilla campaign would utilize violence to achieve the desired political ends. Hundreds of imperial police, British elites, and innocents would die as a result of terrorism from both the IRA and its opponents. Irate at the Irish defiance, Lloyd George and *Winston Churchill* (the colonial secretary) sent various types of irregular and paramilitary forces to Ireland, including the *Black and Tans* (ex-soldiers who had recently fought in Europe in the Great War). The atrocities between British forces and the IRA went back and forth. In August 1920, the British government passed the Restoration of Order Act which called for an end to for both sides to end anarchy in the south. In the same year, the *Government of Ireland Act* was passed to bring political solidity to Ireland. It did not achieve that result as Sinn Féin continued its war and in 1921, after devolved elections in both the north and south, Ulster set up its first parliament.

Box 3.1: Michael Collins (*Mícheál Ó Coileáin*)

Michael Collins was the young, yet tough founder of the Irish Republican Army (IRA). An ardent nationalist, he joined forces with Éamon de Valera and was a combatant in the Easter uprising of 1916. He was also a member of the Dáil, the elected underground Irish government that was proscribed by the British in late 1920. Realizing that parliamentary measures were going to slow down Ireland's attempt at independence, he organized young men into the guerrilla force that became the IRA. Unlike most paramilitary groups, the IRA was a force of plain-clothed irregulars. They took their orders from Collins and by early 1921 had committed widespread acts of terror, mayhem, and assassination. Collins, himself from West Cork, eventually was asked by the Dáil to negotiate Home Rule with David Lloyd George and Winston Churchill in London. Like Leon Trotsky in Russia, he had gone from revolutionary to recognized politician in bringing the British to bend in the lawless context that he had helped create. After Home Rule was achieved in 1922, the Dáil split and Collins chose the gradual course to complete Irish independence. With de Valera against him and the IRA split, he was assassinated in an ambush near his home in western Ireland in 1922 (at the young age of 31) ironically trying to take the gun out of Irish politics and usher in a period of peace. His leadership, draconian tactics, anguish, and convictions are portrayed well in the 1996 feature film, "Michael Collins," starring Liam Neeson.

Finally, at the end of 1921, the impasse was too much and the coalition decided to deal directly with Sinn Féin. Something the Gladstonian and Lloyd George-like Labour leader Tony Blair would do nearly 80 years later in 1997 in attempting to solve "the troubles" in Northern Ireland.

Although the Sinn Féin leader *Éamon de Valera* had met with Lloyd George prior to the Home Rule talks, where both attempted to impress the other with their mastery of their native Celtic tongues (de Valera with an Hibernian dialect of Irish and Lloyd George the ancient Welsh language), the latter eventually sat down with Sinn Féin representatives Arthur Griffith and the IRA boss, "the big fellow," Collins. The treaty that was produced in December 1921 gave Ireland:

1) A partitioned country—with the north and south getting separate parliaments.

2) The *Irish Free State* in the south got 26 counties; the unionist Ulster, or Northern Ireland—a distinct region in a unitary United Kingdom—as it would later be called, got 6.

3) The Free State had dominion status under the British Empire like Canada.

4) The Free State got an English governor general with members of the Dail giving a Parliamentary oath to the British crown.

The treaty was narrowly adopted in the Dáil (64–57) and the minority faction led by de Valera stormed out. It was too much of a sell out to this minority. It had wanted more control for the Irish over the southern Free State. Immediately, a civil war broke out with a split manifesting in the IRA. Collins was killed in an ambush and Griffith died naturally. So the two major conciliators with England could not lead a charge for gradual change. However, de Valera could not hope to beat the new Free State army supported by the military power of Britain. So, de Valera accepted a piecemeal approach to Irish political development and the Free State moved toward republican independence as an eventual sovereign republic by the late 1940s.

Box 3.2: Sir Winston Churchill and the Celts

Winston Churchill was the probably the most famous British prime minister of the twentieth century (of course two of the most recent ones, Margaret Thatcher and Tony Blair, will go down in history as challengers to Churchill's legacy). With his daring leadership during the dark days of the Second World War, Churchill rallied the British nation with his stirring and eloquent speeches. His prose has been called some of the greatest commentary in the English language, as good if not better than William Shakespeare's. With his dogged determination to stave off the Nazi threat and his willingness to defend the British Isles against extinction from Hitler's Luftwaffe, Churchill saw Britain as a multinational state, yet one that was definitely Anglo-centric. His defense of "England" and her "Island race," was a defense of all things Anglo-Saxon and its historically "English" system of democracy and monarchy. Thus, few have discussed Churchill's relationship to the Celts and his ambivalence toward certain groups of Celts, like the Irish and Welsh. Historian John Ramsden has written an interesting book on how Churchill has been perceived in the Anglo-Saxon democracies (Ramsden 2003). In that work, he writes about Churchill's relationship with the Celts. According to Ramsden, Churchill got on well with the Scots, tolerated the Welsh, and had a very stormy relationship with the Irish. Of course, with the latter, he favored a partition between north and south to provide for Home Rule for both, but still keep Ulster's Protestants happy in linking them with the British state. Churchill got on well with the Scots since he held a Scottish seat in parliament from 1906 to 1922. His Liberal Party seat at Dundee was more politically expedient than part of a devotion to the Scots. But, when he was sacked at the Admiralty for the Gallipoli disaster during the Great War, he took a commission in a Scottish regiment and talked warmly of the heroic nature of the Scots fighting men in battle. What's more, Churchill's wife, Clementine was part Scottish herself. As for the Welsh, Churchill had little time for Welsh nationalism and rarely even set foot in Wales, only in the south on a few occasions to stump during elections. However, in 1951 he spoke publicly his only words in Welsh when railing against the idea of Welsh Home Rule (as a unitarist Tory), he said "nothing doing" in Welsh to an amazed House of Commons. The Irish problem was more thorny for Churchill. He despised Éamon de Valera, refusing to meet with him until his last premiership in the 1950s when both he and de Valera where in the twilight of their vast and somewhat controversial careers. Churchill had called de Valera (both the prime minister of the Irish Free State and president of the new Republic of Ireland after 1949) a "murderer and perjurer." The Irish had not forgotten that then-colonial secretary Churchill had sent the Black and Tans to Ireland to stoke continued conflict in his attempt to shut down the lawless Irish Republican Army after 1919. Churchill's commitment to empire stuck like bad glue to the nationalist-minded Sinn Féin and its supporters in the south of Ireland. Despite the bad blood, Churchill had a certain reverence for the Celts who he acknowledged were separate "races" and part of an Anglo-Saxon-dominated multi-national state that could not be run without them.

Home Rule as a Model of Regional and Symbolic Identity

Scotland after 1999

Scotland's politics changed dramatically after 1999. The historic elections in May of that year led to an elected parliament of 129 members. *Devolution* has been defined by the Scottish Parliament Education Service as the following: "Devolution is the delegation of power from a central body to local bodies. This enables decisions to be made at a level closer to the point at which they will have an impact" (Scottish Parliament Public Information Service 2002). This may seem like a simplistic definition, but the concept and process of devolution is much more complex than it appears on the surface. Since the early twentieth century, calls for devolution had grown in Scotland. By 1997, Scots overwhelmingly supported some form of devolution. The re-creation of a Scottish executive with administrative oversight of low politics issues (largely domestic economic and social ones) governed from London had occurred in 1885. The original Scottish secretary position had ended in 1746. This administrative semi-devolution that created the *Scottish Office* and the high profile Scottish Secretary of State (by 1926) was thought, at the time, to allow government to react to local issues and pressures without devolving too much authority away from the central government at Westminster. The Scottish Office was located in Edinburgh in 1939. Of course, the Second World War was near and the UK public and both major parties (Conservative and Labour) were rigidly unionist in their constitutional outlook.

Devolution proved difficult in some respects and liberating in others. The relationship between Edinburgh and London changed, but the fog of politics left several questions unanswered. Which powers would the Scottish parliament have and which did London have? Some argued that Westminster had "reserved" powers like those implied in the United States Constitution given to Washington, DC and the American states. But, overlap still confused. For example, in the area of regulation, which government had final authority? What's more, the European Union (EU) played a curious role in working with both the Edinburgh devolved Scottish cabinet and the Westminster government. As will be seen in Chapter Six, multilevel governance was at play, but it seemed to confuse while clarifying the scope and depth of Scottish commitments politically and economically in Europe.

Wales after 1999

Welsh devolution was different from Scotland's. It did not have the broad consensus of groups and parties as the Scottish Constitutional Convention had. It was largely a product of a unilateral move after 1987 by the Welsh Labour Party (*Plaid Llafur Cymru*—Wales Labour). In 1994, *Plaid Llafur Cymru* created a Constitutional Policy Commission to look at how a Welsh national assembly would evolve. By 1997, the Welsh Secretary of State Ron Davies said that a Welsh legislature would be elected based on proportional representation (PR) and that the assembly itself would be approved by a vote of the Welsh citizenry. No particular percentage of vote would be needed as in 1979 (in both Scotland and Wales). Moreover, since the assembly would have limited powers, no second vote on tax powers would be needed (as seen in Scotland in 1997). Also, a Welsh vote would be held one week after the Scottish vote in order to gain momentum from what was expected as a victory in Scotland that might encourage the tepid Welsh.

The Welsh Assembly would not be a parliament. It would have less power and the Government of Wales Act provided for executive devolution. Wales was to be conceptualized as a region rather than a nation. Thus, the Welsh had the ability to create secondary legislation as opposed to primary legislation. Thus, the Assembly had the power to pass and scrutinize laws related to agriculture and fisheries, culture, economic development, education, environment, health, highways, housing, sport, tourism, water, and the Welsh language to name several. The National Assembly could also create regulations for the administration of 300 acts of the Westminster parliament that were directly related to Wales. Other types of functions such as making appointments to quangos (such as the National Health Service Trust in Wales) and acquiring property (an American-like Fifth Amendment eminent domain function) to improve infrastructure and build new roads was permitted as well.

The election for Wales' devolution was a nail-biter to say the least. The election took place the week following the overwhelmingly successful Scottish referendum vote in September 1997. Unlike the Scots (who voted on establishing a devolved parliament with taxing powers), the Welsh were asked only if they wanted a smaller-scale devolved assembly. The Labour Party, the Nationalists, and the Liberal Democrats all supported the measure while the Tories opposed it. The 1979 referendum had failed miserably in Wales. This time round the vote squeaked by just barely as 50.3% voted "yes" and 49.7% voted "no" with the Labour-voting valleys of the south and the Welsh-speaking areas of the north in favor and the Anglicized coastal belts and the border lands generally opposed. As a result, the Labour government in London passed the Government of Wales Act in 1998 and set in motion the creation of the Cardiff-based 60-seat legislature with limited devolved powers. For the first time in almost 600 years, since the start of the fifteenth century *Cynulliad* ("gathering" in Welsh) under

Owain Glyn dŵr at Machynlleth in the north-central Wales, the Welsh had their own legislature.

Home Rule as Stasis

Northern Ireland 1922-72 and 1998-2002

The end of British domination of the Emerald Isle came at a huge price. Not only did 1922 see civil war in Ireland, but a border commission that enabled unionists in the north to withdraw and partition the country into northern and southern segments. With the creation of a "statelet," Northern Ireland was the de facto (actual) power over the six counties in the north. Thus, this new version of Ulster was Protestant and loyalist. The Free State to the south had control over the other 26 counties on the island, but it still paid the piper in London as a dominion. It was not until 1937 that de Valera's constitution declared the entire island (all 32 counties) part of a de jure (legal) indivisible Éire. It was not until 1949 that Éire (no longer the British creation Ireland) would go its own way and leave the British Commonwealth and demand control over all the island. Of course, this was to no avail.

Box 3.3: Éamon de Valera (*Éamonn de Behailéara*)

Born Edward George de Valera of a Spanish-Cuban father and Irish mother in New York City in 1882, de Valera grew to become perhaps Ireland's most important political figure in its history. A powerful orator, he was one of the chief spearheads of the independence movement and was narrowly saved from execution at the hands of the British after the 1916 Easter Uprising in Dublin. Had it not been for his American birth, the British would have shot him and his name would be little known today. Despite his rabble-rousing, he helped lead the illegal Dáil and challenged the United Kingdom in the chaotic context of 1919–21 in which de Valera, the Dáil president, authorized his loyal lieutenant, Michael Collins, to form the terrorist Irish Republican Army. Given Collins and de Valera's leadership, Sinn Féin got the British government to sit and discuss peace terms and the end to the uprising in Ireland. However, de Valera, always the cunning and crafty politico, sent Collins and Arthur Griffith to sign the peace treaty with UK premier, the Welshman Lloyd George, and the colonial secretary, Churchill. De Valera, knew the outcome would be short of full independence and he blamed his colleagues, Collins and Griffith, for selling out. Thus, Sinn Féin split and "Dev" was now at odds with his loyal compatriots. The 1922 Irish Civil War saw 4000 deaths and eventually de Valera would become the premier of the Irish Free State. By 1949, after forging total independence for Éire, he became the nation's president (a title Sinn Féin had given him in 1921, although not recognized universally and it was not until 1959 that we won the post democratically in the Republic's election). De Valera was involved in Irish politics for 63 years and was president until he was 91 years-old in 1973. His impact on Irish politics cannot be understated. He was an excellent organizer, a stickler for detail, and had a broader vision for the Irish beyond its relationship with Britain. The party he founded in 1926, the nationalist Fianna

Fáil (Soldiers of Destiny) party, developed a virtual one-party monopoly on Irish politics until the late 1970s when genuine multipartism came to the Republic.

A unionist, predominant party system and one-party state (more will be said about this in Chapter Four) evolved in Northern Ireland. The Government of Ireland Act created essentially a kind of federal form of government in Ireland with a guaranteed two-house legislature in Belfast and one in Dublin. The Ulster government would be tipped in favor of unionists who favored the majority Protestant population in the Six Counties. Successive acts of the UK parliament such as the Special Powers Act of 1922 were created to combat Irish Republican Army (IRA) terror, but they were kept in place after the IRA left the scene in the 1930s. A Local Government Act of 1922 was used to do away with PR so as to give the majority (Protestants and loyalists) the lion's share of the seats in the Ulster assembly. According to historian James Loughlin, by the end of the 1930s, Ulster was controlled by unionists with each community (Catholic and Protestant) diametrically opposed and isolated from each other. Each had their own schools, sports, churches, health care facilities, businesses, newspapers, and sectarian fellowships such as the nationalist Ancient Order of Hibernians and the loyalist Orange Order, thus the statelet was crystallizing (Loughlin 2004). The status quo was to persist for years, despite a rekindling of IRA fervor in the north in the 1950s. Even animosity between Ireland's leader, the prime minister, de Valera, and the British leader during the Second World War, Churchill, did not help matters. Ireland's neutrality during the war was seen as treasonous by Churchill and in 1941 he even referred to de Valera, according to historian John Ramsden, as a "murderer and perjurer" (Ramsden 2006). After Ireland left the fold completely in 1949, Churchill did see de Valera formally at 10 Downing Street in their only official meeting in 1951 (a convivial affair, despite years of rancor).

The one-party, semi-democratic Stormont government was a major beneficiary of devolution during the 50-year period of de facto Northern Irish independence. One reason that the British government (especially Tory ones) did not attempt to reign in the unionists in Ulster was the fact that Tory governments relied on the Ulster Unionists for political support at Westminster since the Tories were a Conservative and Unionist Party until dropping the latter title much later in the twentieth century. Most English wanted the Ulster problem to go away and felt that the Northern Irish ought to handle their own affairs without British interference; even Labour governments pretty much maintained the status quo in allowing the statelet to move ahead as a de facto independent government over that 50-year period. As we shall see in Chapter Five, Ulster was the largest beneficiary of net government aid for all sorts of purposes, both to help the region's decent economy of the 1950s and 1960s, but also to police and keep security after 1969. By the time direct rule was imposed by 1972, even Tory governments were growing critical of the Ulster Unionist governments which led to intra-Conservative squabbling on the British mainland and in Ulster. Can a Home Rule government become static? The case of the 1922–72

Stormont assembly may suggest that its curious evolution and less than inclusive nature was a bit of a problem for ensuring quality governance in the region. That is why the next experiment in home rule in 1998 (after 26 years of direct rule from London) was going to be handled differently by the UK government.

The 1998–2002 era is discussed in detail in Chapter Four, but it is a different era from the original Stormont model based on the predominant party system and quasi-democratic approach of the Ulster Unionists. It was to be modeled after the post-1972 stop-and-start assemblies that were to be consociational. This kind of consociationalism was always good in theory, but oftentimes had a difficult time getting off the ground in practice. The Ulster Unionist-Social Democratic and Labour Party (SDLP) government that was formed in 1998 was somewhat short-lived, but it did signify a hope that some intra-communal governance and power-sharing could occur in Ulster. Most importantly, as seen below in this chapter, the Americans got involved and began to treat the Northern Irish question as a foreign policy problem, not a British domestic issue. This offended the Major government in London, but it was a point for congratulations from the rest of the world which wanted the troubles to end. Most on the Celtic fringe were glad to see some changes move forward in the fractured province.

The 1993 Downing Street Declaration to the 1998 Good Friday Agreement and Beyond

The election of Bill Clinton as president of the US led to a change in American policy toward the UK on the Ulster question. Upon taking power in 1993, President Clinton, a descendant of the *Scotch-Irish* in Ireland (like President Ronald Reagan), injected a serious effort toward improving the seemingly ongoing negotiations between republicans and unionists in the north. Prime Minister John Major and Taoiseach Albert Reynolds signed the *Downing Street Declaration* in December 1993, but like other initiatives before it would not progress until the Americans intervened much to the British government's chagrin. Clinton's approach was less pro-British than his predecessor George H. W. Bush. Clinton put Jean Kennedy Smith (JFK, RFK, and Ted Kennedy's sister) in as ambassador to Dublin. He replaced Bush's ambassador to the *Court of St. James*, Raymond Seitz, with fellow Arkansan Admiral William Crowe. And most importantly, he allowed his national security adviser, Anthony Lake, to coordinate Irish policy and the direction of the policy moved away from a pro-UK position to a more neutral one which saw the importance of getting the IRA to the bargaining table. Much to dismay of the UK government, talk of issuing a visa to Sinn Féin's Gerry Adams commenced and the Major government was none too pleased taking UK-US relations to their lowest point in decades. The IRA declared a ceasefire on August 31, 1994. By 1995, former US Senator George Mitchell, a Democrat from Maine, headed up an inquiry into the Ulster question and after studying the troubles propounded six principles:

1) Peaceably and democratically solving political disputes;

2) Complete disarming of all paramilitary groups in Northern Ireland;

3) Verifying via independent commission all disarmament;

4) Each group must take a stand against the use of force by itself and oppose its use by any other group in Northern Ireland in attempting to leave and impact on the all-party talks;

5) Agree to the outcome of the all-party talks and to peaceful and democratic means at any alterations that arose due to differences among parties once the results of the talks were put forth;

6) Speak out against communal and retribution attacks and murders and take concrete actions to stop them.

Adams visited Washington in February 1996 and took the time to gain publicity for the republican cause. The reception was historic in that US governments had never attempted to alienate the British, especially with the standing policy of censorship of Adams and Sinn Féin and the IRA members which had been proscribed in the UK media since the Thatcher-era and the *Official Secrets Act*. The Adams visit, which had been delayed since November 1995, was orchestrated by Lake who had always advocated a mixture of idealism and realism in the foreign policy realm. He was a political scientist who wrote and taught against the views of Hans J. Morgenthau, the great founder of the realist school in international relations in the US, yet he applied realism to various situations to force governments' hands diplomatically (such as was the case in Haiti and Bosnia during the Clinton administration). Despite his interest in working with the British, he also favored using diplomacy to bring outsiders to the table. Thus, getting Adams into the picture directly helped the next government (under Tony Blair) move closer to a settlement on Ulster. Lake's actions, although risky, were actually what spurred Sinn Féin and the IRA to talk and the UK government to press the unionists for more compromises.

After Prime Minister Blair led the Labour Party to victory on May 1, 1997, his government did not change radically UK government policy toward the Irish question. Yet, within a few months of becoming premier, he had Sinn Féin back in talks with unionists and an attempt to get the *Mitchell principles* put into effect was made. On September 23, 1997, British and Irish officials, along with eight political parties sat down at the negotiating table. It was the first official meeting between republicans and unionists in 75 years. By January 12, 1998, the Irish and UK governments had agreed to a proposal that would be the basis of the 1998 Belfast Agreement, or *Good Friday Agreement*. The sticking point for republicans and unionists was powers in the proposed Northern Irish assembly. Just who would have power in the various legislative and consultative bodies became very important to both loyalists and nationalists. With unionists wanting the Northern Irish legislature to have power over the issues dealt with jointly by the north and south and nationalists wanting the consultative North-South Council to be substantive and not a mere talking shop. The abolition of the Government of Ireland Act of 1920 would not radically alter the relationship of Northern Ireland to the UK. This made unionists happy. The SDLP became the main negotiating voice for republicans on the final agreement. Sinn Féin had been involved in the initial talks, but this played into Sinn Féin's tactics and long term strategy. It got positive public relations for sitting down with the unionists, yet it could back away from sticking points that the SDLP agreed to if they were not far-reaching enough. This would help them with both moderate and militant nationalist factions. The situation mirrored the 1921 treaty talks and Adams and McGuinness' position was similar to de Valera's whereas the SDLP leader John Hume's was similar to Michael Collins and Arthur Griffith's. De Valera sent Collins and Griffith to 10 Downing Street to negotiate with Lloyd George and Churchill, knowing that Sinn Féin started from a position of weakness. He then could attack the treaty as a sell-out, which he did. A similar context occurred in 1998, although, the republicans in Northern Ireland were not as interested in civil war given the exhaustion of nearly 30 years of the troubles. Adams and Sinn Féin would have to tread lightly.

The Good Friday Agreement was the fulfillment of the static Downing Street Declaration of 1993. The three-pronged peace process called for three major areas of implementation. The first was the legislative and executive process. It called for a new assembly for Northern Ireland with 108 seats. It would have executive and legislative control over issues related to Northern Ireland. It would select Members of the Legislative Assembly (MLAs) by proportional representation (single transferable vote from the constituencies determined by the existing ones from the UK parliament). The assembly was still to be called Stormont named after the building and grounds used in Belfast from 1922–72. In an example of consociationalism, major issues would have to have at least 40% of both nationalist and unionist parties to pass. Secondary issues would only require a majority vote. These secondary issues dealt with intra-Irish relations. A North-South Council was proposed where cross border ministerial-level consultation would occur. Much like the Council of Ministers in the EU, the southern Republic's ministers would meet the Northern Irish ministers in a consultative council and six areas of importance would be discussed: agriculture, tourism, transportation, health, environment, and education. Like the EU, the new consociational Ulster government was a hybrid of the old and traditional Stormont pro-Unionist settlement and a newer consensual EU-style approach to governance with non-majority government playing a role at times (like in the European Parliament and Council of Ministers after the 1997 Amsterdam treaty) in order to place both the majority and minority communities in Northern Ireland.

Analysis: Devolution as a Transition to Independence, Federation or Confederation

As will be seen in the final chapter (Chapter Seven), a model of Celtic politics presupposes several governmental structures playing an important role in the political life of Scots, Irish, and Welsh simultaneously. This broader conceptualization of governance has gained currency in the realm of international relations given the multiple levels on which government (and governance) are playing out. The concept of Home Rule, although dating back to the drive by Irish nationalists in the 1860s for devolution in the British Empire, is still a salient concept and one that requires much descriptive and analytical contemplation. Devolution to the English, Scots, Irish, and Welsh is an important concept for several reasons. First, it is an important descriptive term. It literally means to delegate or pass (devolve) legislative powers to a localized legislature (or as political scientist Philip Norton has said "subordinate assemblies") (Norton 1994). One can look at this term in the American context in the relationships of the states to the counties and cities. An example of legislative devolution occurs when states control counties and municipalities. In the late 1980s, the state of Illinois took over the troubled city of East St. Louis in order to get its financial house in order. Once that occurred, the state devolved power back to the city and allowed it to run itself. Second, devolution is important for analytical purposes. The interposition of devolution into the British and Irish contexts historically is a unique political event in which the British constitution becomes profoundly affected. Home Rule in 1921 for Ireland and the murky status of the Six Counties in the north of Ireland after the boundary commission of 1922 create a divided Ireland and a semi-implemented devolution that seemed to work somewhat for Ulster until the 1960s; but, the imperfect arrangement is from an imperfect constitutional setup in the UK that is based more on bargains, ad hoc actions, and fuzzy geo-politics. Thus, Éire began as a Free State with fits and starts, Ulster became a one-party colony, and the UK was not able to have the kind of control over either that it would ideally have liked. Finally, devolution is an empirical policy of government that alters the UK constitution and continues to play an important role as we have seen in the UK context especially after 1999.

As for devolution as a stepping-stone toward confederation, federation, or independence, these concepts are all important to students of political science. *Confederation* is a governmental setup where the central government derives all of its legal power from the member or constituent governments (the United Nations or the rebel government in the American States during the Civil War from 1861–65 are examples of a confederation). Confederations are weak governments. The EU is an example of a confederal government. Its constitution, proposed by the former French president (1974–81) Valéry Giscard d'Estaing, would give it more of a federal footing as that great international organization attempts to federalize into a united states of Europe. Ireland after 1922 was quasi-confederal with an official government in Dublin as the de jure standard for the new dominion and a northern province that was a de facto independent power within the dominion. Given King George V's visit to Belfast to Stormont in 1922, a certain amount of de jure recognition was inferred thus muddying the constitutional waters further given the relationship of Ulster to both Ireland and the UK.

A *federal form of government* is one in which the central government holds political and legal power in its sphere of influence and constituent or member governments (like the American states) hold legal and political authority in their spheres of influence. Thus, both may perform overlapping responsibilities and certain powers will be concurrent. This is reality in federal governments when it comes to such powers as taxation, education, standards and certifications, law-making and enforcement, and the like. Thus, the possibility of a federal Britain given the devolutionary policies of the late twentieth century may not be, at least under Labour (or Labour in partnership with Liberals) governments in the twenty-first century, as far away as once thought. Political scientist Stephen Haseler argues that devolution stoked a kind of English regionalism that has led to a resurgence of overtly English nationalism and that it may unleash long untapped English regionalism (of the historical German kind) that pits regions from northern to mid to southern England against each other as one would see in the United States where the states bid for federal largess and multinational capital to grow and develop both economic prosperity and state-wide identities and cultural pride (Haseler 1996). For anti-EU conservatives, unionists, and unitarists (those favoring a *unitary form of government* like the UK's) and those favoring a strong centralized state, this is a cause for concern. The EU continued in the late twentieth and early twenty-first century to promote European economic and social regionalism (all the while promoting EU political centralization qua federalism) in order to not only meet localized needs in Europe (as we will see in Chapters Four and Five regarding Wales, Scotland, Ireland, and Northern Ireland) while solidifying the regions to Brussels and developing loyalty via the backdoor rather than through the central government. A Committee of Regions was created in 1994 and Wales, Scotland, and Ulster all had representatives on it (thus, giving the Celts their first real pan-Celtic representation outside of Westminster). Will all this lead to legislative and executive independence and sovereignty for Celtic polities? That will be addressed in more detail in Chapter Seven.

Suggestions for Further Reading and Research:

Haseler, Stephen. 1996. *The English Tribe: Identity, Nation and Europe*. New York: St. Martin's Press.

Bogdanor, Vernon. 1999. *Devolution in the United Kingdom*. Oxford: Oxford University Press.

Driver, Stephen and Luke Martell. 2002. *Blair's Britain*. Cambridge: Polity Press.

Loughlin, James. 2004. *The Ulster Question Since 1945*. New York: Palgrave.

Pilkington, Colin. 2002. *Devolution in Britain Today*. Manchester: Manchester University Press.

Wilford, Rick. "Regional Assemblies and Parliament, " pp. 117-41. In Paul Mitchell and Rick Wilford, eds. *Politics in Northern Ireland*. Boulder, CO: Westview Press, 1999.

CHAPTER FOUR

Party Politics in Scotland, Ireland, Wales, and Northern Ireland

Emerging Party Politics in Celtic Regions of the British Isle

In this chapter, the party politics and political party systems in Scotland, Wales, and Ulster will be referred to as emergent since new devolved systems arrived in the late 1990s. That does not mean that old political cleavages and party dynamics were not relevant when devolution occurred. What's more, Irish politics from Dublin, long a stable democratic system, has also seen some changes, especially since the 1998 Good Friday Agreement (GFA). Certainly, British politics has affected and continues to influence party politics in the Celtic nations. Simply because three of four cases are still ensconced within the United Kingdom (UK) system, party politics ipso facto in Scotland, Wales, and Northern Ireland evince the effects of broader UK issues and structures on these systems. To even talk about separate indigenous political party "systems" at all was dubious to many political scientists prior to devolution in 1998 (resurrected after 26 years of direct rule from London) in Ulster, and 1999 in Scotland and Wales. Because politics in these areas were regionalized, the broader UK unitary structure was seen as all-encompassing, and even though parties had some regional variations, analyzing party politics as distinctly Scottish, Welsh, or Northern Irish was, in the former two cases, only done after the electoral success of nationalist parties at Westminster in the 1970s. The British political party system was one that emphasized a two-party system with the single member district (SMD) or first-past-the-post electoral system. In this system of electoral politics, electors (as the British call "voters") selected candidates and the winner would get either a plurality of the vote (if more than two candidates were running) or 50% plus one if it was between two candidates from two parties only. Usually in UK politics, unlike American politics historically (although changes are occurring), multiple candidates from several parties challenge for constituency seats in the House of Commons (646 members at the 2005 general election). In the latter half of the twentieth century, the British party system was conceptualized, by many political scientists, as homogeneous. That is, the system was simple and straightforward, essentially because the two major parties had widely recognized and supported candidates and agendas, the populace voted for either the Tories, the dominant party in government in the twentieth century, or the second strongest party in the past century, created in 1900 as a UK-wide party—Labour. Empirical results reflect this assertion. From 1950-70, less than 14 seats out of 625–

630 seats at Westminster, during each general election, went to parties other than the Conservatives or Labour, thus confirming the dichotomous "homogeneity" thesis and the fact that smaller parties were not as important in the British SMD system (Kellas 1989). This would change somewhat after 1970 largely due to the influence of politics on the Celtic fringe.

The English-dominated political system was a class-oriented one whereby politics was tied to socio-economic class and the identification by electors with the proletarian politics of the Labour Party or the middle and upper-class politics of the Tories. Of course, these are overgeneralizations, but political scientists found that this dichotomy contributed to the dualism in the electoral and party systems. As the post-industrial global economy matured by the 1980s, class-based politics began to ebb somewhat forcing Labour to rethink its commitment to socialism. Broad socio-economic changes also forced the Tories to rethink some of their ancient organic approaches on social status and class in Britain. With the advent of *Thatcherism* from 1979–1990 (named after Margaret Thatcher, the daughter of a lower-middle class grocer, who rose to be prime minister and she was followed in 1990 by John Major, himself a high school dropout and the son of a circus performer and maker of cement yard gnomes, unheard of in Tory politics, just 10–20 years earlier), class appeared to be lessening as a major factor in voting, but the divide between north and south in Britain led to acrimonious politics not only in the UK in general, but in the Celtic fringe where many felt disenfranchised where unemployment was higher, although new services and light manufacturing and aid from the now-European Union (EU) was flowing to prop up the periphery's economic fortunes. Finally, the British party system saw a consensus on the welfare state emerge between 1945 and 1979, and the constitution was not much of an issue in the immediate aftermath of the Second World War. It was not until the 1970s that constitutional issues reared their heads again as they had at century's start. Thus, Scotland's party system evolved, as it had previously, in some different directions than the homogenous English-dominated system. The Scottish party system is one that has some major differences from the UK system. Historically, the Scots were a three-party system (compared to the UK's two party system).

Scottish Party Politics: A Three or Four Party System

*The Scottish Labour Party (*Pàrtaidh Làbarach na h-Alba*)*

In 1959, the Labour Party, which was coming into its own in Scotland since its rise in 1888 (12 years before the advent of the UK-wide party) under *Keir Hardie*, became Scotland's top political party. It held this distinction at the dawn of the twenty-first century. The party successfully garnered 40–50 seats (out of 72) at Westminster at each general election from 1959-2001. It received 41 of 59 Scottish seats at Westminster in the 2005 UK general election—a net loss of five seats. The law was changed in 2004 to lessen the number of Scottish seats in

London given the nation's own legislature for local matters in Edinburgh. Scotland eventually became, by the 1980s, Labour's power base where it had created safe seats in the House of Commons. With this transformation, Labour rode high in Scotland, but this also brought some divisions over distinctly Scottish issues such as devolution. Eventually by the 1990s, the party had been forced to decentralize in its Celtic regions due to devolution and the rise of nationalism espoused by not only the small nationalist parties like the Scottish National Party (SNP) or Plaid Cymru in Wales, but also the major parties which had become regionalized. The concept of "tartanization" was now used to describe national (regional) politics advocated by the Scottish Labour Party and many of its members. The party was deeply divided given Labour's history of centralization and advocacy of UK unity under democratic socialism. In the late 1980s and early 1990s, Scottish Labourites like George Galloway (who went on to be ousted from the Labour Party and form his own party over the Iraq 2003 war) wanted overt devolution for Scotland much to the chagrin of the Labour leaders in London.

The Scottish Labour party combined with the Independent Labour Party (ILP) in 1894. From 1899 to 1909, the Scottish Trades Union Congress put forth candidates under its own Labour party and in 1909 it merged with the UK *Labour Party*. The UK-wide Labour Party, although a centralized, socialist organization at the dawn of the twentieth century, was actually somewhat federated as trade unions and indigenous Labour parties sent representatives to the UK Labour annual party conference historically. Since the Great War (1914–18), Scots have voted primarily for Labour giving them a plurality or better in 19 of 24 UK general elections (up to 2005). In England, the Labour Party has only controlled seven elections in the same time frame. As in Wales, the 1922 election in Scotland was a breakthrough for Labour as it got 29 of 71 seats with the Liberals the next closest competition at 15 seats at Westminster. The history of the radicals of the ILP who left *"Red Clydeside"* for London in 1922 is a story of growth and collapse for the socialist militants of the ILP who would be all but gone by the end of the 1930s. The ILP attempted to go it alone as UK Labour overcame the ILP's relatively weak challenges. During the 1920s and 1930s, most of Scotland's constituency associations within the Labour family were affiliated with the ILP. When the ILP left Labour's UK-wide federation in 1932, Scottish influence within the Labour Party attenuated. This presaged a historical dialectic seen in the twentieth century between Scottish Labour parties and their large UK neighbor. Scottish ILP politics were certainly more leftist and radical than the mainstream of the Parliamentary Labour Party at Westminster. The Clydeside ILP leadership of John Wheatley, David Kirkwood, Emanuel Shinwell, Patrick Dollan, James Maxton, and others helped guide the party despite the centrifugal forces generating within the Labour federation.

Labour did well in Scotland in the 1923 (34 seats) and 1929 (36 seats) UK general elections (but the party's fortune's did drop in 1924—26 seats, and fell off dramatically in 1931—7 seats—although several Labourites in Scottish seats were in the *Ramsay MacDonald*-led coalition with the Tories). In 1945, Labour got 37 of 71 seats in Scotland (the next highest were the Tories with 27 seats). By 1959, Scots Labour had 38 seats at Westminster and the era of the Labour Party as Scotland's national party had emerged. It would be the dominant party in that nation into the twenty-first century. Given the fact that the Labour Party in Scotland has a national executive council (now known as the party's Scottish Executive Committee) it gained more importance by 1968 when it was allowed to discuss issues related to national (UK-wide), not just regional, themes and foreign affairs. Much of this decentralization in the party was done to placate devolution supporters in Scotland and party members who favored Home Rule, although between 1947 and 1974 it was staunchly anti-devolutionist and moved away from devolution as a UK-wide position. The UK-wide party began to see a greater number of Scots and other Celts have a greater impact on the UK Labour Party. The party's quintessentially English character (cut from the mold of Clement Attlee, Hugh Gaitskell, and others) changed by the late twentieth century as its leadership after 1976 (and the end of Englishman Harold Wilson's long tenure as party head and premier) saw Welshmen James Callaghan (1976–79), Michael Foote (1979–83), Neil Kinnock (1983–92), and Scotsman John Smith (1992–94) give the UK party a distinct Celtic flavor. Of course, many might consider *Tony Blair* an Englishman given his Oxford education, Anglican loyalties, and parliamentary representation of northeastern England's Sedgefield constituency. However, with an Irish mother and Scottish father, he was Celtic in background (including having gone to primary school in Edinburgh where he was born) and surrounded himself with many powerful Scots including UK Chancellor of the Exchequer (kind of like the American secretary of treasury post) and eventual premier (by 2007) *Gordon Brown*, Foreign Secretary Robin Cook, and defense minister (and subsequently NATO secretary general and then on to the House of Lords as "Lord") George Robertson after the 1997 Labour triumph at Westminster. Much of Labour's rise in Scotland after 1959 is not only due to differences in Scottish and English political culture, but as sociologist David McCrone believes the long-term decline of Tory support in Scotland after 1959 (McCrone 1992). This helps explain the growth of Labour electorally. The swing toward Labour eventually saw Scots return no Conservatives in 1997 and 2001, although Tories did get a few seats in the Scottish Parliament in 1999 and 2003. During the Thatcher years, Labour's "tartanization" in Scotland was more acute after 1987 as the party had 50 of 72 seats and Scotland became the political stronghold for Labour and increasingly anti-Tory in sentiment. In July 1988, the Labour Party in Scotland joined with others to set up the Scottish constitutional convention which aimed at getting a legislature for Scotland. Scots Labour led the convention along with the Scottish Liberal Democrats, Greens, and Communists. The SNP stayed away since the convention was not radical enough in delivering independence and the Tories opposed based on their historical strong UK unionist perspective. The 1979 referendum had angered many, especially the vocal minority nationalist groups and the SNP; of course, this was manifested when the SNP pulled its support from Labour's minority government in London and it collapsed. But by June 1992, some radical Scottish Labour MPs, such as the rebellious George Galloway, met with SNP MPs in London to discuss ways to delay parliamentary business in the House of Commons until the Conservative government would yield on Home Rule. This rhetoric was not welcomed in the Labour Party's parliamentary leadership not only because of the ties with the independence-minded SNP, but because of the division it brought in the UK-wide party where some Labourites were anti-devolution and more statist and centralizing in their politics. After the Thatcher/Major years, Blair's tepid support of devolution was not greeted well by Scots Labourites who did not want a referendum in Scotland. They wanted a direct imposition of Home Rule from London by government decree. But, the Scots had nothing to worry about as the referendum of September 1997 passed overwhelmingly. Scottish Labour, under its regional leader *Donald Dewar*, took power and invited the Scottish Liberal Democrats into a coalition with them after the 1999 election to the 129-member Edinburgh-based parliament.

Box 4.1: Tony Blair

Anthony Charles Linton Blair was born in 1953 in Edinburgh. However, like Gladstone, he was raised in the Anglican Church in England (Durham). He attended an elite prep school in Edinburgh. Although his father Leo Blair, a barrister, had been a Tory sympathizer, Tony Blair was to lead a major transformation of the Labour Party in Britain after 1994, when he took over the party leadership from the late Scotsman John Smith. Blair's ethnic and religious identity were questions of speculation since he was born to a Scottish father and Irish mother (she was from Donegal in the north of Ireland—contiguous to the six modern counties of Ulster, but since 1922 part of the southern Free State). With a Scottish name many thought he would be somewhat Scottish in his sympathies, but like Gladstone, he was thoroughly Anglicized, a British citizen of England, and he had a law degree by 1975 from Oxford. His wife, Cherie Booth, a barrister, was Catholic, and with raising their children Catholic, it was thought that he might be somewhat akin to the Stewarts with secret sympathies for Catholicism (which could be illegal for a British prime minister according to the 1829 Emancipation Act which says the monarch's advisers had to be Protestants). He did eventually convert to Catholicism after leaving No. 10 Downing Street in 2007. At any rate, Blair appeared to be the perfect twenty-first century prime minister in a multi-cultural, European Union (EU)-oriented, and post-Unionist Britain. His religious beliefs were hard-to-pin-down and as a Celt (and more importantly Labour politician) he was willing to devolve chunks of power to the Celtic regions of the UK. He even moved toward restoring Home Rule in Belfast under a new peace agreement in 1998. His heartfelt rendering of I Corinthians 13 at the funeral of the Princess of Wales in 1997, at the onset of his premiership, helped persuade Britons that indeed a liberal Gladstonian type figure had returned to British politics. His passionate leadership and call for war with Saddam Hussein and Iraq in 2003 also reconfirmed the neo-Gladstonian assumptions as well. The son of Celts had indeed brought Britain and its Celtic regions into a post-Union and supranationalizing EU era. His term in office ended in 2007 (after turning power over to his fellow Labourite, Scotsman Gordon Brown) after ten years as premier, the longest serving Labour prime minister in the party's history.

The Scottish Labour Party's 2003 manifesto focused on education, health, safety, and social justice. It also focused on business development and community partnerships. Like the UK Labour Party, the absence of the use of the word "socialist" or even the discussion of overtly statist approaches to economic development has been one of the major changes for Labour at both the national and regional levels in Britain under Blair and Brown. For instance, the 1997 UK Labour Party manifesto was the first in the party's history not to have the word "socialist" in it. Blair moved the party to the center and even to the right in the area of economic development keeping many of Mrs. Thatcher's conservative macroeconomic policies in place, although the party has done its share of public spending on health, defense, and technology. The limited spending on education and the emphasis on private entrepreneurship (fitting in with the EU's capitalist process) has meant that Labour has changed to become similar to the Liberal Democrats historical position on economic issues. Of course, the issues that matter to Scots are similar to the average Briton, but the issue of greater sovereignty for Scotland continues to be debated as Labour argues that Home Rule works and gives Scots just the right amount of self-government whereas SNP supporters say it has not gone far enough and the Tories still argue that the union is the way to solve the UK's problems. Of course, the Liberal Democrats maintain that Home Rule is good, but it would be made better and more European if proportional representation (PR) were adopted for Westminster and more devolution (with English regional assemblies—creating a real British federation á la the US) for the rest of the UK would be created by London.

The Scottish Labour Party structure is similar to most modern mass political parties with localized branch associations that are fed from the ward level (street by street in Scottish cities, towns, villages, and rural areas) from this representatives to national councils and annual regional party conferences can also be selected from constituency association (which geographically make up a legislative district from which MPs or MSPs are elected). The party has various policy forums that are open to members and it has a national executive committee of twenty-nine. Of course, this body has close ties with the UK Labour Party leadership in London.

Box 4.2: Gordon Brown

He is the son of a minister of the Church of Scotland. He earned a doctorate in political history at the University of Edinburgh. His pious upbringing in Scotland with an obsession with politics, meant that Gordon Brown would be an activist politico from a young age. His interest in Labour politics were drawn from his religious upbringing and its concern for social justice and his training in the disciplines of history and political studies (political science) and their concern for critical inquiry into power. Like the author, Brown was a college political science instructor in Scotland prior to his entry into politics. In June 2007, Brown found himself, after years of patient waiting in the Labour party ranks, of leading the United Kingdom (UK), despite his Celtic roots and the fact that his people, the Scots, appeared to be souring on the 300 year-old union with England. Not only was he saddled with this personal paradox (a Scot leading an English-dominated union when the Scots and English were not getting on as well as they had in years past), but he ascended to Number 10 Downing Street when faith in his party was at a 10-year low (given his predecessor and fellow Celt, Tony Blair's unpopular actions on the 2003 Iraq war and its aftermath, scandal tied to Labour's handling of peerages in the House of Lords, and the weight of losing public confidence after a long time in power—much like the Tories from 1979–97). It was an historic moment for Brown since he was the first overtly Scottish prime minister and first representing a Scottish constituency to run the UK since Sir Alec Douglas-Home in 1964 (Blair considered himself an Englishman, despite his Celtic roots). Brown's remarkable career since entering the House of Commons in 1983 (representing Dunfermline, a city just north of Scotland's capital Edinburgh in the eastern Central Lowlands) has been one of rising up the Labour ranks. By 1997, he had reached the apex of his career as the chancellor of the exchequer (like the American treasury secretary, but even more important as the number two post in the British government akin to the vice presidency). His career has seen him move from the far left ideologically (an old-style Labourite) to the center as he was behind the elimination of state control of the Bank of England and liberalizing the monetary policy of the state in 1997 under Labour which would have been unthinkable for an historically social democratic party with socialist origins just a decade earlier. However, as premier, Brown promised to govern differently than Blair and he was much more of a Euroskeptic (questioning the supranational growth of the European Union) including his opposition to Britain ending its use of the pound sterling and joining the euro zone and using the euro currency.

The Scottish National Party (Pàrtaidh Nàiseanta na h-Alba)

The *Scottish National Party* (SNP) continued the Scottish tradition of a three party system in the late twentieth century. Labour had been the third party in the early part of the twentieth century. Liberals had fallen to third party status in Scotland in the 1930s (as it had throughout the UK). By the middle 1970s, the SNP was battling Liberals and Tories for recognition and eventually became one of the top three or four parties in the Scottish party system. The SNP has a detailed history. The seed of national political identity, in the form of a party, was sown in 1928. John MacCormick believed the British parties would never adhere to Scotland's concerns sincerely. As a result, he founded the National Party of Scotland (NPS), the SNP's forerunner, to advocate a policy of political autonomy and independence for Scotland. In 1932, a separate political entity, the Scots National League, changed its name to the Scottish Party. This organization was more cultural in its orientation and its membership reflected varying political views from left to right on the ideological spectrum. In 1934, the Scottish Party and the NPS combined to form the SNP. MacCormick, the prime leader of the NPS and the SNP from 1928 to 1955, was ostentatious and a gifted speaker. He helped form the SNP while a student at the University of Glasgow. Ever a pragmatist politically, he gave up the idea of attaining total independence for Scotland early on. He opted for NPS/SNP legitimacy through the electoral system after Westminster refused to grant Scotland Home Rule after World War I. His authoritarian control of the party and overly pragmatic approach in attaining SNP goals soured many party supporters. Between 1928 and 1934, the NPS lost more deposits at elections than it saved. In that time span, the party gained no more than 16% of the vote in any single by-election. Of the 15 candidates contesting seats at the 1929, 1931, and 1935 general elections, nine of 15 lost their deposits.

As the 1930s progressed, the rise of fascism in Western Europe and the ominous specter of war precipitated a tightly held opposition to all forms of undemocratic governance by members of the SNP. The SNP also passed a resolution at one of its yearly conferences admonishing its members, and the men of Scotland, to refuse military service in defense of the Kingdom. However, after the war commenced, a majority of party members supported Britain's war efforts. As the SNP entered the 1940s, it began to experience growing dissension from within. The 1942 party conference saw a cleavage emerge as a result of the election for party chairman. MacCormick was stepping down from the top position and his hand-picked successor, William Power, was running against Douglas Young, a representative of the dissident element in the party. Young was elected and MacCormick, Power, and their faction resigned and formed a new organization, the Scottish Union, later to be named the Scottish Convention. The SNP split largely along the lines of Home Rule proponents and fundamentalists (who wanted separation from the UK), as was to be replicated in the late twentieth century in the party. The party had allowed members and leaders to affiliate with other parties and this was a bone of contention with many members. MacCormick and his faction advocated more of a pressure group orientation to the SNP tactics; hence, conceiving the party's modus operandi as a movement. The fundamentalist element resented the paternalism by the major British parties, mainly the Labour Party. By the late 1940s, the SNP and MacCormick's Scottish Convention battled Labour at the polls. Though unsuccessful, both organizations continued to push for Home Rule. Yet, losing MacCormick and his following had not hurt the party as much as had been anticipated. Aided by the wartime truce, the SNP improved in wartime by-elections; it took 37% at Argyll in 1940 and 41% at Kirkcaldy in 1944. On April 12, 1945 the SNP won its first-ever *by-election* at Motherwell in central Scotland. Due to the death of the district's Conservative incumbent and because the party ignored the major parties' wartime electoral truce, the SNP edged Labour 51.4% to 48.6%. The new MP, Dr. Robert McIntyre, would later serve as party chairman between 1947 and 1956. In that by-election, McIntyre had campaigned for independence, converting Prestwick airport into an international airfield, and building a bridge over the Firth of Forth. The latter two policy goals eventually came to pass. However, the seat was retaken by Labour two months later on June 15, 1945 in the general election. Nevertheless, the SNP, though struggling to survive, had proved to be a thorn in the major parties' sides north of the English border.

The SNP had been a collection of groups with a broad nationalist agenda at its founding. By 1967, and *Winnie Ewing*'s upset by-election victory at Hamilton (the SNP's second seat at Westminster in its history), the party was starting to make electoral inroads. Of course, the 1974 elections saw the breakthrough that the SNP hoped for with seven MPs elected in February and 11 in October. The October 1974 election saw the zenith of SNP electoral support in elections for the House of Commons. The party got 30.4% of the Scottish vote, its highest output ever. It received almost nine percent more of the vote from the February election (21.9%) and nearly tripled the 1970 vote (11.4%) which was the highest since the party's founding and the first time the party had gotten double-digit numbers. After the 1974 elections, the party's fortunes dropped electorally until 1992 when 21.5% voted for the party, but only three MPs were returned. The landmark 1997 election, which saw all Tory seats in Scotland and Wales erased and a large Labour triumph after 18 years in the wilderness saw the SNP get 22.1% and its third largest output in seats at Westminster with six, a net gain of three seats. The 2001 British general election saw the SNP's fortunes decline marginally as it dropped to 20.1% and five seats in London. Of course, by 2001, the political and electoral context in Scotland had changed as the SNP was the number two party in the newly-devolved Scottish parliament. The party had finally got its wish at challenging for control of a devolved Scottish legislature. According to political scientist Peter Lynch, the 1990s saw the consolidation of the gradualist position within the SNP. The ideological debates since the 1970s in the party over gradualism and fundamentalism were vitriolic and divisive. The gradualists wanted a devolved parliament as a stepping-stone toward Scottish independence and the fundamentalists wanted "independence, nothing less." The failure of the 1979 referendum on devolution in Scotland and Wales left a sour taste in the mouths of nationalists and it inspired some fundamentalists to challenge the gradualist orientation of the party's leadership (Lynch 2002).

Box 4.3: The Celtic Race (Part III): Double Minorities or Multicultural Scots?

The ethno-nationalist phenomenon that spurred Scotland to greater self-governance in the late twentieth century also saw the evolution of a new phenomenon in the Celtic fringe. That development was major immigration from the developing world to Britain where internationals settled in all parts of the UK and some in Ireland as well. Africans, Afro-Caribbean nationals, south and east Asians, and even other Europeans were coming in increasing numbers. This is ironic given the number of Celts who migrated to North America, Oceania, South Africa, and the like in the nineteenth century. It has been estimated that America alone has 25 million Irish-Americans and five million Scottish-Americans. By 1992, the Scottish National Party was actively courting immigrant groups in its social democratic program to prove that it was a multicultural party. Moving away from a narrowly conceived idea of ethnically Celtic Scots, the party used a visible public relations and political communications campaign to woo the "minority Scot" vote in the 1992 general election as seen by its active courting of "Asian Scots," "Black Scots," and even, "Chinese Scots." Much like liberal multiculturalism in the US, the SNP decided to let non-native citizens of the Scottish region of the UK know that they were welcome in a big tent nationalist camp. Elsewhere in Scotland, some immigrants were taking to Scottish customs and traditions. Baron Sirdar Iqbal Singh moved to Scotland from what is now Pakistan where he was born in 1936. The Sikh baron came to Scotland to study medicine, but became a successful businessman. He went on to buy a Scottish manor, a Scottish island, and created his own tartan for his family named Singh (the most prominent Sikh name—Sikhs are the world's fastest growing religion in terms of aggregate percentage and they are a religion with a mixture of Islamic monotheist ideas and Hindu cultural orientations.) He helped translate the eighteenth century poems of Robert Burns, Scotland's national poet, into Punjabi. Like historian Benedict Anderson talks about in his *Imagined Communities*, the concept of Celticness is one that appears to be as much about perception and subjective interpretation as it is, or more so, about ethnicity. This fuzziness may not be bad in terms of bringing people together in the Celtic parts of the UK and Ireland.

By the early 1990s, party leader *Alex Salmond* (the banker and MP from Scotland's rural northeast who headed the party from 1990–2000 and came back to lead the party in 2004 taking over from John Swinney), was committed to socialism, making the SNP compete with Labour nationwide, and making the party a modern, technologically-advanced one. He succeeded in keeping gradualism toward a devolved Scottish legislature on course and even brought the SNP to beyond parity with the Scottish Conservatives, but the SNP was still far from being Scotland's governing party. With the party's growing popularity by the late 1990s and its ability to compete toe to toe with Labour in its heartland in Clydeside (and despite losing most seats to Labour and Liberal Democrats as it was second or third in most Scottish constituencies in the 2005 Westminster vote), the SNP still had to overcome electoral issues that small parties face in SMD electoral systems. Fortunately for Salmond, by 2007, the party had improved its fortunes (given the unpopularity of Labour) and he was able to become the first SNP first minister of the Scottish government in Edinburgh. Although running a minority government, the Nationalists had reached a major goal under Salmond as party and government leader.

In 1997, Labour got 45.6% of the vote in Scotland (the SNP got 22%). However, this translated into 77.8% of the seats for Labour (of the 72 Scottish seats at Westminster) versus 8.3% of the seats in London for the SNP. In 2005, Labour got 39.5% of the Scottish vote which meant 69% of the seats in London. The SNP got 17.7% of the vote and 10% of the Scottish seats at Westminster. Thus, large, UK-wide party status had its advantages in the UK system.

The growth of Scottish nationalism saw the SNP improve its popularity. In 1962, the party had 2000 members. By 1983, it had around 20,000. It had a traditional mass party organizational format with a national headquarters in Scotland's capital, Edinburgh. It also had a yearly national conference, bi-annual national council meetings, a national executive committee with 25 members. By the 1990s, the party had a full-time chief operating officer (the party's managing executive who coordinated administrative activity for the party as opposed to its political leader), a professionalizing and bureaucratic organizational structure, started in-depth fundraising (á la development approaches like non-profits in the

United States such as colleges and universities and the like) replete with large advancement campaigns to strengthen the party's coffers, improved and technologically-advanced political communications (as the internet age began), a full campaign and party staff at headquarters. By 1992, the SNP had called on Scottish actor *Sean Connery*, a.k.a. "James Bond," to openly support the party in its quest for "independence in Europe." Not only did Connery oblige, with his voice used from audio recordings blaring from atop SNP campaign autos moving through Labour neighborhoods in the Central Lowlands, but 10 years later he was giving the SNP a monthly grant of just over £4800 ($9,753). The paradox of the actor who had played the quintessential English intelligence operative supporting a party that was accused at times, by its adversaries, as being anti-English and Crown, was not lost on many even casual observers of British and Scottish politics.

The 2003 SNP manifesto for the parliamentary elections called for connecting all of Scotland via high-speed internet. It pledged to spend £46 million to complete this objective. The party wanted to make Scotland Europe's high-tech center (which would include a University of the Highlands as a kind of high-tech center for education). The party sought to do away with Labour's privatization of hospitals and schools and build quality health and educational services through not-for-profit philanthropies and organizations. It wanted more of a focus on the public side of private-public partnership in building a stronger National Health Service. The SNP also sought to raise the pay of nurses by 11% over the pay of other professionals in the UK to keep nurses from leaving Scotland. Because crime had increased and prosecutions had declined, according to the party, it advocated putting 1000 more police officers on the street in Scotland to deal with crime. The party also wanted to deal with prison overcrowding and try to figure out ways to put lesser offenders in programs that did not require full incarceration. The party claimed that 37% of all prisoners in Scottish jails had defaulted on fines for minor offences. In education, the SNP would cut class sizes to 18 students at the elementary school level. The party, as a social democratic one, continued to advocate the greening of Scotland and said its economic agenda would be tied to friendly environmental policies and to keeping nuclear power stations and nuclear weapons out of Scotland. Last, the party favored a Scottish-wide referendum on independence that would give Scots a chance to vote to separate from the UK. The party said that little had been done in the four years of Home Rule and that expectations in the devolved legislature had not been met.

Like any modern mass party (as classified by sociologist Maurice Duverger in 1951), the SNP has a very elaborate structure as it has grown. Its party structure has branch and constituency associations and eight regional associations. It holds a bi-annual national council meeting (like a national executive committee meeting). The national council is around 200 SNP members (similar to a central committee) and within it the national executive committee has representation from several groups in the party, such as a women's organization, young Scottish Nationalists, etc. A national party conference is held yearly at which general policy changes and initiatives forwarded from the national council are voted on and discussed. Like Labour, the Liberal Democrats, the Tories and other parties in Scotland, this hierarchical process has become the norm in modern party evolution and development. The 2005 Westminster election saw the SNP improve its number of MPs at Westminster from five in 2001 to six. However, the electoral output continued to wane as it had got 17.7% of the vote in the 2005 Westminster election which was down from 20% in 2001, 22.1% and six seats in 1997, and from the 21.5% and three seats in 1992. However, the overall drop in constituencies from 659 in 2001 to 646 in 2005 was due to the reduction in seats for Scottish and Welsh MPs. Scotland dropped from 71 seats to 59 seats in 2005 thus the SNP's smaller percentage may not be as bad a sign for the party given the reduction in seats at Westminster.

By mid-2005, the SNP had nine female MSPs in Edinburgh and no female MEPs in Strasbourg or MPs at Westminster. It had been one of the first parties at Westminster to have high-profile women in its leadership with Winnie Ewing winning her seat in 1967 and later taking a European Parliament (EP) seat. Winnie Ewing was the longtime president of the SNP (a largely honorific title). She had become known at the EP as "Madame Ecosse," French for "Mrs. Scotland". Her daughter-in-law, Margaret Bain Ewing, had won a seat in the realigning Westminster elections of 1974 and stayed in parliament until 1979 and she returned in 1987. Margaret Ewing then won a seat in the Edinburgh legislature in 1999, but resigned due to internal party factionalism. Both had played major roles in helping the SNP become a left-of-center, pro-female party. Of 15 in the party's national executive leadership, one-third was women. In 2004, the party elected a female deputy leader, Nicola Sturgeon. Sturgeon was an MSP for Glasgow and was elected to the Scottish Parliament in both 1999 and 2003. She got involved in nationalist politics as a law student at the University of Glasgow. She was born in Irvine in the Ayrshire region of southwestern Scotland in 1970 and was part of the youthful energy among the party's up and coming leadership. She served as a solicitor in Glasgow prior to politics. Sturgeon spoke out on several issues including Orange Protestant marches (similar to the ones in Northern Ireland) that were arranged in Scotland. She criticized the trend toward sectarian division in Scotland that she saw in 2005. In the same year, she also criticized First Minister Labourite Jack McConnell for joking with school children about getting drunk occasionally. She claimed that alcohol led to destruction and domestic violence in many Scottish homes and that a message of that nature was not permissible. Sturgeon became the deputy first minister (the number two cabinet post in the Scottish government) in May 2007 when the SNP took power in Edinburgh. The SNP in power as a minority government had its ups and downs. It garnered a certain amount of respectability as it followed its center-left agenda which in the Fall of 2009 included improving health care access via the NHS, children's advocacy in judicial affairs, and finally starting the debate on a national referendum on independence from the United Kingdom, in spite of the fact that Labour, the Liberal Democrats, and the Tories were opposed to the referendum (and opinion polls showed that only 30% of the Scottish public favored independence at the time of the worst recession in the UK since the Second World War) meant the initiative by the Scottish government was not going to go very far (*Financial Times* September 3, 2009).

The Scottish Liberal Democrats

From 1832–1910, the Liberal Party under leaders like the Scotsman William Ewart Gladstone and Englishman Herbert Henry Asquith (who sat for a Scottish seat at Westminster) won a majority of Scottish seats (the lone exception was 1900). It was an age of reform, democratization in Britain, and imperial growth. The Home Rule debate burst on the scene in Ireland, but discourse on Scottish Home Rule was never as salient an issue during this era. Indeed, Liberals would become the most staunch and consistent defenders of devolution by twentieth century's end. The Liberal Party held sway in Scotland, as it did in Wales, in the latter nineteenth century. Like the late twentieth century and its preoccupation with Ulster (and the proverbial "Northern" Irish question), the period of 1868–1894 saw the UK and its distinctly "English" politics focused on Ireland. With somewhat sympathetic Scots, Gladstone could forge ahead in trying to rectify what he saw as wrongs for the Irish. Despite the division over Ireland in the party, Liberals were able to use their power base in Scotland and Wales to affect government change with their progressive brand of politics (which included various enfranchisement bills, social and humanitarian laws, and constitutional change by 1911). But, as in Wales, Liberalism began its long descent after 1918 and the end of the Great War due to the increase in labor unions' political activism and the rise of the Labour Party nation-wide and the ILP in Scotland, especially in Clydeside. After 1918, the Liberal electoral fortunes dropped dramatically in Scotland. The Liberal Party vote after 1945 in Scotland was virtually nonexistent until 1983. With the start of "the Alliance," conceived by the Gang of Four (Scotsman David Steele, Welshman Roy Jenkins, and Englishpersons William Rogers and Shirley Williams, all former Labour cabinet ministers), moderate Labourites bolted from the party and its leftward lurch in 1981 during the early Thatcher years to form the Social Democratic Party (SDP). They eventually formed the Alliance with the UK Liberal Party to fight elections in 1983. The Alliance got 24.5% of the vote which was better than any Liberal Party output at a general election since 1923 when the party got 28.4% in Scotland and 22 Scottish seats. The Alliance vote was more than double any returns for the Liberal party since 1945. The Scottish Alliance also got eight seats in 1983 better than the five the Liberals returned from Scotland in 1966. The Alliance saw its share of vote in Scotland drop to 19.2% in 1987, but its seat total at Westminster rose to nine. By 1992, the parties' electoral alliance was formalized as a new party, the *Liberal Democrats*, and the party saw a drop off in its vote total in Scotland to 13%, though it kept its nine seats in London. The party's fortunes improved in 1997 with 16.3%, putting the Tories in fourth place in Scotland. The party managed to keep its 10 seats that it had had since 1997. Certainly, the narrow, yet crucial battleground in the Highlands was becoming more important and tougher to asses given the Liberal Democrats, Conservatives, and the SNP's battles over the years in places like Banff and Buchan, Moray, the Western Isles, and the Shetlands and Orkneys. Some Labour politicos had made minor inroads in a few of these areas over the years; but, for the most part, northeast rural Scotland and Highland constituencies were lost to the Liberal Democrats or the SNP at the dawn of the twenty-first century with the Tories' influence in the Highlands on the wane (as it was all over Scotland).

Scotsman Charles Kennedy was the party's UK-wide leader from August 1999 to January 2006. He helped rebuild the party's image and its electoral fortunes. Kennedy was born in Inverness and attended the University of Glasgow where he joined the SDP. He graduated in 1982. He worked in the early 1980s as a BBC journalist in the Highlands. He also traveled to Indiana University in the United States on a Fulbright fellowship. In 1983, at the age of 23 he was elected, as the youngest MP at the time, to represent the Western Isles for the SDP. Kennedy's goal has been to make the UK Liberal Democrats the official opposition party. He attempted to focus on regional campaigning rather than UK-wide campaigning in targeting Conservative constituencies for Liberal Democrat takeover. The 2003 Iraq war and the Liberal Democrats staunch opposition to it also helped gain new converts to the party throughout the UK and by 2005 the party's fortunes were improving as evinced by its performance in Wales and Scotland where it got two additional seats in both regions in the 2005 Westminster election (the party got 11 seats in Scotland and four in Wales in 2005). The Scottish party was in coalition with Labour in the Scottish Parliament and it was plowing ahead with its staunch agenda for electoral reform for all UK elections (including Westminster elections). The party want all elections to be of the proportional (PR) variety. The charismatic red head with a thick Scottish brogue, had gained some fans with his perorations and parliamentary tirades against Prime Minister Blair's war in Iraq and support for American president George W. Bush. Unfortunately, after the birth of his son in December 2005, a BBC story was prepared to expose Kennedy's battle with alcoholism and he decided to admit to the nation his problems with drink prior to the story's airing. The fallout from the admission led to his resignation as party leader. He was replaced by fellow Scot, *Sir Menzies Campbell* (pronounced: MING-iss CAM-Bull). Born in 1941, Campbell, who grew up in Glasgow, is a lawyer and former Olympic sprinter. He led the Scottish Liberals after 1975 and finally got into the House of Commons in 1987. Campbell took over the helm of the UK-wide Liberal Democrat Party in March 2006. At 64 years of age, Campbell had been involved in the leadership of the Liberal Party and Liberal Democrats since 1975 when he was named chairman of the Liberal Party. In 1997, he was named shadow foreign secretary when the Liberal Democrats decided to have a *Shadow Cabinet*. In 2000, he was considered for the position of the Speaker of the House of Commons when Labourite Betty Boothroyd stepped aside, but that did not materialize. In 2002, he was diagnosed with cancer and after chemotherapy made a full recovery. Campbell came to power in the party in 2006 with the support of such famous Liberal Democrats as Paddy Ashdown, David Steel, and Shirley Williams. A Scottish lawyer by training, he took MA and LLB degrees from the University of Glasgow where was a student with other famous Scottish politicians, Labourites John Smith and Donald Dewar. As a famous Scottish sprinter, he competed for the UK in the 1964 Summer Olympics in Tokyo. He ran the 200 meter run and held the British 100 meter dash record for eight years in the late 1960s and early 1970s. His tenure leading the UK Liberal Democrats was short-lived and ended in 2007 when he stepped down after 15 months on the job. He was replaced by Englishman Nick Clegg, who went on to be deputy prime minister under Tory premier David Cameron in the Conservative-Liberal coalition government after the 2010 United Kingdom general election.

Scottish Liberal Democrats had 17 seats after 1999 and 2003 elections in the Scottish Parliament. Although their share of the constituency vote (SMD) had gone up one percent by 2003, its share of the regional (PR) vote had dropped by just under one percent. After 2003, the party had five government ministers, including the deputy first minister, Jim Wallace of Orkney, who was the minister of enterprise and lifelong learning. Of the four other ministers, various portfolios included transport, education, finance and public services, and environment and rural development. Only two of the Liberal Democrats' MSPs were women by 2004. The party is a modern mass party with various constituency organizations in Scotland at the grass roots. As a federated party nationally (UK-wide), Scottish Liberal Democrats have their own structure and the party's national executive committee consists of 37 voting members and five non-voting members. The Scottish Liberal Democrats were holding party conferences twice a year at the start of the twenty-first century. These conferences would produce party resolutions on a wide range of issues of interest to the party and its members. Ideologically, like its UK parent and Welsh cousin, the Scottish Liberal Democrats issued a manifesto for the 2003 Holyrood elections that favored a focus on creating a context for business growth in Scotland; fighting crime; a better deal for rural Scotland focused on recruiting more general practitioner physicians to the Highlands; developing a broader, more comprehensive fisheries policy in Scotland; and developing organic farming (a link to the Liberal Democrats' interest in environmental issues). The Scots party manifesto also called for keeping the Scottish Parliament intact at 129 members (a direct challenge to the Tories attempt to cut the number of MSPs) and to revive an all-party constitutional convention to look long term at the effectiveness and improvement of devolved government in Scotland. The party continued to advocate for and play an important role in devolution in Scotland given its consistency in supporting devolution over its history.

The future of Scottish Liberal Democrats looks decent. But, its attempts to combat Labour in its stronghold in Clydeside and the Central Lowlands is not an easy task. What's more, the party has enjoyed an upsurge throughout Britain in the early twenty-first century given the natural public opinion drop for the relatively long-term New Labour government (in power since 1997). The 2003 Iraq war gave it a boost among left-wingers of varying parties in the UK. But, the party still had much work to do in Scotland and the UK to become the opposition to Labour in both Scotland and at Westminster.

The Scottish Conservatives

From 1918–55, the *Tories* won a plurality of votes in Scotland. Given the Conservatives' collapse in Westminster elections by 1997, it seems hard to believe that the party was influential in Scotland, but it was successful due largely to its policies of unity during the two world wars and its use of Scottish industry on the Clyde for industrial development and imperial purposes. Several famous Scots also held important governmental offices under the Tories such as prime ministers Harold Macmillan (1959–63) and his successor, Alex Douglas Home (1963–64).

The Conservative Party has long been a key player in Scottish politics. Scottish Conservatives have had less impact historically on the UK party vis-à-vis Scottish Labourites on their national party. But, Conservative Party politics have been no less salient despite less seats at Westminster or since 1999 in the Scottish Parliament in Edinburgh. It was Conservative governments that set up the first attempts at modern administrative devolution. They set up the Scottish Office and a Scottish secretary of state post in the 1880s. To further appease home rulers, they let the secretary have full cabinet status and moved the Scottish Office from London to Edinburgh in 1939. The Tories in Scotland have long opposed devolution, with some minor exceptions. Of course, after 1974 and the rise of the SNP, devolution became the top issue in Scottish politics until 1997. The secretary of sate for Scotland under Mrs. Thatcher and John Major, Lord Lang of Monkton (Ian Lang) argued the Scottish Tory line on devolution in his memoirs, *Blue Remembered Years* (2002). He said that: 1) Scotland is already over-represented at Westminster vis-à-vis England (although, as mentioned above, Lord Lang's wish was granted in 2004 by Britain's parliament); 2) the governmental administrative apparatus dealing with Scottish issues included the Scottish Select Committee, the Scottish Standing Committee, the cabinet post and four junior ministers, and special legislation affecting Scotland; and 3) increased expenditures for Scotland (Lang 2002). This argument says that devolution not only lost or curbed much of this "administrative" devolution, but now the Scottish Parliament and especially the post of first minister have lost ties with the rest of the UK due to Home Rule, thus losing its efficacy and legitimacy vis-à-vis the Westminster government (where ultimate political and legal power still reside).

The Scottish Conservatives were arguably the most powerful party in Scotland from 1918–55 as they won pluralities at most elections. The 1924 elections saw the Tories take 36 seats out of 71 and 47.6% of the vote. Coalition governments ruled Britain during the depression years of the 1930s and war years of 1940–45 and the Tories were the key element in those governments. In the July 1945 general election, while Labour under Attlee were impressing England and the rest of the world, Tories held their own against Labour in Scotland by getting 27 seats and 41% of the vote (to Labour's 37 seats and 47.6% of the vote). The 1951 election saw an even split in UK politics with 48.8% of the vote going to both major parties, but in Scotland the Tories got 48.6% to Labour's 47.9%. This did not translate to an advantage for the Conservatives as they split evenly 70 seats, one Liberal was elected as well. The height of Conservatives' fortunes in the twentieth century in Scotland came in 1955 when they got 50% of the vote and 36 seats at Westminster to Labour's 46.7% and 34 seats. The party would govern the UK for nine more years, but Labour's ascent (which had increased and decreased at times after 1918) would begin in 1959 and stay on course by the dawn of the new millennium. Labour would roughly double the Tories' seats at Westminster in each election from 1964–83. It would get worse for the Conservatives in Scotland as they would see their share of seats plummet further after 1983 and Labour would get four to five times as many seats by 2001. The Tories were shut out completely for the first time in 1997 as they managed only 17.5% of the vote a substantial drop from the 25–28% they had gotten in the general elections from 1983–92. In 2001, their share of the vote in Scotland fell further to 15.6% (in fourth place behind both the SNP and Liberal Democrats). The only good news for the Conservatives is that they did regain one seat at Westminster of the 72 Scottish seats. That seat was Galloway and Upper Nithsdale (in Southwestern Scotland), but they claimed it by a razor-thin margin of only 74 votes. At the start of the twenty-first century, things looked bad for the Conservatives in Celtic mainland Britain. With no seats at Westminster in the general election of 1997 in both Wales and Scotland (an unprecedented first) and only one in Scotland and still none in Wales in 2001. The 2005 Westminster elections saw only one Tory returned in the borders constituency of Dumfriesshire out of the scaled-back 59 seat representation in Scotland. The party had a long way to go to convince Celts that it had answers for them in terms of national consciousness and UK linkages as well.

In terms of party organization, like Labour and the SNP, it is a fully functional modern mass party. It has constituency organizations and a separate Scottish party office in Edinburgh. A Scottish Tory conference is held yearly. In the 2003 Scottish elections for the Edinburgh parliament, the Scottish Tories focused their policy goals on several broad areas which included: 1) Scottish government reform; 2) crime; 3) health; 4) the economy; 5) agriculture and rural areas of Scotland; and 6) education. The party called for making the Edinburgh parliament more efficient by scaling the 129 MSPs in Scotland's legislature down to 108 (the same as the post-1998 Stormont assembly in Northern Ireland), reducing the number of executive ministers in Scotland's government from 20 to 10, cutting government costs back to 1997 levels to save £100 million ($182.87 million), and strengthening relationships between the nations of the UK. The party sounded time-honored Thatcherite themes such as cutting tax rates for business to stimulate indigenous Scottish development. But, they also called for more expenditures on roads and infrastructure to the tune of £100 million to lure more development to Scotland. The party also called for local control of fishing and more choice for students in education. Thus, the party has tried to maintain its staunch limited government persona (regarding economics) and general unionist (pro-UK) vision since the Thatcher days in order to rebuild itself in Scotland.

For the Scottish Tories to be competitive in the twenty first century several things must happen. First, the party must find ways to get more women involved in politics. Labour and the SNP with their large female support and active membership bases (including large numbers of legislators in both Edinburgh and London) have a major edge in the gender area. In early 2008, of the 17 Tory MSPs five were women. A good start for the Scottish party, but one that must see more women get involved to appeal to Scots and non-Tory voters. The party appeared to be getting the message as it appointed its first-ever female leader in October 2005 when Glasgow-born lawyer Annabel Goldie took over the Scottish Conservative Party helm. Second, the party must find a way to deal with the EU in a palatable way to an electorate in Scotland that seems more pro-Europe than the historical English skepticism over Europe. Third, somehow the party must be able to show Scots that they can be unionist and devolutionists simultaneously. Given the number of politicians that have flip-flopped on this issue (including major parties like Labour as a whole) over the years, this can be done without appearing to be too pro-unionist. Fourth, the party must try to deal with political apathy among its historical electorate and in UK and Celtic societies in general. Finally, the party must figure out a way to sell the Conservative party, essentially an English-oriented party throughout its history, to Scots who the vast majority are becoming even more wary of Westminster and English-oriented politics. This does not mean the Tories cannot rebuild and compete in Scotland. The SNP and Liberal Democrats have had great success in the Highlands and parts of the borders fighting Conservatives and taking away Tory seats in the latter part of the twentieth and early twenty-first centuries. With the right politics, rural Scotland could return to the Tories if they could get a coherent EU policy that helps the rural areas and fishing industries.

Scottish Socialists (Pàrtaidh Sòisealach na h-Alba)

The *Scottish Socialist Party* (SSP) came out of nowhere in 2003 and won six seats in the Scottish Parliament. It had won a single seat in the parliament in 1999. The party got only one percent in the constituency (SMD) vote and two percent in the regional (PR) vote in 1999. But in 2003, it got six percent in the SMD vote and nearly seven percent in the PR vote. This was a major breakthrough for a party that was both new and one that did not appear to be a potential threat to Labour in Scotland. The party was founded in 1998 out of the Scottish Socialist Alliance, an amalgamation of socialist and communist groups, and its 2003 manifesto called for an independent "socialist" Scotland, progressive taxes of varying types on the rich, and a minimum wage of £7.32 ($14.87). The minimum wages at the time were £4.20 ($8.53) for those 21 years-old and over) and £3.60 ($7.32) for under 18–21 year olds. The American minimum wage in 2008 was $6.55/hour (£3.22) which then was to rise to $7.25/hour in 2009

(£3.57). The manifesto said the party agreed with the French Socialists in wanting a 35-hour workweek (which was law in France by 2003, but was coming under criticism due to labor and capital pressures a year later). The SSP also called for no privatization of public industries and services. Its social agenda favored a pro-marijuana stance, opposition to imperialism and war (especially the Iraq war of 2003) and an end to racism. It also called for "solidarity" with Palestinians and others needing justice around the world. Certainly, the 2003 vote saw the SSP do well given the animus toward the UK Labour party over Prime Minister Blair's staunch support of the US in taking down Saddam Hussein in Iraq.

The Scottish Socialists were not a major threat to Labour as they were perched clearly to the left of Labour on the radical fringe. The SSP did get four percent of the vote in the 2004 European Union elections, up from three percent in the 2001 Westminster elections. In 2003, the Rail, Maritime, and Transport Workers Union (RMT) in the UK allowed its workers to affiliate with the SSP in Scotland, thus ending the monopoly the UK Labour party had on it. This led Labour to expel the RMT from it. In January 2004, the Labour party held a special meeting and upheld the decision to expel the RMT from its ranks.

The SSP's leader was Tommy Sheridan who represented Glasgow, the party's power base (reminiscent of "red" Clydeside of the early part of the twentieth century). Sheridan had been elected in 1999 as an MSP and the only Scottish Socialist. He was born in Glasgow in 1964 and took a degree from the University of Stirling. He was active in radical politics from an early age and part of the Labour party's Militant Tendency—a group of Trotskyites in favor of nationalization of the means of British production and vehemently pacifistic on defense issues, but also oriented toward unconventional protest. Sheridan himself was jailed several times for protesting the *poll tax* (officially called "the community charge"—a regressive property-like tax from the Thatcher era) and the presence of British nuclear subs in Scotland. Sheridan himself eventually left the party after a personal scandal in 2006. This hurt the party and in the 2007 Scottish elections, the SSP lost all of its seats at Holyrood. The SSP may be a protest party that is ephemeral in its electoral appeal. But, the SNP started out in a similar vein and Scottish socialist groups come and go like the Haggis consumed on Burns night in January. Indeed, the SSP was adding color to the new Scottish party political landscape.

Scottish Greens (Pàrtaidh Uaine na h-Alba)

Like the SSP, the *Scottish Greens* had one seat after the 1999 Scottish parliamentary elections. They got just 3.6% in the regional (PR) vote and no support in constituency (SMD) voting. But, 2003 saw a slight adjustment upward for the party as it nearly doubled its share of the regional vote and added six seats to share fifth place in the Scottish Parliament with the SSP. Again, the Greens were shutout in the constituency vote. Certainly, as the Greens did in Germany in 1980, just getting above the five percent threshold was a major victory for them. Green parties in the UK have never been a force electorally for a variety of reasons. First, the SMD system at Westminster frowns on them. Second, the major left-of-center parties (such as Labour and the Liberal Democrats) take their issues on the environment away from them making the Greens less than appealing as perceived *"single-issue" type parties*. Finally, Greens are seen as too radical on various issues and not in the mainstream. But, with Greens in power in coalition in Germany after 1998 and Ireland after 2007, the time for Greens to play a role in Scottish politics seemed to have arrived. Despite their marginal influence, the Scottish Greens became the first ecology party in UK electoral history to have a major impact at a regional or national level.

The Scottish Green Party was formed in 1979 as the Scottish Ecology Party. The UK Green Party had begun in 1974. In 1986, the Scottish variation changed its name to Green Party and by that time it was fused with the English party. Yet, it continued to address Scottish environmental issues. Scottish Greens got 7.5% of the vote in the 1989 European Community (now EU) elections. The British SMD system kept it from joining European Greens in Strasbourg. In 1990, the Scottish party broke loose from the UK-wide party. After 2003, The party represented four central and southern Scottish areas and two Highland areas in the Edinburgh legislature. Its first MSP was Robin Harper and he was the leader of the Scottish parliamentary Greens. The party did several things in the 2003–04 Scottish Parliament: tried to eradicate genetically modified food from Scotland; produce better conservation of nature in Scotland; dealt with toxic chemicals and their effects on the public; sought to improve renewable energy sources; and tried to augment hate crimes legislation in Scotland. The party in the 2003–07 parliament had five males and two females. Like its German cousin, it sought ways of taking democracy to the people and innovation in participation in the party. Trying to unseat Labour and the Liberal Democrats on environmental issues was not easy in Scotland (or in other mature post-industrial democracies), but certainly the rise of the Greens in Scotland suggests that some voters are very issue-oriented and the environment is a major rubric under which salient issues fell for some Scots.

The Scottish Party System: Limited Pluralism in a Three or Four Party System

Political scientist *Giovanni Sartori* has called party systems like Scotland's one of *limited pluralism* (Mair 1990). Under this model three-to-five parties compete for seats in the national legislature. Of course, this was the case of twentieth century party politics for Scots at Westminster, but in 1999, a genuine system of limited pluralism evolved when elections for the Scottish Parliament occurred on 1 May. Governments formed from party systems that are of the limited pluralist variety have coalition governments (as was the case in the Scottish Parliament from 1999 to 2007 with the Labour-Liberal Democrat government). Sartori says these may be conceptualized as "feeble" governments, even if they are not temporary, as has been the case in Scotland. The Lib-Lab Pact from February to October 1974 in London would empirically verify this assumption. Opposition parties did not form a united bloc (like the SNP, Scottish Socialists, and the Scottish Tories in the Scottish Parliament), opposition tends to be "unilateral," hence, a kind of *moderate pluralism* evolves, as opposed to extreme polarized pluralism where centrifugal forces can destroy a party system. Hence, much of the focus in the system is on centripetal competition and in Scotland each party has more or less agreed to the devolved settlement, although the new governing party after the 2007 Scottish elections, the SNP, would like to see the system evolve toward separation from England at some point. Thus, ideological fragmentation, like a Weimar German system (1919-33), does not appear in the Scottish party system after 1999. What's more, segmentation, or ideological distance between parties based on multiethnic or religious rivalries, has not been as important an issue in terms of ideological space in post-1945 Scotland, or the salient issue, in Scotland as it is in Ulster. That does not mean that ethnicity in general is not important as it is for various nationalist movements and for the SNP and nationalists in other parties. What's more, in localized partisan politics in places like Glasgow (Scotland's largest city), Protestant versus Catholic politics have at times been salient where Labour has tapped into working class Catholic sentiment and the SNP has garnered support from middle class Protestants. However, in the main, ethnic and religious rivalry that translates into political volatility in the party system is not as salient as it has been in Ulster (or other European contexts such as Belgium). In segmented pluralistic party systems, a consociational approach is usually adopted. We will visit that concept under Northern Ireland party politics.

Scottish Parliament Elections

After 1999, Labour controlled the newly created Scottish Parliament in coalition with the Liberal Democrats. Under the former Scottish secretary (after 1997), Labourite Donald Dewar, who served as first minister, Scotland had its first parliament since 1707. Dewar would die in 2000, but the coalition politics would deal with issues of importance to Scots that were specifically devolved to them by UK legislation, such as taxation and educational bills. Perhaps, the biggest issue of all would be the creation of a separate Scottish Parliament building and its costs (see Chapter Four). The rise of the SNP as Scotland's second party in the Scottish Parliament (the Liberal Democrats served in a capacity as a kind of brokering party of government, much like the German Free Democratic Party did for years, in aiding Labour with governing in Scotland) from 1999–2007 would have ramifications in terms of the politics related to left of center environmental controls, statist approaches to economic development and the distribution of resources, and devolution itself. However, the SNP's shock victory in the 2007 Holyrood elections was as much about the Scottish electorate rejecting Prime Minister Blair's Labour Party (after 10 years in power in London and eight years in power in Edinburgh) as it was about embracing nationalism. With a one-seat advantage and a tenuous minority government, the SNP first minister Salmond had to tread lightly in moving Scotland forward.

Ireland: From Predominant Party System to Moderate Pluralism

Irish party politics distanced itself from the British model after 1921. The Home Rule party (Irish Parliamentary Party) dissolved and due to the Irish Civil War which began in 1922, new political parties emerged. Sinn Féin's (Ourselves Alone) dominant position ended when it split over Home Rule. The issue of the agreement that created the Free State, as a devolved entity under the British Crown, was what split Sinn Féin. One group (headed by Michael Collins and Arthur Griffith) wanted a gradualist settlement to independence, the other (headed by Éamon de Valera) wanted outright separation from Britain. This rift was not only the cause of the Irish Civil War, but would be the most salient issue for parties at election times in the 1920s. Although 40% of the population voted for non-Sinn Féin candidates in 1922, by 1927, with Fianna Fáil's evolution as a parliamentary party in Dublin, the issue of the treaty with London was clearly dominating Irish politics. Thus, party politics after 1921 in Ireland were quite unlike Britain's. Britain's electoral politics were divided between rural and urban, as well as class-oriented cleavages in politics. Ireland's electoral politics focused on mainly rural issues and the nation's constitutional arrangements vis-à-vis Britain. These were the dominant themes for parties.

Ireland was to see a party system evolve that would be dominated by one party, with two other parties having relevance. The *Cumann na nGaedheal* (Society of Gaels) was formed in 1922 headed by pro-treaty Sinn Féin leaders Collins and Griffith. De Valera's party, Fianna Fáil (Soldiers of Destiny), would become the dominant party in Ireland. It was an off-shoot of the anti-treaty Sinn Féiners and it formed in 1926. Fine Gael ("Gaelic Nation" or "United Ireland"—pronounced: FEE-nuh GALE) formed in 1933 when *Cumann na nGaedheal*, the Centre Party, and the National Guard (a paramilitary group that was formed to combat IRA violence, pejoratively called the Blue shirts in reaction to leaguist paramilitaries in fascistic states such as Hitler's Germany or Mussolini's Italy) merged. It took its present name in 1933. It was made up of pro-treaty politicos and partisans. From the time of the vote for Home Rule in the Dáil Éireann in 1921 (when de Valera's camp walked out opposed to devolution), Irish party politics were set on a bipolar course revolving around Irish constitutional issues.

Fianna Fáil

Since 1927, *Fianna Fáil*'s electoral support has been strong at 40%–50% of the Irish people. Its evolution has seen it change from a hard line separatist party to a modern *"catchall" party* of bureaucratic government. Its first decades were concerned with legally ending its ties to Britain politically. It saw splits and fissures based on means and ends. Other anti-treaty groups like a revived Sinn Féin pursued a more radical approach to uniting all of Ireland. From 1932 to 1973, Fianna Fáil controlled Irish politics, largely due to de Valera's imprint on the system. Its presence as a kind of national movement in the capacity of political party kept it in a position of authority. Sartori might call the Irish party system of this era a *predominant party system*. Whereby one dominant party controls politics, but smaller ones do have a role to play (which would keep Fianna Fáil from being classified as a directive party in a hegemonic system as communist parties in central and eastern Europe were classified after WWII until 1989–90). In 1985, Fianna Fáil split and the Progressive Democrats were formed. The Progressive Democrats favored neo-liberal (conservative free market) economic policies and the party eventually began to play a role similar to the Free Democratic Party in West German and German politics from 1948–98 as the fulcrum for balancing center- left and center-right governments in the German party system. Fianna Fáil eventually lessened its hard core position on the constitutional settlement as the constitutional issue became less relevant after independence from the UK Commonwealth in 1949. The party then evolved as a business-friendly center-right conservative party that lost support in some rural areas and gained support in other areas because of its moderation.

Led by *Bertie Ahern* (see more about him in chapter four), the youngest Taoiseach in the history of the Republic at 45 in June 1997, Fianna Fáil (called by its members the Irish "Republican party" because of its support for a 32-county or all-island "Republic") was the first government since 1969 to win back-to-back elections (1997 and 2002). The party secured a third straight election victory in May 2007 and Ahern became the longest serving Taoiseach since the mid-1960s. Fianna Fáil was a modern mass party that had evolved from a nationalist movement into a moderate-to-conservative mass party.

In the early twenty-first century, the party defended itself by arguing that it had led Ireland to unprecedented economic growth as a powerful "Celtic Tiger" economy. It felt that its policies in the area of agriculture had helped rural Ireland by getting 20% of foreign net earnings from food exports. The party, as the leader of government, had doled out millions of euros to help build educational programs and facilities at all levels. The party began to move toward providing high-speed internet to all towns of over 1500 people in Ireland. The plan called for spending €25 million to improve Eire's e-commerce and access. The party hoped to utilize the public facilities and organizations that would improve the delivery of services that would help people learn the Irish language. The party, led by the party leader and Taoiseach Ahern, held the European presidency in 2004 and led the way in promoting EU expansion and integration.

Fianna Fáil had 78 *Teachta Dálas* (pronounced CHOCK-tah dawlas) (deputies in Irish) in 2005 (after winning 81 in 2002). Of the 78 TDs, five were women and one was Síle de Valera, the granddaughter of the party's founder and nationalist hero—Éamon de Valera. She was born in Dublin in 1954, went to University College Dublin, and was a career guidance counselor prior to entering politics. She was first elected to the Dáil in 1977 and held a five year seat as an MEP in Strasbourg after 1979. She quit the party in 1993 when the US-Irish Shannon Airport stopover policy was abolished, but she rejoined the next year and was appointed to the frontbench as an arts and heritage minister in Bertie Ahern's Fianna Fáil government. Politics ran deep in her family, she was succeeded as government minister in 2002 by her cousin, Éamon Ó Cuív, a longtime Fianna Fáil TD. She remained as a junior minister and TD.

Fine Gael

Fine Gael came into office in a minority government in 1948 as part of a protest coalition against Fianna Fáil. These *"rainbow" coalitions* would govern Ireland from 1948–51 and 1954–57. In 1973, Fine Gael governed as the dominant partner in a coalition with the Irish Labour party until 1977. A similar coalition was achieved in 1981–March 1982 and December 1982–87. Fine Gael, although a catchall party (a broad umbrella grouping of tendencies within a party in order to appeal to many in the electorate) like Fianna Fáil, was to start creating ideological space between itself and its rival Fianna Fáil. Both are seen historically as conservative nationalist parties. From the 1960s, Fine Gael evolved from a party perceived by many Irish as more conservative than Fianna Fáil to one of social democracy which was moderately centrist. It began to focus on justice and democracy issues and by the mid-1980s Dr. *Garret FitzGerald* tried to move the party away from its conservative base. Under a Fine Gael-Labour government in the 1980s, Éire attempted to solve the troubles with the United Kingdom over Northern Ireland, take a more social democratic route on economic and social issues, and moderate the position of the state church, the Roman Catholic Church, in society. Some success occurred on the constitutional issue with the signing of the Anglo-Irish agreement of 1985 (between Margaret Thatcher's Conservative government in Britain and FitzGerald). A recession hurt the Irish economy and state capitalist approaches to macroeconomic policy. The failure of referendums on abortion in 1983 and divorce in 1986 undercut Fine Gael's attempt to alter the political culture and the party's historical support base. Abortion would be allowed by judicial decree and divorce would be constitutionally sanctioned in the 1990s.

In the early twenty-first century, Fine Gael's policies continued to favor further integration into the EU, supporting the European Constitution that 25 member states were either submitting to referendums or votes via national legislatures. The party was actively supportive of giving 0.7% of its GDP to the developing world for assistance and furthering the peace process via the GFA in Northern Ireland. Fine Gael supported an enterprise economy, but not at the expense of cutting large numbers of public services. The party favored a more moderate approach to economic development. The party called for aiding farmers in improving the exportation of beef, expediting payments to farmers, and providing grants to encourage young farmers to stay in the agricultural business. The party hoped to find ways to encourage youth to work initiatives and helping youth find work. Finding ways to promote education and safety for children was a priority for the party as well. Fine Gael's accent on social responsibility in the areas of business, health, and education made them similar to Irish Labour and other left-of-center parties in Celtic polities. But, its historical moderation in government made it more of a centrist party of government like the two American parties (Republicans and Democrats) prior those parties becoming increasingly more ideological by the late twentieth century.

The party's organization mirrors a modern mass political party. It has a 28-member executive council (like most parties' NECs). Representation on the executive council includes party vice presidents, regional representatives across Ireland, representatives from the party's youth wing and women's group. Of the 32 Fine Gael TDs in the Dáil in 2005 (31 were elected in 2002 and one independent TD had joined the party in 2004), only two TDs were female (one representing a Dublin constituency and one Laois-Offaly in central Ireland). The party had one female Senator who represented Dublin. Fine Gael had dropped drastically from 54 seats in the Dáil in the 1997 parliament. Soul-searching began in the party and Kenny, who had served as a government minister under Fine Gael Taoiseach John Bruton from 1994–97. After the 2004 EP elections, Fine Gael had five MEPs with one of those a woman. The Fine Gael delegation in the EP was part of the People's parties and Christian Democrats bloc in Strasbourg.

Irish Labour

The Irish Labour Party (*Pàirti an Lucht Oibre* in the Irish) is the only pre-1921 settlement party that continued after the Irish Civil War. It was founded in 1912. Like most European social democratic parties, it has waffled between pragmatic politics and calculating its chances for junior partner status in center-right and center-left coalitions with Fianna Fáil and Fine Gael, respectively. It has also had moments where its radicals wanted it to pursue a policy of separation from the conservative parties. Its socialism has never been militant or radical, and its has always favored social democracy for Éire. It has never been able to build a solid following among rural workers or farmers and because the proletariat was less important politically in agrarian Ireland, Irish Labour did not have the same political efficacy historically as its proletarian cousin had in Britain.

In 2005, the Irish Labour Party said that the highest earners in Ireland should pay a minimum of 20% of their earnings in income taxes. The party also said it would eliminate unfair tax shelters and prosecute those who cheat on their taxes. In education, the party wanted to encourage savings for children to give people a better chance at financial success as adults. It called for better recreational opportunities and playground equipment for children at schools and day-care centers. It said that the maximum number of children in an elementary school class should be 25. The party favored policies that would deter anti-social behavior and help neighborhoods guard against crime and hooliganism. Under Irish Labour, Ireland would integrate further into the EU and give 0.7% of its GDP to developing world countries for aid. It would work to provide better housing opportunities for all and create a fair and rational immigration system with a viable green card process for non-nationals.

The party is a modern mass party and has active participation at the branch and constituency levels. It has a 15-person national executive committee (NEC) elected at the national party conference (held every two years). The NEC consists of the party leader, deputy leader, president, chair, national treasurer, and representatives of various groups such as the party's women's organization and trade unions (like traditional European Labour parties). The national conference is not usually held in Dublin. Its representatives are elected from branch and constituency levels, as well as from the women's and trade unions groups. Labour has a youth group which covers the ages of 16–26. Teachers, legal, and social services groups also have representation in the party. The party's headquarters are in Dublin.

In 2002, the party got 21 seats in the Dáil, the same number it received in 1997. The party had unqualified success in the early 1990s with high profile leader Dick Spring, who guided the party from 1982–97, leading it to 33 seats and over 330,000 votes, its most ever, in the 1992 elections. Spring became Tànaiste (deputy prime minister) and foreign minister under Fianna Fáil and Taoiseach (prime minister) Albert Reynolds from 1992–94. In 1994, Labour then joined a "Rainbow Coalition" government with Fine Gael and the Democratic Left party. It was Irish Labour's sixth time in participating in governing Ireland since independence. *Mary Robinson*'s high profile election (see more about this in chapter four) as Irish president, the first female to be so honored, was another bade of honor for the party. In 2005, one-third of its 21 frontbench TDs were women including the deputy party leader, Liz McManus. McManus got her start in Irish politics in local politics. She then became a TD in 1992 as a member of the Democratic Left party. From 1994–97, she served in government and held the cabinet post for housing and urban renewal. In 1999, that party fused with Irish Labour. Outside of politics, McManus has been an accomplished writer winning several awards for her fictional works and she served as a newspaper columnist from 1986–92.

Progressive Democrats

The *Progressive Democratic Party* (*An Páirti Daonlathach*) has become an increasingly important party in the Republic's political system. Founded in 1985, the party has played a major role in four coalition governments. Each government was led by Fianna Fáil: 1989–92, 1997–2002, 2002–07, and after 2007. The party is part of the European Liberal Party family that fashions itself as neo-liberal (conservative in the American sense) on economic issues calling for reduced taxes for companies and citizens to stimulate capitalist macroeconomic growth in Ireland. It is also socially liberal (in the modern American sense) in wanting to keep government from regulating personal behavior and safeguarding individuals' civil liberties. In this regard, it now plays a similar role as the junior coalition partner in Irish government that the Free

Democrats (also known as the Liberals) did in the Federal Republic of Germany with the center-right Christian Democratic Union-Christian Social Union parties from 1949–56, 1961–66, and 1982–98, and with the center-left Social Democrats from 1969–82. The Irish party came into existence under the ex-Fianna Fáil minister Desmond O'Malley who was expelled from Fianna Fáil. The party leader and Tánaiste (by 2002) *Mary Harney*, a co-founder of the party with O'Malley, was open to serving in government with Fianna Fáil or the more centrist (and usually major opposition party) Fine Gael. The party's electoral fortunes have see-sawed as it had 14 seats in the Dáil immediately after 1985, but has seen those numbers drop. In 2002, the party gained four seats to double its number of TDs at eight (despite losing aggregate votes).

Like Irish Labour's Mary Robinson, Harney was first in the Seanad in 1977. She took over the Progressive Democrats in 1993 and became a government minister (enterprise, trade, and employment) in 1997. She hails from County Galway and received her college education, like Robinson, from Trinity College, Dublin. In 1977, she ran for the Dáil with Fianna Fáil but lost. The same year Taoiseach Jack Lynch appointed her to the Seanad as she became the youngest member of the upper house in the nation's history. In 1981, she won a seat in the Dáil. After voting against the Fianna Fáil-led government in favor of the Anglo-Irish agreement in 1985 she was ejected from the party. With O'Malley she helped found the Progressive Democrats and eventually played an instrumental part as a minister of state with a portfolio on the environment in 1989. In this post, she ended the sale of coal in Dublin thus halting the smog problem in Ireland's capital. In 1997, she was named Tánaiste—the first female to ever hold the post and she also continued as a government minister after 1997 as well.

The Progressive Democrats' 2002 election manifesto, *Manifesto 2002: Value for Your Vote*, focused on economic growth, keeping taxes low, and making sure public monies were spent well and efficiently. The party called for investing in health service, supporting the disabled, improving pensions, improving the education system and making it more up-to-date, and making Irish society more tolerant and unified. It called for selling state assets that no longer needed to be in public ownership, creating a fund to deal with privatized monies (from assets that would be liquidated) and fees from state licenses and other items that raise money for the Irish government. The Progressive Democrats favored lower taxes on autos that have lower carbon dioxide emissions. Thus, putting the party in the capitalist, yet environmentally-concerned camp. The party hoped to improve the amount of money it could give to social welfare payouts to improve income for those on social welfare. It also hoped to increase child support payments for those on social welfare. The party wanted to increase the old-age pension amount to help those living on fixed pensions as their main source of income. The party also encouraged immigration to make Ireland more diverse. It hoped to end racism by making the body (the Reception and Integration Agency) that helped facilitate asylum seekers permanent. The party wanted to see more women in leadership roles. The 1992–

97 Dáil had 20 female representatives of the 166 TDs. The party called for a plan to allow for greater female participation in politics by creating a quota system for appointments to state boards. The party strongly supported EU enlargement and maintaining the existing Common Agricultural Policy (CAP) to benefit Irish farmers. Progressive Democrats supported the Belfast agreement of 1998 and believed the ties between Ireland and the UK should be strengthened.

As a party that came to power in the mid-1980s on the promise to try to abolish the Irish state's upper chamber, the Seanad, it saw its liberal credentials evolve to include many liberal policies with market economics, a sustainable environment, and improving society via progressive social policies at its forefront. By 2002, over 50% of its TDs were female, one-third of its candidates in the 1997 election were female. By 2002, party membership had grown by 25% and by 2004 its membership was 6,000 (both statistics according to the party). In the middle of the 2002–07 Dáil, the party had eight TDs, four senators, two cabinet ministers, and two junior ministers. The party had a full-time general secretary and two party communications and research officers at its party headquarters in Dublin. The party was a full-fledged modern mass party with a national executive and annual party conference. After the May 2007 elections, the party's fortune's sagged electorally as it won only two seats in the Dáil, but it still hung on to participate in the three-party Fianna Fáil-led coalition along with the Greens. The Progressive Democrats got one portfolio in the new government (the continuation of Harney's role as minister of health and children).

Sinn Féin in the Republic

Sinn Féin was founded to take Ireland out from under British rule. The party broke apart in the 1920s in the Republic as seen in Chapter Two. It came back to life as the parliamentary arm of the IRA in the 1950s and 1960s, and its major impact was felt in its politics and paramilitary focus in Northern Ireland. The party's operational focus, policies, and party organization are described below in the Northern Irish party system since it has been more relevant in recent years in that party system. It has played a role in Republic politics as a party of nationalist outbidding (ironically given its fringe role vis-à-vis the nationalist, yet conservative parties, Fianna Fáil and Fine Gael.) It won its first seats in the Dáil, as the newer post-independence Sinn Féin, in 1981 and 1982. Sinn Féin's role in Dublin's politics have ebbed and flowed over the years, but at the dawn of the twenty-first century the party was making a bit of a comeback. The party won five seats in the Dáil in 2002 and four in 2007. It got over 120,000 votes and 6.5% of the vote in the Republic's elections in 2002 and 142,000 votes and 6.9% of the vote in 2007. All four of its TDs in the Dáil in early 2008 were male, but its two MEPs elected in 2004 were both women: Mary Lou McDonald for Dublin and Bairbre de Brún for the Six Counties constituency of Northern Ireland. Ireland is divided into five regions for EP elections and it sends 16 MEPs to Strasbourg and for European purposes no difference is made between Northern

Ireland and the Republic. McDonald studied several subjects including English literature and European studies at three Irish universities. She worked for non-governmental organizations tied to economic and European issues. She also worked directly for Sinn Féin in organizing elections in Éire.

The December 2004 bank heist by IRA militants in Belfast netted £26.5 million ($53.84 million or €39.18 million). Immediately, Sinn Féin tried to distance itself from the IRA action. The Taoiseach issued a stern statement criticizing Sinn Féin and he said that the leaders (Gerry Adams and Martin McGuinness) had not been acting in good faith when they met with him on peace talks over the future of the Six Counties. In February 2005, the Dáil passed a resolution condemning Sinn Féin for its ties to the IRA and the thievery. The 2004 bank robbery was followed by a late January 2005 IRA hit on a Catholic man in Belfast. That too brought widespread condemnation and a protest march took place in East Belfast and the sisters of the slain man were invited to the White House by American president George W. Bush to celebrate St. Patrick's Day. Incredibly, the IRA said it would execute its members for killing the Catholic Belfast man. Irish, British, and American governments were outraged at the insensitivity and lawlessness and Adams was not allowed to come to Washington, DC for St. Patrick's Day given the imbroglio his party and the peace process faced due to these invidious events.

Irish Greens

The *Comhaontas Glas* (Green Party in Irish Gaelic) was formed as the Ecology party of Ireland in 1981. The party won two European Parliament seats in 1999, but lost them five years later. After 2002, the party had six TDs: four in Dublin proper, one in a suburban area of Dublin, and one in urban Cork in southern Ireland. Amazingly, for a small, seemingly unimportant party, the Single Transferable Vote system (explained more in Chapter Five) had helped the environmental party, which had done well in rural and picturesque areas of Europe, to do very well in the urban areas of Ireland. This should not be a surprise given the liberal values, levels of education, and concern about pollution in the metro areas of Ireland and Europe.

The party, like its mother Green party in Germany, is not surprisingly focused primarily on environmental awareness and socialization. But, by the early twenty-first century its policies were focused on genetically modified foods, agriculture, preserving wildlife, biodiversity landscapes in rural areas, sustainable economic development, keeping minimum wages tied to growth in the consumer price index, and keeping monopolies from occurring by letting market fairness occur. The party also sought to deal with the teaching crisis, as it perceived it, in Ireland by training and keeping teachers in schools and improving comparable worth policies for women in the workforce.

The Green party is a modern mass party. It has constituency associations, a national council that works on party policy, a NEC, and a national convention, known as the *Ard Fheis* (like Sinn Fein's). The NEC runs the party on a day to day basis, somewhat different from other NECs. It consists of only four people:

a national coordinator, two party TDs, and the party's treasurer. The party was located in Dublin. The party leader after 2001 was TD Trevor Sargent who represented Dublin North. Sargent joined the Greens in 1982 and was first elected to the Dáil in 1992. Sargent was a teacher and speaks Irish fluently. In 2005, of the 29 elected Green party local councilors in Ireland, nine were women including the deputy party leader, Mary White. White was elected a Carlow County councillor in 1999. She ran for a Dáil seat in 2002 and canvassed over 3000 miles on foot. She also ran for a Seanad seat in 2002 and lost that race as well. She was educated at Trinity College Dublin. As a *left-libertarian party* (to use political scientist Herbert Kitschelt's phrase), the Greens continued to promote the environment and a slew of leftist approaches to politics in working to move Ireland in a green direction (Kitschelt 1988). The Greens won places for six TDs in the 2007 Dáil elections and were invited surprisingly into the three-party governing coalition by the Fianna Fáil Taoiseach, Bertie Ahern. The party got two portfolios—environment and energy. It was the first time the Greens had ever helped govern the Republic.

The Evolution of the Irish Party System

From 1927 to 1973, roughly the years of de Valera's dominance and influence in Irish politics, the Republic's political party system was one controlled by Fianna Fáil. The party was distinctly nationalist and the smaller parties played a secondary role to the party that de Valera helped form. Sartori would classify the Irish system during the early years of the Republic as a "predominant" one (as political scientist Basil Chubb has stated) (Chubb 1992). Clearly, the predominant party system in Ireland had smaller parties that served to confront and challenge the dominant party, Fianna Fáil. Of course, Fine Gael, was the major opposition party with Irish Labour serving in an oppositional role as well. Over time, the dominant party wins a majority of the seats in parliament and this was the case in Éire with some exceptions noted above (in the rainbow coalitions of the late 1940s and early 1950s). These types of systems can evolve out of two party systems or fragmented systems and the latter appears to be the case with the split in Sinn Féin which caused the Civil War immediately after the signing of the treaty with Britain in December 1921. According to Sartori, predominant party systems include some Latin American examples historically (Mexico, Uruguay, and Paraguay) and the Democratic Party's control of the American South until the 1980s. However, the predominant party system in Éire began to change to a party system of limited pluralism after 1973 where three-to-five parties have relevance in the party system. Like Scotland's devolved politics after 1999, Ireland has seen the maintenance of two major parties (Fianna Fáil and Fine Gael) and their roles in governance, but both Labour and the Progressive Democrats (after 1985) have played important roles as coalition partners in government. Moderate pluralism is characterized by coalition governments in which no party receives a majority of the seats in the legislature. At times, minority governments will evolve, but the system may imitate a two-party one despite the role of small parties in helping create coalition governments. This is precisely the system found in Ireland today. In moderate or limited pluralist systems, no viable anti-system parties (those wanting to radically alter the constitution or replace democracy itself) are found. In the Republic, the modern Sinn Féin party may be seen as a kind of anti-system party with its insistence on uniting all 32 counties of Ireland, but in reality, the only element that makes it an anti-system party is its paramilitary arm, the IRA, which has used unconventional means to solve political disputes over the linkages between the Northern Irish government and the Republic. Yet, Sinn Féin's role in the Dáil is marginal in practice since it has so few seats. What's more, the IRA's disavowal of terror has put Sinn Féin out of the anti-system category. Also, in limited pluralist party systems, opposition parties can come together to challenge the government. Bilateral opposition parties that may be found at left or right ends of the ideological spectrum are usually not seen (such as communist or neo-fascist parties). In Ireland, the parties are more centrist in both their governance and ideological orientations (save Sinn Féin which is more radical on constitutional issues and overtly socialist, or anti-capitalist, on economic issues). Thus, Éire has not evolved into a segmented party system that would yield a polarized pluralism (rather than a moderate or limited pluralism) as Sartori calls it. In the UK and Ireland, only Ulster would be close to a polarized pluralist party model. But, even then, Northern Ireland's parties would be more akin to a limited pluralism given the longstanding dominance of unionist parties in Ulster since the late nineteenth century.

Clearly, political culture affects party systems and more will be said in Chapter Six about political culture. But, the prevalence of authoritarian attitudes in Ireland historically and the predominant party system that prevailed in both the Republic and Ulster after 1922, may in an ironic way have led to a muting of segmentation in Éire and the rise of a limited pluralism in the party system that has brought stability in Irish political life. Ulster, although having similar authoritarian values at its devolution in 1922, had problems with segmentation due to the religious cleavages in the north and when placed on top of the pluralism in the system, is the variable that has led to more volatility in Northern Irish politics and the eventual use of force and unconventional means, after 1969, to solve political issues in the Six Counties of Ulster.

Wales

Welsh Labour (Plaid Llafur Cymru)

The Labour party got its start in Wales in the 1900 general election when the Labour Representation Committee fielded candidates throughout Britain. Wales had one Labour politician elected from the industrial district of Merthyr in southern Wales. That candidate was the Scotsman Kier Hardie (1856–1915) who had formed the Scottish Socialist party in 1888 and was an avowed Christian as well. Thus, Hardie helped bring democratic socialism to both Scotland and Wales and the Celtic fringe would never be the same. Ironically, in the Liberal Party's greatest moment in Welsh and broader UK politics, the 1906 election, Labour put itself on the map as it got 29 seats in Britain (only one of those seats was in Wales.) Although this may have seemed insignificant at the time, with the Liberals in control of 377 MPs (including some Labourites) at Westminster (the opposition Conservatives had 157), Labour was at its inchoate stages starting to make electoral gains and within 15 years would have control of the coal pits of south Wales due to trade union affiliation with the party. By 1912, the ILP created a Welsh section. This came at the time of the Great Unrest (1910–11) with numerous strikes and worker agitation. Certainly, this helped Labour as it sought to convince Celts that they could be socialists and Christians, which was not an easy thing to do given *Karl Marx*'s (1818–83) atheistic belief that religion was the "opium of the masses." Certainly, Labour's socialism had a profound impact on Wales's political culture. The early twentieth century saw coal miners in southern Wales unionizing and the UK's trade union membership was at 8.25 million by 1920. As a result of labor activism, the future appeared bleak for the Liberals who were falling behind Labour in Wales. From 1920–22, Labour won six by-elections. The Representation of the People Act had increased the franchise to younger adult males and females over 30 could vote for the first time ever. Thus the 1922–23 general elections were a breakthrough for Labour UK-wide, especially in Wales and Scotland. In Wales, Labour continued to get more votes and seats at Westminster. After the general election of 1923, Welsh Labour had 20 MPs versus 12 for the Liberals and four for the Tories. Historian John Davies notes that the Welsh Labour party tended to tap into the class and nationalist sentiments of the Welsh far better than the Liberals or Tories (Davies 1994). The latter were the predominant party in every general election for the English from 1918–35. Liberals had fallen abruptly, but broader regional and national (British-wide) economic trends with greater industrialization, unionization, and the salience of Welsh mining and agriculture allowed Labour to supplant the Liberals in Wales in the 1920s. The public's preference for Labour in representing it at Westminster and then controlling Welsh politics after 1999 in legislative devolution would still be firmly ensconced in the political culture at the turn of the new millennium.

The 1945 UK general election, Labour's greatest victory up to that point (prior to 1997), saw 25 of 36 Welsh seats in the House of Commons captured by Labour. Given the immediate demands of the post-war context, devolution was a backburner issue and Wales's native son, *Aneurin Bevan*, longtime Welsh trade unionist, got the health portfolio and fellow Welshman James Griffiths, was named minister of national insurance under Prime Minister Clement Attlee. Under Bevan, the National Health Service (NHS) was created in 1946 which, at the time, was to provide compulsory health care for all regardless of status or ability to pay. Eventually, within a few years, the NHS would be forced to ask Britons to pay for some prescriptions due to the demands on the system. It was leaders like Bevan who extolled the virtues of a socialist state that was centralized and not federated. This longstanding Labour position, rooted in the old Marxian, class-based, internationalist thinking, was unpalatable to many Welsh nationalists of varying stripes from PC supporters to Liberals to even some Labourites.

By the early 1960s, Plaid Cymru's electoral improvement gave Labour a cause for concern in Wales. Many Welsh Labour politicians began to advocate administrative devolution and some, following the Scottish Labourites, called for legislative devolution as well. In 1973, the Kilbrandon Commission called for an assembly for Wales. Something Labour had being championing in Wales since 1966. The 1979 referendum failure in Wales, which (unlike Scotland's which was mired in controversy) was an outright rejection by the Welsh, was hard for many nationalistic Labourites to swallow. Despite these events, Labour continued to dominate Welsh politics despite a drop in support in May 1979 with the advent of the Thatcher era. From that point until 1997, it was the Labour Party in the Celtic fringe that stood as outposts for the hope that political change could occur in Britain. Of course, Labour under ethnic Celt Blair would try to lead Labour nationally, Labour would recapture its zeal and ability to appeal to Britons from all regions of the UK-state. It is not surprising that the six Labour leaders after 1976 (over a more than twenty year span) were Celts given the importance of the Labour Party base in the Celtic fringe. After the 1997 devolution referendum victory in Wales, Welsh Labour set out to lead Wales into a new era in the newly devolved assembly in Cardiff.

Welsh Labour (*Plaid Llafur Cymru*) sought to continue to do much as the party of government in Wales and the UK. Its policies by 2005 focused on decreasing inflation, putting people back to work (which it claimed 125,000 had got jobs since 1997 under its policies), improving the NHS which had put 350 physicians and 5000 new nurses in Wales under Labour, increasing the number of teachers in Welsh schools (some 1600 more since 1997), and fighting crime by putting 850 police officers on Welsh streets since 1997. The Welsh Labour Party is a modern mass party with branch and constituency associations. It still referred to itself as a democratic socialist party on the regional party website. The Welsh Executive Committee is the overseeing arm of the national Labour Party that runs the regional party. It is made up of AMs, MPs, and others who set local policies for Labour in Wales. Of the 30 Labour AMs in Cardiff after 2003, 16 were women. This was not surprising: 1) given Labour's affirmative action-style quota system to improve female representation; and 2) the fact that 30 of the 60 *Cynulliad Cenedlaethol Cymru* (Welsh National Assembly) seats were held by women (see Box 4.4). The Welsh cabinet in 2005 had five of nine positions held by women. They included a former college professor who grew up in England (but settled in Wales in 1971), a director of a health care quango, a former English teacher, a former trade union leader, and a former public social services manager. Labour's emphasis on putting women in higher profile roles in politics has been somewhat divisive even within the Labour Party in Wales. In May 2005 at the British general election, a disaffected former Labour Welsh AM and MP, Peter Law of Blaenau Gwent, who became an independent because he had been deselected by Labour due to his opposition to all-female shortlists for Labour candidates for the Westminster legislature, overturned a 19,000-seat majority in Labour's safest seat (Blaenau Gwent) in southeastern Wales near the heart of the historical mining country. He was expelled from the party and in May 2005 after his spectacular election, 20 of his supporters were expelled from the party as well. Several supporters had protested at the Labour Party's shortlist meeting where Maggie Jones, Law's opponent, was selected prior to the general election. The protestors included both male and female supporters of Law. Thus, Law's resignation from the Labour Party in April 2005 gave Welsh Labour only 29 out of 60 seats in the Cardiff legislature. The party vowed to fight on with its minority government in Cardiff. Welsh Labour continued its dominance of Welsh politics in the 2005 British general elections by taking 29 of 40 Welsh seats at Westminster. The party got 42.7% of the vote (down from 48.6% in 2001) and it dropped five seats. Despite its decline, the party was still the dominant party in Wales in 2007 as it won the regional elections and continued to hang on to power in Cardiff.

Box 4.4: Welsh *Senedd* or National Assembly?

Some textbooks and newspapers refer to the Welsh Assembly as the *Senedd* (parliament in Welsh). Most journalists and scholars have continued since it came into existence after May 1999 to refer to it in the English as the Welsh National Assembly or the Welsh equivalent—*Cynulliad Cenedlaethol Cymru*. However, the issue is not merely one of semantics or linguistic eccentricity. The debate is more substantive than those. Like the Irish Dáil Eirrean, when that Dublin-based legislature was formed illegally prior to the 1921 treaty that created the Irish Free State, proponents of a Welsh legislature with equivalent powers to their Celtic cousins in the north, the Scots, want a Welsh *Senedd* with more powers. Long a separatist party, Plaid Cymru has called for this for several years. Some Welsh Labourites echo the nationalists' sentiments. But, even some Welsh Tories have called for greater amounts of devolution. AM David Melding, Conservative member from South Wales Central, resigned his shadow minister's role that he had held in the 1999–2003 assembly to protest the lack of power of the Cardiff-based legislature. As a matter of fact, he was the only Tory AM (out of 10) in Cardiff after the 2003 elections without a shadow portfolio. He willingly accepted his backbench status in order to advocate more power for what might become a *Senedd*. Melding exhibited an interesting minority position in Conservative politics in the UK which is historically very much opposed to devolution. He claimed that the post-1999 constitutional settlement of Labour had left Wales powerless. He argued a Scottish-type parliament might rectify Welsh concerns since the current assembly (or none at all if the Tories were to quash it) could give the impression that Cardiff essentially enforces the "English" will in Wales. Of course, given the tepidity of the Welsh toward Home Rule, continued murkiness over a weak assembly or empowered *Senedd* may be the nation's political will into the foreseeable future. However, after Plaid Cymru joined Welsh Labour in ruling Wales in 2007, both parties were committed to a Welsh parliament in the future.

Plaid Cymru

Plaid Cymru (PC), the Party of Wales or better known as the Welsh Nationalists, was founded in 1925 and did not win a seat at Westminster until 1966. However, it was formed by activists who wanted to take Welsh cultural and linguistic nationalism and channel it toward self-government for the Welsh. Like the SNP, PC was somewhat anti-English, but its leaders sought to bring distinctly Welsh issues to the table which they believed were not being addressed by the longstanding major parties in Wales; namely, the Liberals and Labour. One of the two dominant personalities in PC's early history was Dr. Saunders Lewis, a Welsh language professor, who was the party's president from 1926–39. He was a moderate socialist who hoped to put Welsh culture and language on the political agenda for Wales. He was also involved in the incident at *Penyberth* in 1939 for which he and nationalism in Wales are well remembered by Welsh historians. However, his philosophies and actions did not translate into any real political power for nationalists. Yet, by 1980, when the Tory government under Margaret Thatcher yielded to demands for a Welsh language British Broadcasting Corporation TV station and with the increase by the twenty-first century in Welsh speakers in Wales reversing the downward trend 100 years earlier, Lewis seemed to be vindicated.

Box 4.5: Penyberth: Unconventional Political Participation and Passive-Aggressive Celts

Political culture on the Celtic fringe is marked by many characteristics and this book makes several assumptions about a general model of Celtic politics. But, the Celtic national character (if one can argue there is such a thing) is somewhat hard to get a handle on and the marginalization and anger felt by Scots, Irish, and Welsh at times has led to political violence and other acts of unconventional political behavior (whether non-violent civil disobedience and passive resistance of Welsh language advocates or outright terrorism by Irish militants). The Scots are known for their stubbornness and the Irish for bad tempers. Of course, the experience of the Irish in the early twentieth century saw a people who had not really attempted to challenge British rule, for seven centuries, until 1916 and the Easter Uprising. With the gun in Irish politics, 4000 died in the 1922 civil war (more than died from 1969–98, in the troubles in Northern Ireland). Thus, unconventional political action took on different forms in Scotland, Ireland, and Wales. But, growing militancy was always a concern of English overlords.

The Welsh academic Saunders Lewis, born in England to Welsh parents, was an active member of *Y Mudiad Cymreig* (The Welsh Movement) in the early 1920s that hoped to propagate a cultural and social native revival in Wales. Lecturing in Welsh language studies at University College at Swansea, in southern Wales, Lewis joined with other nationalists to form *Plaid Genedlaethol Cymru* (the National Party of Wales) in August 1925. The formation occurred at the National Eisteddfod at Pwllheli. A Home Rule movement already existed, but Lewis and others at Plaid's founding wanted a Welsh voice in London that would articulate Welsh issues from a Welsh perspective. Plaid rejected incrementalism and Westminster's intergovernmental approach and above all the backburner status of the Welsh language as a medium of cultural, social, and political articulation. Lewis guided the party toward conducting all activities within it in the native tongue (which would be a point of conflict in Wales as the twentieth century persisted). He also took control of the party as president from 1926 to 1939. Despite the fact that Plaid was seen for years as a political small-fry in Welsh and UK politics (it was not until July 1966 in a by-election that it won its first parliamentary seat and in 2007 it got into the coalition that governed Wales at the regional level—its first-ever attempt at governance), the advent of Plaid began the modern political march toward eventual structural change in Welsh and UK politics by 1999.

Penyberth is a key event in twentieth century Welsh politics. On September 8, 1936—400 years after England and Wales had formed the political union under Henry VIII—the British army facility there was victimized by arson as nationalists Lewis, D. J. Williams, and Lewis Valentine were caught and put on trial. It sent shockwaves through England, but many in Wales saw the nationalists as heroes. Lewis and company had argued against the facility since it was to be a "bombing school" for the Royal Air Force to train its pilots. Plaid was militantly anti-war and the nationalist and cultural overlay exacerbated tensions further. What's more, English pacifists had kept the school from being built in Dorset and Northumberland. So, its placement in backwater Wales added further insult to Welsh nationalists. The three men were sentenced to nine months in jail and upon release in late 1937 were greeted by 15,000 cheering comrades at Caernarfon. Lewis lost his job at Swansea as a university instructor, but the message was clear: the "Fire in Llŷn" was the first unconventional political response in just over 500 years, since Owain Glyn Dŵr, that Welshmen had fought back at the English.

Thirty years past Penyberth, Welsh militancy recrudesced as the Free Wales Army took part in several bombings in 1968–69. *Mudiad Amddffyn Cymru* (Movement for the Defense of Wales) saw two of its members killed at Abergele in 1969 waiting to blow up the train carrying Charles Windsor, soon to be the Prince of Wales. *Cymdeithas yr Iaith Gymraeg* (Welsh Language Society) in its second iteration after 1962 became involved in a less violent means of unconventional political participation in the late 1960s by painting over English-only sign names with the Welsh. These acts of vandalism were not widely embraced by the populace, underscoring the democratic nature of Wales's political culture. Although, the Welsh did not go down the militant path that the Irish nationalists had in the preceding decade, the thought of another angry Celtic group did not ease the concerns of legislators in London. In 1950, four nationalist students from Glasgow, Scotland motored up to Westminster Abbey in the wee hours of Christmas morning and stole the Stone of Destiny. The three males and one female took the stone north and hid it until April 1952 when they called authorities and left it at Abroath Abbey on the northeast coast of Scotland. When officers arrived a Scottish flag was placed over the stone. None of the four were prosecuted. The stone was sent back south in time for the 1952 funeral of King George VI. The next Celtic group to upset the UK apple cart, albeit marginally, was Wendy Wood's Scottish Patriots, a kind of militant, yet fairly innocuous, nationalist group (this was not an equivalent to the IRA in Ireland in the 1919–22 era or the post-1969 IRA in Ulster). Wood had been born in Kent in southeast England to Scottish parents. After her expulsion from the Scottish National Party in the late 1940s, she became more radical and oriented toward extraparliamentarism. After Queen Elizabeth II's accession, the Scottish Patriots were not happy with her title since she was Scotland's first, *not second*, Elizabeth! So, these nationalists after 1952 began a campaign of blowing up mailboxes with "EIIR" symbols on them. The vandalism was short-lived, but nonetheless is remembered as a small example of unconventional politics tied to Celtic nationalism.

The other major figure in PC's early history, who bridged the party's early days with more recent growth and success, was the hardworking Dr. *Gwynfor Evans* who at 31 was Plaid's president in 1945. Evans served in this capacity for 36 years and was PC's first MP after a by-election upset in July 1966 (its first Westminster by-election victory in its history) when he replaced the deceased Lady Megan Lloyd George, the Labourite MP and daughter of the former Welsh UK premier. Evans was educated at Oxford and Aberystwyth and joined Plaid as a university student in 1934. He said his adoption of nationalism was like a religious conversion. His politics were to the left of Lewis's. Evans embraced socialism, pacifism, and although an efficient party leader, was not seen as a visionary. His views did affect the gradual leftward drift of the party, similar to the development of the other major Celtic nationalist party in British politics, the SNP.

Political scientist Laura McAllister, herself a PC activist, argues that although the party did not fare well throughout most of its existence electorally, it finally got seats at the general elections of February and October 1974, the same ones that saw the SNP rise as a force to be reckoned with north of England's border (McAllister 2001). In those elections, PC got two and three seats at Westminster which translated to 10.7 and 10.8% of the Welsh vote. The 1970 general election was the apex of PC electoral support in UK-wide elections at 11.5%, but it did presage continued support for PC in elections for the House of Commons which never dipped below 7.3% (1987) from 1970 onward. This was fairly impressive for a party which only got, at its peak, 5.2% (1959) from 1945–69 in British general elections. The February 1974 elections saw PC gain two north Wales constituencies, Meirionnydd and Caernarfon, the latter the sight of the Edwardian Conquest of 1283 and Edward I's investiture of his son as the Prince of Wales in 1301. The party also lost Carmarthen by just three votes. The constituency it had won in the 1966 by-election in South Wales.

Despite some growing influence in the north of Wales, where the Welsh language was strong, the party, between 1959–66, started contesting more seats in UK general elections and thus became more of a threat to Welsh Labour and the Welsh Tories. By 1974, with both PC and the SNP winning more seats at Westminster, the combined 14 seats won in October that year put the Celtic nationalist parties ahead of the Liberals in Wales who won only 13 seats.

Ideologically, the party moved away from a broad nationalist movement based on culture and language and suspicion of the English-oriented political process. Like Sinn Féin, it refused, from 1925–31, to take seats, if elected (which did not happen), at Westminster. However, Evans's gradualist and socialist (social democratic) vision was inculcated in the party and like the SNP by the early 1990s, the left had won out and a party that looked much like the leftwing of the Labour party, with a nationalist tilt had evolved. What's more, as the party became more of a bona fide party moving away from a broader catchall-type movement in the capacity of a political party, it began to focus on administration, developing its finances, tactics, and strategy, lessening ideology to a certain extent. Plaid's 2004 EU election manifesto called for a national parliament in Wales by 2007, a greener Wales via sustainable development, accentuating Wales's rural heritage and agricultural economy, growing indigenous business, and Welsh approaches to greater business growth, which placed it to the right of the SNP on economic issues, but similar to the moderate Thatcherite policies of New Labour under Blair after 1997.

By the start of the twenty-first century, Plaid had 10,000 members in 220 local branches. Its national headquarters are located in Cardiff and it held a national conference once a year and a national council meeting bi-annually. It is governed by a NEC of 25 members. It has a standard party organization that can be found in modern mass political parties in the UK, Ireland, and the United States. Plaid's 1999 election success in the National Assembly for Wales (where it got 17 seats and just over 28% of the vote in the constituency and just over 30% in the regional lists) marked an evolution that has seen the party come from a movement-based agglomeration of groups in 1925 to fighting every Welsh constituency in 1970 (and receiving its highest percentage of vote in UK elections) to providing a legitimate alternative to Labour in Wales. PC followed up its 1999 assembly electoral success by getting close to 30% in the European Parliament elections (the first ever held under the PR electoral system in Britain). The party got two of five Welsh seats in Strasbourg. Of its 12 seats after the 2003 National Assembly elections, it showed that it was truly a national party with five seats in constituencies in northern Wales, five in southern Wales, and five in mid-Wales. The Welsh Nationalists had seen themselves evolve slowly, but by 1999 and the start of home rule in Wales it was firmly ensconced, like the SNP in Scotland, as the number two or three party in a three-or-four party system in Wales. By 2003, the party had seen success but it was also dealing with internal issues including a divisive election for party leader (which saw the long time leader Dafydd Wigley retire). The new leader Ieuan Wyn Jones was not as popular as Wigley. He was a lawyer from Anglesey and cut from the same cloth as many nationalists from the north with a view of old Wales (including chapels, labor solidarity, etc). He was challenged by a dynamic single mother from the south part of the nation, AM Helen Mary Jones—a feminist and peace activist. The choice for the party crystallized the historical bridge over the nationalist party's past from old-fashioned to modern, conservative to radical, male to gender-inclusive. With Ieuan Wyn Jones's victory, the party continued to fight on, but certainly, left-of-center nationalism in both Wales and Scotland was seeing a changing face with more women in the fold by the late twentieth and early twenty-first centuries.

PC finally realized its longstanding goal of governing Wales in July 2007 when it entered the coalition government with the Welsh Labour Party. Ieuan Wyn Jones was named the deputy first minister (the number two ministerial post) in the Welsh Assembly Government.

Welsh Liberal Democrats (Democratiaid Rhyddfrydol Cymru)

The Liberal Party came on the scene in the UK in 1859 when the Whig Party joined with Liberal radicals. The new party championed a more egalitarian society in terms of labor-capital relations, healthcare, freedom of religion, education, and better social benefits—which by the twentieth century included pension and unemployment benefits. Liberalism evolved in the late nineteenth century under the Scotsman Gladstone who had left the Tories in 1859 to take a post in Lord Palmerston's (Viscount Henry John Temple) Liberal government. In the 1880 UK parliamentary elections, Liberals got 29 of 33 Welsh seats. In that election, the Liberals had a majority of 137 over the Tories and Gladstone returned as prime minister for the second time with Irish Home Rule again on the agenda.

Although Gladstone was revered by the Welsh, both as a fellow Celt and for his morality and Christian altruism, Welsh Home Rule never got far under Gladstone and the Liberals who paid it lip-service. Out of the Liberal successes of the late nineteenth century rose Wales's greatest political figure of the twentieth century, David Lloyd George. Lloyd George would lead the UK Liberal Party to its greatest electoral and political successes including victory in the Great War (1914–18). Lloyd George would not become prime minister until the middle of the war in 1916. The party took 33 of 35 Welsh seats at Westminster in the 1906 elections and no Tories were returned to London (this would occur again in 1997 and 2001). The first decade of the twentieth century was the highlight of Liberal governance of Wales. But, the party would start to ebb and take a backseat to the Labour Party in Wales by the start of the 1920s. Just weeks after the 11 November 1918 Armistice, the premier was rewarded by the British with a large majority in his coalition. In Wales, 25 seats were won by Lloyd George supporters (including 20 Liberals). However, from 1920–22, the Liberals lost six by-elections to Labour and the transition to Labour's permanent control of Welsh politics began. The 1922 elections saw Labour take 15 seats in the coalfield districts of southern Wales. Scotsman Ramsay MacDonald, who would be Labour's first premier in a coalition government in 1924 for nine months, was elected to a seat from Wales. Labour got 41% of the vote in Wales versus 31% in 1918. The Conservatives got three seats and Liberals hung on to 11 seats. In the 1923 election, Labour got 20 MPs to 12 for the Liberals and four for the Tories. By 1924, Labour started capitalizing on disenchantment with Liberal policies and the inability to combat Tory unionism in both the area of Home Rule and Welsh national and cultural issues. Out of this context grew a plethora of nationalist groups and more Labour unitary evolution under a socialist model which appeared to be contradicting each other; however, this would lay the groundwork for Labour's softening on Home Rule by the 1970s and its movement toward the implementation of devolution by 1997.

By 1959, the Welsh Liberal Party was fighting for its survival as Labour continued to make gains in traditionally held Liberal areas. By 1974, the Welsh Nationalists had arrived on the electoral scene and also provided an almost identical ideological voice to that of the Liberals, just a bit more radical in terms of devolution, independence, and cultural issues. To counter nationalistic influences, the UK-wide Liberal Party became federated and in 1966 a separate Welsh Liberal Party was founded. The party still had federal ties to the UK Liberal Party, but it had more autonomy in terms of policy articulation and formulation. From 1970 to 1979, Welsh Liberals got under an average of two MPs in each of the four parliamentary elections during that decade. Things did not change radically for the party when in 1981 moderate Labourites, Scotsman David Steele, Welshman Roy Jenkins, and Englishpersons William Rogers and Shirley Williams, the so-called "Gang of Four" (all former Labour cabinet ministers), bolted from the party and its leftward lurch during the early Thatcher years to form the Social Democratic Party. The party had little success in the 1983 election at the UK-wide level despite the newly formed "Alliance" with the Liberals. The Alliance did not yield much for Wales's Liberals as the height of its electoral wins was the 1983 election with three MPs for Wales. But, in 1988, the Alliance formerly fused itself together as a parliamentary and nationwide party known as the *Liberal Democrats (Democratiaid Rhyddfrydol Cymru)*, thus transforming the Liberals into a broader party. The 2001 British general election saw Liberal Democrats get two seats in Wales (the same as 1997), but its percent of the Welsh vote increased slightly from 12% to 13.8%. It still took a backseat both in terms of vote percentage (14.27%) and number of seats at Westminster (4) to Plaid Cymru. The party improved its fortunes in Wales in the 2005 UK general election by getting four seats and its vote total went to 18.4% and increase of 4.6% from 2001. The party continued to do better not only on the Celtic fringe but in England as well as its opposition to the 2003 Iraq war had helped it gain ground on Labour and nationalists in Wales and Scotland.

The 1999 Welsh Assembly elections saw Liberal Democrats play an important role in the evolution of the newly devolved "administrative" assembly. The party got six seats the smallest number of seats of the four main parties. Despite this, in October 2000, the Liberal Democrats' legislative leader in Cardiff, Michael German AM, negotiated a secret deal with Labour first secretary, Alun Michael, that put Labour in coalition with the Liberals (a Lab-Lib pact) which allowed German to become Deputy First Minister, as Michael changed his title from first secretary to first minister (a la the Scottish model). Liberal Democrat AM Jenny Randerson was also named Welsh minister of culture and sport in the coalition, the only two portfolios for the Liberal Democrats. In 2003, the Liberal Democrats WNA votes increased marginally in both constituency and regional (second) votes from the 1999 elections, but its seat yield remained the same (6). After 2003 elections, Welsh Labour decided to rule as a minority government with exactly half of the seats in the assembly (30 of 60). Thus, Liberal Democrats were left to think about their role as a tertiary party in Welsh politics. Despite electoral problems, Liberal Democrats had done better in UK elections and by-elections in 2001 and the run up to Britain's war with Iraq in 2003. Thus, the potential of the Liberal Democrats playing a brokering role as they had in both Scottish and Welsh legislatures after 1999, much like the German Liberals (Free Democrats) in the Bundestag from 1948–57 and 1969–98 did seem possible even in UK-wide politics. Of course, the chance at greater participation seemed greater in the devolved Celtic contexts given the PR electoral systems used at the devolved levels of government in Britain.

Ideologically, Welsh Liberal Democrats, like the UK Liberal Democrats, continued to champion many of the same issues they had championed since the days of Gladstone. Economic opportunity and equality were persistent themes in party manifestoes. Greater focus on Welsh approaches to solve issues related to Welsh business and a focus on global trade was a staple of old liberal views from the nineteenth century. However, the EU and environmental issues had taken the party toward actively seeking peace and cooperation with the United States and attempts to persuade the US to ratify the Kyoto global climate treaty and to focus on a greener Europe. In this area the Liberal Democrats, both in Wales and in the UK, had stiff competition with PC and the Welsh Greens (*Plaid Werdd Cymru*). Concerned with fighting poverty, Liberal Democrats continued to advocate equality of outcomes and community-based solutions to entrepreneurship and thus its capitalist orientation was not in question (although it was a kind of capitalism with a human face as socialists and radicals might see it). With a strong defense of devolution, as compared to outright independence, and a vociferous call for PR throughout the UK at all levels, the Welsh and UK Liberal Democrats carried their message forward in Wales via the devolved party politics of the party's federated structure (which is different than the Tories, Labour or the Celtic nationalist parties in Britain).

Welsh Conservatives (Ceidwadwyr Cymreig)

The *Welsh Conservatives* were the second party of governance in Wales at Westminster after 1945 behind the Labour Party. Labour, for all intents and purposes, became the country's national party (as Labour evolved into in Scotland after 1959). The Tories consistently got over a quarter to nearly 30% of the electorate until 1997 when its fortunes sagged to under 20% (19.6%). Exactly like Scotland, the 1997 and 2001 elections represented a sea change for Conservatives in Wales and Scotland. In Wales, Tories did marginally better than in Scotland in those two elections and even saw their percent of the vote rise in 2001 back to 21% (still behind the 32% they got in 1979 when Mrs. Thatcher came to power). Yet, despite having higher vote totals than the Liberal Democrats in 1997 and 2001, the Conservatives received no seats at Westminster while the Liberal Democrats got two Welsh seats in both elections. Thus, the Tories with 19.6% of the vote in 1997 got no candidates into the House of Commons, but Plaid Cymru with 9.9% of the vote got four seats at Westminster. Thus, the argument that the SMD electoral system hurts small parties reversed itself and the concentration of PC's vote helped it gain seats at the expense of Conservatives and other parties ensuring that the Tories would be victimized by the electoral system they had favored for decades.

The Welsh Conservative Party after 1997 and 2001 had maintained its position as the second most voted for party in Wales after Labour, but it fell to fourth behind PC and the Liberal Democrats in terms of seats in London. This strange development did not follow the same path in 1999 and 2003 for the National Assembly. In 1999, the Tories were third behind Labour and PC in terms of voting percentage. The Conservatives got 16.2% in 1999 and 19.5% in 2003. They narrowed the gap on PC which saw its electoral support fall in four years by nine percent to 20.5% in 2003. By 2003, the Tories were still third in seats at Cardiff with 11 behind PC's 12 (PC had fallen from 17 in 1999). Indeed, much like Scotland, the Tories had fallen fast since 1997 in Westminster elections, but still managed to hold on somewhat in devolved elections. The 2003 elections also provided a referendum on Labour's national politics which were unpopular due to the Iraq war (whose formal phase had wound down with the toppling of Saddam Hussein's regime in Baghdad). Thus, in Wales, the Conservatives still had some support in suburban areas and the continued diffidence that some Welsh showed toward devolution helped the party make some electoral inroads at the start of twenty-first century politics.

The 2005 Welsh Conservative manifesto focused on education and parental choice (like the American voucher debate) and efforts to improve discipline in British schools. It also called for improving the cleanliness of hospitals and giving patients more choice in healthcare. The party also called for more police officers to combat crime, tougher sentencing of criminals, and more accountability on immigration rules. The party hoped to continue to argue, as it had in Scotland, for a curbing of the WNA's powers and more control for local councils in Wales. The 11 Tory AMs in the Cardiff assembly after 2003 had two female legislators among them and one ran the family hotel in Aberystwyth for 18 years prior to election in 2003 and the other Laura Anne Jones was Britain's youngest legislator at 24 when she was elected in 2003. She studied politics at Plymouth University after growing up in Monmouthshire. She joined the Welsh Tories in 1996 and was active in Tory student politics. As an avid sportsperson and follower of Cardiff City soccer and the Welsh national rugby team, she was the Welsh Conservatives' spokesperson on sports in the 2003 Welsh assembly. As AM Jones demonstrates, many Celtic politicians gain their start at very early ages.

The 2005 British general elections saw the Tories do well and improve their share of the vote to 21.4% up slightly 0.4% from 2001. Yet, the Conservatives which had got no seats in 1997 or 2001 in Wales received three seats (Clwyd West in the north in the heart of Welsh Nationalist and Labour country, Monmouth in the southeast, and Preseli Pembrokeshire in the southwest). All three were incredible gains for the Tories who had suffered much in the SMD elections in Wales since 1997. By 2007, with Conservatives gaining slightly in the percentage of the vote from the 2003 Welsh Assembly election, the party began to play the national card by making its website fully bi-lingual with equal Welsh-language material and English-language material. The Tories were understanding how to "play the game" in the historically social democratic Celtic regions.

The Welsh Party System: Moderate Pluralism like the Scots and Irish

The inchoate Welsh party system after 1999 bears a striking resemblance to Scotland's. With Labour holding the predominant power, although after 1999 in coalition with Liberal Democrats (as was seen in Scotland) until 2003 when Welsh Labour opted for a minority government, the system is one of essentially four parties vying for control of the legislature. Although Labour and PC were the top two parties after each election, the gap narrowed between PC and the Tories in 2003. The Liberal Democrats were marginal in terms of seats, but their role as junior partners in the first coalition government (1999–2003) gave it disproportionate influence over the Welsh government. The same occurred for Plaid Cymru after it entered the Red-Green coalition with Welsh Labour in 2007. Like Scotland, Sartori's application of limited pluralism in Wales is appropriate given the fact that three-to-five parties contend for power and the rivalry is great, but the existence of unilateral oppositions (such as PC) does not serve to create fragmentation that could turn the system into a polarized pluralist one. Unlike Northern Ireland where fairly severe bilateral polarized oppositions are found (in the unionist and republican camps), Wales and Scotland are evolving into "European-style" political systems replete with PR, a multi-party system, and a normal set of rules and conditions for democracy. What will test Wales's political system as it evolves will be the question of its capacity to absorb greater responsibilities (moving from devolution of a mixture of legislative and administrative responsibilities to full-blown parliamentarism) and how the system will handle (including the political culture) the transition to new parties in power (when Labour is ousted and the Nationalists, Conservatives or Liberal Democrats take the lead at some point in the future).

Northern Ireland

Ulster Unionist Party

The *Ulster Unionist Party* (UUP) has been the dominant party throughout the history of the Northern Irish sub-state. Form 1921–69, the UUP won every single election held for the Stormont assembly in Belfast. Given the sectarianism and communalism that was overtly manifested in the region's devolved party politics, the state quickly became a majoritarian Protestant British one as opposed to dual Protestant-Catholic *Irish* one. Every UUP cabinet minister in the region's first 48 years (save three ministers) were members of the historical *Orange Order*. The order began in 1795 after Protestants and Catholics battled at Loughgall in County Armagh. The next year, the order began commemorating publicly the Battle of Boyne every July twelfth. The society went on to become a major force among Protestant politicians and workers in Northern Ireland. With the use of the UK's SMD electoral system, the UUP appeared to be a majority party and as political scientist Feargal Cochrane has argued, elections were more a census reflecting communal (Catholic versus Protestant) strength instead of the articulation of philosophies, policies, or ideologies in a democratic process (Cochrane 1999).

The UUP was founded in Belfast in 1905 at Ulster Hall when the Ulster Union Council was formed to facilitate connections between Ulster Unionist constituencies (already represented by Unionist MPs at Westminster) and other affiliated unionist groups in Ulster. In general, Ulster Unionism had evolved out of three distinct constituencies that were primed for reactionary response against the forces of Home Rule. The working classes were brought into the Ulster Union Labour Association (UULA) to, on the surface, eradicate Bolsheviks, but also to put Protestant labor in line to work with loyalists political interests such as the British Empire Union headed by Edward Carson by 1918. Aside from the UULA, the remnants of the Ulster Volunteer Force created in 1913 to defend against the British government's plans for Home Rule in Ireland. The other force was *Orangeism* which was an overlay on the labor, military, and political template under which the growing sectarianism and nationalism (both British unionist and Irish republican) had flowered. Carson along with James Craig saw to it that Ulster held its own against the IRA and other nationalist and Catholic groups trying desperately to keep the six counties up north from separating from the rest of the troubled island. By February 1921, soon after the 1920 Government of Ireland Act, Craig headed an Ulster Unionist government at Stormont and Northern Ireland was controlled by the UUP until 1972.

Within the UUP and in the Unionist community in general, fissures evolved and by the early 1960s, the UUP's premier Terence O'Neill attempted several reforms to lessen the oppositional actions of Catholics in Northern Ireland who were victimized by Unionist policies. Political historians and academics Paul Bew, Peter Gibbon, and Henry Patterson argue that O'Neill represented a modernizing faction in the UUP and that although he was chosen as UUP premier, the modernizers were not successful in keeping him in the saddle (Bew, Gibbon, and Patterson 2002). O'Neill came to power in 1962 and although a traditional unionist, realized the Northern Ireland Labour Party was making gains on the UUP (due somewhat to its bi-confessional nature and proletarian politics). With the onset of a Catholic civil rights movement due to discrimination in the workplace, O'Neill tried to use economic planning as a mechanism to divert attention from other issues and consolidate support within the Unionist camp. Ultimately, the rise in Catholic politics and unconventional action by the Provisional IRA led to a hardening of UUP politics alongside other unionist parties. In 1972, Stormont was prorogued and it was not until 1998 that the assembly was reopened. Assembly elections were held in 1973 and 1982, but the legislature was not reconvened.

The UUP's importance in Northern Irish politics was seen as it continued to dominate electoral politics by getting seats at Westminster. It got the largest slice of the vote, with a range of 32.3% (February 1974) to 54.3% (1970), in UK general elections of all Northern Irish parties from 1970–2001. It was still a major player, despite, as political scientist Paul Mitchell states, the fact that the Unionist share of all votes in various elections, including Westminster, had declined from the 1970s where unionists of all stripes got an average of 59.4% (to the nationalists' 25.8%) to the 1990s where unionists got 50.5% (to nationalists' 37%) (Mitchell 1999).

By 2001, the UUP was the only one of five relevant parties in the Northern Irish system that predated 1970. The party was one historically where the party elites were from the Northern Irish landed Protestant gentry, with generally deep religious convictions, and the supporters were largely working class. Into the 1970s, unionism in general began to fragment and the UUP had a difficult time as it was forced into intra-communalistic battles with other unionist parties such as Ian Paisley's Democratic Unionist Party (DUP). The rise of the Provisional Sinn Féin saw intra-communalist fissures come to the Catholic camp as well in Ulster and nationalist and loyalist outbidding in both republican and unionist camps led to disaffection over Conservative (*and Unionist*) UK government actions in 1985 (the Anglo-Irish Agreement) and 1993 (the Downing Street Declaration).

In 1995, the UUP elected a new leader, *David Trimble*. Trimble replaced the aged James Molyneaux, who headed to Britain's House of Lords. Born in 1944, Trimble was a law professor at Queen's University of Belfast. He had cut his unionist teeth in the Ulster Vanguard Party and had helped bring down the consociational experiment in Northern Ireland in 1974. After the Vanguard Party collapsed, he joined the UUP. He had played the "Orange card" to ensconce himself as the UUP's next leader. Eventually, he was coaxed to the bargaining table by the UK premier Blair and worked out the power-sharing agreement in 1998 known as the GFA. For this he won the 1998 Nobel Peace Prize which he shared with the Social Democratic and Labour Party (SDLP) leader, John Hume. Despite this grand humanitarian gesture, the decommissioning of IRA weapons was a slow go. The post-1998 assembly got off to a rocky start, shutting down only two months in. But, it was resurrected in 2000 (although Trimble, who was the government's first minister, had to unilaterally remove Sinn Féin from its positions of ministerial responsibility) and by 2002 the assembly was prorogued once again. Unfortunately, politics appeared to be the same as usual by 2003 when new elections for the Stormont assembly were held as the top two parties (the UUP and SDLP) were replaced by the more hardened communalistic parties, the nationalist Sinn Féin and the loyalist DUP, as the top two vote getters in Northern Ireland. The party did have one of three Northern Ireland European parliament seats. Its MEP, James Nicholson, was elected in 2004 and was part of the EP bloc that aligned with the European People's Party and European Democrats (the equivalent of Christian Democrats). The 2005 Westminster elections continued the decline of the UUP as the chief party in Ulster. The party lost five of six seats it held in London in 2001 and incredibly its leader, the Nobel laureate Trimble *lost* his seat in Upper Bann. This seemingly ended the UUP's 80-year dominance of Ulster's politics. Many pundits speculated that Trimble had tumbled due to his willingness to negotiate with Sinn Féin (the IRA's parliamentary arm) and enter government with it after the GFA had been implemented.

The UUP fought the 2003 elections by arguing in its manifesto that it was trying to extend Northern Ireland's influence beyond Britain and the Irish island to Brussels. After 1998, the UUP had helped lead in opening a Brussels office at the EU so Northern Ireland could directly lobby the EU itself for its own development as a Celtic polity in Europe. The party also increased the health budget of the UK sub-state by £1 billion. Also, the party helped create a government post to advocate for children's needs known as the children's commissioner. The party also authorized and had its members sign a document known as the "Ulster Unionist Charter" which was a kind of Northern Irish Unionist contract with her citizens—like Newt Gingrich and the Republican Party's "Contract with America" in 1994. Among several of its planks, it called for an inclusive and democratic assembly for Northern Ireland; working toward erasing both unionist and nationalist paramilitarism from the society; opposing amnesty for fugitives from justice; policing and anti-social behavior legislation that would keep pace with the UK's; the sub-state would remain part of Britain and an integral part of the UK; and the improvement of the social and economic base for all living in Ulster. By 2003, the party had evolved into a modern mass party with professional administration and staff in Belfast. It had the original Ulster Unionist Council (made up of 900 members—the equivalency of a party national governing council, albeit larger) which comprised of both party faithful and members of associated unionist groups. The party had a national executive committee of 120 members and 13 party officers. Certainly, the distinction between the UUP and other British or Irish mass parties is that it still had the aura of a mass movement while operating as a mass party, which is not all that difficult to conceptualize since unionism is a broad diffuse force in Northern Irish society. Ironically, the Republic to the south saw its major party of dominance, Fianna Fáil, start as a similar party out of various nationalist groups in the late 1920s. The mass nationalist or loyalist movement continues to shape the fortunes of political parties in both parts of the Emerald Isle.

Sinn Féin in Northern Ireland

The split in the IRA occurred in late 1969. That rift was between the *"Provisional" IRA*, or "Provos" as they are known, and the *"Official" IRA*, known as "Officials." Immediately after this secret division, the IRA's parliamentary wing, the modern radical nationalist party, Sinn Féin (Ourselves Alone), broke in two as well in January 1970. The split in the party occurred in Dublin when the party met and the Provos were more interested in emulating the traditional modus operandi of the IRA and Sinn Féin. They wanted to continue to fight the constitutional arrangement that had been foisted on it after 1921 by the UK. They also objected to forming a united front with various leftist parties and organizations, such as the Republic's Communist Party. As the divide in the IRA and Sinn Féin grew, more began to side with the Provos, although the label had been officially jettisoned by the faction. At that point, the Provo leader, Sean MacStiofan (born John Stephenson to an Irish mother in England) called for both defensive and offensive actions to combat the Protestant militants in Ulster.

The IRA had offered a ceasefire in Ireland from 1962–69. But from 1969 to 1971, it resumed violence on a minor scale (throwing rocks, Molotov cocktails, etc.), but after this, the radical underground group began in 1971–72 to move away from street fighting to more of a Michael Collins-type war of attrition. As journalist and historian Tim Pat Coogan has said the Provos' policy became three-pronged: 1) shooting troops and police in Ulster; 2) using propaganda; and 3) using bombs—some big, some little, and focusing on industrial and commercial sites (Coogan 2000). This type of terrorism was applied to cause maximum anger and anxiety among the Westminster government's leaders and the British citizenry. In late summer 1971, the Provos adopted a political policy, largely advocated by its members from the south, in favor of a quasi-socialist arrangement throughout the island. Most Provos from Northern Ireland were generally not as in favor since it was felt this might redirect the armed campaign in the north. From this point, one month later Provisional IRA leaders met with the Tory government's William Whitelaw and laid demands before the British government. Those demands included the UK ending violence against the Irish, abolishing Stormont, releasing Irish political prisoners, free elections for a regional parliament for Ulster that would be a stepping stone toward unity for all of the island's 32 counties, and reparations to Irish who were hurt by the UK in various military and security operations. The meeting which included many of Provisional Sinn Féin's leadership—including young Martin McGuinness and *Gerry Adams*, were the first time the UK government had met with republican rebels since 1921 (when Collins's newly formed guerrilla group, the IRA, had forced Lloyd George and Churchill to the negotiation table.) The events failed to yield any political headway and the self-styled freedom fighters, the IRA, resumed their long campaign of attrition in getting "England out of Ireland."

Box 4.6: Gerry Adams (*Gearóid Mac Ádhaimh*)

Gearóid Mac Ádhaimh (Gerry Adams in the Irish) was born in 1948 and rose to the rank of leader of the republican movement under the aegis of the Sinn Féin political party in Northern Ireland and the southern Republic. He grew up in West Belfast and was socialized into a large Catholic and nationalistic family and his grandfather and uncles had fought the British during the tumultuous era of civil conflict in the late teens and early 1920s. Adams was tending bar as a young man when he joined the Irish Republican Army (IRA) in the late 1960s and he was interned by the British in the early 1970s for seditious and unconventional political activities. Adams continues to deny any direct links to terrorist activity. But, his real fame began in 1983 when he was elected to the British House of Commons for a seat in West Belfast under the Sinn Féin banner. He refused to take his seat as a sign of defiance toward London (a policy since continued by other nationalist politicians in Northern Ireland). Since the early 1990s, his radicalism has abated, but his nationalism has continued, although Sinn Féin under his guidance has attempted to engage loyalists in Northern Ireland and the British government to bring about peace and a power-sharing assembly in Belfast (which occurred in 1998, although Adams had no seat in the regional legislature). In 1995, Adams was invited to the White House to toast St. Patrick's Day with President Clinton, a move reminiscent of David Lloyd George's willingness to sit down with Éamon de Valera in the Spring of 1921 to talk Home Rule at 10 Downing Street. By 2006, Adams had moved Sinn Féin, the IRA's parliamentary arm, further away from weapons and was attempting to settle the violent "troubles" in his homeland via the ballot box and diplomacy, rather than by the gun.

Sinn Féin as a parliamentary wing of the IRA was not a major player in terms of legislative politics because it refused to contest seats in what it saw as illegitimate parliaments in London and Belfast. Even south of the border, it was essentially persona non grata due to most Irish abhorring violent solutions to the island's political quandaries. Indeed, it was not in the mainstream of the nationalist movement in Ulster taking a backseat to the Nationalist Party from 1921–69 and the SDLP after 1969. However, its controversial policy of encouraging IRA prisoners to go on hunger strikes in 1980–81 got the party sympathy from nationalists all over the ideological spectrum. In April 1981, the hunger-striking prisoner Bobby Sands won Sinn Féin's first-ever seat at Westminster in a by-election in Northern Ireland. He along with nine others would die for their beliefs in the protest. Sinn Féin refused to let its politicos take their seats at Westminster in defiance of that body's politics. Yet, Sinn Féin realized that engaging in electoral politics could give the IRA more legitimacy in its "war" with the British and also subtly strengthen the party's goals by appealing to broader segments of the nationalist electorate and thus radicalize the electorate toward supporting greater militancy in ending UK rule in Ulster and undercutting "softer" nationalist groups, such as the SDLP, that were willing to compromise with the British.

This policy appeared to start working in the early 1980s as Sinn Féin started winning some elections (Gerry Adams took West Belfast from the SDLP in 1983 in the House of Commons elections, although he did not go to London to take his seat due to his party's policy) refusing Westminster legitimacy over Irish seats and increasing its percentage of vote in the nationalist electorate. After only getting one-third to the SDLP's two-thirds of the vote in the 1981 Stormont election, Sinn Féin got 43% of the nationalist bloc vote (to the SDLP's 57%) in 1983. This was a cause for concern to both soft nationalist and unionist opinion given the apparent radicalization of the nationalist voter at the time. In subsequent elections, Sinn Féin vote fell back into the 30% range on average from 1984 to 1996. But, in 1996, the Forum elections along with the 1997 Westminster and local government elections saw it gain from 40–45% of the nationalist vote. Clearly, the prospects of a settlement after the John Major government's Downing Street accord of 1993 and the prospect of a conciliatory Labour government after 1997 appeared to help Sinn Féin as some nationalist voters appeared to want more than just incrementalism from Northern Irish and UK politicians.

The increase in the nationalist vote was presumably tied to the rise in the Catholic population and efforts to improve franchise opportunities for Catholics. In the 1960s, Northern Ireland was two-thirds Protestant and one-third Catholic. By the mid-1990s, Ulster was 58% Protestant and 41% Catholic in terms of population. Thus, the nationalist bloc grew in terms of the electorate's voting preferences from an average of nearly 26% of the votes in the 1970s to 37% in the 1990s. The corresponding unionist vote dropped from an average of nearly 60% in the 1970s to just over 50% in the 1990s. Sinn Féin saw negligible gains vis-à-vis the SDLP throughout most of the 1980s and early 1990s, but it got over 40% of the nationalist vote after 1996 and it appeared its electoral fortunes were improving. Sinn Féin has been supported by younger and working class Catholics whereas the SDLP got support from the middle classes and older population in Northern Ireland's Catholic community. Sinn Féin's policies have centered on the argument that unionists are a minority in Ireland and should have minority status and rights. This contrasts with the SDLP's "constitutional" approach which sees unionists as an integral part of Northern Ireland and thus changes in Ireland's de jure and de facto make-up must have some overt unionist approval. Sinn Féin's resorting to violence to achieve its political ends via the IRA, its paramilitary arm, has alienated it from forming a Catholic nationalist electoral alliance with the SDLP. After the 1994 IRA "first" cease-fire, some SDLP activists and supporters wanted a united nationalist front with Gerry Adams and company, but it did not happen. As a matter of fact, in the complex STV PR-based electoral system in Northern Ireland (see chapter five for a further explanation of the voting system of the post-1998 Belfast sub-national government), SDLP supporters tended to split their votes and support unionist or unionist-leaning parties rather than Sinn Féin. The intra-segmental rift in the Catholic political community appears to be greater than in the unionist political community.

Born in 1948, Gerry Adams grew up in the Falls Road area of West Belfast. Although his family had deep republican roots, his upbringing was not steeped in much overt political socialization as a youth. It was not until the mid-1960s that he started working as a bartender and got active in the Catholic civil rights movement. He also began participating in unconventional political activity (tossing Molotov cocktails at police and loyalist paramilitaries, etc.) He was seen by journalists as a leader, charming, intelligent, and a capable negotiator (in the Michael Collins mode). But, he was also as tough as nails and appeared to support the work of the IRA as it used terrorism to further republican aims in Northern Ireland. He was part of the northern leadership that took control of Sinn Féin in the early 1970s and by 1978 was the party's vice president. He was first arrested in 1972 held on a British prison ship and then arrested again spent four years (1973–77) in the Long Kesh prison in Ulster. He has claimed that he was never a member of the IRA, but declassified Irish and British intelligence reports indicate that he had a role in the IRA's northern operations. Adams was largely responsible for disconnecting Sinn Féin's overt linkage to the Provisional IRA. In 1988, he began secret talks with the SDLP's Hume. At this point, he was interested in trying to work his nationalistic agenda via parliamentary politics. He held West Belfast at Westminster from 1983–92 (although never taking his seat out of protest). He was defeated in 1992 by under 600 votes when unionists tactically voted him out by supporting the SDLP candidate. Still, Adams most salient role was yet to come in 1995 when he got a temporary visa to visit the United States and meet at the White House with President Bill Clinton at the White House, much to the UK government's chagrin. However, coaxed on by the US, the UUP, SDLP, and Sinn Féin reached an all-party agreement in 1998 (the Good Friday or Belfast agreement) which led to power-sharing in Northern Ireland, a rewording of the Irish Republic's constitution regarding de Valera's famous de jure claim to the Six Counties (which now called for gradualism in the north), and Sinn Féin's jettisoning of its policy of not taking its seats in parliaments it holds them in. For its participation, Sinn Féin got two ministers in the power-sharing government (like the SDLP) it chose not to have the all-Ireland party leader, Adams, take a portfolio, but its Belfast assembly leader, McGuinness (who had been the IRA's chief in Derry during the *Bloody Sunday* event in 1972), did take the post of Northern Ireland's education minister.

Box 4.7: Bloody Sunday(s)

The concept of "Bloody Sunday" has repercussions in Irish history and it is a term that has been used to describe civil unrest and government action, seen as unjust in the Irish cases, to quell unconventional political action. The first Irish "Bloody Sunday" incident occurred on November 21, 1920, the day after Michael Collins directed the Irish Republican Army's (IRA) notorious assassination of 14 British intelligence officers in Ireland. British troops descended on Croke Park in Dublin where a Gaelic football match was being played. The British home secretary, Winston Churchill, had sent various forces to Ireland, including auxiliaries (who were at the sporting event that day) and the infamous "Black and Tans." As the game got under way before 10,000 fans, the military moved into the park and shots were fired, largely by angry British troops in retaliation for the previous day's events. The unauthorized use of force killed 14 including women and children in attendance. The British officials in the Castle in Dublin were not happy with the reaction of the troops. Churchill was vilified as a warmonger, as was Lloyd George. The incident undoubtedly helped the IRA under Collins recruit more men into its ranks.

The second Irish "Bloody Sunday" occurred on January 30, 1972. The Derry Civil Rights Association hosted a peaceful march through the streets of Derry to protest the housing and disenfranchisement of Catholics in that city and Northern Ireland in general. The march was led by the Protestant Republican politician, Ivan Cooper. As the thousand or so marchers protested in peace, British soldiers showed up and when some of the more radical protestors started throwing rocks soldiers panicked and only a handful charged the crowd arresting protestors and firing their weapons. Fourteen were killed. The military claimed that the IRA had planted some provocateurs into the crowd and that weapons had been brandished and even fired. It was a terrible moment in the growing sectarian divide in Northern Ireland. Both of these events 1920 and 1972 are remembered now as movies featuring both events have been released: "Michael Collins" (1996) and "Bloody Sunday" (2002). The former takes many liberties in the short scene where the 1920 event occurs, but it is a powerful portrayal nonetheless. The latter is an emotional and quite factual manifestation of that terrible day in 1972. Actual participants in the protest thirty years earlier were used as extras in the film. The idea of Bloody Sunday as a salient event in unconventional political protest and state authority was not new to the world when Ireland first saw the 1920 event. Russia had experienced "Bloody Sunday" as it has become known on January 22, 1905 when Czar Nicholas II's dragoons led a cavalry charge on a huge mass protest against the government. The protestors, some 80,000 strong were marching to give a petition of grievances to the czar. It is estimated that 1,000 to 4,000 were killed. Other Bloody Sundays have occurred in England and the United States. The former occurred in 1887 in London and was tied to the internment of Irish nationalists; the latter occurred during the civil rights protests of the 1960s. Unfortunately, a day that is supposed to be one of rest and peace has become synonymous with civil unrest and government repression in not only Ireland, but other parts of the world as well.

Sinn Féin's party politics have seen growth in its electoral and representative fortunes. Referring to the Ulster legislature as the "Six County Assembly," the 2003 Manifesto, *Agenda for Government (Clár Rialtais)*, for the Belfast government's elections said that the party favored a green paper on Irish unity, building on the Belfast agreement and continued talks with unionists, trying to get voting rights in the Dublin legislature for citizens of Northern Ireland, intensifying political relations with unionists, the development of an unarmed policing service (similar to Britain's historical approach—although that has changed somewhat in the last decade), ending the use of plastic bullets, completely overhauling the justice system in Northern Ireland, creating a "Department of Equality," reconfiguring the Northern Irish human rights commission, modeling human rights legislation on the Republic's in the south, improving educational and health care services, focusing economic development on areas of "need," calling for taxation powers in the northern assembly (similar to Scotland's), creating an all-Ireland transport system, making St. Patrick's Day an all-island holiday and day of reconciliation, improving women's access to public sector positions and childcare, forwarding anti-racist initiatives, and continuing to move forward on the Belfast agreement, especially the all-Ireland aspects of it.

In 2005, the party had four MPs at Westminster, including Adams for West Belfast and McGuinness who had won a seat from Mid-Ulster. As mentioned above, in the June 2004 European elections, it won two seats and placed two MEPs in Strasbourg both female (one from the southern Republic and the other from Northern Ireland) aligned with the parliamentary group known as the European United Left and the Nordic Green Left. The party had 24 of 108 MLAs in the Belfast legislature and around 250 elected local government officials throughout the Emerald Isle—north and south. Michelle Gildernew was the lone female in the MP. She was elected by only 34 votes in 2001, at the age of 31, to a seat (Fermangh/South Tyrone in Northern Ireland) at Westminster. Married with a young son, she traveled in Europe, the US, and worked in Australia for a year before coming back to enter politics and serve on Sinn Féin's national executive. She was elected as an MLA in both 1998 and 2003. In the Belfast assembly after 1998, several women played important roles as Sinn Féin MLAs. They included a former political prisoner and activist from North Belfast, a political science PhD from Upper Bann, a teacher from West Belfast, a non-governmental organization and humanitarian aid worker from South Down, a mother of nine and a community activist involved in a "relatives of nationalist prisoners" group seeking better treatment from the British, and Gildernew who was a professional party worker. Women were playing a significant role in the nationalist agenda of Sinn Féin and the party had reached out to women in order to promote gender equality in both the north and south.

Its national executive, the *Ard Chomhairle*, consisted of 20 persons led by Adams. Its national offices are located in both Dublin and Belfast (on Falls Road in West Belfast). It held a yearly national party conference, the *Ard Fheis* which functioned like a modern mass party's national party convention or conference as seen in Britain or the United States.

Amazingly, by September 2005, Adams and Sinn Fein were attempting to make good on a pledge to disarm its paramilitary wing, the IRA. General John de Chastelain, the Canadian, announced to the world that the IRA had completely destroyed much of its vaunted weapons cache. Rifles, mortars, pistols, machine-guns, missiles, and explosives were all turned over or liquidated. De Chastelain had been involved in monitoring IRA decommissioning attempts since 1997. Along with the general, the IRA allowed two other witnesses, a Catholic priest and a Methodist minister, to verify its decommissioning. Officials from the US and Finland took part in the process. Politically, some remained skeptical as the original 1998 GFA had called for the scuttling of the IRA's arsenal by 2000. The top party in Ulster by 2005, the DUP, and its 79 year-old leader Paisley said they did not trust the IRA to decommission fully and de Chastelain admitted that other IRA weapons caches could exist and that the actions and rhetoric of Sinn Féin and the IRA were taken in good faith. UK Prime Minister Tony Blair and Éire's Taoiseach Bertie Ahern were pleased with the announcement and felt is was a major jump start in the peace process. Sinn Féin's top negotiator Martin McGuinness hopped a plane to Washington, DC to talk with the American leaders about peace and power-sharing in Northern Ireland. The decommissioning process had faltered after 2003, but the move by Sinn Féin's leader Adams was a bold one akin to Michael Collins's attempt to broker peace with the UK in 1921 or Yasser Arafat's actions in the Palestinian resistance movement after 1988 in working through diplomatic rather than unconventional political means.

Democratic Unionist Party

The *Democratic Unionist Party* (DUP) was formed by Reverend *Ian Paisley* and Desmond Boal in late 1971. Paisley had been active in the Ulster Defence Association which aimed to help minority Protestants in predominantly Catholic areas of Ulster. Like Catholics in the 1950s and 1960s, these Protestants were victimized by fire bombs, street thuggery, and overt discrimination. Northern Ireland at the start of "the troubles" resembled Bosnia from 1992–95, although Bosnia saw some 200,000 perish in its horrific civil war (Ulster saw 3000 deaths from 1969–94). The UDA was a kind of equivalent to the various Catholic groups agitating for civil rights. Paisley, who had played a role in several provocative marches for Protestant rights in various Catholic areas including West Belfast and Derry in the 1960s (many leading to major civil unrest and burned out neighborhoods), was growing tired of the Unionist government's concessions under O'Neillism. Thus, his new party, conceived at the start of "the troubles," was as much a movement around him as a charismatic politico as it was a bona fide political party. It was to be right-of-center on issues related to Ulster's constitution and left-of-center social issues. Paisley's preaching led the party toward an overtly Protestant tenor with ties to his Free Presbyterian Church, evangelical fervor, and radicalism (anti-Catholic) in the social relations in Northern Ireland. Paisley was known for his lengthy diatribes against the Pope in Rome (not all that unfamiliar territory for descendants of Scottish Presbyterians with the 400 year-old tradition of John Knox's leadership and oratory on their side). The DUP got support from working-class Protestant voters in Belfast and Protestants in the rural areas. After the party started making greater electoral inroads after 1979, its electorate was young, not very religious, and poorer than those voting for the DUP's main rival, the UUP. The major upshot of intra-unionist electoral battling in Ulster was what Sartori would call "nationalist outbidding." Both the UUP and the DUP would fight elections on the premise that each believed they were the better party to eradicate Sinn Féin and the IRA from Ulster by getting tough and undermining and ending ongoing Irish Republic-UK peace talks. Thus, the centrifugal forces of inter-party competition in the unionist camp were every bit as vitriolic as the nationalist camp and the DUP did its best to make the UUP appear soft on constitutional issues.

The DUP emerged as a major political player in the Northern Irish party system in 1979 when Paisley won a European Community (now EU) seat in Strasbourg. Interestingly, the PR system has worked in the DUP's favor as it got 61% to 55% of the unionist vote in the European elections from 1984–94. It has done much poorer in unionist competition for Westminster elections getting 37% of the unionist vote in 1983 (to the UUP's 63%), but less than 30% in subsequent elections. The SMD system has not been kind to the DUP. Also, Paisley was more popular than his party historically, thus hurting the party at the polls at times. The party has had a second fiddle status (to the UUP) historically as a kind of rightist anti-politics vote, somewhat akin to the Danish People's Party under Pia Kjaersgaard as a coalition partner with Anders Fogh

Rasmussen's center-right Liberal Party in the Danish government after 2001. Despite constantly getting in the teens in terms of percent of the Ulster electorate for most elections in the 1980s and 1990s, the party surprised many observers when it got 29% and took a plurality of the vote in the November 2003 Stormont assembly elections. Of course, Sinn Féin was second in terms of votes and seats, thus making the polarized pluralist system in Northern Ireland one of continued segmentation and centrifugal evolution. The DUP originally participated in talks spurred by US Senator George Mitchell that led to the Belfast agreement in 1998, but the party pulled its support when Sinn Féin was allowed to participate in talks after the IRA ceasefire. It was also opposed to the referendum on the GFA which occurred in May 1998 (which passed 71% to 29% with a voter turnout of 81% in Northern Ireland).

Born in 1926, Paisley has been at the center of the party's evolution and continued to make an impact as a veritable institution of unionist politics in Ulster from the time he founded the Free Presbyterian Church in Belfast in 1951. A longtime opponent of concessions to Catholics and what he perceived as the British government selling out to the Dublin government, Paisley was known for his bombastic oratory and staunch opposition to unionist parties trying to alter the status quo in Ulster. He and Ulster prime minister Brian Faulkner addressed rallies after the 1985 Anglo-Irish accord (signed by Taoiseach Garret FitzGerald and UK premier Margaret Thatcher) by using the catchphrase "Ulster says no." Paisley's dogmatic defense of Ulster's constitutional position got him a very close personal following in the region. It also made him enemies on the republican side. He was a tough political fighter and as a sitting MEP even heckled Pope John Paul II when he addressed the European Parliament. Ever an enigmatic political figure, he detested Catholicism, but worked with the SDLP's Hume both to further Northern Ireland's position in Europe (while both were in the European Parliament). He also had private social gatherings at his home with Hume and their spouses in the 1990s. He also was seen as someone who would help constituents with their pet problems and concerns irrespective of Protestant or Catholic backgrounds. When Hume retired in 2000, Paisley gave a long, glowing tribute to the Nobel Prize winner. Thus, the hard-core Ulsterman, who had winked at Protestant violence in the past, and mortal enemy of Sinn Féin and the IRA, had a complex political persona. He temporarily retired from politics in 2004 leaving his EP seat vacated, but returned to win his seat at Westminster in 2005. Like his polar opposite Adams of Sinn Féin, he had worked on the fringes of paramilitarism at times in his career (tacitly and even overtly endorsing various groups and their use of weaponry and counter-terrorism). But, overall, his impact has been marked and by November 2003, he retained his seat as an MLA in Belfast and watched his party secure its greatest legislative triumph in its history by taking a plurality of the vote and seats in the election. Health and age appeared to have taken its toll and the Free Presbyterian Church moderator decided not to run in the 2004 EU elections. He was reelected to Stormont in 2003 (which was prorogued after 2002). However, after the 2007 Northern Ireland elections, the octogenarian DUP leader took the helm as first minister of the Belfast government in a bi-confessional coalitional with Sinn Féin. The Calvinist firebrand had come full circle and now sat with his fellow co-nationals in power. It was a remarkable and breathtaking moment in the statelet's history.

The 2003 DUP party manifesto, *Election 03: Fair Deal Manifesto 2003*, rails on the negatives of the 1998 Belfast agreement. It argued that the agreement failed for the following reasons: 1) a less than accountable executive where decisions were made that were not accountable to the Stormont legislature; 2) "terrorists" (Sinn Féin) were allowed to participate in government; 3) the implementation organizations of the agreement were not accountable to Stormont; 4) the Belfast government had become incoherent and unable to deliver decent government; 5) north-south cooperation in Ireland was haphazard and Belfast government ministers could do whatever they wished; 6) the NMSC (all-Ireland) council was not accountable to Stormont; and 7) less than balanced regional relationships between north-south, east-west (many meetings occurred on the north-south relationship in Ireland occurred with few focusing on the relationship of Belfast to Great Britain). Amazingly, by 2007, the DUP had reversed itself on most of these claims. Aside from the constitutional issues the DUP called to provide free use of public transport for those over 60, keep a handle on taxes and public costs, free home health care for the elderly, improve educational standards and maintain solid elementary schools in Ulster, make sure increased health care expenditures equates with higher quality, improve the planning process in government making it more efficient, and lessen the strictures of planning laws for those in rural areas. The DUP was diametrically opposed to decentralizing police and judicial systems as proposed by Sinn Féin. It focused on tougher sentences on anti-social behavior, gangs, and terrorists. It especially was vocal about its opposition to Sinn Féin politician Gerry Kelly taking the justice and policing portfolio because of his past ties to the IRA. The party promoted tourism in Northern Ireland as a means through which economic development could occur. The party promoted its focus on Northern Ireland's farmers by saying it would try to get the best deal for its beef and dairy exports to other parts of Europe under a newly revised CAP in the EU. It also played up the fact that Paisley was the head of the agricultural committee in the Belfast assembly thus ensuring the party's clout in making decisions that would help farmers in Ulster. In the cultural realm, a volatile area in Ulster, the party was in favor of making sure freedom of speech and assembly was maintained in order to permit marching by Orange groups and it criticized the parades commission on its lack of accountability. The party sought the promotion of "Ulster-Scots" dialect as a way of promoting another Celtic language in the UK and Ireland. It also sought to build a national stadium for the Northern Irish national soccer teams. It also wanted to see race car driving promoted in the province. The party also called on Northern Ireland to resume its attempts to get Belfast deemed as an EU cultural city in order to get more monies for the arts and to bring diverse people to the region. An attempt to gain this status was denied in the past. The party called for increased linkages between business, industry, and higher education institutions to improve the kinds and access to tertiary education for students. It also called for a "minimalist" bill of rights in terms of human rights which would devolve human rights issues and management to Belfast away from London.

The party's electoral fortunes improved dramatically in November 2003 as it won a plurality of seats (30 of 108) in the Stormont assembly. It also did well in the May 2005 Westminster elections taking nine of 18 seats and garnering 33.7% of the provincial vote (up 11.2% from 2001). In 2004, Jeffrey Donaldson defected from the UUP thus giving the DUP six seats at Westminster to five for the UUP. Sinn Féin had 4 and the SDLP 3. In the May 2004 European Union elections, Paisley stepped down and Jim Allister won Paisley's old seat winning one of the three UK seats in Northern Ireland by the largest vote total of any of the three. The DUP member did not affiliate himself with any of the major blocs in the EU parliament.

Social Democratic and Labour Party

The *Social Democratic and Labour Party* (SDLP) was the successor to the Nationalist party that operated in Northern Ireland's predominant party system from 1921 to the 1960s. The SDLP first competed in elections in Northern Ireland in 1973. It got 13.4% in the local government elections (behind the UUP's 41.4% and the Alliance party's 13.7%) and it won 22.1% in the consociational legislative elections (behind the UUP's 29.3%). The latter outcome conferred an important status on this largely Catholic, yet inter-confessional, party as a key player in what was thought to be a new era in Northern Irish politics. Of course, the nature of Ulster's internecine communalism undercut positive consociationalism. The SDLP was formed by a transformation in the Catholic community in Northern Ireland. The younger activist Catholics who were products of the civil rights movement left the more passive politics of their forbearers and took a stand for the minority in Ulster. In the 1973 legislature, 42% of the SDLP's representatives were younger than 39. The SDLP was not only a successor to nationalist political organization and aspirations, but it was Ulster's first modern mass political party replete with bureaucratic and administrative components and a detailed policy program. The SDLP was also the first party made up of primarily Catholics to recognize that a settlement in Ireland would not be dictated by the majority on the island. As nationalists, they embraced the unorthodox position of seeking to help govern the statelet along with the unionists. The SDLP has sought to attenuate the emphasis on the importance of electoral demographics (as controversial as those are) and focus on altering the region's institutional landscape. In the 1970s, the SDLP ensconced itself as the representatives of the nationalist section of Northern Irish society. Its European social democratic politics and parliamentary approach was more in line with late twentieth century mass democratic politics than early twentieth century nationalistic and unconventional politics in the island's south that won freedom from the UK. After 1969, violence escalated and even the inchoate electoral fortunes of the SDLP were eventually challenged by 1982 as the Provisional Sinn Féin contested seats in the Northern Irish assembly and Gerry Adams won the West Belfast seat at Westminster in 1983. Thus, intra-communal discord on the Catholic side of the ledger had forced the SDLP to fend off the more militant nationalist contender, Sinn Féin.

As the nationalist bloc grew in terms of percentage of the vote (from 33% in the 1960s to just over 40% by the early 1990s), the SDLP maintained its position of electoral advantage as the top nationalist party in Ulster. In Westminster elections, it got 17.9% (1983) to 24.1% (1997) and the 1998 election to Stormont saw it returned as the number two party behind the UUP; thus, putting it in the province's power-sharing government.

John Hume was born in 1937 and rose in the civil rights movement in Northern Ireland in the 1960s. A college graduate, he had intended on going into the priesthood and chose to teach high school French. In 1968–69, his participation in civil rights marches in cities like Derry (where he was born) where he was accosted by police and loyalists led him into politics. He was elected as an independent to Stormont in 1969. He went on to become the foremost nationalist voice in Ulster and eventually the SDLP's president from 1979–2001. He won seats in the European Parliament and House of Commons as well. His willingness to take a stand for Catholic rights in the face of the Protestant majority, and just as importantly, diplomatic skill at working to bring about truces between loyalists and nationalists over a thirty year period, led him to share the *Nobel Peace Prize* in 1998 (with Trimble) after the Belfast agreement. In November 2001, Hume stepped down as party leader and Seamus Mallon did likewise as deputy party leader and deputy first minister in Ulster's assembly. Mark Durkan was elected deputy first minister and party leader at the time.

Box 4.8: John Hume

John Hume was the leader of the Social Democratic and Labor Party (SDLP), a moderate republican, and winner of the 1998 Nobel Peace Prize for bringing about a new peace agreement with the Ulster Unionists in Northern Ireland. Hume, born in 1937, was a teacher from Derry who tried to bring about better civil rights for Catholics in Northern Ireland, based on actions of Martin Luther King and the Civil Rights Movement in the United States. He joined the Stormont legislature as an independent in 1969 and by 1971 was protesting British internments and law and order policies. He helped found the SDLP in the 1970s and he always tried to bring the communalistic problems and sectarian divisions in his homeland to an end. He has been lauded for giving the intellectual impetus behind the Good Friday Agreement that helped bring republicans and unionists closer together and restart the long-failed Stormont assembly. He retired from politics in 2001.

The party's 2003 Stormont election manifesto focused on reforming government in Northern Ireland and improving public services. The SDLP said in the manifesto that it was "100% for the Good Friday Agreement." It claimed to be the only party to have abided by the protocols of the accord. Thus, it said it was opposed to any renegotiation of the Belfast agreement. It hoped to see complete implementation of the agreement in the areas of equality, community relations, the Irish language, north-south partnerships, human rights demilitarization, victims' rights, and decentralization of law and order. The party called for a united Ireland, but with a kind of devolved Northern Ireland assembly where both Protestants and Catholics kept their own identity. The party sought a referendum on a unified Ireland while seeking to assure unionists that they would be protected in a unified island. The SDLP sought "all-Ireland" cooperation and fusion in economic development initiatives, marketing of Irish goods, fishing policies, agricultural programs related to various initiatives such as food marketing and animal health, unified law and order and creating a pan-Irish sexual offenders register. A focus on culture called for a coverage of southern Irish television in the north and strategies to improve Irish arts and culture. Investment in public infrastructure (roads, health programs, schools, etc.) was advocated as a solution for job creation via the public sector. Thus, the party's identification with the time-honored social democracy movement in Europe (as a derivation from the old democratic socialist party family) was found in the party's 2003 platform. Aside from general calls for improved environmental protection and greater investment in renewable energy sources, one area of salience related to "the troubles" was a call for a beefed up sectarian hate crimes law that would increase penalties for offenders who committed crimes motivated by sectarianism—thus the rhetoric of hate crimes legislation in other Western legislatures had reached Ulster in a tangible way, at least in theory. One way the SDLP proposed to do this in its platform was to proscribe sectarian chants at soccer matches. In EU affairs, the party was staunchly in favor of increased ties to the EU for both Ulster and Ireland. It proposed an EU committee for the Stormont assembly and favored inclusion in the Euro-zone for monetary and macroeconomic purposes. In foreign policy, it had a broad and diffuse agenda. It highlighted its Westminster MPs unified vote against UK participation in the 2003 US-led Iraq war and it called for a Palestinian state. It also called for continued support of the statesman Hume's work in Sri Lanka to end violence there and for the channeling of globalization toward ending poverty.

The party is a modern mass party and its organization is made up of various constituency associations at the local levels. It has an annual party conference in the Fall and it has both policy forums held at various times throughout the year and various party standing committees (an eight-person general council and committees on political management, organization, communications, elections, fundraising, and policy). The party also has a youth wing and a women's organization. The party membership (according to the party's website) is made up of 47% women and by 2004 the party had improved its female representation on local councils in Northern Ireland from 20 to 31 women. The party also put six females forward in the 2003 Stormont assembly elections and five were returned: a nurse from south Belfast, a mental health services administrator from Foyle, a chef from Langan Valley, a legislative assistant from South Down, and an occupational therapist from Upper Bann. The party's recent former deputy leader was a woman as well. Brid Rogers, one of the party's cofounders and longtime SDLP politician in both Westminster and Stormont assemblies enjoys golfing and follows Manchester United in soccer. She had been an influential figure in Irish politics both north and south of the border. She was minister for agricultural and rural development after 1999 and had worked in all-party talks for regional stability in 1996. She was also held a seat in the Irish senate (the upper-house of the Oireachtas) from 1983–87. By 2004, the party had 50% of its executive posts (5/10) filled by women. It has a centralized party staff with professional party administration in its headquarters in Belfast.

Northern Ireland's Party System: From Predominant Party System to Limited Pluralism

Northern Ireland's political party system is a fragmented one. It has a certain amount of stability in that the communalistic divide between *Republicans* and *Unionists* has led to fairly predictable ethno-nationalist and socio-religious politics since the end of the monolithic control of the party and electoral system by the UUP after 1969. The start of *"the troubles"* brought with it new forms of protest and political mobilization in the form of conventional and unconventional groups, armed paramilitaries, and political parties from both ends (republican and unionist) of the political spectrum. The 1921–69 period can be safely referred to as a predominant party system. According to Sartori, a predominant party system is one that has a longstanding dominant party within a pluralistic political environment that includes other parties (Mair 1990). The party can obtain an absolute majority of seats at each election and continues to wield power over time. The UUP, much like Fianna Fáil in the south, was essentially the creator of a predominant unionist state in Northern Ireland until 1972. The reason the label one-party or hegemonic party system should not be applied to this era in Ulster's politics is due to the fact that Northern Ireland was a democracy under British auspices and not an authoritarian one-party state and it was not a hegemonic political party system, like many of the communist systems from 1946–89 in central and eastern Europe, because the UUP did allow other parties to operate and overtly participate in the political system. Communist parties behind the Iron Curtain did so as well, but as parties of government were largely the masters pulling the puppet strings of smaller agricultural or Christian parties. Those parties had no real authority or say in governmental directions. Republicans will level the same charges at the UUP-dominated state from 1921–69, and despite irregular franchise problems and unfair gerrymandering against Catholics, Republicans got more say in government especially after 1970 once the SDLP and Sinn Féin rose to the fore.

After 1972, the party system changed somewhat from a fairly stable predominant one to an unstable polarized pluralist one. Political scientist Paul Mitchell states that the Northern Irish party system is one that sees both types of competition "between" and "within" the communalistic and sectarian groups. Mitchell says the Northern Irish party system is a polarized, segmented "ethnic" party system where the ethnicity factor ties to nationalism and the republican (Irish) bloc and the unionist (British) bloc. Of course, this is an overlay of the sectarian differences that see nationalists (republicans) and loyalists (unionists) side with Catholicism and Protestantism respectively. These identities have created large fissures in the social and political system in Northern Ireland that have led to the creation of a "dual" party system. This dual system is known for fierce competition among the sectarian sides, but just as fractionalizing are the rifts that have evolved within the two blocs: nationalist and loyalist. The latter fissure is where most of the salient politics in terms of understanding Northern Ireland's stability and political culture development have occurred since 1969 and the start of the Troubles. Mitchell contends that the scope and depth of the intensity of the partisan political competition has to do with the nature of the STV PR system and its divisions in the province (Mitchell 1999). But, of course, at least the STV system gives the voter a somewhat realistic (although it has still been gerrymandered in the unionists favor) look at the deep divisions in the society. Yet, a straight SMD system, like Westminster's, gave the UUP dominance for years and the electoral system itself was a topic of displeasure for republicans. However, the electoral system is a double-edged sword and the segmentation that produces the polarized pluralist party system in Ulster is one that may be difficult to overcome.

Polarized pluralism has seen itself evolve in problematic ways at times in other European polities, such as Germany from 1919–33 and France from 1870–1940. But, consociationalism has worked in Belgium (until a party political impasse in the summer of 2007) among segmented minorities (Flemings and Walloons) and even though it has had fits and starts in Northern Ireland going back to 1972, the chances of real political change and peace in Northern Ireland may be approachable if the 2007 bi-confessional consociational agreement between Sinn Féin and the DUP and supranational entities start playing a role in the region. However, the return to nationalist outbidding could occur at any point given the region's recent history since 1969.

Conclusion

A common theme runs throughout the Celtic nations' political party systems. Scotland, Ireland, and Wales have a limited or moderate pluralism, to use Sartori's classification. These systems have evolved toward European-style party systems with three to five relevant parties, unilateral oppositions that do not appear to present a threat to systemic operation. As the SNP gained power in

2007, Scots might get radical system overhaul (separating Scotland from the UK). When the Slovak National Party (SNS) got power in Slovakia after 1993 it had to rely on other parties to further its militantly anti-EU agenda and this was not in the offing. In fact, the opposite happened, the SNS was full of corruption, saw its leader deposed, and the political culture turned toward moderation, pro-EU perspectives, and voted the left into power. Comparing the SNP to the SNS is akin to comparing apples and oranges, but the broader point is that the SNP has been a unilateral actor whether in government or opposition because of its nationalism (unlike Plaid Cymru who was able to get Welsh Labour to invite them into a governing coalition in Wales in 2007). The Greens have supported the SNP (but not in a formal coalition government), but radical change will most likely depend on the SNP's ability to work with whichever party is running the UK in London and independence may take several years. The political party systems in Scotland, Ireland, and Wales all have unique challenges ahead for themselves in the twenty-first century. The nationalist card will always affect these systems. With relatively stable limited pluralism, a Weimar-type (Germany's 1919–33 wayward polarized pluralist republic) reaction is not in the offing soon. Despite the role of the EU in these societies, a nationalist backlash against the EU could bring some of the same animosities to the fore that each of these three Celtic systems saw in their histories in contending with the English for political power over their lands.

The outlier in terms of these four party systems is Northern Ireland. Not only do recent political culture and terrorism affect its current party system development, but the fact that it can be classified as a polarized pluralist system according to Sartori's classification leads to concerns about its development and stability. Indeed, the attempt to create a kind of consociational system may help. However, this was done in 1972 and failed in 2002 as well. Trying to mitigate the ideological space between republicans and unionists as bilateral oppositions which leads to fragmentation in the Belfast party system is what must be done to create systemic stability. How that is done is another question which the Irish, British, and Americans have all worked on and some successes have occurred since 1998. Of course, the use of PR (which is marketed by its proponents as more democratic and fair), European style governance (with coalitions and other tactics, including elite bargaining), addressing EU issues of importance, and recognizing the regionalization of the EU and the Celtic fringe's place in it as distinct parts of Europe (both historically and culturally) does lend itself to the view that these party systems are related to the English model at Westminster, but have more in common with their European neighbors on the continent which may bode well for further political integration with the EU and identification of Celtic systems as unique and increasingly semi-independent (in the case of Scotland, Wales, and Ulster).

Polarized Pluralism	Moderate Multipartism	Twopartism
Northern Ireland (Sub-national, PR)	**Scotland (Sub-national, PR) Ireland (National, PR) Wales (Sub-national, PR)**	**United Kingdom (Westminster) (National, SMD)**
Characteristics:	**Characteristics:**	**Characteristics:**
System is fractionalized	Similar to continental European	System mutes factionalism systems—consensual not adversarial and excessive pluralism
System can only find consensus through consociationalism (elite bargaining)	Moves parties to center to create	System undermines outliers coalitions and stability (both pro and anti-system)
Opposition parties are more hardcore than political parties of government (e.g. anti-system parties like Sinn Fein and DUP)	Plays to Celtic communalistic orientation (unlike English individualistic [liberal] orientation)	System is based on a responsible party government process of a majority party ruling and a loyal opposition
Operates in a divided political culture that can be both democratic and semi-democratic	Operates in a democratic political culture	Operates in a democratic political culture
	Elements of these systems political culture may be tied to Scandinavian influence of these systems both historically and more recently	

Table 4.1: Celtic Party Systems Continuum*
*Concepts of polarized pluralism, moderate multipartism, and twopartism are based on Giovanni Sartori. 1976. *Parties and Party Systems: A Framework for Analysis*, Vol. I (Cambridge: Cambridge University Press).

Suggestions for Further Reading and Research:

Chubb, Basil. 1992. *The Government and Politics of Ireland*, 3rd ed. London: Longman.

Drucker, H. M. 1979. *Multi-Party Britain*. New York: Praeger.

Cochrane, Feargal. 1999. "The Past in the Present," In Paul Mitchell and Rick Wiltford, eds. *Politics in Northern Ireland*. Boulder, CO: Westview Press, pp. 1-28.

House of Commons (Matthew Leeke). 2003. *UK Election Statistics: 1945-2003*, HL Paper 3-59 (Her Majesty's Stationary Office, July 1) <www.parliament.uk>.

Kellas, James G. 1989. *The Scottish Political System*, 4th ed. Cambridge: Cambridge University Press.

Lynch, Peter. 2002. *SNP: The History of the Scottish National Party.* Cardiff: Welsh Academic Press.

Midwinter, Arthur F., Michael Keating, and James Mitchell. 1991. *Politics and Public Policy in Scotland.* Housdmill, Basingstoke: Macmillan.

Mair, Peter, ed. 1990. *The West European Party System.* Oxford: Oxford University Press.

McAllister, Laura. 2001. *Plaid Cymru: The Emergence of a Political Party.* Brigend, Wales: Seren.

Mitchell, Paul and Rick Wilford, eds. 1999. *Politics in Northern Ireland.* Boulder, CO: Westview Press.

Party Websites:

Scottish Labour Party: *www.scottishlabour.org.uk*
Scottish National Party: *www.snp.org*
Scottish Liberal Democrats: *www.scotlibdems.org.uk*
Scottish Conservative Party: *www.conservatives.com/people/scotland.cfm*
Scottish Socialist Party: *www.scottishsocialistparty.org*
Scottish Green Party: *www.scottishgreens.org.uk*
Fianna Fáil: *www.fiannafail.ie*
Fine Gael: *www.finegael.com*
Irish Labour: *www.labour.ie*
Irish Progressive Democrats: *www.progressivedemocrats.ie*
Sinn Féin: *www.sinnfein.ie*
Comhaontas Glas (Irish Green Party): *www.greenparty.ie*
Ulster Unionist Party: *www.uup.org*
Democratic Unionist Party: *www.dup.org.uk*
Social Democratic and Labour Party: *www.sdlp.ie*
Welsh Labour Party: *www.waleslabourparty.org.uk*
Plaid Cymru (The Party of Wales): *www.plaidcymru.org*
Welsh Conservative Party: *www.conservatives.com/wales*
Welsh Liberal Democrats: *www.demrhydcymru.org.*

CHAPTER FIVE

Celtic Institutions

Legislative and Executive Politics

Conceptual and Analytical Approaches to Studying Celtic Institutions

In comparative politics, political scientists were concerned historically with the study and analysis of foreign governments. The time-honored legal-historical approach which focused on understanding history, political structures, and functions, as well as the ways in which societies evolved with reference to legal affairs and constitutional development (both written and unwritten—regarding government and society's makeup) continue to be applied in the sub-discipline. The behavioral revolution in the 1950s and 1960s began to change the way political scientists thought about causation and the role of theory in scientifically analyzing politics. Instead of only looking at historical foundations and normative variables (for example, political ideologies), political scientists began to look at questions related to "why" and "how" and more abstract conceptualizations of government and the state began to hold sway in order to: 1) understand empirical forces affecting politics and political outputs; and 2) analyze holistically all variables (forces) within or between political systems to permit greater explanatory capabilities. Thus, political scientists set off down a path of trying to utilize more theory-based approaches (or conceptual models) to look at and explain politics to students and to each other. *Behavioralism*, although fraught with shortcomings, enabled political scientists to bring both normative components of political science (assumptions, values, and goals) and empirical aspects of politics (the actual context of politics in the state or states under investigation) to enable political scientists to analyze in greater detail and explain more fully how, when, and why politics occurred as it did in various national settings. The study of Celtic politics can be understood through various conceptual lenses used in the discipline of political science.

The study of legislatures and executives on the Celtic fringe can be done in concert with several behavioral and other models. Not only can legislatures be studied from a structural-functionalist approach or legislative behavior (studying the voting behavior of legislators on various issues) but an historical approach is useful to understand continuity and national receptiveness or antipathy to legislative bodies. The institutional model helps us conceptualize what legislative bodies do and how they do it. *Institutionalism* also enables us to analyze how parliaments or assemblies are affected by outside forces both tangible and intangible. It also helps us look at a legislature's impact on government and society. Institutionalism can do several things in terms of explaining parliamentary behavior: As political scientist Ruth Lane argues, it can help us see that:

1) Individuals have multiple goals and these goals are multifaceted.

2) Institutions are developed by people and cannot be conceptualized in and of themselves. We have to look at the context they evolve and operate in as well as their histories.

3) The role of other institutions on an institution under examination is important since people and institutions and contexts change.

4) Institutional analysis is at its core "political." Because institutions do not evolve in a vacuum, the political forces that shape institutions allow us to make comparisons across national boundaries.

5) Institutionalism as a conceptual analytical approach is not as concerned with finding appropriate statistical data and confirming empirical assumptions, but rather findings ways to systematically and scientifically analyze how institutions evolve, live, breathe, and even die (Lane 1997).

Scottish Parliament and Executive

The *Scottish Parliament* was not a novel concept. Prior to 1999, the last time Scotland had a parliament was 1707. The rise of political nationalism in Scotland in the 1960s and 1970s brought about renewed calls for Home Rule. When Tony Blair's Labour government took power in 1997 it followed through on its pledge to bring devolution to the Scots. Like the minority Labour government in 1979, it promised a referendum on Scottish self-rule. This was delivered within months and on September 11, 1997, 700 years since William Wallace had beaten the English at Stirling Bridge, the Scots voted overwhelmingly for Home Rule. The March 1979 vote had called for 40% of the *entire* Scottish electorate to vote "yes." When only 32.9% did the referendum was nullified, despite a 52% to 48% vote in favor of devolution. In 1997, the two questions received an extraordinary majority of support. The first question as to whether a parliament should be established in Scotland saw 74.3% in favor and 25.7% opposed. The second question asked if the parliament should have taxing powers. It got 63.5% in favor and 36.5% opposed. The Scottish Parliament was to have 129 members elected by the semi-proportional representation system known as the *additional member system* (AMS). Members of the Scottish Parliament (*MSPs*) were to hold four-year terms. The legislature was to be headed by a cabinet with ministers and a *first minister* (the rough equivalent of a prime minister in the Westminster model). The legislature had limited powers in fiscal areas (taxing and spending), education, health, culture, and many other areas. It did not have powers in areas reserved by the Westminster parliament such as foreign affairs, defense, macro-economic policy, employment, and the United Kingdom's (UK) constitution. It was a much more robust legislature than the devolved ones in Belfast or Cardiff.

The 1999, 2003, 2007 Scottish Parliament elections went as follows:

Party	1st Vote (%) (Constituency)	2nd Vote (%) (Regional)	Seats
May 1999 Election			
Labour	38.8	33.6	56
Scottish Nationalists	28.7	27.3	35
Conservatives	15.6	15.4	18
Liberal Democrats	14.2	12.4	17
Scottish Socialists	1.0	2.0	1
Scottish Greens	0.0	3.6	1
Others	1.6	5.7	1
May 2003 Election			
Labour	34.5	29.4	50
Scottish Nationalists	23.7	20.9	27
Conservatives	16.6	15.6	18
Liberal Democrats	15.3	11.8	17
Scottish Socialists	6.0	6.7	7
Scottish Greens	0.0	6.9	7
Others	3.8	8.7	3
May 2007			
Scottish Nationalists	32.9	31.0	47
Labour	32.2	29.2	46
Conservatives	16.6	13.9	17
Liberal Democrats	16.2	11.3	16
Scottish Greens	0.2	4.0	2
Others	1.0	10.2	1

Table 5.1: Scottish Parliament Elections (1999–2007)

In May 1999, Labour got 36% of the vote thus securing a plurality of seats (56) in the Scottish Parliament. It then asked the Liberal Democrats (who got 13% of the vote and 17 seats) to join in forming a coalition government in Edinburgh. The Scots used the AMS system, a semi-*proportional representation (PR)* electoral system, which allows for a first "constituency" vote to give constituents in legislative districts to elect MSPs based on a *Single Member District (SMD)* electoral process (like voting for MPs at Westminster or Americans voting for congresspersons in Washington, DC). The second vote was a "regional" one that saw voters cast a vote for a party list in a broader Scottish parliamentary region. The latter is a PR-based vote (like other European systems). In general, the Scottish electoral system for the Scottish parliament is exactly like the German electoral process in balloting for the Bundestag.

Box 5.1: West Lothian Question

This question was raised by Tam Dalyell, Labour MP from Scotland, who opposed devolution. Dalyell came to the House of Commons representing West Lothian in 1962 after beating the Scottish National Party's leader Billy Wolfe. By 2001 and the retirement of former prime minister Ted Heath, Dalyell became the "father of the House"—the seniormost member of the House of Commons. He argued that under legislative devolution that Scots and Northern Irish representatives could vote for legislation affecting the English at Westminster in London, but the English could not do the same in Edinburgh or Belfast. One way to handle this was to cut the number of Scottish MPs in the House of Commons. In 2005, this happened when the number of Scots MPs dropped from 72 to 55 according to the 1998 Government of Scotland Act. The second way to keep the "West Lothian Question" from going into effect was championed by the former Conservative Party leader William Hague (1997–2001) who argued to let only English MPs vote on English laws. But this is difficult when you get to laws related to high politics issues such as defense and foreign policy of the UK. Certainly, Dalyell's concern was a valid one that still proposes a quandary for a regionalizing and federalizing UK with a salient Celtic fringe. For Dalyell, he announced in January 2004 that the 2001 parliament would be his last and that he would retire from politics despite the fact that the West Lothian question would remain at least partially unanswered even after 2005.

The Scottish Parliament had a muddled relationship with the UK government after 1999. Although its purview of legislative powers included transport, health, education, housing, agriculture, justice, food standards, local government, police/fire services, environment, training, social work, fisheries, and an agglomeration of tourism, culture, and sport. The issue-areas reserved by the Westminster government were traditional high politics issues of defense, national security, and foreign affairs. Other powers included gas, coal, drug laws, social security, equal opportunities, broadcasting, and electricity and nuclear energy to name several. Given the new role of the legislative oversight in Scotland, issues of regulation and investigation in these political areas caused MSPs and others to raise questions over original jurisdiction both in terms of legality and politics. The European Union's (EU) role became increasingly important as it intervened at both regional and national (central government) levels to impose its will on Scots and UK legislation that affected its policies, especially in the all-important areas of fisheries, agriculture (where the Common Agricultural Policy represented over 50% of the EU annual budget by the start of the twenty-first century) and human rights.

The symbolic value of the Scottish parliament was not underestimated by devolution proponents. Once the 1997 devolution referenda had succeeded, the would-be first minister and New Labour Scottish Secretary Donald Dewar decided that the new Scottish legislature would be built near the Holyrood Palace, instead of housed in the Royal High School hall in the Scotland's seat of government—Edinburgh. From 1999 to late 2004, the Scottish parliament was housed in the Kirk's Assembly Hall in the Old Town section of Scotland's capital city, not far from the last Scottish parliament building which had become the nation's highest court. Once construction began in 1999, cost overruns grew wildly and Scots and others south of the border began to sound off against what appeared to be a botched boondoggle of a project. By late 2003, the total cost of the new parliament was to be £50 million, but the Scottish government put the cost at nearly £7 million over that figure. Thus, the problems of the inchoate national parliament in Scotland were seen as metaphorical for a legislature that many wondered whether it was truly delivering the results it was supposed to. Despite the rancor, one poll said Scots felt (51% to 31%) the newly devolved Edinburgh legislature was more important than the House of Commons in terms of Scots politics. The beautiful new parliament building was eventually opened in September 2004.

Though Scots had some troubles adjusting to the new parliament, the first election for a Scottish parliament was nothing short of historic. For the first time in nearly 300 years, Scots were going to have control of much of their domestic affairs. In March 2000, for the first time in 600 years, another remarkable event occurred at the infant Scottish legislature. The first use of Scottish Gaelic in a legislative debate occurred. The bilingual proceedings were as much about symbolism as substance, but MSPs wanted to make good on promises tied to Gaelic education in Scotland. Interestingly, only two in the 129-person chamber were fluent in the language. Alasdair Morgan, a SNP MSP, was one of the Gaelic speakers and he opened the proceedings by stating he was proud of the return of Gaelic use in the Scots legislature. Morgan would win the Western Isles seat in the House of Commons in 2005—the first time in 31 years that the SNP had beaten Labour for a Scottish seat at Westminster. MSPs struggled to keep up with the translators, but several politicians had been studying the ancient language on their own. Gaelic is known only by one percent of Scots and those are largely found in the peripheral areas such as the Highlands and Western Isles. The language was recognized as one of Scotland's chief languages by the parliament, but MSPs must notify the speaker in advance if they intend to use it in legislative discourse. The parliament was going to appoint a Gaelic official and a committee on parliamentary procedure was to review the use of motions in Gaelic, Scots, and English.

In 1999, several MSPs had objected to the British Sovereign, Queen Elizabeth II, attending parliament's opening and sanctioning the legislature's right to exist. Like Ireland after 1920, some saw this as an affront to the Scottish nation. Others as a mere formality that would, in time, take care of itself as it had for fellow Celts across the Irish Sea. In May 2003, with the addition of six Scottish Socialist MSPs, the protests at the swearing in ceremony were pronounced. The leader of the Scottish Socialists, Tommy Sheridan, declared that his party was for an independent Scotland: a Scotland for the Scottish citizens, not "subjects." One of his colleagues, Collin Fox sang a Robert Burns (Scotland's national poet—hero of the eighteenth century) poem and was rebuked by the presiding officer, Liberal Democrat Sir David Steel. Another, Rosie Kane, put her oath in writing on her hand and pledged to bring some figurative fireworks to the parliament. The Greens were no less respectful of Westminster's authority. The SNP saw its members begrudgingly pledge to the Crown, despite statements of loyalty to the Scottish nation alone.

Within days, Scottish Labour Party leader and first minister Jack McConnell had struck a deal with Scottish Liberal Democrat leader Jim Wallace and another "Lab-Lib" government was established. Two areas where sticking points had occurred and compromise was sought were Labour's interest on cracking down on youth criminal activity and the Liberal Democrats wanting electoral reform for council elections in Scotland. The UK-wide Liberal Democrats have wanted PR for all elections throughout the UK.

The May 2007 elections saw a major revolution in Scottish politics. For the first time ever, the SNP won a plurality of Scottish votes and seats in an election. It was the best electoral outing for the nationalists since October 1974 when the party won over 30% of the vote for the House of Commons in London. That translated into 11 seats. However, the Holyrood elections of May 3, 2007, were a major victory for the party as it nearly doubled its number of seats in the Edinburgh legislature going from 27 (in 2003) to 47 seats. It was the first major electoral setback for Labour in Scotland since 1955 (if one includes Westminster elections). The nationalists, under Salmond as first minister, went into government running a minority government with the consent of the Greens which supported independence for Scotland and some SNP initiatives, but eschewing full participation in government. The Greens agreed to a "confidence and supply" approach with the SNP in power. That is, the Greens would support the SNP in votes of confidence and on budget issues. The Greens would support Salmond as first minister as long as the SNP would make the Greens conveners of an environmental committee at Holyrood. The two parties would work together on reducing global warming and opposing nuclear power plant production in Scotland. They would also support expanding the scope and power of the Holyrood parliament. The agreement stopped short of demanding Green ministers in the government. Another interesting aspect of the 2007 elections was the 140,000 spoiled ballots that led to an American-style wrangling among the parties over Scotland's tainted election procedures. Confusion over ballot papers which had as many as 23 parties on them and two systems of voting for both regional and constituency seats led to much finger-pointing among Scots. Glasgow, Scotland's biggest city, had the most problems and this led to enmity among the parties given the fairly close margin of difference in terms of seats at Holyrood between the SNP and Labour. A few days after the historic elections in 2007, SNP leader, Salmond, was elected 49–46 to serve as the new first minister of Scotland. He was the first non-Labour leader of Holyrood since devolution began in 1999. The vote was narrow due to the fact that only SNP and Green MSPs voted for Salmond and Labour MSPs voted against. The Tories and Liberal Democrats abstained. Thus, adding to the increasing tension of Scotland being governed domestically by a minority nationalist government. Also, in an interesting twist, the seat that gave the SNP the one seat plurality over Scots Labour in the Edinburgh legislature was won by Angela Constance, MSP who took the Livingston seat from Labour. However, Constance was pregnant and announced she would take maternity leave early in the government's life and thus negate the government's one vote advantage over Labour. Salmond suggested that the situation was not that big of deal given that the SNP was in the minority anyway. The complication seemed to empower the former SNP MP, Margo MacDonald, who was the Scots legislature's only independent MSP. She left the SNP in 2003 to run as an independent for Holyrood. MacDonald was the former daughter-in-law of SNP MEP and MP Winnie Ewing (the victor at Hamilton in 1967) and wife of former SNP MP Jim Sillars.

The Oireachtas, Taoiseach, and President in Éire

The *Oireachtas* (Parliament) is the bicameral legislature of the Irish Republic. Consisting of two chambers, a lower house (*Dáil Éireann*—Chamber of Deputies of Ireland) and an upper house (*Seanad Éireann*—Senate of Ireland), the *Oireachtas* has functioned as a relatively modern parliament since 1937 when Éamon de Valera's Constitution created a new upper chamber. The Republic's first legislature was unicameral and it began operation illegally in 1919. After 1921, and the creation of the Free State as a dominion of the UK, an upper-chamber (senate) was included and the idea was to allow the senate to function as a channel of representation for Protestant northerners. When the senate blocked some legislation, the nationalists were not happy and by 1936 de Valera led the charge in jettisoning the upper body. However, a year later when de Valera's Constitution was promulgated, a new *Seanad* was created.

The Dáil has 166 members and the average size of each legislative district in Ireland is 21,000 people. Compare this to the *House of Commons* in Britain at 69,000 per MP and the United States (US) at 260,000 per Congressperson in the House of Representatives. The Irish lower house is elected, by law, once every five years. The legislative process in the Republic has evolved into a standard, Western democratic one. According to political scientist Basil Chubb, bills are normally fairly well-developed and usually presumed passable before debate on them. The view that bills are open to amendments, the principal behind them open to attack at all stages of their evolution, is not part of Irish legislative mores. The Irish generally expect the government and its ministers to provide bills for the Dáil to accept or reject, rather than the more two-way street seen at Westminster or in Washington, DC with many bills coming out of the backbenches. The Dáil generally allows the government to move bills through the process to a vote on the legislature's floor with little hindrance (Chubb 1992). Thus, the Dáil allows for the government to become more powerful vis-à-vis the institution itself which has led to the argument that the Dáil may be perceived more as a kind of rubber stamp at times in Irish history than other legislatures in

Western democracies. What's more, the Irish lower house has occasionally acted like a biennial southern state government in the United States (such as Texas and Kentucky in the past) that met every other year or so. The body only met 90 or so times a year for 20 years from the late 1960s to the early 1990s. The fact that the philosophical foundations of the Free State were forged by de Valera and Fianna Fáil's dominance also led to the charge that Éire's political culture imbued with nationalism and authoritarianism affected the less than mature legislative evolution that did not see European pluralist party politics as part of its normal recurring party political process on a regular basis until after 1973.

The *Seanad* has 60 members and like the French Senate (the upper chamber of the French bicameral legislature) is indirectly elected and takes on a nearly identical function and role in the Republic. The majority of senators (43) are elected by a group of around 1000 politicians. This electoral college is comprised of local councilors at county and borough levels, as well as *Teachta Dálas* (deputies in the Irish), known as TDs (pronounced: CHOCKTA dawlas), who are the Dáil legislators. These groups are divided by interest areas (agriculture, commerce, education, labor, etc.) and TDs. Thus, in effect the selection process is similar to some judicial selection processes in the US such as the Missouri Plan (used in many American states) where an American Bar Association-approved panel selects judge candidates for the governor to choose. Six senators are selected by graduates (Irish citizens) of the two universities in existence in 1937 (the National University of Ireland and Dublin University's Trinity College). Graduates of both select three senators. The last 11 senators are chosen by the Taoiseach (prime minister). Thus, the selection process is quasi-democratic despite the fact that the *single transferable vote (STV)* system is used within the Electoral College to select senators. Selecting Irish senators does remind many of the pre-1999 method of picking peers for the *House of Lords* in Britain since the Taoiseach can select senators who can deliver majorities in the *Seanad* so as not to thwart the will of the government. This process is not unlike what has been seen at times in Britain when the prime minister has tried to pack the House of Lords with like-minded peers as Prime Minister Herbert Henry Asquith did in 1911 in order to undercut the veto of Liberal Party legislation in the House of Lords. British Prime Minister Tony Blair did something similar in abolishing most hereditary peerages in 1999. The *Seanad* can deal with many bills, but basically has little power to stop the will of the Dáil majority. The upper house may be successful in hindering the lower house's bills if the Irish president forces her or his hand on a bill of vital national interest or importance and he or she fails to sign it.

The electoral system in the Republic is the same as Northern Ireland: a PR system with a STV process for multi-member districts. The STV system was championed by Sinn Féin's founder Arthur Griffith who was a staunch advocate of PR and agreed to the STV system for unionists in the southern Free State which the UK wanted. This was agreed to by December 1921 when the treaty was signed. The STV PR system has remained in Ireland despite Fianna Fáil's attempt to change the electoral system in 1959 and 1968 to a SMD system (like the UK's and US's) which failed in national referendums. The STV allows voters to vote for one or more candidates and rank order their preferences and as candidates achieve the quota to be elected or fail to achieve the quota and are defeated. But, this "top-up" system allows for votes to be transferred as various counts occur to determine the winners. Votes will go to the top candidate and after he or she wins a seat, votes for him or her will go to the next candidate in the party (unless preferences were listed by the voter.) Thus, legislative districts are multi-member and have more than one TD representing them. Éire has 42 constituencies and with 166 Dáil seats this translates into an average of nearly four seats per constituency. Thus, areas with over 30,000 citizens must have at least one, and usually more than one, TD representing them and constituencies with less than 20,000 voters must have no more than one TD representing them. These caveats are law in Ireland. The latter restriction is a rarity in early twenty-first century Ireland given its growth both in population and governmental operations over the years.

The *Taoiseach* (pronounced: tee-SHOCK) is the Irish prime minister. In ancient Irish Gaelic the term means "chief" or "leader." The deputy prime minister is called the *Tánaiste* (pronounced: taw-NISH-ta). The Tánaiste in the 2002 government was Mary Harney of the Progressive Democrats. This was the first time a party outside of the three major and more senior parties (Fianna Fáil, Fine Gael, and Labour) had held the post in post-1937 Irish history. It is selected from the ruling party in the Dáil. The Taoiseach plays a role like modern European prime ministers. The Taoiseach may lose power if her or his government loses on a vote of no confidence or he or she asks the President to dismiss the parliament. The Irish prime minister got more power after 1937 and the adoption of the new constitution. He or she may remove government ministers and conduct the day-to-day affairs of the government. Prior to 1937, Ireland was governed by an Executive Council. The chief executive was found in the post of President of the Executive Council (held for many years by de Valera). The post was more of a first among equals with much less authority and charged with chairing council meetings. The pre-1937 Council president could not dismiss council (cabinet) members. This changed after the adoption of a new constitution. The Taoiseach may be defeated on a "loss of supply" vote. This occurs when the Dáil denies the government funds from the budget for which it has primary legislative competence and control. This occurred in January 1982 when the lower house voted a "loss of supply" to the Fine Gael-Labour government under Taoiseach Dr. Garret FitzGerald. Normally, under these circumstances, the Irish prime minister would resign and/or call for new elections. FitzGerald got the Irish President Patrick Hillery, who held the presidency from 1976 to 1990, to end the Dáil and his government ended in March 1982 and elections were held which Fine Gael lost. But, FitzGerald and Fine Gael would be returned a few months later in November 1982 and take power again the next month.

The Taoiseach after the 2007 election was Bertie Ahern who had been in the chief executive post since 1997. Ahern had led Fianna Fáil to three straight election victories. It was the first time since 1966 that Éire had a three-term premier. Born in 1951, Patrick Bartholomew Ahern (Parthalán Ó hEachtairn in Irish Gaelic) started out as a backbencher in Dáil after winning election in 1977. A member of the longstanding party of nationalist governance, Fianna Fáil, he began to make his way to the top of the party's ranks. In November 1994, Ahern was elected as Fianna Fáil's leader, the sixth in the party's history. Ahern expected to jump into the premiership immediately, but Labour's Dick Spring ended discussions with Fianna Fáil and formed a minority "Rainbow" coalition government that was to last until 1997. This made Ahern the leader of the opposition, despite having the largest slice of seats of any party in the Dáil. In June 1997, at 46, Ahern was elected to the chief executive post in the Dáil. He was the youngest Taoiseach in Irish history. Ahern was known for moving Ireland ahead in the EU and in 2004 was discussed as a serious candidate for the presidency of the European Commission (which turned out not to be). But, his major accomplishments included moving Northern Ireland and the Republic closer together in working with Tony Blair's government in passing and promulgating the Belfast Agreement in 1998. Ahern also helped jump start the Irish economy and moved it forward as a vastly improving service economy with large technology sectors evolving despite the history of economic sluggishness in Éire due to a predominantly rural agricultural economy. Ahern left the premier's post in 2008 after a financial scandal and was replaced by Brian Cowen.

The Irish *presidency* like in many European systems of politics takes on a largely ceremonial role in Éire. Unlike the Dáil (where residents with UK citizenship may vote), only Irish citizens can vote for the presidential post. The election is a form of STV, despite the fact that only one candidate ultimately wins (unlike the lower house of the Irish legislature in Dublin). Although the role of head of state takes on various functions, some real power can be exercised by the Irish president. He or she is the commander-in-chief of the military, yet that power is directed by the government. This is very much unlike France and the US, where the president holds de jure and de facto power, the Irish leader takes a back seat to the Taoiseach and the government. The president appoints the cabinet and opens parliament. He or she can, upon request from the prime minister, dissolve government and fire government ministers. The president signs bills into law and rarely opts to veto legislation under special reserve powers. These reserve powers can give the president some real power such as turning bills over to the Irish supreme court, taking bills to the public for their approval in referendums much like the Gaullist Constitution of 1958 for France's Fifth Republic (such as the attempt in 1968 by Irish President de Valera to change the STV PR electoral system to SMD), the right to speak to the Oireachtas (either house or both jointly—de Valera exercised this right once, Mary Robinson twice, and *Mary McAleese* once), not allowing the Dáil to be dissolved (which has never happened), lessening the time the *Seanad* can take to hear a bill, and creating a committee of privilege (or conference committee as in the US) for both houses of the parliament to solve legislative issues. Like the French and US presidents, the Irish president receives foreign ambassadors and may act on behalf of the government in foreign affairs. Unlike French and US presidents, this latter action must be coordinated with the government. Much like the monarch's speech that opens parliamentary sessions at Westminster in London each year (which must have the government's blessing, and usually is written for the monarch by cabinet ministers and their staffs), the Irish president must run all of his or her public speeches before the government (cabinet) for its approval. The president is also not allowed to leave Éire without government approval.

The Irish president had long had a history of running disagreements over its institutional title with its old colonial overlord the UK. The position was conceptualized by politicians in the Dublin government as consisting of an official title of "President of Ireland." This implied that the Irish presidency was the head of state for all 32 counties on the green island. The British disagreed and in 1953 when Queen Elizabeth II was crowned the Republic government took umbrage at her title as queen of "the United Kingdom and Northern Ireland." Thus, the Irish president, Sean T. O'Kelly (Sean T. Ó Ceallaigh in Irish Gaelic) refused to attend a party at the British embassy in Dublin in honor of the Queen's coronation. The symbolic rift continued as President Hillery (1976–90) refused to attend the nuptials of Lady Diana Spencer and the Prince of Wales (Charles Windsor) in 1981. On both occasions the Fianna Fáil-led government advised such a course of action. These high-profile diplomatic rows have waned over the years with recent presidents, such as Robinson (1990–97), being received regularly in Britain. Ireland has had eight presidents since 1937. All but one has been from the dominant nationalist party, Fianna Fáil: Robinson of the Labour party. Two have been female—Robinson and McAleese.

Robinson was Ireland's first female president and one of Europe's first major female political leaders after Britain's Margaret Thatcher. Born Mary Bourke in 1944 in Ballina in County Mayo, she studied law in the 1960s at Trinity College Dublin despite a law against Roman Catholic students taking courses there. That changed formally in the 1970s. She then became a law professor at the college upon graduation. She championed several women's issues such as the right to use contraceptives, placing women on juries, and fighting a law that forced women who had married to resign from the national civil service. She also served as an attorney for a group advocating homosexual rights. Championing these causes was not vogue in a conservative Ireland in the 1960s and 1970s. Although her ancestors ties to the Church of Ireland (the Anglican Church in Ireland), her own immediate family's Catholicism was an issue when she married Nicholas Robinson, a member of the Church of Ireland. Spending her Irish political career in the *Seanad*, Robinson started out as one of Trinity College's three members in the early 1970s. She then joined the Labour Party in the mid-1970s and when the party joined with Fine Gael in coalition in 1982 it was thought that she would win a cabinet post. To no avail, she stayed in the senate until 1989, although she resigned from Labour to voice her displeasure over the Anglo-Irish Agreement of 1985 which she felt gave no chance for the unionist majority in Northern Ireland to be brought into the decision-making process. In 1989, Labour asked her to run for the presidency of the Republic. She obliged and pulled a stunning upset over Tánaiste and minister of defense Brian Lenihan, who became the first Fianna Fáil candidate to ever lose a presidential election in Ireland. Robinson made headlines as president. She was the first Irish president ever to visit Buckingham Palace and Queen Elizabeth II and she hosted the Prince of Wales in Dublin. She also traveled north to chat with Sinn Féin's Gerry Adams in his West Belfast constituency. She also spoke to the houses of parliament twice (only done once before by de Valera in 1969). Remarkably, from her left-of-center political perspective on many social issues, she got to sign into law a bill legalizing homosexuality and one allowing for the use of contraceptives, both long taboos in the strictly Catholic state. Her popularity rating was over 90% during her years and she eventually turned power over to Fianna Fáil's McAleese, who had followed her as the legal counsel for the same gay rights group she had fought for in the early 1970s. What's more, McAleese held the same post at Trinity in the law faculty that Robinson had held years prior as well. Robinson left office a few months early in 1997 early to take a new post as the United Nations High Commissioner for Human Rights. She had paved the way for a new generation of women politicians and others hoping to see Ireland change socially and politically.

The May 24, 2007 elections in Éire saw Fianna Fáil and Taoiseach Ahern returned for a third term in a row. Ahern thus became the longest serving premier since Fianna Fáil's Seán Lemass held the post from mid-1959 until late 1966. Ahern was set to surpass the Republic's longevity record as Taoiseach which was set by de Valera during his three terms as premier (all served successively) between 1937–48 at the start of the Free State's new constitution. His term ended just prior to the birth of the independent Republic was born in 1949. Fianna Fáil entered into a coalition with the Progressive Democrats just as it had in 2002. But, there was a new twist. The coalition also had the Greens and some independent TDs which led to a more moderate government. It was the first time ever that the Greens had helped govern Ireland and the first time Fianna Fáil had been in a three-party coalition.

The 1997, 2002, 2007 Dáil elections had the following results:

Party	1st Preference Votes (%)	Seats
June 1997 Election		
Fianna Fáil	39.3	77
Fine Gael	27.9	54
Labour	10.4	17
Progressive Democrats	4.7	4
Greens	2.8	2
Sinn Féin	2.5	1
Others	12.3	11

May 2002 Election		
Fianna Fáil	41.5	81
Fine Gael	22.5	31
Labour	10.8	21
Sinn Féin	6.5	5
Progressive Democrats	4.0	8
Greens	3.8	6
Others	11.0	14
May 2007 Election		
Fianna Fáil	41.6	77
Fine Gael	27.3	51
Labour	10.1	20
Sinn Féin	6.9	4
Greens	4.7	6
Progressive Democrats	2.7	2
Others	6.9	6

Table 5.2: Irish Parliamentary Elections (1997-2007)

Welsh Assembly and Executive

The campaign for a devolved assembly in Wales was never as salient as it was in Scotland. The Welsh, after years of direct linkages and integration with England's political system, had a divided political culture and the issue of a Welsh legislature was divisive by the advent of "New Labour's" government in May 1997. With the promise to bring a newly devolved parliament to Scotland a similar overture was made to Wales. Tony Blair's government, in July 1997, then published White Papers (proposed government policy) on devolved legislatures in both Scotland and Wales. The latter's was entitled, *A Voice for Wales*. The Scots and the Welsh had had referendums in 1979. In that year, the Welsh had voted overwhelmingly against a separate Welsh legislature, 80%–20%. Although the Scottish referendum was overwhelmingly supported by Scots, the Welsh were much more tepid and when the question was put as to whether the Welsh wanted their own assembly with differing powers from the parliament offered to the Scots, but unlike 1979, the Welsh voted in favor, just barely, 50.3% to 49.7%. The turnout was poor at just over 50% as well. Predictably, divisions in Wales occurred with the more traditional northern part of the region more likely to support the government's policy and the more Anglicized and cosmopolitan areas of southern and eastern Wales, including the capital Cardiff, opposed to Home Rule. Wales had not had its own legislature since 1406. But, the referendum forced the government in London toward the passage of the Wales Act of 1998 and the eventual elections in May 1999 for the National Assembly for Wales or as it is known in Welsh—*Cynulliad Cenedlaethol Cymru.*

The Welsh Assembly was quite different from its Celtic parliamentary cousin to the north in Scotland. The Welsh legislature was to be a creature of unique British administrative devolution; that is, a kind of mixture between a council and a parliament. It was not to be a body with the kind of parliamentary powers seen in Scotland after 1999 or in the House of Commons, especially in fiscal powers. Its executive was to be a grouping of committee chairs, or an executive committee led by a first secretary. It had some executive powers, but no taxing powers. It had some authority over various issue areas such as education, health and social services, environment, agriculture, transportation, economic development, and housing. The Welsh secretary of state, who had political authority in Wales, was to retain his/her cabinet spot in Blair's government.

The Welsh Assembly would not be a parliament. It would have less power and the Government of Wales Act provided for *executive devolution*. Wales was to be conceptualized as a region rather than a nation (as political scientist Vernon Bogdanor said) (Bogdanor 2002). Thus, the Welsh had the ability to create secondary legislation as opposed to primary legislation. Thus, the assembly had the power to pass and scrutinize laws related to agriculture and fisheries, culture, economic development, education, environment, health, highways, housing, sport, tourism, water, and the Welsh language to name several. The National Assembly could also create regulations for the administration of 300 acts of the UK parliament that were directly related to Wales. Other types of functions such as making appointments to quangos (such as the National Health Service Trust in Wales) and acquiring property (an American-style eminent domain function) to improve infrastructure and build new roads was permitted as well.

According to political scientist Colin Pilkington, the role of the first secretary was to do several things: 1) work with the Welsh secretary (from the UK cabinet) to create Welsh legislation at Westminster; 2) serve as party leader and put into effect the party's manifesto (platform); 3) lead the national assembly; 4) lead the national assembly executive and create a Welsh cabinet; 5) hold a "Question Time" in the national assembly; 6) represent the national assembly at the House of Commons in London and Europe; and 7) give a state of the nation speech each year (similar to an American governor's state of the state address) (Pilkington 2002).

The first two first secretaries, Ron Davies and Alun Michael, held both the first secretary and Welsh Secretary posts. After Michael was ousted on a no-confidence vote (31 "for," 27 "against," one abstention) in February 2000, he was replaced. The vote had been called for by Plaid Cymru. He was replaced by Rhodri Morgan.

The assembly had six subject committees: agriculture, economic development, two education committees (pre-16 and post-16), environment, and one committee for health and social services. Five non-subject (functionally oriented) committees: audit, European affairs, legislative scrutiny, regional, and standards and conduct. Committees were to engage in discussing and making policy, oversight of administrative actions, amending pending legislation, scrutinizing Westminster and EU legislation that affects the committee's purview (much like the function the House of Lords plays in the legislative process in the UK vis-à-vis the House of Commons). Finally, committees were to summarize legislation and provide their views to the Welsh cabinet.

According to Pilkington several problems existed in the early days of the devolved Welsh legislature. First, no formal method for collective conversation on given issues was available. Second, power was held by a few individuals (notably the first secretary). Third, little accord existed by the political parties on how the Welsh administration should guide the devolved assembly. Fourth, no real way to make decisions was found in the assembly since most decisions were subject to the Welsh executive in both Cardiff and London. Fifth, no venue for the creation of policy existed. These hurt the nature of the Welsh assembly and the hopes by some that it might gain more power in the years ahead (Pilkington 2002).

The assembly was to have 60 *AM*s (Assembly Members—40 elected from constituencies and 20 from party lists). Each was elected to a four-year term and members were to be paid around £35,000/year ($71,211), compared to £43,000 ($87,488) at Westminster. The assembly was to be elected by a modified of proportional representation (PR) system known as the additional member system, which allowed voters to cast two votes (one for their constituency and one for a party list). In the constituency, seats were won based on the single member district electoral system (or first-past-the-post system used in both for elections to the House of Commons and at all levels of government in the United States). In each region of Wales, the votes won by parties were totaled after a second vote and the last 20 seats were awarded based on the percentage each party got in the second vote—a more pure PR system). This system was used in Scotland's elections for its parliament after 1999. And it is very similar to the STV system of Ireland and Northern Ireland's electoral systems.

The 1999, 2003, and 2007 *Cynulliad Cenedlaethol Cymru* elections yielded the following results:

Party	1st Vote (%) (Constituency)	2nd Vote (%) (Regional)	Seats
May 1999 Election			
Labour	37.6	35.5	28
Plaid Cymru	28.4	30.6	17
Conservatives	15.9	16.5	9
Liberal Democrats	13.4	12.5	6
Others	4.7	5.0	0
May 2003 Election			
Labour	40.0	36.6	30
Plaid Cymru	21.2	19.7	12
Conservatives	19.9	19.2	11
Liberal Democrats	14.1	12.7	6
Others	4.8	11.8	1

May 2007 Election			
Labour	32.2	29.6	26
Plaid Cymru	22.4	21.0	15
Conservatives	22.4	21.5	12
Liberal Democrats	14.8	11.7	6
Others	8.2	16.2	1

Table 5.3: Welsh Assembly Elections (1999-2007)

The May 1999 election saw Labour win a plurality of the seats in the Welsh Assembly. Because it was short of an overall majority with 28 of 60 seats, initially it chose to form a minority government with no coalition partners. Many in Wales had expected Labour to govern with a majority of the seats in the Cardiff-based assembly. However, when Ron Davies, who had been tapped to be the initial first minister of the assembly, resigned as secretary of state for Wales in the Fall of 1998 (the first Blairite cabinet official to resign due to an alleged scurrilous personal scandal), the Welsh Labour Party saw a bitter struggle for power between London's man, Alun Michael, and Rhodri Morgan, a Labour backbencher who Blair and his cabinet colleagues did not want running the Welsh party. Thus, Plaid Cymru took advantage of the wrangling and took 17 seats and just under a third of the vote on both ballots. Its leader Dafydd Wigley was popular and many supported its nationalist and cultural campaign that not only called for greater Welsh identity, but also argued that Labour was too rightwing on economic issues for the left-of-center Welsh political culture. After only six months in office, Michael was forced out and Morgan replaced him. In 2000, Labour shifted its legislative tactics at Cardiff and entered into a coalition government with the Liberal Democrats. This coalition maintained itself until the 2003 elections.

The 2003 election saw Labour improve its fortunes adding two extra seats at Cardiff and the surprise winners electorally of the assembly race were the Conservatives who saw their percentage rise by four percent in the first vote and three percent in the second vote. They also gained two seats to come closer to the lead opposition party, Plaid Cymru, who lost dramatically by dropping to 12 seats in the Assembly. In 2003, Labour did an effective job of getting disaffected voters to return and it, along with the two other non-nationalist parties (Tories and Liberal Democrats) did an effective job of painting the Plaid as a militant, anti-English nationalist party. In 2003, Welsh Labour's Morgan distanced himself and the party from Blair's government in London—partly because of the war in Iraq (unpopular in much of the Labour Party, especially among Welsh Labourites) that was winding up as the nation went to the polls. All Welsh parties played the ethnic identity card, but Welshness was downplayed somewhat in order to paint the Plaid Cymru as extremist in that party's concern over immigration into rural Wales by non-Welsh. This anti-Plaid rhetoric played well in the southern areas of Wales which are more English-speaking than northern Wales. It put Plaid on the defensive and it gave the appearance that much of Plaid Cymru's agenda was not pro-Welsh, but racist and anti-English. This seems to explain Plaid's sudden drop in the vote and seats at Cardiff.

In the immediate aftermath of the 2003 assembly election, Morgan opted for a minority government for Labour with 30 of 60 seats at Cardiff. The Liberal Democrats were left out in the cold and Welsh Labour, more "red" than the UK-wide Blairite party, was concerned about the rise in Conservative Party support throughout Wales.

Two of many issues that the Welsh Assembly dealt with during its first year were agriculturally related ones. They both demonstrate the complexities of the relationship between devolved legislation in Cardiff and its relationship to both Westminster in London and the *EU's Commission* in Brussels. In the Fall of 1999, Wales saw an increase in the number of cattle born despite falling livestock prices. The assembly created a £750,000 scheme to help cattle owners. The Welsh agriculture minister, Christine Gwyther, went to Brussels hoping to enjoy the confidence of both the Welsh office (tied to Westminster) and the EU, but the EU declared the law a no-go given the problems of applying EU law to regions within member states. Unfortunately for Gwyther, she was criticized as was the first secretary, Michael. A vote of censure on Gwyther and a vote of no confidence on Michael failed. In early 2000, the issue of genetically modified (GM) crops became salient in Welsh politics. The London-based Department of the Environment, Transport and the Regions allowed GM seeds to be planted in Wales (although the company doing the sowing had an English address). As a result, the Welsh Assembly declared *Cymru* should be free of GM products. The declaration by the legislature led to a political and legal row over jurisdiction between London and Cardiff. It also highlighted the differences between nations (Wales and England). Thus, the political and legal challenges that devolution brought to the Cardiff assembly were pronounced.

The Welsh Assembly was beset with some rather quirky issues as well. After 1999, wanting to make sure the assembly left a lasting impression in Welsh, UK, and European politics, Welsh AMs were concerned about the legitimacy of the legislature. In the Summer of 2000, First Secretary Rhodri Morgan claimed that one problem facing the infant legislature was that is was boring. He likened its process to looking at drying paint on walls. Concern over the impact the assembly was having on Wales vis-à-vis Scotland's parliament was part of the problem. Not only was Scotland's legislature well-received, but it had more popular support than the Welsh one which had about a quarter of the Welsh nation's backing. In 2003, after elections in May, the Welsh Assembly was criticized for planning a 12-hour debate on where AMs would sit in the legislative chamber. Although some saw this as substantive, others decried it as a waste of time. Concern over whether the legislature's planned debate would run past 5:30 PM, the closing time agreed on to make the 60-person chamber more conducive to family schedules, also arose. Various parties in opposition had delayed 800+ amendments in order to kill the planned debate. These actions were similar to the notorious filibuster in the United States Senate.

Box 5.2: Women in Politics: Celtic Nations Changed the Game

Politics in the Celtic fringe as in most parts of the globe was traditionally a man's world. However, the late twentieth and early twenty-first century saw unprecedented changes in executive and legislative politics in various parts of the world including the Celtic areas of Britain and Ireland. The 1997 Labour landslide saw more women enter the House of Commons than ever before. This was ironic ideologically since Conservative Party leader Margaret Thatcher was Britain's first female prime minister and she governed from 1979–90. Women were not as front and center in Celtic politics until Mary Robinson burst on the scene in Éire in 1990 as that nation's president. In the late 1990s, many leftist and center-left parties began to impose a kind of American-style affirmative action on party list seats at election time, such as *le Parti socialiste* in France. However, the role of women in both Scottish and Welsh legislatures has become pronounced. In the 2003 elections, 39.5% of the MSPs in Edinburgh were women (51 of 129 seats)—in the top five in the world in terms of female legislators winning seats in elected democratic bodies. Wales had even more remarkable results in the 2003 balloting. The Welsh Assembly became the first-ever legislative body worldwide to see gender parity achieved. The May election that year saw 30 women seated at Cardiff out of the 60 seats available (50% of the available seats). The Welsh had surpassed the Swedes who had 45.3% of their parliamentary seats occupied by women. What was more remarkable is that none of the Welsh parties had imposed an affirmative action policy. Even more amazing was that until 1997 only *four* women had ever represented Wales at Westminster in London in over 700 years of English parliamentary politics. So, clearly the development of equal opportunities in politics in Wales and other parts of Celtic Britain sent the message that men and women could work side by side in politics and that it was no longer a game for men only!

Like the Scots, who had attempted a Gaelic debate in the Scottish Parliament in 2000, the politics of language showed up in the Welsh Assembly. One study showed that the use of Welsh in the assembly had declined by one-third since 2000. On October 1, 2003, a three hour-long legislative session saw only three minutes of Welsh used in the political discourse. Only about one-third of the 60 AMs elected in 2003 actually spoke Welsh. Many of the Welsh-speaking AMs believed that speaking Welsh (instead of English) would not get them quoted by the media. Thirty translators were employed by the assembly after the 1999 elections. Many AMs tried to learn Welsh as well. But, this issue continued to vex, even if symbolically, and led to some divisions among parties. Thus, life in the devolved legislature in Cardiff was cohesive at times and incoherent at other times given the fuzziness over administrative devolution. Just how much power did London want the Welsh to have over their own affairs? Or were the Welsh all that interested in gaining more power to pursue broader national and Celtic interests?

The May 2007 elections yielded an interesting return in Wales. Like Scotland where Tony Blair's UK-wide Labour government was a liability, Wales saw Labour's power reduced, but Welsh Labour still retained a plurality of the seats in the *Senedd* (assembly). The Welsh Labour leadership immediately began to discuss coalition government possibilities with other parties after winning 26 of 60 seats (a reduced plurality from 2003). The Welsh executive brought in the health minister from the Labour Party-led government in New Zealand to help it figure out how to lead as a minority government as it moved to the same status the SNP embarked on in Scotland in mid-2007. The major change in Wales was the slight rise by about two percentage points in both regional and constituency votes of the Welsh Nationalists and Tories (as had occurred in 2003). This gave the *Plaid* three new seats and the Welsh Conservatives one new seat. The Liberal Democrats had remained remarkably flat lined since 1999. The vote appeared to be almost a stalemate in accentuating the status quo. The Welsh Nationalists proclaimed victory, but in reality, their numbers were nothing like the 28–30% of the vote they got in 1999. Labour had continued to hang on, just barely, despite Blair's unpopularity, and the rise of Conservative appeal given its UK-wide oppositional appeal, especially in southern Wales and England.

In late June 2007, Plaid Llafur's leader Morgan and the Plaid Cymru's head Ieuan Wyn Jones agreed to a "Red-Green" coalition government which would work toward an independent Welsh parliament (with more legislative power than the current assembly). This led to squabbling inside the Welsh Labour Party and the party voted overwhelmingly in favor of the deal at an ad hoc summer meeting in July 2007. Some 78% of Welsh Labour affiliates (representatives of trade unions, women's forums, and local party branches) voted to enter the coalition with the Plaid. The Plaid saw 95% of its membership support the coalition and the historic vote put the Nationalists in power for the first time in their 82-year history.

Northern Ireland's Stormont Parliament

As seen in Chapter Two, the Ulster parliament between 1922–72, was a devolved one that essentially functioned as a national parliament. It allowed the UK to stay out of Northern Irish affairs and it gave Ulster more say over its domestic politics and economics—which led to the region developing as one of Britain's most advanced economically. "The troubles" led to the suspension of the *Stormont legislature* in 1972 and for 26 years direct rule from London was imposed. The election of Labour in Britain in 1997, after 18 years in the wilderness, brought changes in the government's regional policies on the Celtic fringe. To attempt to end the internecine fighting in Ulster and IRA *terrorism*, Prime Minister Tony Blair made a good faith effort to find peace among the warring factions in Northern Ireland, and his government helped refashion the Stormont legislature to reflect a new consensus among the parties and groups in Ulster. Political scientists would call the 1998–2002 assembly a "consociational" setup.

Post-1998 Northern Ireland Parliament: Consociationalism

Political scientist Arend Lijphart's consociational model, or *consociationalism*, of democratic political systems is appropriate for understanding some of the general dynamics of Northern Ireland's fragmented political culture and system. Lijphart argues that highly segmented (fragmented in the ideological, racial, or religious sense) societies where deep-seated cleavages on issues has led to systemic destabilization or, in the case of systems that have not collapsed, inertia may be able to find political stability through the bargaining of political elites who cooperate in finding middle ground on deep seated divisions in society (as seen among the masses) (Lijphart 1969 and 1977). One might argue that this abstract conceptualization occurs in all democratic countries, but what makes a consociational model different is that the cleavages are not deep-seated with a promise that sides will argue over them, but usually ones that provoke violence or longstanding disagreement that impedes governmental functioning (as we have seen historically over religion in Lebanon, language in Belgium and Switzerland, or ethnicity, religion, and socio-economic status in Nigeria). Cultural divisions oftentimes provide some of the most profound disagreements in both authoritarian and democratic systems. In Ireland, political violence as part of the political culture was inherited from various groups' willingness to use the gun in Irish politics and resistance to colonialism from Britain. However, solving problems democratically, although sought by the majority of citizens, did not appear to be in the offing after 1922. While the Republic in the south got on with its democratic development, the loyalist north saw an upswing in violence in the 1960s and by 1969 and the start of the troubles, Ulster was a fragmented political context with little hope for democratic solutions to its vexing religious, ideological, and civil rights problems. Britain's attempt at fixing these problems, at least temporarily, in 1998 was a first move at recognizing the legitimacy of the various participants in the governmental process in Ulster. Each group with a stake in the region which represented different subcultural views (and those that could translate those views to the masses in Northern Ireland) was brought in and allowed to have a say in the general power-sharing agreement which reconfigured Stormont into a consociational democracy. Through classical elite bargaining, differences were set aside and former enemies became a bit more familiar with each other. Clearly, the problems were not fixed as Sinn Féin, the IRA's political arm, was to negotiate with the major unionist parties (as well as the London government). When the US president Bill Clinton invited Sinn Féin's leader Gerry Adams to the US in 1995, it signaled a change in not only American policy, but UK policy as well. Adams, the former defender of unconventional political action (including violence), was now seen as a legitimate statesman. It was a remarkable moment in Irish history, not unlike the 1921 invitation to Sinn Féin to meet with Lloyd George and Churchill in London to end the IRA's war on British control in Ireland.

Consociationalism as an analytical model is important for many reasons: a) It allows political scientists to understand the problems of segmented democracies as it can be used as a purely descriptive approach, and heuristic device, in studying segmented democracies; b) it serves as a conceptual model that extends theorizing about segmented and fragmented political systems beyond the boundaries of those states to other nations in allowing for comparative analyses to develop; c) it can serve to help us analyze in greater detail, the relationships between variables in democratic societies and their connection to each other and their connection to elite and mass opinion; and d) finally, it can serve as a normative applied approach to good governance as a model for actual government, not just the study of democratic governments in segmented societies.

The Good Friday Agreement of 1998

The Good Friday Agreement (GFA) of April 1998 has its roots in several recent attempts at beginning and implementing a framework for peace between Protestants and Catholics in Northern Ireland. The 1985 Anglo-Irish agreement, signed by UK premier Margaret Thatcher's Conservative and Dr. Garret FitzGerald's Fine Gael-led governments created an intergovernmental conference, à la the EU Council of Ministers, to get British and Irish (from the south) government ministers to begin a dialogue about political and legal affairs. In 1990, the British government attempted to get Belfast and Dublin's political parties to begin a discourse on issues in Northern Ireland. This was hampered by sectarian violence. However, under American president Bill Clinton, the United States became directly involved in Ulster's peace process, much to British prime minister John Major's chagrin (since it was viewed by Downing Street as a UK domestic problem, not an international one). However, in December 1993, the Taoiseach Albert Reynolds and Major signed the *Downing Street Declaration*. This eventually got the IRA to declare a cease-fire and two years later, George Mitchell, the former US senator from Maine, had brokered a new model for talks among the parties and groups in Ulster. Also, Sinn Féin's leader, Gerry Adams, was invited to the White House to meet with Clinton at the behest of American national security adviser, Tony Lake. Despite vacillation by the UK Tory government and the IRA, the peace process lumbered forward under the new Labour government after 1997 and in April 1998 the GFA was signed.

The agreement was enforced by plebiscites in both the north (where 71% supported it) and south (where 94% supported it). Movement toward restoring a newly configured Stormont parliament (which had sat prorogued since 1972) began with elections in July 1998 that called for power-sharing among Protestant and Catholic parties. This consociationalism would allow Catholic and Protestant parties to be represented in the regional legislature's executive arm. Also, the agreement called for releasing prisoners from both communities which was implemented by Blair; confronting the problems of policing in Ulster which was also tied to *decommissioning* the IRA's arms; and finding an objective way to handle security issues with the establishment of a non-partisan policing board.

Finally, the issue of parades during the notorious summer Protestant marching season was broached in order to find ways to lessen this cultural threat that has led to much violence in both Catholic and Protestant areas over the years.

Consociationalism had been tried in 1974 in Ulster. A 10-person multi-party cabinet with guaranteed places for both Protestant and Catholic parties was implemented. It was short-lived. The exact same model was applied after Good Friday in 1998. Using a STV electoral system, a modified PR system, in which voters ranked the preferred candidates in multiple-seat districts. Like the Republic in the south, which has the STV system, each district in Ulster's six counties, may return 3–5 candidates to the 108 seat Northern Irish parliament. It is different than a traditional PR system where voters (or electors as they are called in Britain) votes for a party list and the party will then get the number of seats according to the percentage of the vote it got in the election. The PR electoral system for Israel's 120-seat Knesset is an example of this system. Some argue that the STV, although a form of PR, limits the ability of assembly to deal with problems of segmentation in Northern Ireland's polity because it places the choice of individual voters over the parties' choices when choosing from a party list.

In 1998, the newly revised Stormont assembly in Belfast had 10 executive posts in its government. Power was shared, just like 1974, by Catholic and Protestant parties. The first minister post was held by Ulster Unionist Party (UUP) leader David Trimble. The deputy first minister was Seamus Mallon of the Social Democratic and Labour Party (SDLP). Sinn Féin got representation in the consociational administration with Adams and McGuinness taking seats, giving Sinn Féin executive representation in Ulster for the first time ever, an historical step for the IRA's legislative arm. By 1999, the deal was in trouble with bickering over decommissioning and other issues. In October 2002, Stormont was suspended by London and direct rule was imposed once again. However, hope for finding a way to correct the problems between Catholics and Protestants was still in the offing. Blair's government had acted in good faith to give Catholics and their representatives, the SDLP and Sinn Féin, about the best opportunity they had ever gotten to end over 30 years of hatred and violence.

Attempt to Resurrect the Stormont Parliament: 2003 and 2007

In October 2003, Blair's government in London called for elections for late November 2003. Stormont had been revived by the April 1998 GFA in which the IRA and unionist parties had made several compromises (as seen above). In 2002, Stormont was prorogued and direct rule from London resumed. The Protestant loyalists and the Catholic republicans had fallen out over the decommissioning of the IRA's arms nearly ten years after they had promised to do so. In 2001, the IRA had begun the decommissioning process. Sein Féin, the political arm of the IRA, had called for peace and its leader, Gerry Adams, had made overtures to the unionists in pursuit of peace. He even met with the UUP leader Trimble in an unprecedented meeting that evinced what most thought was a new thaw in post-Good Friday Catholic-Protestant relations. But, the inability of the decommissioning commission to verify the number and the location of IRA weapons was a stumbling block. The head of the commission, a Canadian, General John de Chastelain, said the IRA had given up various guns from semi-automatic ones to machine guns as well as various types of ordnance and semtex (the light, but volatile Czech explosive used by Libyan terrorists to bring town an American jet over Lockerbie, Scotland in December 1988). The IRA claimed to have given up 100 tons of weapons in all. However, no video verification was offered. Backed into a corner by his colleagues and by other parties that refused to work with Sinn Féin, Trimble recoiled and put the move toward Protestant power-sharing with Catholics in abeyance. Trimble who had been much more open about working with Sinn Féin and calling for democratic transitions toward multipartism and toleration (in an O'Neillist fashion), was assailed by opponents in the unionist camp, even in his own UUP. Paisley's Democratic Unionist Party (DUP) continued to call for the end of the GFA and a refusal to work with Adams and McGuinness. Despite the revelations, the British Labour government decided to go ahead with the Ulster elections in late November, much to the chagrin of the Unionist parties.

The elections to the Northern Irish Assembly of November 26, 2003 yielded fairly predictable results. Given the increased distrust between communalistic factions and parties, the two moderating forces in Ulster society, the UUP and the SDLP saw their share of the vote fall and, hence, their allotment of seats declined as well. The two polar ends of the devolved Northern Irish party system saw gains with the DUP gaining nearly 28% of the vote to Sinn Féin's 23.52% of the vote and both saw gains in the assembly. Clearly, the electorate manifested a return to sectarian communal politics. The UUP lost some as did the SDLP given the recrudescence of violence and the perception in the unionist community that the Sinn Féin would never disavow the IRA as its paramilitary arm (something seen as antithetical to democratic politics). The Belfast assembly had 108 members with each elected to a five year term. Each Member of the Legislative Assembly (MLA) was to be paid £31,817 ($65,185). But, because the assembly was suspended even as elections occurred, MLAs were getting 70% of their annual pay to deal with constituent issues and the assembly was spending £1.93 million ($3,954,075) per month after it was suspended. The 1998, 2003, and 2007 Northern Ireland Assembly elections results are as follows:

Party	Vote (%)	Seats
June 1998 Election*		
SDLP	21.97	24
UUP	21.25	28
DUP	18.14	20
Sinn Féin	17.63	18
Alliance Party of NI	6.50	6
Others	11.52	13

November 2003 Election*		
DUP	27.71	30
Sinn Féin	23.52	24
UUP	22.67	27
SDLP	16.98	18
Others	5.60	3
Alliance Party of NI	3.68	6
March 2007 Election*		
DUP	30.1	36
Sinn Féin	26.2	28
SDLP	15.2	16
UUP	14.9	18
Others	8.3	3
Alliance Party of NI	5.2	7

Table 5.4: Northern Ireland's Assembly Elections (1998-2007)
*First preference votes only.

Despite the 2003 elections, the Ulster assembly did not start due to the suspicions found among both nationalist and loyalist sides. The political polarization ideologically was a continued problem. After over a year and a half of bickering, in April 2006, British PM Blair and Irish Taoiseach Bertie Ahern delivered an ultimatum to the parties of Northern Ireland. That an ultimatum said that parties in Ulster needed to elect a new power-sharing assembly or the Stormont assembly would be shutdown. The regional legislature itself had been prorogued since October 2002 when the governing coalition of right-of-center and left-of-center parties (UUP and SDLP) broke after an IRA spying accusation. The Irish and British governments stated that the Belfast legislature would start again in May 2006, but a power-sharing government would have to be viable by late November 2006. Of course, that proposition was difficult with the DUP and Sinn Féin, led by bitter rivals Ian Paisley and Gerry Adams respectively. Blair promised an externally imposed solution to Ulster's politics after November if a newly constituted legislature failed to function in Belfast. Of course, this led to a new round of direct rule from London which had been the case from 1972–98 and from 2002 until 2007. However, in late January 2007, Sinn Féin voted to stop its boycott of the Northern Ireland police. The party had treated the police as "legitimate targets" in carrying out the terror campaign (via the IRA) in getting "England out of Ireland." This monumental vote did not come without opposition. Adams admitted that the party's youth arm, Ogra, was opposed to the vote. The action put the onus on the DUP to counter as it had not wanted to enter a ruling coalition with Sinn Féin until it recognized the authority of the Ulster police and law enforcement system. On January 30, 2007, the UK government dissolved the suspended Northern Irish legislature and called for new elections for March 7, 2007. Blair and Ahern had met in Scotland in December 2006 to set the timetable for new Northern Irish elections and a new attempt at multi-confessional party governance in Northern Ireland by the end of March 2007.

Box 5.3: Bertie and Tony

Tony Blair and Bertie Ahern were an unlikely pair. Blair was the leader of the left-of-center social democratic Labour Party (formerly an avowedly Marxist party) and Ahern the leader of the nationalist right-of-center Fianna Fáil party in Éire. Blair represented the 1100 year-old constitutional monarchy of England and its global power. Ahern represented the 50 year-old fledgling Irish state that had spent 700 years fighting Blair's country as a colonial overlord. The political marriage did not seem logical, let alone interesting. But, the Six Counties in the north of the Emerald Isle led these two unlikely leaders to sit down and figure out how to restore order to Northern Ireland and bring peace to the island. To be sure, the two had some things in common. Both had come to power in 1997. Both had been quick climbers through their respective parties and governments' systems. Both were charismatic and charming. Both were Celts with Irish ancestry (Ahern was a full-blooded indigenous Irishman and Blair's mother was from Donegal in the Republic's north). Both supported the European Union and its role in European and global affairs. Both even had scandals taint their administrations toward the end of their careers (Blair's was a scandal revolving around peerages in the House of Lords allegedly "for sale" to the highest bidder in terms of party support and Ahern allegedly took cash gifts from businesspersons which were also called "loans" that he did not repay). Both men faced ethics charges as a result of the scandals. Despite all of these issues, Ahern and Blair may go down in history as the first two premiers (Ahern as Taoiseach and Blair as prime minister) of Ireland and the UK respectively to actually provide concrete solutions to the intractable Irish question that has dumfounded politicians since 1969. The restoration of the prorogued Stormont assembly in March 2007 and the ensconcing of Sinn Féin in power with Ulster's Democratic Unionist Party led to widespread hope that peace was taking place in Northern Ireland.

The March 2007 election for the Northern Ireland assembly yielded nearly identical results to the 2003 elections in Ulster. And, it produced an even greater number of votes and seats for the polar opposite sectarian communal dominant parties—the DUP and Sinn Féin. The most surprising development was the installation of Paisley as first minister of the Stormont legislature in May 2007 alongside the deputy first minister of Sinn Féin, the former IRA operative and newfound peacemaker in the capacity of government minister, Martin McGuinness. The consociational setup proved to be a major historical undertaking after nearly five years of prorogued legislative governance in Ulster and the endless hours of work by the governments of Britain's Blair and Ireland's Ahern turned the tied toward peace and democratic peaceful cohabitation in Belfast. Watching the one-time sectarian Protestant pit bull Paisley settle into cohabitation with the IRA's parliamentary wing under Adams and McGuinness was a true sight for sore eyes after nearly 40 years of sectarian bloodshed and 3600 deaths in the region. Despite Blair's and Ahern's shortcomings as leaders, this would be remembered as one of their finest achievements.

Conclusion

New legislatures and executives in Scotland and Wales after 1999 and in Northern Ireland after 1998 brought renewed hope for Celtic citizenries. Having seen nationalist sentiment grow for years in Scotland and Wales, "New Labour" led by Prime Minister Blair in the UK delivered on long sought promises for devolution. According to most experts and pundits, Home Rule in the Celtic parts of mainland Britain was a mixed bag. Important political issues related to fiscal, health, and social affairs could be dealt with close to home in Edinburgh and Cardiff. Family-friendly policies that allowed female legislators to be both full-time mothers and politicians helped as well. The policies also helped fathers of young children at Holyrood. Women played greater roles in Celtic politics with the Welsh assembly the first ever 50% female representative body at a national level for any democracy globally. Yet, many problems came with devolution. Scandals dogged both the Scots and the Welsh and the anger over which political base London or the Celtic ones in Cardiff or Edinburgh would control the newly devolved executives ensued. The transitory nature of the first several months of the devolved executives at the start of the twenty-first century hurt the legitimacy of the devolved institutions in the eyes of the public. But, eventually both the first minister in Scotland, Labourite McConnell, and the first secretary in Wales, Labourite Morgan, had had time to develop some continuity and both had been in power long (McConnell for six years before being ousted by the SNP in 2007 and Morgan for seven years by the end of 2007) as Home Rule leaders for their nations so some continuity was coming.

The prospect of a return to consociational governance in Northern Ireland appeared to be very positive in 1998. But, problems with decommissioning of weapons and other inter-communalistic thorns continued to see a bipolar factionalism grow and even breathtakingly the electorates moving past the two major powers of Northern Irish politics (the UUP and the SDLP) to embrace the bilateral opposites, Sinn Féin and the DUP. This appeared to moot much progress in Ulster's long drawn-out peace process. However, the events of 2007 in Northern Ireland may suggest consociationalism may work as the lion and the lamb knelt together to bring Paisley and Adams together to attempt to end years of bloodshed and start a new chapter in the region's (Ulster's) politics. In the south of the green island, public opinion may be shifting somewhat and the growth of a viable government with oppositions and stable institutions in the Taoiseach and presidency in the Republic and integrating EU institutions playing a role in bringing Ireland together, institutional progress may continue to evolve. Celtic institutions may be similar to British ones, but the use of PR electoral systems and the political culture (which will be addressed in much detail in the next chapter) may help explain the institutional development as Celtic regions and institutions continue to mature democratically despite the problems manifested by each political context.

Suggestions for Further Reading and Research:

Collins, Neal and Terry Cradden. 2001. *Irish Politics Today*, 4th ed. Manchester: Manchester University Press.

Gallagher, Michael, Michael Marsh, and Paul Mitchell, eds. 2003. *How Ireland Voted 2002*. Houndsmill, Basingstoke, Hampshire, UK: Palgrave Macmillan.

Keating, Michael. 2005. The Government of Scotland: Public Policy Making After Devolution. Edinburgh: Edinburgh University Press.

Kissane, Bill. 2002. *Explaining Irish Democracy*. Dublin: University College Dublin Press.

Mitchell, Paul and Rick Wilford, eds. 1999. *Politics in Northern Ireland*. Boulder, CO: Westview Press.

CHAPTER SIX

Political Culture, Economics, and Culture in Celtic Life

Political Culture

Political culture is a key empirical component of any political system. The concept has been defined in numerous ways, but, in general, it is seen as the attitudes, values, and orientations of individuals toward their political system. Because it is fundamentally a psychological concept, it is the successor to the earlier concept known as "national character." The behavioral revolution in political science in the 1950s and 1960s refined national character somewhat to broaden its scope, yet make the study of political psychological orientations more precise. Thus, political culture was born with political scientists Gabriel A. Almond and Sidney Verba's seminal work, *The Civic Culture* (1963). The study of political culture entered its fifth decade after the start of the new millennium and despite its shortcomings, still enabled students to look at variables that may go a long way in explaining why citizens feel as they do about politics in given publics in both the developed and developing worlds. The concept of political culture enabled students to look at politics not just from elite perspectives, or time-honored legal-historical approaches, rather from an empirical approach to citizens' attitudes and feelings. Almond and Powell identified three key characteristics: 1) cognitive orientations; 2) affective orientations; and 3) evaluative orientations. The first describes political knowledge and beliefs of citizens; the second feelings of participation or negativity regarding politics; and the last describe opinions about politics. Citizens may evaluate their political systems based on these three categories and students may be able to study differences in the political cultures that in turn affect systemic evolution in politics in various societies both democratic and non-democratic alike.

Analytically, political culture is a key variable in explaining why some societies may evolve democratically and others may not. In the case of the Celtic fringe in the British Isles and Ireland, it may help us make sense of decidedly English political variables and processes vis-à-vis Celtic ones. However, the concept is not without its problems as it is at times a subjective one (lending itself to "nominal" status in a statistical analysis rather than the more quantitative "ordinal" data). Its tendency toward becoming a self-fulfilling prophecy explains why many find its place in political analysis to be subjective. For example, democratic political cultures such as the United Kingdom or the United States may be democratic and participatory because they are democratic states.

Of course, the logic of this circular reasoning is troublesome analytically and may condemn non-Western or non-democratic states to a permanent second class citizenship precisely because they do not have a mature or developed democratic polity and political culture. This then allows the critique of ethnocentrism to be leveled at Western political scientists. However, these weaknesses do not undermine the utility of political culture as an heuristic device or as a variable that helps us see the similarities and differences between Celtic political cultures and England's or the US's political culture.

Tied to political culture is the concept of political socialization. Political socialization is the process through which individuals learn about politics and their political values. In political science, the main agent of political socialization historically was the family. Other agents included schools, peers, religious institutions, and media. Also, the government itself and the community (or when both are combined—the polity) may affect how individuals learn about politics. In looking at these variables, one could see ways in which the varying institutions of Celtic politics may affect political cultures and make them distinct from Anglo-Saxon political culture. Some may argue that to talk about Celtic or Anglo-Saxon political cultures in the twenty-first century where globalization and multi-ethnic regions and sates see growing numbers of non-Celtic and non-English people assimilating into the British Isles and Ireland, such as South Asians in England or the Chinese in Scotland, is an atavistic conceptualization. However, the concepts are not meant to connote only ethno-cultural identification, but a broader socio-cultural and political identity tied to territory, structures, political beliefs, and post-industrial culture as well. The classical conceptualization of *Celtic political cultures* as parochial (narrowly defined along racial or cultural lines) as many developing political cultures were classified in the early twentieth century, has given way to a broader definition of subject and participant political cultures.

Scottish Political Culture

Scottish *political culture* has been shaped by institutions, ideologies, and myths, but most importantly to the Scots, their history, cultural traditions, and territory set them apart from the other nations and regions of the Celtic fringe and the UK. Unlike the Irish, who have historically had elements of authoritarianism within their political culture, the Scots pride themselves in a democratic political culture. Although, *the Kirk* (Church of Scotland) was seen historically as a conservative force, and even somewhat authoritarian in the *Scottish Reformation* era under *John Knox* in the sixteenth century, the Presbyterian nature of the Church led to a more egalitarian structure and ethos that filtered into Scottish political and social life. This cleavage was due to the hierarchical, conservative nature of the Anglican Church and the more democratic nature of the Kirk, which was still affecting Scottish and English politics and societies at the dawn of the twenty-first century, despite the fact that church attendance in the UK had dwindled to

12% of citizens who attended church once a week (compared to 47% in the United States).

Box 6.1: John Knox

John Knox, the fiery Calvinist preacher, has been elevated to hero status in Scotland largely due to his defense of the Kirk and his willingness to challenge the Scottish Catholic queen, Mary (she reigned from 1542-67). His interest in creating an autonomous church unfettered from English or French control and papal authority led him to rail against Mary and political settlements that would undermine Calvinism (a Christian doctrine which stressed predestination of the elect and removed itself from the interpretation of doctrine by Rome). Knox's petulance got him in trouble and put in jail, but it also laid the foundation for the Presbyterian form of Christianity without the hierarchy of Catholicism or the Episcopal model eventually adopted by the English in the wake of Henry VIII's break with Rome by 1540. Today, one can visit the John Knox house on High Street in Edinburgh. It is small and simple, dour and austere, much like Knox himself must have been.

The historical tension between liberalism and socialism, especially after the rise of Kier Hardie's Scottish Labour Party after 1888 and the impact of the UK Labour Party after 1900 evinces Scottish politics' links directly to political culture. A similar transformation occurred in Wales as industrialization led to a partisan electoral shift away from the devolutionary, free trading, and socially altruistic Liberal Party to the centralizing, Marxist, workers-oriented Labour Party over a 50 year period. By 1959, Labour had become Scotland's national party and much of this transformation was due to the growth of Scottish industry in the central lowlands where shipbuilding in Glasgow and metals mining were proliferating. Still, with Edinburgh as one of the UK's capitals of education, finance, law, and services, the liberal, progressive strain of politics was still in operation leaving Scotland with a kind of dualistic political culture that evinced a blending of liberalism and communalism.

The historical institutions of the Kirk of the mid-nineteenth century endured fissures as evangelicals broke free to form offshoots that were more literalist in their interpretation of scripture. First, the Free Presbyterian Church of Scotland (the "Wee Frees") and then the *"Wee Wee Frees"* (who broke from the Free Church) due to doctrinal disputes, saw the Kirk fragment much like many mainstream denominations in the Protestant world in the latter part of the twentieth and early twenty-first century. The Church of Scotland provided education in the Scottish school system and these schools were sectarian, but this has changed somewhat over the years.

Scots law, the brand of civil or code law applied to the legal context in Scotland is qualitatively different from Anglo-American common law. Scots law is based on codified rules that derived from the amalgamation of Scottish legal precedents and common law-based actions (inherited from Scotland's links with England). Today, some statutes from the pre-1707 Scottish parliament still stand

and these are still referred to in Scottish law although they are written in the Scots language. Scots law came from several historical origins including ancient Celtic law from the 1000s and laws from the areas of Viking control in northern and eastern Scotland, including the Udal law found in the Orkneys and Shetlands. This law is a Norse-based legal system that is occasionally recognized by Scottish judges in the cases dealing with tort (property) law in these northern Scottish isles. Scots law, which was based on code law which came from the Romans, got its modern-day origins in the advent of the Scottish parliament in the late 1200s. Today, some differences between English common law and Scots law persist in the area of property and one major difference is in the criminal law where sentencing can produce a "guilty," "not guilty," or "not proven" verdict, the latter two resulting in acquittal. The last verdict, "not proven" is unique to Scots law and would be loosely analogous to the plea of "no contest" in American courts (when a defendant will not admit guilt, but will bear a light punishment). In the "not proven" verdict the defendant walks free and no subsequent trial can occur (like American double jeopardy) if a jury cannot prove the charges. A case in a court in Perth, Scotland found a 21 year-old man innocent of murdering his mother in 2005 based on a "not proven" verdict. The decision was controversial with the woman's family angered by the verdict and advocates of her son saying not enough evidence could be found (despite him having a poor alibi and blood on him—the outcry was similar to the 1995 OJ Simpson trial in the United States, although less sensationalized). Scotland's system of law is seen as an amalgamation of legal approaches and it is similar to legal systems in the Republic of South Africa, Quebec, and the American state of Louisiana. Today, a combination of codified law, English common law, and European Union (EU) law all factor into the interpretation and promulgation of Scots law, thus making it part of the political context in Scotland that affects the distinct Scottish political culture.

Scots tend to be cooperative and accepting of bargaining in a democratic sense on issues related to politics and economics. The great question related to Scottish political culture is the relationship of individualism (liberalism) and communalism. As was championed by many thinkers and writers in the eighteenth and nineteenth centuries (such as the famous Scottish novelist *Sir Walter Scott*), Scotland was conceptualized as a bastion of *liberalism* (later to be translated literally into political power in Scotland by the Gladstonian party that held sway there in the late nineteenth and early twentieth centuries). This liberalism was seen in the individualist intentions of the Scottish crofter (small farmer) who was doggedly independent, devout religiously, and a dutiful UK citizen, despite his or her interests in maintaining a distinct national Scottish identity. The individualism persisted in a kind of rise of a meritocracy in Scotland via the *Kailyard culture* of the late nineteenth century (roughly 1880–1914). This culture was displayed when in Scotland's small villages and rural areas, the local minister, who was often the local school teacher, would help promote youth from rural crofting families up through the local ranks of the educational system on to Edinburgh, Aberdeen, or Glasgow for university training and then on to professional careers in the Church, medicine, politics, higher education, the law, and other professions. This function of Scotland's professions gave the Scots the proud achievement of saying their educational system was superior to other Celtic ones in Britain as well as the English system. As sociologist David McCrone says there is some truth to the fact that Scots were better educated than their English compatriots and this feeling persisted into the nineteenth century. He argues that that the Kailyard culture led to a conservative meritocracy that was not as egalitarian as many nationalists like to reinvent (McCrone 1992). But, certainly, this may be one area of political culture that is similar to the United States, where merit was a consideration over class at times (unlike England prior to the twentieth century and even into the early years of that century) where youth could achieve professional status via advanced levels of education. Sir Robert Strachan Wallace is an example of the effects of the Kailyard culture. Wallace was from the small Highland hamlet of Kinknockie, Scotland (literally about four farm houses). His father was the blacksmith for the local laird's family farm spread over many acres in the rolling farm land along the North Sea just a few miles north of Aberdeen (one of the few places in the world where one will see seagulls perched atop cows!) After education in local schools around the wee northeastern Scottish burghs of Old Deer and Clola, Wallace, was from an evangelically devout Free Presbyterian family which had 13 children and several went on to serve as Free Presbyterian ministers (one ministered in Liverpool, England to the local Scottish diaspora), went to university first in Aberdeen and then to Oxford where he took masters degrees in English. He then joined the teaching profession and took a professorship at the University of Melbourne where he became one of Australia's leading Shakespeare experts. He also served in the ANZAC—joint Australia-New Zealand—forces in the Great War and eventually ended up at the University of Sydney (Australia's top university). In 1941, he was named vice chancellor of the University of Sydney (the equivalent of the American college or university president). He served in that capacity until 1947 and given his service he was singled out for honors from King George VI who knighted him in 1946. This may evince the meritocratic rise of peasant youth in the Kailyard culture. Interestingly, another feature of Wallace's story was that some in his own family back in Scotland were less than enthused given the "English" king's gesture which did not sit well with their Scottish sensibilities!

Box 6.2: The Highland Clearances

Perhaps one of the most notorious of events in modern Scottish history is the removal of peasant families from the land they farmed and tended by the Scottish landlords from around 1790–1830. The landlords had taken their marching orders from the English aristocracy for centuries. They decided to toss the peasants and replace their work on the land with sheep farming in order to make more money and use of the land for grazing. This event seems to stick in the memories of Scots, especially Highlanders, like other political initiatives in European history, such as the great Potato famine in Ireland in the 1840s or the collectivization of agriculture in Stalinist Russia in the early 1930s. It was this event that stoked what would become modern Scottish nationalism, although it would be more cultural and literary in the nineteenth century.

We shall return to nationalism, but first the concept of *communalism* is one that many Scots link to egalitarian culture, which some argue is a staple of Scottish political culture, and others argue is more a myth. Given Labour's political dominance in Scotland since 1959 and the Liberal Party's rise prior and its increasing challenge to Labour and the Scottish National Party (SNP) since 1999 in both Scottish parliamentary and Westminster elections, many political scientists would argue that Scotland is much more communalistic than England. Cultural anthropologist Jonathan Hearn argues that Scotland has been shaped by competing individualist (liberal) and communalistic claims by political and social forces and its own institutions over its history. Thus, much of what is found in the political culture are self-fulfilling prophecies of how groups and elites have dictated the political discourse and created distinctly Scottish institutions to make Scotland what it is. Scotland's communalism may be tied to an egalitarian strain found most prominently in the Kirk where the Presbyterian model reflects a more broadly defined, democratic agreement among ministers who even today try to inject their political views into the church and society at several levels. The importance of religion in Scotland has seen tension historically between Catholics and Protestants (like the conflicts in Ireland and Ulster), especially during the British Civil Wars. But, the nineteenth century saw Irish Catholic immigrants descend on Scotland and Catholics played an important role in the growth of the Labour Party in Scotland, as Hearn notes (Hearn 2000). Much of Labour's historical socialism in Scotland may have less to do with Marx's teachings and more to do with communalism that is colored by the hue of Catholic doctrines on social, economic, and moral issues. Political scientists Ian Budge and Cornelius O'Leary's important study (1973) comparing Glasgow and Belfast suggests a major difference between the Northern Irish and Scottish contexts. Both cities have virtually the same religious demographics, but Scotland is more of a democratic political culture compared to Northern Ireland. What accounts for this? Despite salient religious tensions and even bigotry (seen in the Old Firm Celtic-Rangers rivalry on the football pitch—see box 6.10), the differences may say more about influences from the south of Ireland as exogenous variables in Northern Irish political life (nationalism) and those from the south on the British mainland (Anglo-Saxon democratic norms—compromise, negotiation, and civility in problem solving) as exogenous variables in Scottish life (Budge and O'Leary 1973).

Nationalism has been an important, yet not indispensable part of Scottish politics since the 1920s. As seen in Chapter Four, the rise of the SNP has brought the issue of independence to the fore in the 1990s, but Home Rule (as seen in Chapter Three) was an important part of the Scottish political discussion. Although most Scots see nationalism as part of the political landscape, rarely have more than 50% wanted outright independence. In 1998, over 50% wanted independence with the numbers trailing off to 42–49% in 1999 and 2000 (see Lynch 2002, p. 245). Unlike Ireland, where Irish Catholics have seen their political culture imbued with nationalism, anti-English colonialism, and anti-British sentiments in Northern Ireland, Scotland's nationalism was always a kind of bourgeois nationalism which would evolve via the ballot box rather than the gun.

Irish Political Culture

For a nation-state of four million, which stood at 6.5 million in 1841, the Republic of Ireland has evolved as a distinct European nation-state, despite 700 years of British overlordship prior to its divorcement from the British Commonwealth in 1949. Several variables affect Irish political culture. According to political scientist Basil Chubb, they include, nationalism, the influence of the British, religion (viz. *Irish Roman Catholicism*), an historical agrarian society (that has given way to a post-industrial service-driven state), an anti-intellectual climate (which he argues is fostered by the Church), and a loyalty to the Free State that has left an indelible mark in the fiercely independent Irish mindset (Chubb 1992). Another variable that may be part of the historical legacy of the English on Éire is the impact on the Republic exerted by the six northern counties.

British control and its roots are discussed in detail in Chapter Two, but Irish assimilation into the UK was always difficult given the religious, linguistic, and social differences between the Irish and British. Although different from other Catholic states and regions, Ireland's Catholic population was constantly on the defensive and threatened by Protestant usurpation once Elizabeth I sent landlords to colonize most of the north of the Emerald Isle. By the nineteenth century, assimilation saw a drop in the number of Irish speakers which in part explained the rise of Irish nationalism that led to both inchoate forms of violence by 1848 and calls for Home Rule via the parliamentary route. This in turn saw nationalism grow and weave its way into the hearts of Irish Catholics who valued the *Irish Gaelic* language, were proud of their *agrarian society* and traditions, and saw the Church as a distinctive institution vis-à-vis the imperial overlords who ruled from across the Irish Sea. The one variable that appears to be significantly different from the democratic political context that evolved in other parts of the Celtic fringe and the British mainland was the inclusion of authoritarian attitudes (as Chubb argues). Some would see this as synonymous with conservatism whereby the Church was more hierarchical, the family was paternalistic with males domineering, and the Catholic clergy controlled the nation's schools. Chubb recognizes the paradox of authoritarian attitudes and the evolving democracy in Éire (Chubb 1992).

However, the role the gun began to play in politics once the IRA burst on the scene in 1919 may suggest a confirmation of this supposition that the *Irish Civil War* of 1922 was a bloody intra-Irish feud (4000 perished) and the excessive violence in the north from 1969–2004 (where 3600 died) may be a reflection of the authoritarian variable in the political culture. Chubb's argument may be problematic given that even Scotland, Wales, and England have seen authoritarianism in their histories, but a normative framework based on theories of democratization and modernization may suggest that the Irish authoritarian values are really more conservative social values based on the importance of family, church, schools, and nationalism and Irish traditions that play important roles in the lives of the Irish. Historically, some have argued that the local Catholic priest (who may have also been a school teacher) was the most important figure in the Irish village up to the mid-twentieth century. This sounds familiar in the supposed Kailyard culture of Scotland in the late nineteenth century where the local Kirk minister played a similar role. Thus, a conservative political culture may be transformed as we saw passage of an amendment repealing the divorce provision in the Republic's Constitution in 1996, a female president (Mary Robinson in 1990), greater tolerance for liberal ideas, and a decline in Church attendance by 2006 (despite a high number of baptized Catholic citizens in Éire). Some Irish may not see some of these as positive, but the state had certainly become more like its British and EU neighbors by the onset of the twenty-first century.

Welsh Political Culture

On the surface Welsh political culture could be characterized by less class consciousness than what was historically seen in England. Like other Celtic political cultures of early modern and recent history, religion, especially non-conformity, has affected the national consciousness, especially after the Welsh revival of the late eighteenth century. Finally, the rise, decline, and comeback, in the late twentieth century, of the Welsh language not only helped develop a sense of Welshness, but began to create a greater collective identity for the Welsh. Although each of these suppositions is true, it does not tell the complete story about Wales's political culture since the nation's political culture is much more complex and a somewhat of a work in progress.

Like Scotland and Ireland (and Northern Ireland), religion plays a key role in the historical and recent foundations of Welsh national character. The importance of Methodism and the *chapel culture* in challenging the basic assumptions of the Anglo-centric socio-political order furthered gains by non-conformists who then by 1920 had gotten political outcomes to codify their religious identity. In this social context, *evangelical Christianity* was very important. It not only reinforced the Christian maxim that God was "no respecter of persons," but that all Welsh were inherently equal as citizens, irrespective of class or economic and social rank. Ironically, the doctrines of the non-conformists (Methodists, Calvinists, Baptists, etc) were, by the nineteenth century, laying the foundations for the Welsh working class's lurch leftward politically by the 1920s and embracing the Labour Party and its socialism based on the teachings of Karl

Marx. The religious teachings also laid the groundwork for the evolution of a nationalist movement made up of a patchwork of groups who saw injustices in England's longstanding dominance of tiny Wales. The English were seen as the economic, political, and social arbiters of the Welsh people, culture, and land. Some Welsh had no problems with this perception; others were angered by it and conceptualized it as reality. Of course, politically, being governed from London did mean Anglo-Saxon-dominated democratic government was English-led for the Welsh. For hard core nationalists, they at times put the English-Welsh relationship into virtual biblical terms (e.g. David versus Goliath).

Although religion is an important aspect of Wales's political culture, even if it is used only to distinguish its national character from England, it may not always help explain the complexity of social and linguistic differences in Wales itself. Wales's social evolution is complicated given the effects of 1283 and 1536 on the nation. Not only did the Normans stick vassals in the Marches after 1066, Edward I and Henry VIII kept English lords in place to govern along with the indigenous Welsh elite. Thus, an Anglo-Welsh identity evolved as well (as opposed to a purely Welsh identity). An example of this can be found in the family of Thomas Jefferson, third president of the United States (Jefferson is one of four American presidents of Welsh origin, the others are James Monroe—father of the US Constitution, Abraham Lincoln—the great emancipator of the slaves, and Calvin Coolidge of the 1920s). Jefferson's family history says the family came from the Snowdonia region of northern Wales near Llanberis (with a population today of 2,100). The family supposedly stayed in the region until approximately 1200 and then moved to Herefordshire, England along the border of Wales to become English squires under the Normans. The Anglicized Jeffersons thus stayed in Herefordshire until the early 1600s when they left rural England for rural Virginia in America. The Jeffersons mirror the complexities of *Anglo-Welsh identity*, similar (in reverse) of Anglo-Irish identity in Ireland after 1600 and the Tudor and Stewart placement of English landlords who became Irish over dozens of generations. Still at the start of the twenty-first century thousands of Welsh live in a *Welsh diaspora* in England, especially in London. This tradition goes back centuries given migration patterns due to social, economic, and other reasons. Thus, Welshness is not an easy thing to empirically identify given the closer history between England and Wales than other parts of the Celtic fringe. Although Welsh nationalists like to minimize this important fact and argue that national identity is all or nothing, in fact, Wales at the start of the twenty-first century saw the schizophrenia of multiple identities affecting it including the role of Welshness tied to language only. With the northern areas of Wales seen as the home of the ancient kings of Wales and home to more indigenous speakers of the Welsh tongue, the south is seen as more cosmopolitan and a mixture of linguistic orientations. This of course is an overlay on the complex industrial evolution in Wales during the late nineteenth and early twentieth centuries as mass migration of miners went from north to south Wales to find work, thus changing the social and political landscape. By the twentieth century's end, national character in Wales could still be thought of as a nation with collective (generally Labour-oriented) sentiments, but with a nationalist tinge in countering England's influence (although the extent to which that influence was rejected was debatable and opinion mixed—much like Quebeckers' narrow vote on separation from Canada in 1995 which saw a nationalist-liberal unionist divide.) Although the chapel culture and Christian nonconformity tapered off in its day-to-day effect in the Welsh psyche (some say due to its devoutness and strictness) and a large drop in attendance and participation (although Welsh churchgoing is still higher than England's which stands at 12% of the adult population attending once a week or more). The mines still play a role today (as some have converted workers and contexts to heavy manufacturing plants), but not the magnitude of the nineteenth and early twentieth centuries. Economics has changed drastically and a post-industrial society in Wales (as in all the UK) has seen a rise in the salience of services (financial, education, legal, retail, wholesale, and tourism). Thus, with greater non-Welsh and non-British immigration Wales is now becoming more multicultural like other parts of the Celtic fringe (although less so than England which has seen large pockets of immigration from Africa, Asia, and eastern Europe in the last 40 years.)

Box 6.3: Welsh Chapel Culture and Men's Choral Tradition

The Methodist, Baptist, and Congregational evangelism of Wales during the nineteenth centuries saw some 5000 chapels built throughout the country. In the nineteenth century some 80% of the Welsh people belonged to a *capel* (the Welsh word for "chapel). Not happy with the narrow Anglo-centric Church of Wales (the Anglican version there) which forced parishioners to speak and listen in English, the nonconformist denominations allowed worship and sermons in the indigenous tongue. Thousands of coalminers and other laborers would toil and sweat by day and worship at night and also pour their own money and sweat into building the actual chapels; some small villages had several. By the late twentieth century, church attendance had dropped off some argue due to modern entertainment replacing the fiery evangelical services others arguing that the once evangelical nonconformist groups had moved to more of a social orientation away from preaching the Bible and its message. This had an effect on the world-famous all-male Welsh choirs which were found all over the nation and grew with the chapel movement. Despite the demise in chapel attendance in the twentieth century, the Welsh all-male *a cappella* style of singing is still popular today with several left in the region, but admittedly, the aging singing force is finding it hard to recruit young men to sing under 40 years of age given other popular forms of music and entertainment. The American-based Society for the Preservation of Barbershop Quartet Singing in America is a vestige of this *a cappella* harmonizing tradition. The two most famous Welsh choral anthems that could be heard in the chapels or coming from the coal pits of south Wales in the 1880s are *Cwm Rhondda* (the Welsh word for the "Rhondda Valley") and synonymous with the great hymn "Guide Me, O Thou Great Jehovah" by the Welshman William Williams (1745) and memorably sung in Welsh at the beginning of the Academy Award winning film, "How Green Was My Valley" (1941) and by a Welsh Choir at Princess Diana's funeral at Westminster Abbey in 1997. The other great Welsh choral song is the military-style march "Men of Harlech" (*Rhyfelgyrch gwr Harlech* in the Welsh) which was composed in the late eighteenth century and is about the soldiers of Owain Glyn Dŵr fighting the English and the Prince of Wales (the future Henry V) in 1408 at Harlech Castle in the northern part of Wales.

Political Culture in Northern Ireland

Because it is divided religiously and politically, Northern Ireland, or the Six Counties that are part of the UK, known to Britons as *Ulster*, has a curious, complex political culture. As Irish journalist and historian Tim Pat Coogan reminds us, the historical Ulster (which republicans in the north and southerners see it as) was the nine northernmost counties of the Emerald Isle (Coogan 2002a). Today, three northern "Ulster" counties (Cavan, Donegal, and Monaghan) are part of the Republic, the other six (Antrim, Armagh, Down, Fermanagh, Londonderry, and Tyrone) are controlled by Britain. To use the term "Ulster" to describe Northern Ireland has politically-loaded ramifications (see Box 6.4 below). Thus, where one sits in the Northern Irish political culture will inform how one responds to this conundrum. Simply put, the communalistic/segmented orientation of the Northern Irish will tell much about where they sit in the Six Counties' political culture. Normally, a Catholic will align with *republicans* and *nationalists* whereas a Protestant will align with *unionists* and *loyalists*. Because the political culture is directly affected, and even driven at times, by exogenous variables such as the government in the south in Dublin and the UK government in London, and loyalty to these external, non-Northern Irish governments, the political culture is much more complicated than a superficial reading of it.

Box 6.4: Loyalists vs. Republicans, Protestants vs. Catholics

In the fractured politics of Northern Ireland, the usage of various terminologies is necessary to understand the historical conflict between Catholics and Protestants. Most Catholics tend to view themselves as Irish republicans. That is, those who believe the Six Counties in the north should be part of the "Republic" of 26 Counties in the south, known today as "Ireland," a country of 4 million with its capital in Dublin. Most Protestants in the north tend to see themselves as loyalists. That is, those who believe Northern Ireland should remain tied to the United Kingdom as a province of the British government (which has 55 million citizens) with its central government in London. Thus, Protestants feel a sense of "loyalty" to the monarchy and British state. The divide between loyalists and republicans corresponds with the terms "unionist" and "nationalist" with the former favoring ties to the United Kingdom and the latter favoring ties to the Republic of Ireland in the south via a nationalist or break-away politics. Making this such a difficult political context is the fact that in 1937, the Irish leader, Éamon De Valera wrote into the Irish Constitution (a written document, like the United States's) that the Six Counties of the north were part of the southern Republic (giving de jure, or legal, constitutional authority in southern Irish eyes to the Dublin government over Northern Ireland). Of course, unionists having won partition in 1920 with the UK's divisive government of Ireland Act which effectively created separate governments in Belfast for a Protestant-dominated region and one in Dublin for nationalists. This political and legal quandary simmered and blew up at varying times from the 1920s into the 1960s, but exploded in 1969. The use of the terms "Northern Ireland" and "Ulster" are fraught with political significance and disagreement among republicans and unionists. Unionists use the term "Ulster" to describe the Six Counties under British rule in Ireland. Republicans point out that the historical Ulster was nine counties in the north (of which three in the north are part of the southern Republic today). So, the use of Ulster has historical and normative connotations for both sides. Towns like Derry (to nationalists) and Londonderry (to loyalists) evince the strong feelings of how each ethno-sectarian community views places through its specific political lens. Most would see this as an intra-Irish conflict and consider all in Northern Ireland Irish, but some Ulstermen and women see themselves as distinctly British and not Irish. Of course, nationalists are proud of their Irish heritage and ties to the southern Republic. The irony is that many of Ulster's Protestants descend from Scottish Presbyterians and thus are fellow Celts along with their Irish Catholic neighbors. There was a sizeable influx of English Anglicans throughout the north as well. But, it was from the north part of Ireland that the Gaels invaded Scotland and knocked out the Picts to make Scotland a land of "Scots" ("Pirates"—in the Gaelic—form Ireland). Making the context of Protestants and Catholics in Northern Ireland more intriguing and muddled was the fact that not all loyalists were Protestant and vice versa. Protestant Ivan Cooper was one of the main forces behind the Civil Rights Association in Northern Ireland and was the main focus of the January 1972 Derry civil rights march which ended with 13 dead. That event is known today as "Bloody Sunday" recreated in an award-wining movie in 2002. Also, some Catholic workers were known to support unionist parties that might work toward bringing home economic benefits in Ulster over the years. Indeed, politics was perplexing, rife with sectarianism, and bloody by the late twentieth century in Northern Ireland. And even though labels and terminology may be confusing, it helps to know them to sort out Northern Ireland's complex political landscape.

For the British in Ulster, national identity evolved into a mixture of responses. Since the Irish and the UK were formally united in 1801, UK identity was generally accepted in four of the six counties of "British" Ulster. Historian Paul Ward argues that three types of national identities are found in Ulster. First, a Gladstonian orientation which saw the UK as a multi-national liberal settlement among the nations of the UK and Ireland and devolution (if it could be delivered by the Liberals) would allow the Irish to figure out their own version of Celtic *Britishness* like the Scots and the Welsh. Second, Britishness would bring the Anglicization of Ireland and a suppression of Irish identity. In some ways, this occurred in Ulster proper after 1922 until nationalists and republicans started agitating in the late 1960s. Last, the idea that Northern Irish identity was based on a regional in the capacity of British identity was important to many Protestants in Ulster (Ward 2004). Thus, London governed politically, but regions whether Celtic or British would have cultural and social differences. This kind of regionalism may have led to a strong kinship between Ulster and England politically and culturally, but it may have outstripped its usefulness as *Ulster Protestants* maintained a Victorian linkage to Great Britain's Empire and

Kingdom, while the English and other Celts moved beyond the anachronistic views and slogans of a bygone era. However, with the EU playing a more prominent role in national and regional politics in European countries, regionalism in the UK after 1997 may have returned to impact each of the Celtic regions (including Ulster) in important ways—governance through the backdoor.

According to Ward, the British identity in Ulster was tied to the Britishness of its capital, Belfast. Belfast was seen as a great imperial English city. Its ambience reflected the culture of the majority of the *Scotch-Irish* people in the city. Ulsterpersons were hardworking, austere, had an air of hospitality, and individualistic (much like their eastern Celtic cousins, the Scots). The Protestants of Ulster were similar to other UK citizens on the British mainland. The minority Catholics in Northern Ireland were not characterized the same way. *Northern Irish Catholics* were seen as communalistic, attended Catholic schools, learned and spoke Irish Gaelic, engaged in *Gaelic sports*, were socialized into nationalism, and learned Irish history (from the Free State's perspective). Protestants were socialized into British culture by learning British history, a love for English football and non-Irish sports (one of the greatest English top division professional soccer players ever was the Northern Irish international star, of the 1960s and 1970s, George Best, who was affectionately known in England at Manchester United as the "Belfast Boy"), they believed Catholics were a threat to the Protestant identity of Ulster, and that Catholics were underachievers (Ward 2004). Protestants celebrated the July 12 provincial holiday of William of Orange's victory over Charles II at the Battle of Boyne in 1690 (in Northern Ireland). This event brought the loyalist marching season to bear and in July 1996 as the British government tried to dissuade Orangemen from the Orange Order from marching in Catholic neighborhoods in Northern Ireland, a standoff with police occurred at Drumcree which saw force applied. The resulting force used on Catholics in their areas was even more resolute and led to an escalation in tensions and the perpetual return to square one in peace negotiations between the UK government and the parties involved.

Because of the salience of the *sectarian division* in Northern Ireland, deep cleavages in the economic, cultural, social, and political landscape emerged as well. Thus, the statelet's political culture was poisoned. It was difficult finding ways to bring the Catholic and Protestant communities together. This continued to be a challenge especially after 1969 and the start of the troubles. By 1998, and the Good Friday Agreement (GFA), several alternatives for the future of Northern Ireland were under serious review by officials in Northern Ireland, the UK, and the Irish governments. Political scientist Lord Norton of Louth (Philip Norton) has identified four solutions to the Ulster question: First, *"direct rule"* from London has been reality since 1972. It stopped briefly in 1998 until 2002 and conflict between the political communities and IRA activity resumed and direct control of Ulster was re-imposed by the Blair government until early 2007. Control from London allows for the UK to impose its will quicker on its wayward province, but it also leaves a lasting impression of authoritarianism and colonialism as well. Second, the UK usually supported devolution and some sort of *"power-sharing assembly."* This assembly was reality between 1998 and 2002 (see Chapter Five) and after early 2007. But, without significant Catholic participation and a North-South Irish component that forces Ulster to interact with the Dublin government, this option has, at times, been problematic. The third solution, a federated Ireland, is generally unpalatable to the Protestants because they would go from being a majority in Northern Ireland to a small minority in Ireland as a whole. Catholics in Northern Ireland would prefer this option for obvious reasons, but again, the socio-political climate is complex and divisions between Northern and Southern republicans may come to the fore if this option were applied. However, the 1998 GFA sought greater North-South dialogue and cooperation along quasi-federal lines with the North-South Council of Ireland. The last option is the one that most English and UK subjects favor, letting the decades-long headache of Ulster go quietly toward independence. Northern Ireland as a sovereign nation-state (autonomous and separate from Ireland and the UK) would be seen as distinctly Northern Irish. Perhaps, it was a bit like an independent Bosnia after 1995 and the former Yugoslav state. Of course that comparison may not bode well for that option, but polls in the UK since the 1980s have shown a plurality (35-36%) of citizens favoring independence; although, this is not a majority of respondents, a full one-third want Britain and Éire out of Ulster and to let the troubled statelet go its own way (Norton 1994). The late UK premier, James Callaghan, who led a Labour government from 1976–79, favored this option. He had also served as secretary of state for Northern Ireland and knew the issue all too well. Most believe this option would be difficult to create given the deep fissures in the society. The most recent consociational solution (see Chapter Two) that was a byproduct of the GFA of 1998 and appeared to be moving forward by 2007. Certainly, the context that had seen much sadness for nearly 40 years was beginning to find peaceful ways to change the region's political culture.

Scotland's Economy

Part of any political culture is a nation's economic orientation. Oftentimes, political scientists, historians, sociologists, and economists, simplify economic variables to one or two key empirical components in a nation's social, political, and economic context. Thus, the picture appears relatively straightforward and easy to conceptualize. For centuries, Scotland has been seen as a rural agrarian nation with a heavy dose of fishing-oriented enterprise to supplement its agrarian ways. At the start of the twenty-first century, in the Highlands, *crofting* (or small farming) is done, but like other post-industrialized regions of the world technology has changed the agricultural economy much.

By the mid-nineteenth century, Scotland began to develop its industrial economy. Ship building, textiles production (from the American colonies' cotton), and various types of mining led to an industrial boom and greater wealth concentrating in and around Glasgow (or the Clydeside area as Scots call it).

This area today is well over 1.5 million people (rivaling Manchester and Birmingham as Britain's largest urban metroplex after London). Today, Glasgow proper has 600,000 people making it Scotland's largest city. In the 1740s, Glasgow had 17,000 citizens and by 1840s it had 200,000. The industrial boom brought Highlanders and immigrants from Ireland to Clydeside. Today, four-fifths of Scottish residents live in the central belt in the Lowlands stretching from Glasgow to Edinburgh. From 1802, shipbuilders were building large steam vessels (similar to the HMS *Titanic*) and sailing them down the Forth estuary into the Irish Sea. In 30 years time 95 ships had been built and several large ocean liners would be used from 1882–1947 to send UK nationals (Scots, Irish, and Welsh) to Ellis Island in New York harbor where many American ancestors landed. Given the demand for iron and coal, two commodities that were indispensable in building ships, Scottish miners become an important labor force. Indeed, by the 1860s the Liberals were tapping into worker disaffection and by 1888 in Scotland Keir Hardie's Scottish Labour Party was poised to represent workers and unions at the political table. After the Second World War, the demand for iron, coal, and ships (with the advent of mass air transit) saw a downward spiral. The post-industrial economy saw the growth in public and private services, tourism, etc. By the early 1970s, as in Wales in the late 1980s, most mining operations were closing and shipbuilding had all but ended. Various types of manufacturing, including multinational capital had started moving into Scotland and the UK years before. One example was the earthmoving and equipment giant Caterpillar. It had a plant at Tanochside that had basic assembly-line work for unskilled and semi-skilled laborers. The plant closed in 1987 and workers rebelled by taking control of the plant and painting a solitary tractor pink! Thus, touching off the divisive politics in Scotland of communalistic working class militancy versus more liberal, yet empathetic moderate social democracy that wants capital regulated, but not necessarily controlled by the state. Although the Thatcher years brought increased unemployment in the aggregate (from 1979–90) throughout the UK, lessening inflation and a monetarist macroeconomic policy brought more investment to Scotland from the rest of the UK and from other parts of the globe. Edinburgh became the Scottish Silicon Valley with the manufacturing of high tech electronic goods. A similar structural result occurred in the Republic of Ireland in the 1990s as it opened its economy more under the EU. Computers, microprocessors, and the like were now part of Celtic economies to go along with Scottish whiskey, Scottish and Irish fishing, and farming in both nations.

For Scots, economically and politically, one of the biggest issues of the post-industrial era has been *oil*. Crude oil was discovered in 1970 in British Petroleum's Forties Field off Scotland's coast in the North Sea. Almost overnight Aberdeen became a boomtown as investment in the harbor and offshore facilities took off. The Aberdeen airport (located in the suburb of Dyce) grew as well and opened a heliport which is now the world's most used. Aberdeen, a city of 400,000, and Scotland's third largest city and the largest city in the north of the UK, grew by 60,000 people in the 1970s and by 1985 around 2.6 million barrels of oil a day were being produced. The next year, oil fell to $10 per barrel and the local economy turned sour. Economic growth in the late 1990s helped the oil industry which is still the staple of the local economy in Aberdeen. Around 10,000–15,000 people live on 130 oil rigs in the North Sea today. Despite stiff competition from Germany, Norway, Denmark, and other British coastal towns, Aberdeen still hauls in a lion's share of Scottish oil that has had a profound impact on the local Scottish and UK economies.

Scotland's financial sector has grown in terms of output, employees, and importance to the European regional and global economies. In the 1990s, Scotland's two main banks, Royal Bank of Scotland (RBS) and Bank of Scotland, were banks of local importance in the UK, but as the twenty-first century began, both grew and acquired other banks. As of 2005, both were in the top 20 banks in the world in terms of market capitalization. From 2000–05, the *Scottish financial services sector* grew 37%, four times faster than the growth of the Scottish economy and twice as fast as the UK financial services economic sector. As Scotland's profile was raised vis-à-vis other European financial centers, Scottish politicians began to take notice and the Liberal Democrats' Jim Wallace, one-time Scottish enterprise minister, called for both public and private sectors to keep up with its fast-paced English rivals, the cities of Manchester and Leeds. He believed Glasgow and Edinburgh should compete with Zurich, Frankfurt, Munich, and London for capital and growth in the financial sector of the economy. By 2005, 51% of Scotland's finance economy jobs were found in Edinburgh and 26% in Glasgow (the UK's second largest city). The Bank of Scotland (*Banca na h-Alba* in the *Gàidhlig*) was created by the Scottish parliament in 1695 and the RBS was chartered by the UK monarchy in 1727. Both have been longstanding rivals. RBS acquired National Westminster bank in 2000 and the Bank of Scotland merged with Halifax bank, creating Halifax-Bank of Scotland (HBOS) in 2001. Both banks joined together, despite their rivalry, to fend off UK treasury action to force Scottish and Northern Irish banks to pay £80 million ($141.893 million) a year to issue their own banknotes. Interestingly, both have become multinational corporations (MNC) with RBS having 18,000 workers in Scotland (a mere 13% of its global workforce). HBOS has 17,759 employees in Scotland (25% of its global staff). HBOS still has its global headquarters on the historical Mound in Edinburgh, contributing to the continued importance of Edinburgh and Scotland as an important UK, European, and developing global financial sector.

With a commitment to social democracy (in the European sense) and a modicum of statism within a liberalizing global economic context, the Scots still have some nationalized sectors. One of those is in the area of water. *Scottish Water* is the nationalized water and sewage service of Scotland. Different from sewer and water services in England and Wales, Scottish water services have not been de-nationalized, they are owned and operated by the devolved Scottish government in Edinburgh. In 2002, the nationalized Scots water system became a conglomeration of regional power systems that were merged together (West of Scotland Water, East of Scotland Water, and North of Scotland Water). By

2006, some £1.8 billion was being invested by the government into 1500 water-based projects in Scotland to modernize the water system and provide improved services to citizens. It gave water and waste services to five million clients in 2.2 million homes and 130,000 business clients in Scotland. As a publicly-owned business, it does about £1 billion in business per year placing it in the top twenty Scottish businesses and it has nearly 3700 employees. Its home office is in Dunfermline, northwest of Edinburgh in the east part of the central lowlands (scottishwater.co.uk).

The Irish Economy

The staple of the Republic's economy prior to Home Rule in 1921 and after was always the family farm. Agriculture took on an importance not only economically in Ireland, but its socio-political relevance was tied to its hold over the livelihoods of Irish people and the symbolic value for nationalist leaders, such as Éamon de Valera, who saw in the Irish peasantry the ultimate symbol of Gaelic culture and tradition. Despite the drop in population, after the Potato famine of the mid-nineteenth century, Ireland remained a peasant-based economy. Largely because the industrial revolution that hit England's large cities in the nineteenth century failed to reach the outer edges of the British Isles and thus a true industrial core and rural periphery ensconced itself in the UK in a way that saw the peripheries of Wales (its western and northern areas), Scotland (the Highlands and islands), and Ireland all remained essentially rural, non-industrialized regions of the Celtic fringe. The economic evolution that brought industrial growth, labor movements, secularization, and greater wealth to the urban areas of the UK failed to materialize in these peripheral Celtic areas. The rural and traditional values, the role of the local church, and the lack of technological and entrepreneurial advancement left the regions largely untouched until the 1970s when the *European Economic Community* (EEC—now EU) began to invest Common Agricultural Policy (CAP) monies into these areas to subsidize farming and in Ireland this led to more prosperity for farmers. Chubb states that it was not until the 1970s that many in rural Éire started getting television sets (Chubb 1992).

Despite the rural economy, the EEC did continue to affect the Irish economy by the 1980s and 1990s. The relatively stagnant Irish economy began to see major changes as a thriving service sector came into existence. Like Scotland in the early 1990s, Ireland developed a Silicon valley type *light manufacturing* of computers and microprocessors. It also became a hub for movie production as Hollywood sought to use its nineteenth century scenery in both Dublin and the state's rural areas for the creation of motion pictures. Labor and supply costs seemed to help this economic transformation. Tourism also grew as the Emerald Isle became a bucolic alternative to crowded, and polluted, London. The Irish government's longstanding decision in 1993 to allow transatlantic flights from North America to land at Dublin instead of Shannon Airport (in western Éire) only was a great expedition of more tourism from across the Atlantic—this was logical with 25 million Irish-American consumers who many were interested in visiting their "homeland" to discover their roots. *Aer Lingus*, the Irish national air carrier (the anglicized form of the Irish word for "air fleet," *Aer Loingeas*), has been owned by Ireland's government since 1936. It has had some minority ownership by subsidiary concerns which were part of British Airways (including British European Airways) after 1946. However, the Irish government always controlled the airline. Although small with only about 60 planes, the airline came to be a symbol of Éire's statist and nationalist approach to economic life, yet willingness to connect to other parts of the world. In early 2006, Ahern's cabinet started discussions on the partial privatization of Aer Lingus. Selling parts of the national airline to private companies was to yield around €300 million ($396 million). With an interest in improving overseas flights and to farther destinations in Asia and the United States, the state-owned carrier's fleet was getting old and the costs to Irish citizens was increasing. The government expected to retain at least a 20% interest in Aer Lingus to satisfy demands from citizens and interest groups that did not want private investors to control the long-standing state-owned entity. Thus, creating a kind of entity like the vaunted German auto manufacturer, Volkswagen, which is owned 20% by the Lower Saxony regional government, 18.50% by Porsche, and the rest by other interests including the Volkswagen entity within the semi-public owned and publicly traded company itself. In Éire, Businesspersons favored a sell-off to make Aer Lingus more efficient and lean. However, as in any political and economic context, some were opposed to privatization including the largest trade union in Ireland, SIPTU. Some 2,300 Aer Lingus workers were part of SIPTU (just under 60% of the airline's workforce). The union argued that after September 11, 2001, that state ownership brought stability to Aer Lingus and the airline industry, rather than the opposite where some airlines collapsed due to the drop in market share and pricing problems due to an overall fall in consumer demand. Of course, the upstart, "Southwest Airlines" of Ireland, Ryan Air, had taken much of the market away from Aer Lingus as well. By 2005, Ryan Air was the most profitable airline in Europe (much like its American counterpart Southwest). Both had reached the heights of a very competitive business by appealing to no-frills and cheaper products for consumers. Ryan Air's attempt to buy a majority of shares in Aer Lingus was stopped by the EU in 2007 due to monopolistic fears.

Another state-owned industry, the Irish Telecommunications Board, created by British statue in 1893 was originally under the postal ministry in Ireland. As *Bord Telecom Éireann* it was the state telephone monopoly until 1999. Privatization of the *Telecom Éireann* began in 1995. When privatized in 1999, *Eircom*, as it is known today, was placed on the London Stock Exchange, the Irish Stock Exchange, and the New York Stock Exchange. In 2002, the company was taken over by a venture capitalist group headed by George Soros. By 2004, it was back on the stock markets. In 2007, 21% of the company was owned by employees. Another 12% is owned by an Australian firm. In August 2005, Eircom bought a rival in the market, Meteor (the third largest telecoms firm in Ireland). By November of the same year, Swisscom, the former state-owned Swiss telephone company—privatized in 1997, was talking about buying the Irish company. Eircom has had some problems keeping up with consumer demand in the area of internet broadband service. When at one time it was the state's major telecommunications provider, the opening of the Irish market has meant a drop in market share for Eircom, but it still retains roughly 44% of the telecoms market in Éire. In late 2005, Eircom was valued at €4.4 billion ($5.3 billion). Eircom is an example of how the formerly statist and nationalized industry-driven Irish economy is changing into a modern, capitalist state in the globalizing EU.

The Irish economy grew incredibly in the 1990s. It was the leader of the *Celtic tiger economies*. The Irish economy grew by an average of 10% per year in the 1995-2000 period. This represented remarkable growth in an economy that was conforming to EU standards and seeing its economy go from one in which agriculture had dominated even after the Second World War and was giving way to the new post-industrial economy of the age. Éire became a haven for high technology firms and jobs for its citizens. Companies such as Apple Computers and IBM began production in Ireland. Other sectors such as financial services began to grow. The decontrol of the economy (in line with EU liberalization policies) helped spur growth as well. Instead of watching many of its youth leave for the United States or England, Ireland began to see many stay home and supply much needed labor (of various types including an increasingly educated and skilled labor force) stay in Ireland and the country benefited from the trend.

Wales's Economy

Like England, Scotland, and Ireland, Wales was a predominantly agricultural economy until the mid-nineteenth century. Wales, like the rest of Great Britain and Ireland, was a region where a few wealthy landed elites owned most of the land. Various parliamentary acts enclosing previously open areas sent small farmers into towns and villages looking for work. Mining on a micro-scale had occurred since Celts came to Wales several thousand years prior. By the middle of the nineteenth century, thousands had moved to the valleys of southern Wales where coal and iron were copious. In the late nineteenth century, it was estimated that a Welsh coalminer was injured every two minutes and one killed every six hours. In and around Merthyr Tydfil in south Wales iron purification and steel production were in full swing. As coal mines opened and steel was refined the demand for increased rail services into and out of Wales increased. This booming industrial context saw many social and economic forces come to the fore such as Methodism, a proliferation of chapels, and the rise of largely English captains of industry owning large quantities of land and capital.

Welsh *mining* was not only concentrated in the south, but found in the nationalist areas of the rural and mountainous north as well. With the growth of mining came trade unions and movements with a range of liberal to more radical politics. Workers started unionizing and this brought about some social fissures as both Anglican and nonconformist clergy were deeply suspicious of socialism due to its intellectual origins in Marx's atheistic, materialist thinking. Welsh coal was one of the world's major staples. Immigration into Wales to work in the collieries was rivaled only by immigration to the United States. In 1913, the coal pits of south Wales produced 57 million tons, double what was extracted two decades earlier. By 1920, Welsh coal mines produced 1/3 of the world's coal. Work stoppages led by unions continued at times as workers struck for better pay and working conditions. An explosion in a mine killed 439 at Senghennydd in 1913. By 1920, there were 620 coal mines in southern Wales and 256,000 men working in them.

The *slate* industry was concentrated largely in the north around Snowdonia. English capitalists owned most slate companies and by 1898 these mines were producing ½ million tons of refined slate each year. Strikes, disease, and poor working conditions affected slate miners and by the 1950s most slate mines were closed. The Welsh still believe their slate is the globe's best, although global capitalism has tightened the market and it is difficult to compete with cheaper slate from Spain. The EU now forces similar types of slate (largely from Spain) into the UK and Welsh markets, although pockets of slate in the north are left uncultivated and Welsh quarrymen have difficulty finding work. Today, slate is used for floor tiles, ashtrays, and road compounds, but it does not hold the market power it once did.

By the time the socialist Labour government under Clement Attlee came to power in 1945, *coal* was still the major industry in Wales despite its declining role in the UK's economy. Labour nationalized the industry as was consistent with its ideological agenda. By 1952, the European experiment that first manifested as the six-nation European Coal and Steel Community (a cartel that would later become the European Economic Community by 1958 and the EU by 1995) still was not producing as much coal and steel as the UK by itself—a testimony to Wales's economy. However, mines began to close as postindustrialism came to the fore. In 1945, Wales had 212 coal mines and by 1989 only 11. In 1994, its last coalmine was in operation but ran by a worker's cooperative. The legendary Welsh coal mining industry was at an end.

Despite deindustrialization in Wales, farming had changed drastically there after 1945. Like other postindustrial nations, the 1960s saw the Welsh small farmer improve his means of cultivation via improved technology: hay bailers, milk machines, and tractors. All allowed for greater work by less people. In 1951, more than 33,000 were farming. Twenty years hence just over 11,000 were working the land. In the same timeframe, women started playing a greater role in the Welsh workforce. Female workers rose by nearly 50% while male laborers dropped by six percent. The use of the automobile allowed for greater mobility of the workforce as by the mid-1960s some 10,000 people a day were commuting from the area of the coalfields in the south to other parts of Wales and England for work. Manufacturing became important in south Wales as did tourism throughout the nation. Cardiff, only the recognized capital of Wales since 1955 by Westminster, was home to numerous services—legal, educational, financial, and governmental. The transformation of Wales's economy not only as postindustrial, but one tied to the global economy saw an exodus of indigenous citizens to other parts of the UK for employment opportunities. It also brought both non-UK immigrants and non-Welsh UK nationals to Wales to work and live cheaper than in England. This trend saw Englishmen and women come into northern Wales to buy second or holiday homes and led to some nationalist backlash. Looking for affordable housing in beautiful vistas, such as the Llŷn peninsula, was thought by some Welsh to commercialize and dilute the culture, especially regarding the use of the indigenous language. In the 1980s, *unconventional politics* reared its ugly head as Meibion Glyndŵr (Sons of Glyndŵr), a surreptitious militant nationalist group, burnt down a number of homes owned by English nationals.

At the start of the twenty-first century, the Valleys (the name for the area of the historical coalfields and coal mining communities in southern Wales) had seen several high-tech businesses invest in the communities that were once populated by men and women who worked around the thick black dust of coal. *Tourism* has grown with the growth of museums, sporting facilities, and cultural festivals to promote community pride and healthy lifestyles. However, some small villages have not seen the economic development needed to rejuvenate their communities. Like other Celtic regions, and most notably Scotland, the postindustrial economy has seen capital concentrate in large urban areas, such as Cardiff and Swansea, and the governments (Welsh, UK, and EU) have tried to steer capital and development into neglected areas, especially in northern and mid-Wales.

One manufacturing area that has grown in the Welsh economy after 1985 is the microeconomic activity associated with the auto industry. Some 300 companies employing 30,000 workers work in Wales in jobs that help support the auto industry. Several MNCs from Germany, the United States, France, and Japan have set up shop in Wales and these business turn out $3.5 billion in profits each year. Ford automotive company produces engines in a plant in Bridgend which are placed in Volvos, Land Rovers, Fords, and Jaguars. The Toyota plant in Deeside ships the Japanese car manufacturer's engines to its Toyota plants in England. Of these 300 companies some produce various automotive products such as power locks, brakes, sensor systems, and seats. Thus, the idea that a formerly depressed area that was reliant on one or two economic sectors (such as coal and slate), has revitalized even in the context of the post-industrial economy and seen manufacturing and jobs tied to traditional unions working with management in the industrial sector return.

Box 6.5: *Eisteddfod*

Although it had its roots in ancient Welsh history, *eisteddfodau* were held from the twelfth century by Welsh kings and were largely drunken events. After 1789, they took on more cultural and national significance and the eisteddfodau in northeast Wales were, by the nineteenth century, gaining in popularity and importance. Eisteddfodau were festivals that focused on Welsh culture; namely, music and poetry. However, some religious and mystical elements were included such as the assembly (*gorsedd*) of the bards which played on ancient pagan (druid) themes. Much of ancient Welsh poetry had been tied to the druids, until the sixth century when Wales became a Christian nation. Welsh music has been known for the all-male choirs largely part of the southern industrial areas (portrayed well in the 1941 Oscar-winning film, "How Green was My Valley." After 1819, eisteddfodau were held in the south part of the country. The increased interest in eisteddfodau was due mainly to ministers in both Welsh-speaking and English-speaking areas who were interested in Welsh literature and preserving the culture. By 1853, local festivals were being held annually throughout Wales and the establishment of a National Eisteddfod had occurred. Not all in Wales welcomed the eisteddfodau. Methodists in the nineteenth century felt they promoted vices such as drinking and reveling and the small northern town of Bala banned them due to Methodist influence. Due west of there, 30 miles or so, the Llŷn Peninsula was still "dry" into the 1990s due to Methodist and temperance concerns since the age of industrialization 150 years ago. Ironically, just down the road from Bala, Llangollen (a town of 5000) in northern Wales, an international eisteddfod has been held every year since 1947. Each July over 12,000 singers and poets come from almost 50 nations to participate in the weeklong event. Along with highlighting the Welsh culture, the event brings in much needed tourist currency into the region, thus stimulating the nation's economy. The eisteddfod certainly helped produce cultural awareness in Wales and reinforced Welsh national identity in ways that supported the political changes in the late twentieth century. Thus, the eisteddfod served to reinforce dualistic aspects of the Welsh culture (tied to both religion and national identity) that divided religious and non-religious Welsh, but ultimately brought most indigenous groups together by the advent of the twenty-first century to celebrate Welshness.

The Northern Irish Economy

Ulster's economy was for many years one of the best economic regions of the UK. Prior to the advent of the troubles in 1969, Northern Ireland's economy was vibrant and a major contributor to the growth of the UK-wide economy. The reformist Ulster Unionist premier Terrence O'Neill tried to emulate UK prime minister *Harold Wilson* by capitalizing on the *"white heat of technology"* and planning the growth of industry for the Northern Ireland. According to historian James Loughlin, from 1964–69, numerous factories were built in Northern Ireland. Six plastics factories were built in the period which were the largest number globally. New manufacturing saw 29,000 jobs created, but as heavy industries declined the balance was not as good netting only 5000 new jobs (Loughlin 2004).

Like Ireland, Northern Ireland's most important economic sector was agriculture. The nature of small family farming left a large imprint on the region as it had in Scotland's Highlands and the American Midwest. Despite the recent violence in the late twentieth century in Ulster, the EU's CAP continued to aid the region. Government aid from London was important too. By the mid-1990s, Northern Ireland was the largest net beneficiary of UK government funds. In the

UK, per capita government spending was higher in Ulster (with Scotland and Wales second and third respectively and England last) according to political scientist Alan Greer (Greer 1999). Paradoxically, the largest per capita beneficiary was not investing as much in the domestic infrastructure and macroeconomy because a larger slice of public funds was going to security. By the 1990s, an attempt to invest in local and regional businesses, lessen public regulation, and create a more liberal entrepreneurial culture (like the Republic's in the south) was occurring and this was encouraged by the EU and both the UK and Irish governments.

The issue of employment equality was always a thorn for Catholics in Northern Ireland and systematic *economic discrimination* was a longstanding problem. Even today, for every Protestant that is not employed, two Catholics are similarly situated. The UK government tried to address the sectarian employment imbalance in 1976 with the Fair Employment Act that hoped to further opportunities for Catholics. This altruistic attempt did not bear as much fruit, but the US government's attempt to tie fairness in investment policies to free trade manifested themselves in the *MacBride Principles* (named after and created by an Irish nationalist who won the Nobel Peace Prize in 1974) which tried to allow more opportunities for economically disenfranchised groups based on religion and ethnicity in Northern Ireland; thus, attempting to rectify the situation for Catholics. This at least brought to light the concerns that Catholics and human rights groups had with government policies and business practices in Northern Ireland and gave these concerns more of a global stage. Probably, the most important aspect of Northern Irish economic development has been the conceptualization of joint North-South economic vision whereby the Irish Council—the North-South body created after the Good Friday Agreement (GFA) of 1998—would promote economic issues that both Ulster and the Republic were confronted with in their domestic economies and the EU. The goal of Brussels was to see the eventual *convergence and harmonization* of Irish regional economies to make them work smoother in the borderless EU economy. These issues included agriculture, fishing, tourism, and developing other macroeconomic sectors. What's more, liberalizing both the Ulster and Republic of Ireland economies was to be an important focus of both regions in the 1990s so as to grow in the EU and begin a steady effort to decontrol both economies (given years of *statism* and *protectionism* in both regions). In the tourism sector (the fastest growing sector by the twenty-first century in all of the EU), a return to the vision of O'Neill and in the 1960s which promoted "Ulster Weeks" to counter the Republic's "Irish Weeks" (promoted by Taoiseach Seán Lemass) when tourism in the Emerald Isle was promoted in mainland Britain by both regions. This was a repeat of history but within an evolving globalizing economic and federalizing EU context.

Religion in Scotland

The Kirk

Although imbued with national pride and character, the Church of Scotland, or Kirk, had been a nominally separate entity from the English Church into the sixteenth century. It was not until 1560, one hundred years before the Civil War, that the Kirk gained its independence and identity that set it apart today from the Anglican Church. After the Scots invited the English to remove the French from Scotland, due to the fear of Mary of Guise's Catholicism and iron-fisted overtures, the Scottish lords signed the Treaty of Berwick with England and by July 1560, England and France had agreed on the Treaty of Edinburgh and the exit of both their armies from Scotland. At the same time, a Scottish parliament ended the Kirk's ties to Rome, invoked a new Church constitution, and a new Confession of Faith. These events were inspired by the Calvinist firebrand John Knox. Thus, the Kirk began to take new form. The Church was to be federated administratively. Within a year, Mary Queen of Scots was on the Scottish throne at Holyrood and her Catholic ways were constantly challenged by the austere Knox. Knox's leadership was resolute and Catholics suffered both spiritually and in terms of traditions (most stained glass in Scots churches were smashed as sinful icons). Despite the excesses of The Scottish Reformation, both Catholics and Protestants could claim victories. Mary would be executed by her half-sister, Elizabeth I of England, in London eventually, but Mary would give birth to the future Catholic King of England, James I (aka, James VI of Scotland) under whom both crowns were united. The Kirk would evolve into not only an identifiably different church from the Church of England, but also an institution that helped bring about political transformation and revolution in Scotland by 1638 in the signing of the covenant. As political scientist James G. Kellas has remarked, the Church of Scotland had a profound effect inculcating Scottish values and a sense of national identity in its citizens via its schools which were actually state financed, but controlled by the Kirk (Kellas 1989). Although the Kirk itself was more corporatist and not a product of overt liberal democratic practices, it helped spur national consciousness (via covenants), favored self-governance (as evinced by its own constitution), and sought to provoke independent thinking in its membership and Scottish citizenry in general. The hierarchical Anglican Church model became the antithesis, whether real or imagined, in the evolution of church-state relations in Scotland. Descended from austere Scotch-Irish Presbyterians, American president Woodrow Wilson lectured for years at Princeton on the topic of democracy and would point to the signing of the 1638 covenant in the Greyfriars church yard as the seminal event in the movement toward democracy not only for Scots, but for Americans as well. Whether this event was indeed a foundation for liberal democracy in Scotland or the United States is debatable, but the fact that the identification and articulation of rights of men and women were tied to actions by Kirk members with church sanctioning does lay an interesting groundwork for both Scotland's and the US's democratic future, despite the fact that the Kirk was not perforce a democratic body. Despite Scottish political change and transformation during and after the English Civil War, the Kirk underwent a great *"Disruption"* in 1843 when evangelicals bolted from it in a battle over secularism, theology and control that created the Free Church of Scotland. Led by the aged Reverend Thomas Chalmers, the "Wee Frees" hoped to challenge secularism and Catholicism in Scotland and especially the former's impact on the Kirk. One-third of the Kirk's ministers left the Church of Scotland to join the Wee Frees. Interestingly, the split lasted less than 100 years as the Free Church of Scotland (which had joined with the United Presbyterian Church of Scotland in 1913) reunited with the Church of Scotland in 1929. As a minority faction in the Free Presbyterian Church of Scotland, the "Wee We Frees" had broken in 1907 and still remain an independent and separate fundamentalist church, devoted to separation from the secular world, sabbatarianism, the UK's monarchy, and adamantly opposed to Catholicism.

Box 6.6: Wee Wee Frees

The "Disruption" of 1843 led to a split in the Church of Scotland (when evangelicals broke ranks largely over church autonomy and secular versus spiritual issues). The fissure resulted in the creation of the Free Church of Scotland which began looking at union with another Presbyterian body, the United Presbyterian Church. Eventually, by 1929, the Free Church had reunited with the Kirk. The Free Presbyterian Church of Scotland was formed in 1907 when a small group of ministers, mainly from the Highlands and islands, left the Free Church over doctrinal issues related to the church's confession. Known as the "Wee Wee Frees," this church's members were strict sabbatarians (no use of motorized transport on Sundays even to church services) and the use of the King James Version (KJV) of the Bible only. By the early 21st century, the church had 21,000 members largely in the Highlands and a seminary in Glasgow. Although not tied officially, the Free Presbyterian Church of Scotland has some similarities with Reverend Ian Paisley's Free Presbyterian Church founded in Belfast in 1951 by the Democratic Unionist Party leader. Both are stridently opposed to Catholicism, both use the KJV Bible exclusively, both encourage women to wear head-coverings during services, and both are doctrinally conservative. The Wee Wee Frees are known for its most famous former member, the Lord Chancellor of the UK, Lord Mackay of Clashfern, who was excommunicated in 1989 for attending a deceased colleague's Roman Catholic requiem mass and for belonging to a golf club that allowed its members to play on Sundays. Lord Mackay ended up leaving the church and helping start a new denomination known as the Associated Presbyterian Churches. As Scottish political scientist James Mitchell has said of political parties, they are like churches with their various factions and tendencies (Mitchell 1988). As can be seen in the Presbyterian churches of Scotland (as well as other Protestant denominations globally), factions and tendencies are part of the mix and splits have been the norm, not the exception, in Christendom since the nineteenth century.

Celtic Languages

With 95% of Britons English speakers, it is not surprising that the Celtic languages have not received the recognition or support culturally or politically that they once had when Celtic nations were autonomous. With the rise of Celtic nationalism in Britain in the late twentieth century, newfound interest in Celtic languages returned and by the beginning of the twenty-first century, increasing numbers of speakers in various Celtic tongues could be found across the British Isles and Ireland. The 2001 British census said that 20% of the Welsh spoke the Welsh language. The same census said that around one percent of Scots spoke Scottish Gaelic (*Gàidhlig*) which is roughly 60,000 people. In Éire, there are over 1.5 million speakers of Irish Gaelic (*Gaeilge*), also known as Irish. This is over one-fourth of the population. In Ulster, seven percent of the population (110,000 people) speak Irish Gaelic according to the 2001 census. Two percent of the Northern Irish speak Ulster-Scots, a dialect of Scots. This language is similar to Scots spoken in Scotland which is a mixture of various types of language streams from Middle English of the Anglo-Saxon era to Northumbrian to strands of Old Norse. As the EU focused on regional issues in the late twentieth century, these minority languages all began to receive official recognition at Westminster and attempts to revive long thought dead dialects began to reemerge. However, Some languages, like Irish Gaelic, actually eroded throughout the twentieth century. Calls for recognition and increasing access to Celtic language training came loudly from nationalist groups and from various corners of the Celtic fringe by twentieth century's end.

Irish Gaelic

Irish Gaelic (*Gaeilge*) was supposed to be the official language of Éire after the passage of the nation's constitution under Éamon de Valera in 1937. It was the official language of the Republic of Ireland. Yet, due to the dominance of English, the Irish Gaelic language (also known as Irish) suffered and English supplanted it in most parts of the Republic. Despite the fact that at the beginning of the twenty-first century over 1.57 million Irish could speak *Gaeilge*, the language was not growing like Welsh was in Wales. Irish was first spoken in Ireland after 1200 BC. It changed and morphed into various dialects throughout the century, but it was the most widely spoken language on the island until the nineteenth century. Combined with the banning of Irish Gaelic and the effects of the Great Famine (*An Drochshaol*), the Irish language began to give way to English as many poorer agrarian Irish starved and left the country. This subset of the population was more likely to speak Irish than those in the cities. Politically, the Irish language took on various connotations and the English perceived it as underdeveloped and a sign of the lack of civilization among the Irish. By the early twentieth century and the growth of the Irish Home Rule Movement, a cultural revival was in full swing on the island. The Gaelic League (*Conradh na*

Gaeilge) had many major political supporters including de Valera, Patrick Pearse, and W. T. Cosgrave (*Liam Mac Cosguir*). The increase in Gaelic sports and increased artistic endeavors, such as Irish-themed theater (although in English), by such cultural icons like Sean O'Casey and William Butler Yeats helped the Gaelic cause in Ireland. In 1914, the Protestant Church of Ireland started offering some worship services in Irish. The branch of the church that facilitated the Irish Gaelic was called *Cumann Gaelach na hEaglaise* (the Irish Guild of the Church).

Interestingly, Irish independence did not coincide with a growth in Irish Gaelic. Despite the populist rhetoric aimed at Gaelic and the fact that the Free State leaders wanted Irish Gaelic as the state's official language, the business of administration was still done in English and by 1926 a commission on language, the *Gaeltacht* Commission (*Gaeltacht* meaning Gaelic-speaking region), advocated the use of Irish as the official language of state, but the British government would not adhere to the commission's findings. As the state became larger, and with its employees speaking English as the first language, the influence of English became more pronounced. A requirement that each Irish bureaucrat have some understanding of Irish Gaelic was merely a political component of government employment and it was oftentimes hard for Irish speakers to interact with bureaucrats, especially in the *Gaeltacht* areas (the parts of Éire that had salient Irish speaking communities—largely in the western part of the isle.) Politically, the early leaders after revolution and civil war were interested in Gaelicizing the state, but as the twentieth century continued few Irish leaders were as competent in Irish Gaelic. De Valera and others of his generation could read and speak the language well, but from the onset of the *Dáil Éireann* hardly any legislative perorations were in Irish Gaelic. Only formal declarations and other formalities were in the Irish tongue. Most Irish leaders, including prime ministers (*taoisigh*) were not fluent in the language. This included Albert Reynolds (*Ailbhe Mag Raghnaill*), John Bruton, and Bertie Ahern. These individuals had difficulty even speaking some Gaelic at major political events. Two recent female presidents of the Republic, Mary Robinson (*Máire Mhic Róíbín*) and Mary McAleese (*Máire Mhic Ghiolla Íosa*) were fluent in Irish and Robinson, tried to improve her abilities in the language by studying it while in office. Each president of the Republic has taken his or her declaration of office in Irish Gaelic, but they do have the right to make the declaration in English. Douglas Hyde, the founder of *Conradh na Gaeilge*, gave his declaration of office in a dialect of Irish Gaelic (Roscommon Irish) that has died out and his speech is the only remaining text and sound in that dialect. Like north Wales and the Scottish Highlands, Éire's *Gaeltacht* has seen an infusion of English speakers in recent decades. This may account for the decline in spoken Irish. Fewer children are learning Irish in the home and Irish as a language of business has declined as well. In some areas in the *Gaeltacht*, such as parts of Galway in the south, a scheme to build Irish speakers homes has been attempted to keep English speakers from overtaking Irish speakers in terms of population. This has not necessarily worked either as English has been the language of commerce and government and thus the Irish speakers, who are bilingual, use English in Irish society, but Irish Gaelic at home in private. Interestingly, despite the setbacks for Irish speakers, the language's unique imprint on Irish culture, society, and politics continues to be felt. In 2005, the EU recognized Irish Gaelic as one of its official languages and it went into effect on January 1, 2007. After 1963 and Vatican II, the Catholic Church allowed the Irish Church to perform mass in Irish Gaelic, not the customary Latin. In 2003, the Quran was translated into Irish Gaelic as Muslims in Dublin and *Foras na Gaeilge*, the all-island organization that oversees the Irish language in Éire, worked to produce the Islamic holy book that is normally disseminated in Arabic only. *Foras na Gaeilge* was created in 1998 as a result of the GFA to serve as a pan-Ireland institution to link the Republic and Ulster in terms of the access, promotion, and growth of *Gaeilge*. The organ replaced the 26-county *Bord na Gaeilge* which did the same in the south.

Northern Ireland: Irish Gaelic and Ulster Scots

The politics of language is quite salient in Northern Ireland. The Catholic community saw many of its sectarian schools teaching *Gaeilge* while Protestant schools oftentimes refused to teach Irish Gaelic. Bilingual signs were not allowed in the province as well. This began to change somewhat after the GFA. Sinn Féin leader, Gerry Adams, started learning *Gaeilge* in prison because of the study of the Gaelic language by IRA prisoners; as a result a *jailtacht* (Gaelic-speaking jail community) was formed. Protestant politicos, like Ian Paisley, were opposed to the teaching and usage of *Gaeilge* in Ulster and they in turn proposed the greater usage of Ulster Scots. Thus, *Gaeilge* slowly became a language with political connotations surrounding the nationalist community and Ulster Scots became a cause celebre for the loyalist community. *Gaeilge* was officially recognized after the GFA and inter-Irish cooperation was implemented in applying the language in both parts of Ireland.

Ulster Scots is a variation of the Scots language spoken in Scotland (largely the lowland parts of the nation). Scots is a derivation of English, but with pronunciations, words, and idioms unique to the language. An English speaker may pick up on much of Scots, but may be confused as to pronunciations and sounds. On the other hand, the dialect, grammar, and syntax may be completely foreign to English speakers. Ulster Scots came to Northern Ireland in the 1600s. Gaelic speakers from Scotland had been in Ireland for 200 years prior to the mainly lowlanders coming in the seventeenth century. Ulster Scots is not a Celtic language (like *Gaeilge* or Scottish Gaelic). It is related to English and various dialects that have affected English down through the centuries. About 30,000 people in Northern Ireland speak Ulster Scots (roughly two percent of the population). In 1999, Ulster Scots was given official legal status as a protected minority language of the United Kingdom. Some republicans and advocates of Irish Gaelic claimed the British government was trying to create a counter linguistic movement to the Irish language. Thus, implying that the recognition was more political and overt than cultural or a matter of empirical realities. Interestingly, the GFA gained legitimacy via the Ulster Scots language. The language was part of the Protestant sub-culture in Northern Ireland and an Ulster Scots Agency to work between north and south was established. The key issue for nationalists was that to them Ulster Scots was not a distinct language but a derivation of Scots, and hence, a foreign import. For loyalists, Ulster Scots was ipso facto an independent language with important cultural merit worth preserving.

Scotland: Scots and Scottish Gaelic

Scotland has long had numerous languages running through its historical landscape from Gaelic to Scots to Norse to Northumbrian to Middle English and others. From Celtic to Germanic languages, the Scots have seen an incredible amount of fusion and fission when it comes to how they communicate with each other and with the outside world. Take a trip to Scotland and drive around the country and you will see evidence of each of these languages with various place names with each having a detailed linguistic and social history in their own right. From Norse settlements dating back to the thirteenth century like North Uist in the Outer Hebrides and in northeast Scotland, Thurso, to North Ballachulish and Bridge of Orchy, Gaelic names, in the West Highlands. Many Viking, Norse, and Pict names have either merged with or been supplanted by Gaelic and English place names over the years. Certainly, learning more about Celtic place names provides a fascinating etymology for those who are into linguistics.

Box 6.7: Celtic Place Names

One of the most entertaining aspects of Celtic culture are the place (or town) names found throughout Scotland, Wales, and Ireland. In Scotland, towns like Spittle of Glenshee, found along the Royal Deeside trail in the Highlands southwest of Aberdeen and due north of Perth, are small burghs in the mountains. Cities like Limerick or Blarney in southern Ireland conjure up references to twentieth century popular culture, with a limerick as a fashionable type of rhyming children's poem and leprechauns kissing the blarney stone for luck. In Wales, the mixture of Welsh and English over the centuries caused place names to vary between the two languages. But, one of the most famous places in the world is found in northern Wales on the Anglesey isle just north of the Menai Strait. The small village there is known as the longest name for a town in the world—58 letters long! The town was called Llanfair P.G. for short, but the name of the town stretches over the top of its railway station. The town, *Llanfairpwllgwyngyllgogerycerndrobwllllanantysiliogogogoch*, is translated to mean, "St. Mary's in a hollow of white hazel near to a rapid whirlpool and to St. Tysilio's Church by the red cave."

The *Scots language* is a branch of English which came to Scotland's lowlands in the 700s. It differed from the Gaelic that was spoken in the Highlands, a distinctly Celtic language, found in Scotland by the fourth century AD. The Normans came in the 1100s and 1200s and most likely spoke some form of English (perhaps Middle English) and French. The dividing line historically for Scots versus other languages in the area came in the 1600s when Ynglis (English), the language of the Anglo-Saxons in Northumbria (the land that now stands on both sides of the Scotch-English border), began to emerge as the language of the lowlands, but with a different dialect and a new name for it, "Scots." This language had been used for over 1000 years prior in *Alba* (Gaelic for Scotland). The term "Scottis" was the word for the inchoate Gaelic language of the Highlands at the time. With the term, Scots now applied to a variation of English, a new name for the Celtic tongue would have to be found. Scots is not an easy dialect to always understand, but some Scots words have found their way into the English language, such as "cuddle," "clan," and "greed." The Scots language has carried on throughout the centuries. Like Ulster Scots, the EU and the UK government recognize Scots as a minority language in the UK. Scots is probably best known culturally in the writings of Scotland's most famous poet, Robert Burns (1759–96). Still to this day, one of the few events where Scots is heard and honored is the annual Burns night dinners throughout Scotland and held all over the world on the evening of January 25th. Since many English speakers see Scots as a derivation of English, the language has not gotten as much recognition or application as Scottish Gaelic (*Gàidhlig*). Some have made comparisons of Scots and English like other languages very close in nature such as Czech and Slovak or Serbian and Croatian (which is essentially known as Serbo-Croatian). Some 1.5 million claim to speak it in Scotland; however, it is not seen as important as English and because it is not as distinct as *Gàidhlig* it does not garner the attention that the Highlands language gets. Scots words such as *cou* for "cow," *guid* for "good," and *schuil* for "school" are all similar to their English counterparts. However, some words are not, including *cuit* for "ankle," *bairn* for child, and *hooseockie* for "small house." Compare the latter to the French *la petit maison* or малинкая дом (*malinkaya dom*) in Russian. Words like loch for "lake" and clan for "family" have stood the test of time in Scotland in both Scots and English.

Wales and the Welsh Language (Cymraeg)

Welsh (*Cymraeg*) is spoken by 20.5% of the Welsh population. The nineteenth century saw the reemergence of Welsh due to the growth of cultural nationalism. A few monolingual speakers existed in the country. But today, most Welshmen and women who speak the language are bilingual. The twentieth century saw the deliberate rise of Welsh as a salient minority language in the British Isles. The rise of political and cultural groups dedicated to the revival of the Welsh language and culture included *Cymdeithas yr laith Cymraeg* (the Welsh Language Society). Politics have affected the propagation of Welsh. The Welsh Language Act of 1993 and the 1998 Government of Wales Act assured an equal footing for the Welsh language. Schools that taught both languages were to be seen as equal. State entities had to promote Welsh and government bodies had to conduct work in both English and *Cymraeg*. The move toward greater Welsh usage in government stems from the creation in 1982 of S4C, the regional BBC channel that produces all its programming in the Welsh language.

Welsh speakers can be traced back to 500 AD. Welsh speakers were eventually truncated geographically by Angles and Saxons and Celtic speakers north of Wales spoke Cumbrian and they spoke Cornish south of Wales. The Welsh language continued its evolution, although the Anglicization of Wales did affect the language and those who insisted speaking it and trying to unify the culture for political reasons as well. A Welsh translation of the Bible in 1588 was a case in point. By the seventeenth and eighteenth centuries, the language was ebbing as English was growing alongside the population in England. But, *Cymraeg* began to rebound culturally in the nineteenth century. Welsh words include *Beibl* for "Bible," *mis* for "month," and *newydd* for "new." Many scholars have speculated that the Welsh people came from the Iberian Peninsula. Certainly, their language is different from the Gaelic languages of Éire and *Alba* (Scotland). As a Brythonic language (a language group of the Celtic family), Welsh is closer in nature to Breton (*Bretagne* in France) and Cornish (in Cornwall in southwestern England) than Irish (*Gaeilge*) or Scottish Gaelic (*Gáidhlig*).

Box 6.8: *Me na vyn cows Sawsnak*!: Cornish Nationalism and the Revival of the Cornish Language

Cornish hens, King Arthur, and palm trees are what most Britons think of when dreaming of a vacation in the rugged, yet picturesque southwestern region of England. To a small number of folk in Cornwall and home to the ancient Celts of *Kernow* ("Cornwall" in Cornish), the revival of the Cornish language became a major issue at the end of the twentieth century and the beginning of the twenty-first century. In Summer 2002, the British government gave the Cornish language legal status as an official tongue and it was protected legally by European Union law. Only 100 or so fluent Cornish speakers were found at the time including only 10 households that regularly used the language in Cornwall itself. However, nationalists, academicians, and Cornish citizens had called for its recognition and also for more political recognition for their region of England; and in 2001, 50,000 signatures were gleaned for a petition for a devolved Cornish legislature. Dolly Pentreath, the last non-English speaking indigenous Cornish speaker, died in 1777. She died in the uniquely named Cornish town of Mousehole (pronounced "mowzle"), which is due south of Penzance. It is believed that she was 102 years-old at death. The last person to understand the Middle Ages-era Cornish dialect (an ancestor of modern-day Cornish) was a schoolmaster John Davey of Zennor (west of St. Ives in the southernmost tip of the mainland of Great Britain) who would practice the language by speaking to his dog. He died in 1891. By 2002, 500 had conversational ability in the language and 3,500 had some knowledge of the tongue. With government endorsement, the language started to gain recognition as a grocery store chain (ASDA—the British equivalent of Wal-Mart) began putting up bilingual signs in their Cornish stores. The novelist Ruth Rendell also was a backer of the tongue. The recognition of the language was a proud moment for Liberal Democrat MP Andrew George, from St. Ives, who had given his maiden speech at Westminster in the Cornish tongue. He said, "It might mean, for instance, that if a Cornish speaker writes a Government department they should receive a reply in their own language." However, the language was not accorded the same recognition that Welsh has which is a mandatory subject in schools and must be used in government reports and documents. Some schools in Cornwall were moving toward teaching the language. Yet, only 42 students took state exams in Cornish between 1986–96. One school, Hayle Community School, started teaching Cornish to 11 year-olds in 2001 and was hoping to expand its language curriculum in the coming years. Cornish thus became the sixth protected indigenous Celtic and British language to be recognized by the UK government. The other five include Scots, Welsh, Ulster Scots, Scottish and Irish Gaelic. And, finally, what does the Cornish "*Me na vyn cows Sawsnak*!" mean in English? "I will not speak English!"

Sports and the Celtic Fringe

Certainly, the most important sporting event in Britain and Ireland in recent history has been the English import, *football* (or as Americans call it, *"soccer"*). Football not only provides a stimulating activity for people, but a competitive product for nations to rally around. The Celtic nations are proud of their national and local professional and amateur football traditions and teams. Ireland has had an improving national team and made the FIFA World Cup finals in 1990 (where they drew England and beat Romania to make it to the quarterfinals where they lost to the hosts, Italy). The team, coached by a member of the 1966 World Cup champion English side, Jack Charlton, was greeted by one-half million screaming Irishmen and women when they returned home to Dublin. The Irish national men's team also qualified for the 1994 and 2002 World Cup finals in the United States and Korea and Japan respectively. In the latter, the Irish proceeded to get to the "knockout" round of 16 where they succumbed to Spain.

Northern Ireland has had some football success and produced several excellent individuals on the football pitch such as the great *George Best*. Best, a Belfast native and consequently known as the "Belfast Boy," is considered to be one of the top strikers in modern football history. He did not have much success in 37 international caps (matches) for Ulster in the 1960s and 1970s. However, his domestic career with several English and American teams, including the fabled Manchester United, was short, yet brilliant. In recent years, Northern Ireland has had problems in international soccer. The national men's team made the World Cup Finals in 1958 (when it advanced to the quarterfinals after beating a strong Czechoslovak side) and it got into both the 1982 and 1986 World Cups and acquitted itself well. In September 2005, the green-shirted Irishmen shocked the much favored and vaunted England side, with English heroes David Beckham and Michael Owen, 1-0, before the frenzied faithful at Windsor Park in Belfast, the first win against England in 33 years. The Football Association of Ireland governs football in the Republic and the Irish Football Association oversees the sport in Six Counties of the north. The latter emerged out of the rift between North and South and these organizations reflect the realities of the division of the Emerald Isle after 1921.

Box 6.9: Man U: Where the Nations of Great Britain and Ireland Converge!

The great English football (soccer) side, Manchester United, has been known since the 1950s for successes on the football pitch. In the 1960s, the team had one of England and Europe's best sides as they won the English top division twice (1965 and 1967) and won the European Cup (today known as the UEFA cup) in 1968. Three players on those 1960s teams represent the fierceness of British sporting heritage: George Best, Bobby Charlton, and Denis Law. Interestingly, each of these amazingly talented footballers was named European footballer of the year during that decade (Best in 1967, Charlton in 1965, and Law in 1962). What made these three unique was that each came from a different region, or country as Celts would say, of the UK. Best was a native of Belfast and thus Northern Irish, Charlton was English and Law was from Aberdeen, Scotland. They were superstars that symbolized not only greatness and athletic prowess on the pitch, but national aspirations for their respective homelands. Best wore the green and white kit for Northern Ireland, Charlton the red and white for England, and Law the blue and white for Scotland. Each had great moments as international footballers. Best's greatest moment wearing the Northern Irish green was a win over Scotland (and his buddy, Law) in 1967, 1-0 at Windsor Park in Belfast. Unfortunately for Best, the Irish Republican Army would periodically call in death threats to him (a Protestant, playing primarily for English sides) and he would be forced to the sidelines. Charlton won the World Cup in 1966 as England hosted the fabled tournament; English sides have never really lived up to the example set by that team. The Scots have had there moments, but none was sweeter than the April 1967 3-2 victory over England at Wembley (England's national football stadium in the London suburbs). Law scored the first goal of the match for the Scots. That victory broke a long unbeaten streak for the defending world champs. Football is an important identifier for Britons and its nationalistic implications grow as the nations of the UK take on their own identity. At the dawn of the new millennium, Man U had a new group of superstars from the various corners of the British Isles, including the side's captain, Irishman Roy Keane (from the Republic of Ireland) who retired in 2006 and went on to a successful coaching career, Englishman David Beckham (who was signed by the great Spanish side Real Madrid in 2003 and then went to Los Angeles to play professional soccer in 2007), and the Welshman Ryan Giggs. History was repeating itself to a certain extent as England and Europe's most famous side was again representative of Britain's multi-national context. Man U continued to find great success due largely to the second great Scottish coach in its history (after the legendary Sir Matt Busby), Sir Alex Ferguson.

Scottish football has a long and storied history. The Scots have had more "footie" success than the Irish nations and the Scots had long epic battles on the football pitch with England in the twentieth century. The Scots have been to eight World Cup finals with the most recent in 1998; however, they have never made it out of the first round during the finals (unlike Ireland, Northern Ireland, Wales, and England). Probably, the nation's greatest moment was the 1967 victory at Wembley Stadium in London against the defending World Cup champion England team, 3-2. The Aberdonian and Manchester United star, Denis

Law, led the charge that day. Scotland's professional football is well known, and like American basketball in the 1980s when the Boston Celtics and Los Angeles Lakers dominated the National Basketball Association every year, *"the Old Firm"* has been the dominant duo of Scottish soccer since 1888. The Old Firm is the colloquial name for the rivalry between the two Glaswegian sides, Rangers and Celtic (pronounced SELL-tick, like the American NBA team from Boston, unlike the title of this book which is pronounced KEL-tick with a hard "k" as in the German name "Kurt"). The two teams have combined for 90 league titles in the Scottish top division. The role of sectarianism in the Old Firm matches is a continued sore spot for many, as the old wounds of religion (Catholicism versus Protestantism), race (Irish versus Scot/Briton), and class (Protestant middle classes versus Catholic working classes) manifest themselves at times in Glasgow. A 2003 Glasgow city council study found that 74% of Celtic's supporters in Glasgow were Catholic versus only 4% Protestants. Rangers were supported by 65% Protestant Glaswegians and only 5% Catholic Glasgow natives. Both sides have diehard supporters in Northern Ireland which has abetted communal violence in the Six Counties at times.

Box 6.10: The Old Firm

In Scottish society, football (soccer) is king. The English invented the game, but the Scots are proud of their long affiliation with the sport. Throughout the hamlets and burghs of the region on can find green football pitches (fields) everywhere. When one thinks of Scottish football the legendary rivalry between the Glaswegian sides, Rangers and Celtic, comes to mind. The duo became known as the "Old Firm" since both dominated the Scottish top league like a monopolistic business! Celtic was formed in 1888 by a Catholic priest as an outreach to local Catholic boys. Eventually the club helped pacify Catholic workers in the Parkhead section of Glasgow where its stadium is now situated. Rangers was formed in 1872 as a way of encouraging working-class Protestants in the Govan section of central Glasgow. The interesting rivalry on the football pitch emulated a much bloodier rivalry after 1969 in Ulster. Of course, the Scots would argue that their political culture is democratic and sport is a proper channel for solving differences of opinion—as long as no one gets hurt. Rangers which sport a blue and red jersey and Celtic which has a green and white striped jersey (the same colors as the Boston Celtics in the US), have had their share of adversity based on overt sectarianism through the years. From 1910 to 1989, Rangers refused to sign Catholic players. Thus, the deep sectarian divide found in this rivalry did mirror the problems in Ulster. Few realized it had gotten that bad in "democratic" Scotland. This longtime informal code held by the club was mercifully broken due to not only great talent locally, but scores of players coming from the Catholic areas of Southern and Western Europe. The animosities of yesterday are not dead, but they are changing as both sides focus on foreign talent and greater money as the Scottish and global game change in the twenty-first century.

In 2004, the Scottish first minister, Jack McConnell warned the Old Firm on several occasions that the Scottish government held the teams and the players responsible for sectarian violence during and after football matches. During a match at Ibrox Stadium in Glasgow on November 20, 2004, Rangers beat Celtic, 2-0, but the fans became unusually boisterous and sectarian chanting broke out. Players from both sides were scolded by the police for inciting reactions after goals during on-field celebrations. Violence broke out after the contest in Glasgow and the first minister threatened to promulgate race and religious hate speech laws to bring the unruliness to an end. It was the first time a Scottish politician had attempted to link Old Firm activities to violence outside of the football stadiums where the Rangers-Celtic games are played in Glasgow. This was not the first time violence had flared surrounding the Old Firm soccer rivalry. Multiple times in recent years in Belfast the game has led to problems with youth gangs attacking supporters who wear the blue shirts of Rangers or the green-and-white striped shirts of Celtic. The rivalries religious dimensions are eerily similar to the divisions in Northern Ireland and it was not until 1989 that Rangers hired its first Catholic player. In February 2005, 12 were arrested for "religious prejudice" at a Celtic-Rangers match. One player was injured when something hit him in the eye. Just a week before, 30 groups, including the two elite soccer clubs, had participated in an inaugural "summit on sectarianism" held at the University of Glasgow. By 2005, Scottish legislators were becoming more proactive in trying to investigate and clamp down on the matter further.

Rugby is a popular sport in the Celtic regions of Britain and Ireland. It is the national sport of Wales. The game is a tough one in which 15 players are on the field for each team (so a total of 30 players are on the field at one time). It is similar to the American game of football in that it is a game decided by which side controls the line of scrimmage. It is different from American football in that no forward passes are allowed. Teams must advance the ball by running it (which may include back or lateral passes) and strategic punts and drop-kicks are allowed. Rugby matches are 80 minutes in length and in rugby union "tries," the equivalent of American football "touchdowns," are worth five points. The "conversion" after the "try" is worth two points (this is similar to the American football single point conversion kick after a touchdown—known as a PAT or "point after touchdown"). It is different from American football in that very little padding or head protection is worn by players in Rugby. Thus, injuries are common and the game is seen as particularly brutal. The sport which is popular in New Zealand, Australia, and South Africa, has grown in popularity in Wales, Ireland, and Scotland, and even, England has seen its growth in popularity to counter soccer and cricket. England even won the Rugby Union World Cup (held in Australia) in 2003. The Welsh love rugby and are known for their fans' zeal about the sport (even more zealous about rugby than soccer). The most famous "try" in rugby history, according to most chroniclers of the game, was Welshman Gareth Edwards' try against the mighty "All Blacks" of New Zealand in 1973. Edwards, one of several Welsh legends playing for a multinational "Barbarians" side based in England. The match was played in Cardiff and the Barbarians (a kind of all star team of rugby greats) were not expected to beat the All Blacks (New Zealand's vaunted national side which has been one of the most dominant in history). However, with Edwards's mad dash to the try line, the Barbarians scored five points and they went on to win 23-11. Several Celts (Welsh, Scots, and Irish) as well as English players were on that Barbarian team. Rugby, like football, brings out passion in the Celtic areas of Ireland and Britain.

Gaelic sports are particularly interesting because of the indigenous elements of them and the politics surrounding them. They are found in both Ireland and Scotland. The game of *Gaelic football (caid)* is very popular. It is a mixture of soccer and rugby. Like rugby each team has 15 players. Like rugby and soccer, each team can pass and kick the ball up and down the field. Like soccer, the sport has a goal and goals can be kicked into it. However, like American football and rugby, standards on top of the goal can be used to kick the ball through for points. A ball that goes over the cross bar is worth one point and a ball that goes in the goal is worth three points. Normally, Gaelic football lasts 60 minutes. The other major Irish Gaelic sport is *hurling (iománaíocht)*. Hurling is a field team sport that, like rugby and Gaelic football has 15 players on each team at a time. It is somewhat similar to American field hockey (as played by college women in the United States) and la crosse (as played by both men and women in North America). The game is played on the same field as Gaelic football and scoring is exactly the same. The major difference is the use of a solitar (a small ball) which is advanced using hurling sticks. The governing association of Irish Gaelic sports, the Gaelic Athletic Association (GAA), *Cumann Lúthchleas Gael* in the Irish, has overseen the development of these sports which are very popular in the southern part of the Republic of Ireland. Hurling does have some support in Northern Ireland. Politics have also kept northerners from playing in Gaelic competitions. But, that is changing due to cultural rapprochement after the 1998 Belfast Agreement. In 2007, the GAA allowed Ireland's all-island international rugby union squad to use Croke Park, the GAA's national stadium, for a match between Ireland and England (the first time and English side had played rugby in Ireland) and the first time a "foreign game" was allowed at Croke (site of the infamous 1920 "Bloody Sunday" event in Dublin). Certainly, Irish sport has seen its fair share of politicization, but some of that is beginning to change with power-sharing in the north and better relations between Dublin and London.

Box 6. 11: *Páirc an Chrócaigh* (Croke Park)

Probably the one of the most famous sporting parks (stadiums) in the Celtic world is Croke Park (known in the Irish as *Páirc an Chrócaigh*). It is known for the infamous event of November 21, 1920 when British colonial secretary Winston Churchill sent the hardcore Black and Tans smashing through the park during a Gaelic football contest and the soldiers opened fire on the players and crowd. Twelve were killed (including three small children). This was done in retaliation for the deaths of 11 British secret agents at the hands of the Irish Republican Army. From that time, the stadium has been a memorial to that notorious event and it has been the temple of Gaelic football and the home of the

Gaelic Athletic Association (GAA). Thus, Croke Park served for nearly 90 years as a symbol of Irishness and the South's culture. In 2007, right after the IRA agreed to recognize the police system in Northern Ireland, the GAA allowed for rugby internationals to be played at Croke including a match between Ireland and its enemy, England. Was the nearly century long animus between the two countries coming to an end? Interestingly, it was not only the political forces in Ireland or England who moved the GAA this direction. In 2002, the GAA allowed players from the Northern Irish security forces to play Gaelic sports. This was done to encourage Catholics to join the police in Northern Ireland to foster integration. Thus, a kind of functionalism, in the international relations sense of the term, occurred in which humanitarian, social, and technical convergence between the North and South evolved and this spurred on the political process toward greater sectarian harmony. Certainly, the GAA was cautious not wanting to stoke sectarian fissures (as seen even in Scotland over the Celtic-Rangers rivalry in soccer). However, with Ireland's rugby and soccer squads playing at a run-down facility (Landsdowne Road) in Dublin, the sparkling, newly renovated (in 2004) 80,000-seat stadium appeared to become even more visible in hosting non-Gaelic sports and entering the globalized age as millions watched on television all over the world. The memory of the Irish War of Independence was still real in Ireland, but a European Ireland on the world's sporting stage meant that Croke Park had a new image to a new generation. That image was not one of colonialism and bloodshed, but one of globalization and Irish pride in the new Europe.

The Scottish game of *shinty* (*camanachd* in the Scottish Gaelic) is another ancient Gaelic game that is similar to hurling. It is only 45 minutes in length, plays on a smaller pitch (field), and utilizes only 12 players per side. It is closer to American field hockey with its shorter crooked stick (*caman*). Hurling was brought to Scotland by the Gaels from Ireland and it is believed shinty evolved from it in the 1300s. Today, the game is popular mainly in the Gaelic-speaking areas of the Highlands and islands where professional leagues are found. A game that is similar to hurling and shinty is *Cammag* played on the Isle of Man. The Manx play the game with as few as four players and upwards of 50 or more. It is played with a *caman* and a ball (called a *crick* in the Manx). So, the Celtic game is played in another Celtic area like the original game of hurling in Ireland.

Conclusion

Celtic cultures are rich and multifaceted. It would be glib to try to generalize about them and say they are all the same and even similar. But, certainly, history shows that Celtic cultures and political cultures have many common threads running through them and they are oftentimes distinctly different from both English and European cultures. Culture is one area that will get academics arguing, especially in terms of how it informs and affects politics and economics in varying contexts. For Scotland, Ireland, Wales, and Northern Ireland, although much in their indigenous cultures is unique, as is seen by the linguistic differences in pockets of each area, the Celts have allowed culture to be a differentiating and unifying force simultaneously. It differentiates in that it allows outsiders to see how different in terms of political culture and culture in general is unique (such as Scotland with its religious and cultural traditions versus a very British culture in Northern Ireland for the majority Protestants). On the other hand, culture can unify and as distinct Celtic nations, each of the four under examination in this book see such areas as sport that help highlight differences, but bring Celts together on the football pitch even playing an archrival like England. This may be one of the few ways in which conflict can be sublimated among fans for each side given the national rivalries between the English and Celtic nations and even among the Celtic nations themselves (there is no love loss when Scotland plays Northern Ireland in a football match!) As posited in this book's model of Celtic politics, the EU is leaving a stamp on the cultures of these areas and this has given rise to claims of greater political legitimacy for the Celtic regions. However, like the English, the Celts have some concern over the watering down of identity and culture as the EU promotes continued economic convergence and cultural (via economic means) homogenization. Despite these qualms, Celtic cultures will remain distinct (despite the multicultural changes due to immigration in Britain and Ireland) and this will even eventually challenge the idea of Scottish, Irish, and Welsh cultures as the globe shrinks and non-Britons and non-Irish continue to make up a greater percentage of these island countries and races.

Suggestions for Further Reading and Research:

Almond, Gabriel A. and Sidney Verba. 1965. *The Civic Culture*. Boston, MA: Little, Brown.

British Broadcasting Corporation (BBC)–Scotland <bbc.co.uk/scotland/>.

BBC *Craoladh nan Gaidheal* <bbc.co.uk/Scotland/alba/> (BBC Scotland's Scottish Gaelic language page).

BBC–Wales <bbc.co.uk/wales/>.

BBC *Cymru'r Byd* <bbc.co.uk/cymru/> (BBC Wales' Welsh language page).

Brown, Mathew, et al. 2004. *Rugby for Dummies*. Mississauga, Ontario, Canada: John Wiley & Sons Canada.

Coogan, Tim Pat. 2004. *Ireland in the 20th Century*, pbk. New York: Palgrave Macmillan.

The Economist (London) <economist.com>.

The Financial Times (London) <ft.com>.

Foer, Franklin. 2004. *How Soccer Explains the World: An Unlikely Theory of Globali zation*. New York: Harper Perennial.

Goldblatt, David. 2002. *DK World Soccer Yearbook, 2002-03*. London: Doris Kindersley.

Goldblatt, David. 2008. *The Ball is Round: A Global History of Soccer*. New York: Riverhead Books.

Kellas, James G. 1989. *The Scottish Political System*, 4th ed. Cambridge, UK: Cambridge University Press.

Kuper, Simon. 2003. *Football Against the Enemy*. London: Orion Books.

McCrone, David. 1992. *Understanding Scotland: The Sociology of a Stateless Nation*. London: Routledge.

CHAPTER SEVEN

Lessons, Hopes, and Concerns

The Break-up of Britain and the Advance of Celtic Nations in Europe?

Four Nations, One State...For How Long?

Political Scientist Stephen Haseler has posited that the United Kingdom (UK) is essentially withering away and in the not so distant future the Celtic regions of this unitary state will move beyond Home Rule or administrative devolution (in Wales' case) and become independent sovereign nation-states. His argument is not as much a normative one as it is empirical. It is based largely on European Union (EU) machinations and political and global economic trends in the UK. He argues that Scotland, for example, may see independence due to several factors. First, it could move toward, what the Scottish National Party (SNP) calls "independence in Europe" if Ulster becomes independent. Second, the Scottish Parliament, which many UK politicians thought might put the breaks on nationalism, may do the opposite and spur greater calls for independence and thus Scotland would move toward ending the 1707 relationship with the other nations of the UK. Third, if the SNP could achieve greater electoral success and actually gain control of the Edinburgh parliament independence could be in the offing (Haseler 1996). However, even Haseler acknowledges the limitations of these causal variables. Northern Ireland was mired in sectarian and partisan bickering after the Good Friday accord in 1998 and, thus, movement toward restarting the prorogued devolved legislature in Belfast (which was suspended in 2002) was laboriously incremental at best by 2004, even after the Fall 2003 elections. The mild confusion after 1999 over where legislative jurisdiction lay on various issues between Edinburgh and London (also seen in Cardiff as well) left many politicos and Scottish citizens scratching their heads. The Holyrood debacle and major electoral and legislative changes (such as proportional representation and European coalition-style government after 1999) may have been more than the average voter could digest vis-à-vis the Anglo-Saxon, single member district, two-party system at Westminster. Indeed, the SNP did somewhat well in the 1999 Scottish parliament elections, but the party's election tactics were problematic. Under then-leader Alex Salmond, the SNP chose to fight the local legislative elections on foreign policy (over Labour's Kosovo war policy at Westminster) which was curious given the fact that the newly devolved parliament in

Edinburgh had no authority over foreign and defense policy. Thus, the seemingly high projections for seats for the SNP in the polls running up to the May 1999 election fell short. What's more, the party, by 2003, had seen its coffers drop drastically. It even had to move from its offices near Edinburgh's historic business district—Princes Street to cheaper confines. However, Labour's popularity plummeted after 2003 and the SNP's gamble on foreign policy paid off and by 2007 the SNP was in power in Edinburgh.

Another issue acknowledged by Haseler is the problem of EU accession. If Scotland, or other nations of the UK, seeks EU membership, how will the break-up of the UK be resolved by London, Edinburgh, and Brussels? The SNP argues that Scotland and the rest of the UK are equal partners and thus membership in the EU should be granted to Scotland and the UK based on the mutual treaty of union in 1707. This may be tricky in a legal sense since Scotland or other Celtic regions might be classified as successor states and in need of new accession agreements rather than the automatic assumption of a place in the Brussels-based supranational entity. Of course, the collapse of the German Democratic Republic in 1990 may be a loose precedent where five länder joined the 11 in West Germany to form a reunified Germany on October 3, 1990 and the old East Germany was ipso facto a part of the EU. Indeed, the nuances of this issue may be tied to Britain's European Economic Community accession in 1973 when it entered as the UK under the Tory government headed by prime minister Edward Heath. Thus, the UK-state is the signatory to the instruments of accession and an independent Scotland, Wales or Northern Ireland may not be able to access the EU immediately given even an English-rump UK-state from London may still be the legal representative of the UK at Brussels. The fact that all three Celtic regions are larger than the smallest EU state, Luxembourg at 650,000 citizens, and especially, Scotland's five million people, its economic clout in agriculture, fishing, and future North Sea oil production (rivaling its north European cousin Norway in size and potential oil resources), it may be hard for Brussels to keep the Scots out of the EU very long. Haseler argues that it will be through the EU that Brussels will eventually loosen the ties of the UK. Certainly, the current devolved context in the Celtic regions of the UK leads political scientists and historians to speculate about not only the UK's future, but the future of Celtic nations in Europe. Regionalism may be the key to change and the undoing of the UK state. The Liberal Democrats have called for a federal UK (which might mirror a federal Europe; literally a United States of Europe). After 1997, New Labour tepidly called for the start of a discussion on English regional parliaments to mollify English concern over too much pandering to Celts on devolution. Haselers argues that the English settlement, which is an asymmetrical UK Anglo-Saxon-oriented one, is on its last legs and Britain is in a European period in its political development. He may be premature given the hostile attitudes in England toward the EU (Haseler 1996). Polls show that a minority of citizens favored continued British membership in the EU. Also, the Welsh are quite tepid about devolution and Scots, although united in favor of devolution, are somewhat divided over outright independence. However,

Haseler is prescient about the fact that the EU at the dawn of the twenty-first century was continuing to deepen economic and political integration after several groundbreaking treaties in the 1990s Maastricht in 1992 and Amsterdam in 1997.

Unitarism, Federalism or Confederalism: Can or Should the Union Hold?

Former UK Conservative Party shadow secretary of state for the environment, transport and the regions John Redwood argued in a thought-provoking book, *The Death of Britain?* (1999), that the UK was experiencing a very severe constitutional crisis and that Tony Blair's policy of devolution to the Celtic fringe in Britain would not only lead to a break-up of the UK, but to an EU Trojan horse working its way into British politics and culture. As a Tory and Euro-skeptic, Redwood believed that further political integration into the EU would destabilize the political system by marginalizing the time-honored monarchy, undermine the House of Lords as a check on the House of Commons, change the nature of UK electoral politics (as was happening after 1999 with PR systems introduced in Wales and Scotland), and enervate Britain's economic and political power as a sovereign state. His counter to the Blairite move toward greater decentralization of UK politics, was to argue for a strong unified UK—as was argued by John Major's Tory secretary of state for Scotland Ian Lang, now called Lord Lang of Monkton (see Chapter Four above)—in his memoirs, *Blue Remembered Years* (2002)—and a confederal EU that allows Britain to remain a global business power and also retain its political power without yielding too much political and economic power and sovereignty to the EU. The unifying theme and question raised by Redwood, Lang, and Haseler, albeit from divergent perspectives, is a very salient one: is Britain due for some inexorable break-up given the move toward devolution and greater EU integration? The Labour government of the late 1990s and early twenty-first century under Blair (1997–2007) and Gordon Brown (after 2007) sought to answer this question by saying that a decentralized UK where "British" values could be found alongside English, Welsh, Scottish, and Northern Irish values would be viable. This fuzzy calculation seems to have worked somewhat, but it does not deal with the continued Euro-skepticism found in the area of both political and economic issues and the concern over what would happen to the country's sovereignty if the euro was adopted and the pound sterling jettisoned. Certainly, a Celtic model of politics does not imply automatically growing Celtic power. Nor does the decentralization of the UK state mean that Celtic nations could become powerful and viable vis-à-vis Europe and England. However, a loose United Kingdom with regional assemblies in the Celtic fringe and England might lead to changes in the way Britain does business with the EU perhaps (mirroring the decentralized, yet federal Spanish model with its 17 autonomous communities). A question remains about EU intentions with regions in Europe and certainly the current devolved setup in Britain allows for the growth of multi-level governance to play its hand further in Britain and the EU in general.

Is Ireland the Best Model for Other Celtic Nations?

Given its violent past in the early part of the twentieth century and continued violence in the north of its island, Ireland is an important, yet perplexing model for Celtic nations. Its people fought bravely for its break from the UK. Yet, the revolution, that began with Éamon de Valera, Michael Collins, and Arthur Griffith that eventually brought independence, put the gun into Irish politics and until early 2007, that gun was still a part of the northern part of the island. Political and social scientists have long wondered why violence was much more a part of the Irish political culture and not a part of the other Celtic political cultures, especially in the twentieth and early twenty-first centuries. One study completed by political scientists Ian Budge and Cornelius O'Leary found that Glasgow and Belfast had the exact same sectarian make-up, yet Glasgow was more democratic, stable, and peaceful than its Northern Irish sister city. What's more, they found that the Scottish political culture was more democratic than the Northern Irish one (Budge and O'Leary 1973). Thus, one can argue that perhaps something in the political and cultural context indigenous to Scotland would make it more democratic. Perhaps, the English influence is one variable that would play into the mix here. Interestingly, despite the perception of stability and democracy in Scotland and instability and violence in Ulster, the *Times* of London reported in late 2005 that Scotland was the "world's most violent" country. A United Nations (UN) report had found that folk in Scotland might be assaulted three times more than in the United States. The study found that three percent of Scots had been assaulted versus 1.2 percent of Americans, 0.1 percent in Japan, 0.8 percent in Australia, and 0.2 percent in Austria. Interestingly, England and Wales were second in terms of the number of violent assaults and Northern Ireland last in ranking the UK nations. This may give rise to a challenge to the belief that Northern Ireland is an intrinsically violent political culture. Unfortunately for the Scots, the study which looked at 21 countries, found a doubling of violent crime in 20 years and that per capita violence was equal to such notorious cities as Johannesburg, South Africa, Rio de Janeiro, Brazil, and Tbilisi, Georgia. The report found that a sample of 2000 Scots told interviewers that they had been victims of crime often (ten times higher than Scottish police figures). The problem area appeared to be the western part of Scotland in and around Glasgow where 160 people had been killed in five years and in the first nine months of 2005 alone 1,100 major assaults, 13 murders, and 145 attempted murders had occurred. Much of this violence was attributed to the Old Firm football rivalry between Celtic and Rangers. What's more, a culture of alcohol and knives had emerged that may have had some roots in history as the skein dubgh (Pronounced: SKEEN-doo), or famous Scots dagger, placed in the knee socks of men wearing the traditional kilts may be part of the reason for the knife culture as more Scots young men are wearing kilts as signs of their national identity, even to football matches at home and abroad. Thus, political scientist Samuel Beer's contention that incivility had led to the end of consensus in Britain may partially explain the rise in violence in Scotland and other parts of the UK.

Certainly, despite these negatives, Scotland was still seen as a democratic culture and one that was attempting to confront its social problems and challenges. Éire had changed much as it democratized after 1937 and grew as an agrarian state into the 1960s. But, its joining of the EU in 1973 helped take it further toward developing a modern services-dominated economy that has not only helped it provided jobs and an improving standard of living for its citizens, but an entrenched and ensconced democratic political culture and political system. As seen in the pages above, its political system has seen parties of the right and left come to power and even share power and thus its original predominant party system under de Valera has given way to a moderate multiparty democratic system that fosters an evolving democratic political culture. In this respect, Éire may be a good model for the other Celtic nations given its size, populace, and relationship with both the UK (which is stable and diplomatic) and the EU.

Positives and Negatives of Small Celtic States in a Europe of Regions

What are the pros and cons of small Celtic states in Europe? The "pros:" First, the Celtic nations would find that their cultural identity would be recognized and accepted, in many ways more so, as independent states in the EU than with the current status quo. Ties with Celts in Brittany in France and some ancient Celtic settlements in Spain (with some Celts found in Galicia and the Basque region in Spain, for example) could help forge greater transnational ties for economic and social purposes. Second, the ability to derive prestige in the diplomatic and political realms as full-blown sovereign nations would help in several ways. Politically, the profile of these states would be raised and in terms of foreign policy old acquaintances (Scotland with France, for example) could resume. Third, the economic fortunes of these states might improve not only within the EU, but with greater access and control of indigenous resources (such as oil for the Scots, fishing for the Northern Irish, and mining for the Welsh). The "cons" are apparent as well: First, losing political linkages to either the UK or Ireland would lead to some unforeseen costs both economically. Infrastructural expenses, government grants, etc. will mean that the indigenous Celtic governments would have to come up with much on their own. Second, cutting political ties with the UK and Ireland could mean a rise in tensions over foreign relations and border disputes and problems as Éire and Ulster have had over the years could lead to problems and even conflict and security concerns for all parties involved. The cooperation afforded under the current status quo appears to work well for all nations. Third, the conceptual problems of controlling decisions on economics, foreign policy, overt political and policy issues could lead to much confusion in a fuzzy, blurry regionalizing EU context, yet fractured UK that has lost one or more Celtic regions. What's more, the power of a large UK with 58 million citizens is more beneficial than a truncated one with a small Scotland and even smaller Wales and Northern Ireland operating in a growing and increasingly uneven EU as eastern European nation-states joined in 2004. Thus, Scotland competing with a 40 million strong Poland for EU grants and recognition, Ulster doing the same with two million strong Slovenia, and Wales competing with three million strong Lithuania may lead to issues that the Celts might want to bypass or at least share with their UK (English) and Irish (Republic) neighbors. Certainly, these are all highly speculative, yet Haseler and others feel that speculation about the future of the Celtic fringe in UK politics and Irish politics is important and a good exercise in "thinking outside the box" given the challenges that devolution have brought to Britain since the Blair government implemented it after the 1997 referendums.

Regionalism

Regionalism can be conceptualized in a number of different ways. Comparativists in political science and historians (historian Sam Goodfellow's conceptualization of regionalism is a good one) tend to view regionalism in an inductive manner (Goodfellow 1998). That is, the importance of the region under investigation is viewed based on the characteristics of that region (e.g. its linguistic, cultural, political, social traditions and so forth and how they relate to the identity of individuals within that region). In the political science sub-field of international relations, regionalism is conceptualized in more of a deductive manner when investigating a grouping of states that have aligned for either economic, social or political reasons or a combination of these reasons. Regionalism is important for students of the EU and small states in Europe because it has returned as a dominant unit of analysis and a major analytical framework (i.e. the region) that help us understand what regions do today and how they interact with various supranational organizations and dominant states.

Political scientist Samuel P. Huntington argues that at the onset of the post-Cold War era in the early 1990s that "regionalism and the regionalization of world politics" had returned to the discourse on politics and international relations. Regional conflict had replaced strictly "global" ones and this was difficult for major powers such as the United States, China and Russia to deal with. Moreover, some smaller powers were redefining their national and defense interests along regional lines, such as Turkey and Sweden (Huntington 1996). Economics were not immune to the regional trend, he argues. Intra-regional trading was as prolific as inter-regional trading and in the early 1990s these trends gave way to the creation of regional trading blocs such as the North American Free Trade Agreement trade regime, Asia-Pacific Economic Cooperation, and a newly augmented post-Maastricht EU. Political scientists David M.

Wood and Birol A. Yeşilada argue that although regional integration theory is an appropriate conceptual approach to the study of European integration and EU evolution, the EU itself is a problematic entity when applying regionalism to the study of the structures, functions and processes related to the development of the EU. First, they say that a number of economic and political variables continue to affect EU development and this has hurt the EU's attempt to carry out a consistent plan of action as a major international organization (IO). Second, Wood and Yeşilada argue that the EU is too complex an organization and social phenomenon to be studied by one type of conceptual approach or model. They believe the EU has a kind of "multi-level character" and this adds to the EU's complexity as a unit of analysis (Wood and Yeşilada 1996).

Political scientist Neill Nugent carefully delineates the literature that has utilized various conceptual approaches to reflect the balance between regional and supranational theories of the EU and its processes. The regional, which sees the EU as a stepping stone just shy of a supranational entity, is embodied by *intergovernmentalism*. Intergovernmentalism is much like the sub-discipline of international relations' view of regionalism: Nation-states will work with each other on topics and issues they have in common. Control over how these decisions are made will affect the sovereignty of the nations and states involved. Some decisions will be made mutually or multilaterally by states and others will be turned over to international organizations (like the EU or the United Nations). This contrasts with the concept of *supranationalism* which sees nation-states working with each other to solve problems and issues and each state cedes some sovereignty over to the international organizations and gives it authority to act on their behalf. This takes international relations past pure cooperative efforts toward integration and the connection of state's decision-making power. Hence, the loss of sovereignty occurs (Nugent 1999).

Critics of regionalism as an applied theory argue that it denies the reality of transnational economic and political events. Huntington argues that regions are geo-culturally oriented and that regions may not succeed in meeting economic and political objectives for nations and nation-states when peoples do not share common approaches to decision-making, peace and goals within a specific region. He argues that, as a matter of fact, regions may cause the reverse, a divorce from what might link peoples together (common cultural outlooks, etc.) and an exacerbation of intra-civilizational conflict, as seen in the former Yugoslavia from 1991–95. Political scientist Inis Claude, Jr. argues that regionalism is tied to the question that is under consideration. Not all issues can be solved by regional approaches to diplomacy and international conflict management. He further states that regionalism may allow for "international solutions" to problems that are carried out by states that are committed to a mutual process of decision-making that is manageable and committed. Oftentimes, the world is too large and "unwieldy" to allow for supranational-level action on issues and problems confronting states and regions. This is why regionalism, in the applied sense, makes sense, according to Claude. However, Claude conceptualizes regionalism an incremental set of steps to supranationalism. Hence, Claude suggests that the regional organization will perhaps end up as a supranational one at some point in its evolution (Claude 1984).

The EU: Is Supranationalism Inevitable?

Regional IOs such as the EU and the North Atlantic Treaty Organization (NATO) are in the process of becoming more universal in their approaches to political decision-making and conflict resolution. By universal, I mean increasingly supranational or global in their actions and processes as IOs. For example, the EU has created trade regimes with various non-European regions including the Africa, Caribbean and Pacific (ACP) trade regime and the Global Mediterranean Policy (GMP) trade regime which has attempted to increase exports and other linkages to North Africa and other parts of the Mediterranean basin. These organizations have been created to extend the EU's scope, at first in a functionalist sense, and secondarily, to achieve greater political and social linkages with the peoples of those areas which those two trade regimes serve. The ACP was created as a result of the first Lomé Convention of 1975. The treaty, signed by the then-European Community (EC), today's EU, and 46 ACP countries, provided for a preferential trade regime for these states with the EU, a five-year aid package largely determined by the ACP states, a number of "consultative institutions" and the Commodity Export Earnings Stabilization Scheme, which gave monies to ACP states whose export earnings from a country's main commodity fell short of expectations due to external variables. The GMP was created in 1972 in order to strengthen economic ties to the non-member Mediterranean Basin countries (NMBCs). The GMP was a move toward a multilateral approach to trade with the NMBCs, treating them as a region rather than separate states. The motives for the GMP were political as well with the clear functionalist goal of using economic carrots to improve regional stability, trade between Europe and NMBCs and the attempt to check Soviet aims in the region. Despite these aims, problems did occur between NMBCs and the EU. One major problem was the incompatibility of lesser industrialized economies in the NMBC states attempting to trade and compete with the industrialized EC/EU states. The EU is not the only European regional IO that has at times moved toward a more global or supranational orientation.

NATO is in the process of evolving into a global organization with its focus on economic development and democracy for all its member and candidate states, as well as subsidiary partner states that include some states not found in the geographical areas of Europe or the Atlantic area. For example, NATO began its so-called "Mediterranean Dialogue" in January 1994 and by December of that year NATO's foreign ministers said they were ready to create "contacts, on a case-by-case basis, between the Alliance and Mediterranean non-member countries with a view to contributing to the strengthening of regional stability." The Dialogue was setup to allow for bilateral talks between participating Mediterranean states and NATO, but also provided for multilateral discussions on an ad hoc basis. By the Madrid Summit in 1997, the Dialogue had moved to a new level with the creation of the Mediterranean Cooperation Group (MCG). The MCG includes the NATO states, Egypt, Israel, Jordan, Mauritania, Morocco and Tunisia. The MCG was a follow-up to the EU's Barcelona Declaration of 1995 which was agreed to by the EU states and 12 NMBCs. The Barcelona Declaration called for an eventual broad-gauged European-Mediterranean alliance that would: 1) create a security and political alliance to allow for peace and stability in a Euro-Mediterranean region; 2) an economic partnership that would encourage prosperity in this region; and 3) cultural, social and civil society linkages to improve social relations between the states involved. Clearly, these examples evince the supranational or universal character of developments within these two important regional organizations and their impact on Europe and other parts of the globe. I will now discuss Scotland, Ireland, Wales, and Northern Ireland's evolution in Europe and the EU.

How Celtic Nations Fit into a Europe of Regions

A Europe of regions began to evolve in the late twentieth century. The charismatic leadership of Jordi Pujol in Catalonia in Spain brought Europe and the globe a heightened sense of Catalonian separatism and the uniqueness of the region's language (Catalans) and its bid to become one of the regional economic leaders and engines of not only Spain, but Europe. Pujol's interest in forging direct economic and political linkages with other regions of Europe, such as Baden-Württemberg in southwestern Germany, led many to comment on the increasing regionalization of Europe. The EU realized the importance of regionalism in Europe and in 1992 when the Maastricht Treaty was promulgated, its attempt to bring about deeper economic, political, and social convergence in the EU led to the creation of the *Committee of Regions* (COR). The body serves as an advisor for subnational governments and autonomous regions in the EU which includes regions like Catalonia, the Basque region of Spain, Scotland, Northern Ireland, Wales, and the various *länder* of Germany. The COR plays a similar role to the Economic and Social Committee (ESC) of the EU vis-à-vis the Council of Ministers and the European Parliament. Both the ESC and the COR represent functional and subnational interests with the ESC representing interest groups and others that have more of an economic focus on policy and the COR representing regions and nations that are part of a group of subnational peoples and regions that want representation for their particular economic, social, cultural, and political needs. The COR may not be as powerful an outlet for subnational interests given that some regions such as the Celtic ones may be more powerful within their own country's political systems than the EU's. However, by 1999, when devolution began in Scotland, the EU had some 50 subnational representatives in Brussels lobbying the EU central government. These 50 diplomatic hubs included Scotland House which the Scottish first minister the late Donald Dewar christened to give Scotland more control over its European policy-making and a greater identity as a quasi-independent state in Europe. The symbolism and the political importance of the move toward more subnational governance within a regionalizing and globalizing EU is important since the EU has worked its way "in the front door" in both UK and Irish politics, but also "in the backdoor" as well, by directly bypassing London in allowing Edinburgh, Cardiff, and Belfast to interact and channel policy-making directly to Brussels. The same can be said of Belfast's relationship to Dublin as well, given the fact that, despite the troubles in Northern Ireland, a cross-party agreement on working closely with the EU was one method of applying a functionalist approach to drawing Northern Ireland into a regionalizing EU. Hence, the identity of Celtic nations is no longer one related and tied only to domestic UK and Irish politics, but to supranational EU politics as well where the subnational Celtic governments have their own interests, channels of interest articulation, places on EU committees (such as COR) for unique Celtic identity, and representation above and beyond the UK or Irish identity. Thus, the Celts continue to see their nations as increasingly semi-autonomous rather than wholly dependent on the politics and economics of the dominant UK or Irish nation-states. With this all taking place in the context of greater global governance and a supranationalizing and globalizing EU, the question remains at what point will the Scots, Northern Irish, and Welsh either break with the dominant nation-states politically or will they continue to decentralize, yet take the best of what a supranationalizing EU and a devolving UK bring? How will the continued quest for peace and power-sharing in Ulster affect that region's relationship to the Republic in the South? These questions may not have definite answers, but the EU and greater integration since 1992 has provided a platform for increased regional and national identity for these Celtic fringe nations. Certainly, the events of the late Spring and early Summer 2005 in which France and the Netherlands rejected the proposed EU Constitution put the movement toward continued integration and an eventual United States of Europe on hold. But, the functional processes through which the EU interacts and regulates policies in Britain and Ireland will continue to bring Celtic nations closer, not farther away from Brussels.

What about the Scandinavian Model for Celtic Nations?

Political scientist David Arter makes the argument that the Scottish parliament may be on the way to becoming a Scandinavian style legislature. Scotland, with Sweden as an exception, is roughly the same size as the northern European democracies. The Scandinavian countries have historical ties to Scotland (as seen in earlier chapters above) and both work together in the context of EU programming. Scotland like its friends across the North Sea face many similar challenges: voter apathy among the young, eroding party membership, ebbing legitimacy in the political process, and cynicism toward politics. One political scientist has called the Scandinavian states "bargaining democracies" and thus negotiations among the parties in Nordic systems are more common than continental systems. Perhaps, Scotland is similar in this respect with the devolved 1999–2007 Lab-Lib governments and Wales with its Lab-Lib government from 1999–2003 and the "Red-Green" (Labour-Nationalist) coalition after mid-2007.

Why is the Scottish parliament a Scandinavian style legislature? According to Arter: 1) In its creation it drew inspiration from several Scandinavian legislatures—the Swedish *Riksdag* and the Danish *Folketing* to name two. It hoped to emulate the parliament in Stockholm as processing much information about government to constituents. It sought to emulate Norwegian custom at that nation's legislative body (the *Storting*) in figuring plenary session speakers by allowing members to register in advance to keep the debate practices more open; 2) the Scottish parliament is unicameral and based on an extensive committee system like the Scandinavian states; 3) like Sweden, Iceland's *Althing* or Finland's *Eduskunta*, the Scottish parliament committees have the right of initiating legislation; 4) 56 of 129 female MPs were elected in 2003 by proportional representation (PR) in Scotland, much like the Scandinavian parliaments. Interestingly, more women are getting elected to the Scandinavian and Celtic legislatures than other legislatures around the world [see Box 7.1; Like Finland, the Scottish parliament is bilingual (5% of Finns speak Swedish and less than one percent of Scots speak Gaelic). Three MSPs could speak Gaelic fluently in the 2000–01 legislative session and used that language in a few debates; 6) Seating is semi-circular (according to party) like the *Storting* in Oslo and *Eduskunta* in Helsinki. Sweden and Norway sit according to geography (constituency representation) and Iceland's legislators draw lots to see where they will sit; 7) a Scandinavian multiparty system is found in Scotland; and 8) like all Nordic states (except Sweden), the Scottish government is a coalition one (unlike the UK government) (Arter 2004).

Box 7.1: Celtic and Scandinavian Legislatures: North European Coalescence?

The Scandinavian heritage of parts of the Celtic fringe recalls the role the Vikings and others played in shaping the cultural and political fortunes of Celtic peoples. Today's Scandinavian parliaments also have direct ties to both longstanding Celtic legislatures and newer ones. The Tynwald, the parliament of the Isle of Man (like Bermuda in the Caribbean, it is a British Crown territory in the Irish Sea), is the longest standing legislature in the world. It goes back over 1000 years and the Celtic Manx claim that it has sat continuously from the time of the Vikings in 800 AD. The Norse controlled the island until the thirteenth century when the Scots took control. What started as a kind of meeting of Viking families in a classic tribal council format (as seen even at the dawn of the twenty-first century in post-Taliban Afghanistan) evolved into a relatively autonomous self-governing legislature. Dublin was initially a Viking town and the Irish tradition of chieftains and large families may explain the dovetailing of Viking and Celtic cultures. The same occurred in Scotland with Viking invasions of both Western Isles and northern Scottish outposts. Thus, today the kinship felt by Scots, Norwegians, and Danes is not surprising, and the move to emulate their Scandinavian friends in terms of parliamentary democracy may be related to the ties between history and culture. So in 1000 years, the Celts and Scandinavians have gone from enemies to friends.

Furthermore, Scotland and Ireland's ties to the invading Vikings from Norway make for cultural and ethnic connections that have been reviewed earlier. In Scotland today, ties to Norway and Denmark have increased especially in Aberdeen, Scotland and the UK's oil capital. One can find daily flights from Aberdeen to Oslo and Cophenhagen in order for business executives working on North Sea oil exploration and other projects which strengthens economic, social, and political ties between Scotland and their Scandinavian neighbors. Flights to and from Scotland on airlines located in Norway, Denmark, and Sweden are now the norm on a daily basis. Certainly, Scots can get flights to other British cities and Paris, but Norwegian City Star Airlines flies to Oslo (the Norse capital), Kristiansund, and Stavanger. Another Norwegian airline, Widerøe, flies to and from Edinburgh and Aberdeen and it flies to Bergen and Stavanger in southwestern Norway. Royal Dutch Airlines (KLM) out of Copenhagen and Scandinavian Airlines System (SAS) out of Stockholm fly direct to Scotland as well. The Scottish capital's airport sees 11 of 26 airlines flying to Scandinavian cities (in Denmark, Finland, the Netherlands, Norway, and Sweden) and to Belfast, Dublin, Shannon, Cork, and Galway on the Emerald Isle. Flights can be found for the EU's capital Brussels as well. Thus, the importance of commercial, financial, cultural, and political linkages with the Scandinavian and European societies are very important to the Scots and Celts in general and underscore the end of a parochial British outlook that now sees a broader attempt to regionalize in Europe than regionalize purely inside the UK.

International *functionalism* as it applies to the Celtic regions could eventually mirror the Scandinavian states. In 1952, these countries formed the Nordic Council which included Denmark, Norway, Iceland, Sweden, and Finland. Greenland and the Faroe Islands (both controlled by Denmark) and Aland (controlled by Finland) are autonomous islands that participate in the IO. Estonia is working toward membership and the Nordic Council has offices in Estonia. These nations sought to forger closer ties on social, economic, cultural, and legal affairs. Two issues of especial importance to the council were environment and transportation. The council has also attempted to align foreign policies and move toward greater cohesion politically by extending intergovernmental linkages and deepening political and economic communication and integration among these countries' executives. This mirrors what the EU has done since 1958, but it could serve as a model for Celtic states and regions that want to look at a range of issues related to the social, political, and economic space shared by Celts and polities on the Celtic fringe. Also, some intergovernmental relationship between Celtic nations and Scandinavian ones may evolve as well—perhaps a loose linkage between a "Celtic Council" and the Nordic Council on issues that appear to be important to both groups such as the environment, North Sea oil and energy resource growth, management, and conservation, shared cultural history under the Vikings, educational opportunities, even social concerns (from sport to religion), cultural change and handling immigrants could help solidify better relationships and greater Celtic identity aside from dominant nation-state identities (such as the UK and even Éire). Of course, a Celtic-like Council exists as a cultural IO—the Celtic League (see Box 7.2).

Box 7.2: An International "Celtic Council?"

Like the Nordic Council, League of Arab States, African Union or Organization of Islamic Conference, could Celts establish an international organization (IO) that would serve an intergovernmental purpose to facilitate social, political, and economic dialogue over Celtic concerns? Where would the headquarters be? Edinburgh (the home of the largest number of Celts) or Dublin—the home of the lone Celtic nation-state? Who could belong? Scotland, Wales, Ireland, Cornwall, Ulster, and Breton in France? A genuine IO that could harmonize relationships between Celtic peoples and traditions might be an interesting step in creative functionalism in terms of international relations. However, like the European Union, would sovereign nation-states like the UK and France find this to be too intrusive into their domestic and foreign affairs arguing that this could divide their countries even further? What is more, given the multicultural melting pot that many Celtic regions have become, is emphasizing "Celticness" a good idea when parts of the Celtic societies are descended from Asians, Arabs, Africans, and other Europeans? In actuality, a Celtic cultural IO has been around since 1961. It is called the Celtic League and it serves to unite the Celtic peoples and regions of Europe largely for cultural and linguistic purposes. But, its efficacy has been minimal. At its foundation, it was hoped that the Celtic League would emulate the Nordic Council. But, that has not happened so far. It is interesting to speculate about, but nonetheless, Celtic international political integration may not be as far afield as some might think.

As political scientist Ann-Marie Slaughter suggests in her book, *A New World Order* (2004), global networks are becoming the norm empirically and the world is shrinking not around a universal model of world government, but one of *global governance* based on decentralized decision-making and policy networks tied not only to expertise, but also to geo-politics where nation-states voluntarily work with supranational and inter-governmental bodies to achieve greater understanding and problem solving capacities among neighbors. Thus, Celtic polities have taken on a unique identity of their own given this global transformation that appears to have begun under the EU, but will probably congeal further beyond the growth of a globalized EU. Is this ideal for the UK or Celtic nations in the normative sense? Perhaps no and yes depending on one's viewpoint; but it appears to be reality in a globalizing age.

Conceptualizing and Understanding Celtic Political Systems

The concept of Celtic politics is one that is not new to political science or other related disciplines. The idea of studying Celts is an ancient discipline whether historical, geographical, or literary. To apply the term "politics" to understanding the Celtic fringe has been a fairly regular focus of various social and political analyses since the advent of nationalist movements in Scotland, Northern Ireland, and Wales since the late 1960s. A model of Celtic politics makes various suppositions about the political contexts in which politics is occurring in the Celtic fringe. One time-honored approach used in political science since the 1950s has been political scientist David Easton's *political systems analysis*. Using an empirical behavioral approach, Easton developed an abstract model centered on the political system. The system was the "black box" or dependent variable that allowed the investigator to make various hypotheses about it. Without the political system were various independent variables such as the "inputs" (a. k. a. "demands" and "supports"), outputs (laws, policies, rulings, etc.), and feedback loop that started the process over again. Ipso facto, the political system was important, but as a way of looking at a Celtic political model, the individual system may be less important than the condition imputed to the functioning and development of the system. Easton argued that four key properties of political systems are found in them. First, the identification of properties within the system allows us to tell whether the system is political or governmental as opposed to social. For example, various units of a system are identifiable (legislatures, executives, political parties, etc.) Also, because systems do not work inside a vacuum other forces affect them making it necessary to set boundaries. Second, political systems have inputs and outputs which affect a system's overall operation. Without either the system will not work and eventually atrophy. Third, a political system will see some differentiation within it. Separating tasks and deciding who does what is part of this process. No two political systems are exactly alike, thus comparing Celtic political systems will inevitably lead to some limitations in analysis. Finally, the integration of a political system is important in terms of creating a certain functioning process and viable units within the system. Without a decently "oiled machine" a political system will sputter, falter, and eventually collapse. This final property can be extended not only to evince the viability of inchoate Celtic political systems whether Scottish or Welsh with low levels of development at the sub-national level in UK politics or more advanced levels of development as in Ireland's case as it plays a more significant role in the EU as a sovereign political system or as a semi-viable, semi-static system as the case may be in Northern Ireland.

Political scientists Zsuzsa Csergo and James M. Goldgeier argue that nationalisms may evolve in various manners and that at least four types (traditional, substate, transsovereign, protectionist) are found in an integrating EU. This takes Easton's last property past self-integration as an autonomous nation or nation-state toward more of an external integration within a supernationalizing IO like the EU. Ironically, for the substate nationalism to evolve, a fully integrated political system is not necessary because IOs may be able to provide a lever of legitimation and integration that allow the sub-state nation to develop outside of normal domestic politics in the sub or national political systems. Empirically, this can be demonstrated in the case of Scotland and Wales.

As for the model of Celtic politics posited in Chapter One, certainly, regionalism does factor in, but cross cutting elements of these assumptions may also explain how growing regionalism both within the EU and within the UK affect the Celtic areas. As was stated in the opening chapter a model of Celtic politics assumes a certain amount of social democracy as part of the Celtic political culture. Economically, this may be important as well, since the Celtic regions of the UK tend to be the most statist of all the regions of the UK. That is, these regions have a higher percentage of laborers working in the public sector than the other regions (especially the southern regions of the UK). As the *Financial Times* reported in March 2006, the UK regions with the largest number of public sector (government) employees were (in order from top to bottom): 1) Northern Ireland (30%); 2) Scotland (24%); 3) Northeast England (just under 24%); and 4) Wales (23%). These were the top four among 12 UK regions with the Southeast England region with the least amount of government workers at around 18%. What is more, the Southwest region of England (which is home to Cornwall and the Cornish) was number six of twelve regions just behind the northwest part of England. So, four historically Celtic areas are in the top six in terms of public sector workforce in Britain. This would help confirm perhaps two assumptions: 1) that those regions have been oriented toward social democracy given the people's interest in having greater government intervention into their personal and economic lives and 2) the rift between the more affluent south of England and the less affluent north of Britain may suggest a need for a greater role for the public sector in those parts of the UK. The latter may be more of an economic explanation rather than an explanation based on assumptions of a model of Celtic politics. But, nevertheless, this trend may continue to accentuate the differences economically and politically between the Celtic fringe in Britain and the Irish state and the concentration of capital in London and the southeast as one pillar of the EU's economic power that concentrates economically in northern Europe from Brussels to Frankfurt to London (the golden triangle). One expert, Andrew Henley of Swansea University, argues that the divergence within the UK economy in terms of growth in the south versus north was greater after 1997 than the years of Thatcherism. Economic growth in the UK since 1997 when Tony Blair took over has been around 2.5%. However, in Scotland and Wales the private sector growth rates have been less. Scotland's at 1.5% and Wales at 1.6%. In the UK, 80% of the economic growth was found in the private sector. However, private sector growth on the Celtic fringe was not as good: Scotland (72%) and Wales (66%). Certainly, this evinced the disparity between the regions. Of course, much of the southeast of England's growth was tied to the banking and financial services areas. These areas are popular in the Celtic fringe too, but capacity and labor market rigidity may explain some of the economic problems related to these issues in the Celtic fringe.

Csergo and Goldgeier's typology can be applied coherently to each Celtic political context discussed in this book. Scotland and Wales appear to fit the substate type well. Northern Ireland is an example of a protectionist region, but purposeful diplomacy has led to some minor movement toward a transsovereign type nationalism in that region. Ireland, as a state, is traditional, but may at times be seen as transsovereign in its willingness to work with Britain and Northern Ireland's leadership on the Northern Irish question. Certainly, since the introduction of a more multiparty type system in Northern Ireland (and especially since the GFA in 1998), Northern Ireland may be seen as a substate actor as well (rather than a UK region that is more traditional in its typology).

Type of Nationalism	Main Objective	View of EU as Alliance of
Traditional	Ensure congruence of political and Cultural boundaries (nation-state)	States
Substate	Strengthen political representation for homeland vis-à-vis state	Nations
Transsovereign	Create institutions to link nation Across state boundaries	Nations
Protectionist	Preserve national culture in face of immigration/social change	States

Source: Zsuzsa Csergo and James M. Goldgeier. 2004. "Nationalist Strategies and European Integration." *Perspectives on Politics* 2(1): 21-37.

Table 7.1: Typology of Nationalisms and View of the European Union

Is There a Distinctive "Celtic" Politics?

Certainly, there is a distinctive Celtic politics found in Scotland, Ireland, and Wales. Whether one can talk about a "model of Celtic politics" would be an important topic of debate in both academic political science and governmental circles in Britain, Ireland, and other places, such as the US. If political scientist James G. Kellas can talk of the "Scottish political system" then it appears that a model of Celtic politics and distinct Celtic politics appears to be an appropriate lens to analyze politics in Scotland, Ireland, and Wales in the twenty-first century, post-Cold War globalizing context in which Britain, Ireland, and EU development are occurring. What's more, the growth of literature and policy on sub-national government in Britain suggests that the inchoate devolved legislatures in Scotland and Wales are in and of themselves forming unique and distinct political units that cohere to both the UK and EU systems. The concept of the political system, mentioned above, helps us understand that systems are both sui generis and organic and thus Celtic political systems may be distinct and unique contexts for political analysis and inquiry given their importance as separate units of analysis in UK, Irish, and EU politics. Certainly, Northern Ireland may be a problem here, but in a strange way, it provides a case that may be important as a "murky or fuzzy" system that does not neatly fit sub-national or national governance models in the EU, UK, Irish, or globalizing context. Its political culture has made it the outlier in Celtic politics with violence and fragmentation, but as a product of both UK and Irish politics, Northern Ireland may grow to be a product not of UK or Irish systems politics, but of EU regional politics as its politicians and leaders (of all parties in that segmented system) fast adhere to EU politics, policies, and linkages as seen above in the discussion of party politics focusing on agriculture, tourism, fishing, and environmental interests and the like. This means that as the EU continues to tinge deeper the politics of these areas, the Celtic model of politics in these regions and states will continue to be of greater importance as political and structural homogeneity may allow for regional identity to continue to come to the fore (as seen in Spain with the Basques and Catalonians and even in regions of Germany, with Baden-Württemberg a growing prosperous region in southwestern Germany that has tried to improve its regional links in economic terms with other regions of Europe). If regionalism continues to grow in Europe then the Celts may be in for continued salience, despite their small numbers vis-à-vis the English and their political importance may increase despite their disproportionate size. Celtic politics is not a new phenomenon. It is a product of the eighteenth and nineteenth centuries and its antecedents are even older when looking at cultural and ethno-linguistic origins. What makes a model of Celtic politics so thought-provoking is that even some British political scientists are now saying that the Westminster model (the "English" two-party system) may now be out of date. Not only is it questionable as a main level of analysis, but the future of British politics as a sub-discipline of political science may hinge on reconceptualizing how British politics is studied in both a global and European context. Structurally, the Blairite system has changed the status quo in allowing devolution to occur in Wales and Scotland. But, analytically and conceptually, the definition of the political in the UK is now broader than it was prior to 1997. One could argue that it was broader academically after 1945 as changes in the post-industrial economy and pressure groups and the newly evolving European Economic Community had a dramatic impact on Britain and Ireland. New theorizing about the UK and Ireland has led many scholars, such as political scientist Gary Marks and others, to question the institutional model that focuses on party power and elites. Instead, a *multi-level governance* model says that multiple decision-making areas occur in governance and that not all lay within the purview of the state. Some lay outside the state and are found in IOs and international networks that affect state-level policy-making as well as sub-state level actions. Thus, Britain is gradually "Europeanizing" and "globalizing" simultaneously and it is no longer a Westminster-based system as it is influenced by external variables that force it to change and adapt. This is why the model of Celtic politics seems conceptually acceptable since not all politics in these regions are driven by UK actions only, but EU ones as well. This underscores the importance of how a decentralizing UK, a regionalizing EU, and a globalizing economy impact these nations. As a geopolitical bloc, the Celtic political systems are distinct and warrant a separate conceptual approach (such as a Celtic model of politics) in order to study the politics in Scotland, Ireland, and Wales in order to analyze and understand those regions better in relation to their dominant neighbors (the English) on the British mainland and even the newer context of the EU that is increasingly as important as the British context for Celts.

Suggestions for Further Reading and Research:

Arter, David. 2004. *The Scottish Parliament: A Scandinavian-Style Assembly?* London: Frank Cass.

Claude, Inis L., Jr. 1984. *Swords into Plowshares: The Problems and Progress of International Organization.* 4th ed. New York: Random House.

Czergo, Zsuzsa, and James M. Goldgeier. 2004. Nationalist Strategies and European Integration. *Perspectives on Politics* 2 (1): 21-37.

Haas, Ernst B. *Beyond the Nation-State: Functinoalism and International Organization.* Stanford, CA: Stanford University Press, 1964.

Haas, Ernst B. *The Uniting of Europe: Political, Social, and Economic Forces, 1950-57.* Stanford, CA: Stanford University Press, 1958.

Huntington, Samuel P. 1996. *The Clash of Civilizations and the Remaking of World Order.* New York: Simon and Schuster.

Marks, Gary and Liesbet Hooghe. *Multi-level Governance and European Integration.* Boulder, CO: Rowman and Littlefield, 2001.

Mitrany, David. *The Functional Theory of Politics.* New York: St. Martin's Press, 1976.

Nugent, Neill. 1999. *The Government and Politics of the European Union*, 4th ed. Durham, NC: Duke University Press.

Wood, David M., and Birol A. Yeşilada. 1996. *The Emerging European Union.* White Plains, NY: Longman.

Bibliography

The sources listed below provided background information and data for the material and ideas presented in the book:

Andrews, Robert with Peter Hack, Kate Hughes, and Bea Uhart. 2004. *The Rough Guide to Devon & Cornwall*, 2d ed. New York: Rough Guides.

Arter, David. 2004. *The Scottish Parliament: A Scandinavian-Style Assembly?* London: Frank Cass.

Beer, Samuel H. 1982. *Britain Against Itself.* New York: W.W. Norton.

Beer, Samuel H. 1974. *The British Political System*, 1st pbk ed. New York: Random House.

Beer, Samuel H. 1969. *British Politics in the Collectivist Age.* New York: Vintage Books.

Bew, Paul, Peter Gibbon, and Henry Patterson. 2002. *Northern Ireland, 1921—2001: Political Forces and Social Classes.* London: Serif.

Bogdanor, Vernon. 2002. *Devolution in the United Kingdom.* Oxford: Oxford University Press.

Budge, Ian, and Cornelius O'Leary. 1973. *Belfast: Approach to Crisis: A Study of Belfast Politics, 1613–1970.* London: Macmillan.

Burnett, Kathryn A. 2003. "The New Clans" in *The Greatest Clans, part two. Sunday Herald* (Glasgow), September 14: 18-21.

British Broadcasting Corporation, "Scottish Politics," May 15, 2007 <bbc.co.uk>.

British Broadcasting Corporation, "Scottish Politics," May 16, 2007 <bbc.co.uk>.

British Broadcasting Corporation, "Scottish Politics," May 18, 2007 <bbc.co.uk>.

British Broadcasting Corporation, "Welsh Politics," May 19, 2005 <bbc.co.uk>.

British Broadcasting Corporation, "Welsh Politics," April 3, 2005 <bbc.co.uk>.

British Politics Group Newsletter (No. 89, Summer 1997): 24-5.

British Politics Group Newsletter (No. 97, Summer 1999): 7.

Brown, Mathew, et al. *Rugby for Dummies*. Mississauga, Ontario, Canada: John Wiley & Sons Canada, 2004.

Bulmer, Simon, Martin Burch, Caitríona Carter, Patricia Hogwood, and Andrew Scott. 2002. *British Devolution and European Policy-Making: Transforming Britain into Multi-Level Governance*. Houndsmill, Basingstoke, UK: Palgrave Macmillan.

The Christian Science Monitor, October 22, 2003.

Chubb, Basil. 1992. *The Government and Politics of Ireland*, 3d. London: Longman.

Claude, Inis L., Jr. 1984. *Swords into Plowshares: The Problems and Progress of International Organization*. 4th ed. New York: Random House.

Cochrane, Feargal. 1999. "The Past in the Present," In Paul Mitchell and Rick Wiltford, eds. *Politics in Northern Ireland*. Boulder, CO: Westview Press, pp. 1-28.

Columbia Daily Tribune (Columbia, Missouri), September 26, 2005, p. 8A.

Comhaontas Glas (Irish Green Party) (website). <www.greenparty.ie>.

Coogan, Tim Pat. *The IRA*, rev. ed. New York: Palgrave, 2002a.

Coogan, Tim Pat. *The Troubles: Ireland's Ordeal 1966-1996 and the Search for Peace*. New York: Palgrave, 2002b.

Coogan, Tim Pat. *Ireland in the Twentieth Century*. New York: Palgrave, 2004.

Czergo, Zsuzsa, and James M. Goldgeier. 2004. Nationalist Strategies and European Integration. *Perspectives on Politics* 2 (1): 21-37.

Dangerfield, George. 1980. The Strange Death of Liberal England: 1910-1914. New York: Perigree Books.

Davies, John. *A History of Wales*. London: Penguin, 1994. Originally published in Welsh as *Hanes Cymru* in 1991.

The Daily Telegraph (London), November 17, 2002 (http://www.telegraph.co.uk).

Democratiaid Rhyddfrydol Cymru (Welsh Liberal Democrats) (website). <www.demrhyddcymru.org.uk>.

Democratic Unionist Party (website). <www.dup.org.uk>.

Dodd, A.H. 1990. *A Short History of Wales: Welsh Life and Customs from prehistoric times to the present day*, pbk rpr. London: BT Batsford.

Duverger, Maurice. 1951. Political Parties *(Les Partis Politique)*. London: Methuen.

Eagles, Robin with Andrew Dickson. 2002. *The Rough Guide Chronicle: England*. London: Rough Guides.

Easton, David. 1990. "The Analysis of Political Systems." In *Comparative Politics: Notes and Readings*, 7th ed, eds. Roy C. Macridis and Bernard E. Brown. Pacific Grove, CA: Brooks/Cole: 48-58.

The Economist. October 25-31, 2003.

Electionworld.org (a site dedicated to election data from democracies around the world; specifically, election information on the May 16, 2002 election in the Republic of Ireland is contained here.)

The Evening Standard (London), May 17, 2007 <thisislondon.co.uk>.

Fianna Fáil (website). <www.fiannafail.ie>.

Financial Times (London), September 27, 2005, p. 2.

Financial Times (London), October 12, 2005, pp. 25-6.

Financial Times (London), November 3, 2005, p. 23.

Financial Times (London), March 20, 2006, p. 11.

Financial Times (London), April 3, 2006, p. 5.

Financial Times (London), November 11, 2006 <www.ft.com>.

Financial Times (London), January 29, 2007, p. 2.

Financial Times (London), February 10/11, 2007, p. 4.

Financial Times (London), May 12, 2007 <www.ft.com>.

Financial Times (London), June 13, 2007 <www.ft.com>.

Fine Gael (website). <www.finegael.com>.

Foer, Franklin. *How Soccer Explains The World: An Unlikely Theory of Globalization*. New York: Harper Perennial, 2004.

Fraser, Antonia. 1973. *Cromwell: The Lord Protector*. New York: Grove Press.

Fry, Peter, and Fiona Somerset Fry. 1995. *The History of Scotland*. New York: Barnes and Noble.

Fry, Peter, and Fiona Somerset Fry. 1993. *The History of Ireland.* New York: Barnes and Noble.

Goodfellow, Samuel H. 1998. *Between the Swastika and the Cross of Lorraine: Fascisms in Interwar Alsace*. DeKalb, IL: Northern Illinois University Press.

Greer, Alan. 1999. "Policymaking." In Paul Mitchell and Rick Wilford, eds. *Politics in Northern Ireland.* Boulder, CO: Westview Press.

Guardian Unlimited (*Manchester Guardian* online). <www.guardian.co.uk> October 26 & 28, 2003.

Harvie, Christopher. *Scotland: A Short History.* 2002. Oxford: Oxford University Press.

Haseler, Stephen. 1996. *The English Tribe: Identity, Nation and Europe*. New York: St. Martin's Press.

Hazelton, William. 2004. "'Election to Nothing': The Northern Ireland Assembly Election 26 November 2003," *British Politics Group Newsletter* 115 (Winter): 6-11.

Hearn, Jonathan. 2000. *Claiming Scotland: National Identity and Liberal Culture*. Edinburgh: Polygon at Edinburgh.

Hewitt, Adrian. 1989. ACP and the developing world. In Juliet Lodge, ed. *The European Community and the Challenge of the Future*. New York: St. Martin's Press.

Humphreys, Rob and Donald Reid. 2004. *The Rough Guide to Scotland*, 6th ed. New York: Rough Guides.

Huntington, Samuel P. 1996. *The Clash of Civilizations and the Remaking of World Order*. New York: Simon and Schuster.

The Irish Echo (online) <www.irishecho.com> March 15-21, 2006.

Irish Labour Party (website). <www.labour.ie>.

Irish Progressive Democrats (website). <www.progressivedemocrats.ie>.

The Irish Times (online) <www.ireland.com> June 14, 2007.

Jefferson, Kurt W. 2008. "Thermidor: The Scottish National Party in Power One Year On." *British Politics Group Quarterly* 132 (Spring): 9-11.

Jefferson, Kurt W. 1993. "Scotland's Post-Election Fireworks: The Rivalry Between Labour and the SNP." *Current Politics and Economic of Europe* 3(1): 71-78.

Jefferson, Kurt W. 1993. "The Scottish National Party and Left-libertarian Politics." PhD dissertation, University of Missouri–Columbia.

Johnson, Lonnie R. 2002. *Central Europe: Enemies, Neighbors, Friends*, 2d ed. New York: Oxford University Press.

Kavanagh, Dennis. 1990. "Politics of Great Britain" in Roy C. Macridis, ed., *Modern Political Systems: Europe*, 7th ed. Englewood Cliffs, NJ: Prentice Hall.

Kellas, James G. 1989. *The Scottish Political System*, 4th ed. Cambridge: Cambridge University Press.

Kerr, Peter and Steven Kettell. 2006. "In Defence of British Politics: The Past, Present and Future of the Discipline." *British Politics* 1(1): 3-25.

King, Anthony, David Denver, Iain McLean, Pippa Norris, Philip Norton, David Sanders, and Patrick Seyd. 1998. *New Labour Triumphs: Britain at the Polls*. Chatham, NJ: Chatham House Publishers.

Kitschelt, Herbert. 1988. "Left-libertarian Parties: Explaining Innovation in Competitive Party Systems." *World Politics* 40(2): 194-234.

Lander, J.R. *Ancient and Medieval England: Beginnings to 1509*. 1973. New York: Harcourt Brace Jovanovich.

Lane, Ruth. 1997. *The Art of Comparative Politics*. Boston: Allyn and Bacon.

Lang, Ian. 2002. *Blue Remembered Years: A Political Memoir*. London: Politico's.

Lange, Peter and Hudson Meadwell. 1985. "Typologies of Democratic Systems: From Political Inputs to Political Economy." In Howard J. Wiarda, ed. *New Directions in Comparative Politics*. Boulder, CO: Westview Press.

Leapman, Michael, et al. 2003. *Eyewitness Travel Guides: Great Britain*, rpr. London: Dorling Kindersley.

Leeke, Matthew. 2003. "UK Election Statistics: 1945-2003." Research Paper 03/59 (House of Commons Library), July 1.

Lijphart, Arend. 1977. *Democracy in Plural Societies*. New Haven, CT: Yale University Press.

Lijphart, Arend. 1969. "Typologies of Democratic Systems." *Comparative Political Studies* 1 (April): 3-44.

Loughlin, James. 2004. *The Ulster Question Since 1945*. New York: Palgrave.

Lynch, Michael. 1993. *Scotland: A New History*. London: Pimlico.

Lynch, Peter. 2002. *SNP: The History of the Scottish National Party*. Cardiff: Welsh Academic Press.

Maclean, Fitzroy. 1993. *Scotland: A Concise History*. London: Thames and Hudson.

Mair, Peter, ed. 1990. *The West European Party System*. Oxford: Oxford University Press.

Marks, Gary and Liesbet Hooghe. 2001. *Multi-level Governance and European Integration*. Boulder, CO: Rowman and Littlefield.

McAllister, Laura. 2001. *Plaid Cymru: The Emergence of a Political Party*. Bridgend, Wales: Seren Books.

McCrone, David. 1992. *Understanding Scotland: The Sociology of a Stateless Nation*. London: Routledge.

McKinlay, Alan and R. J. Morris, eds. 1991. *The ILP on Clydeside, 1893-1932: From Foundation to Disintegration*. Manchester: Manchester University Press.

Mitchell, Paul. 1999. "The Pary System and Party Competition." In Paul Mitchell and Rick Wilford, eds. *Politics in Northern Ireland*. Boulder, CO: Westview Press.

The National Post, November 18, 2002.

NATO Handbook. 1998. 50th anniversary ed. Brussels: NATO Office of Information and Press

New York Times, September 26, 2005, p. A10.

Norton, Philip (Lord Norton of Louth). 1994. *The British Polity*, 3d ed. White Plains, NY: Longman.

Nugent, Neill. 1999. *The Government and Politics of the European Union*, 4th ed. Durham, NC: Duke University Press.

The Observer, July 28, 2002 (http://observer.guardian.co.uk).

Parker, Mike and Paul Whitfield. 2003. *The Rough Guide to Wales*, 4th ed. New York: Rough Guides.

Pilkington, Colin. 2002. *Devolution in Britain Today*. Manchester: Manchester University Press.

Pittock, Murray G.H. 2001. *Scottish Nationality*. Houndsmill, Basingstoke, UK: Palgrave.

Plaid Cymru (Party of Wales) (website). <www.plaidcymru.org>.

Powell, David. 2002. *Nationhood and Identity: The British State Since 1800*. London: I.B.Tauris.

The Press and Journal (Aberdeen), December 3, 2003: 8.

Psephos.adam-carr.net (a site with information on the June 6, 1997 election in the Republic of Ireland).

Ramsden, John. 2003. *Man of the Century: Winston Churchill and His Legend Since 1945*. New York: Columbia University Press, 2003.

Redwood, John. 1999. *The Death of Britain?: The UK's Constitutional Crisis*. New York: St. Martin's Press.

Roberts, Clayton, and David Roberts. 1985. *A History of England: Prehistory to 1714*, vol. 1, 2d ed. Englewood Cliffs, NJ: Prentice-Hall.

Rose, Richard. 1964. *Politics in England*. Boston: Little, Brown.

Sartori, Giovanni. 1990. "A Typology of Party Systems." In *The West European Party System*, ed. Peter Mair. Oxford: Oxford University Press: 316-49.

The Scotsman (Edinburgh) Online, November 23, 2004 <www.sport.scotsman.com>.

The Scotsman (Edinburgh) Online, March 17, 2005 <www.scotsman.com>.

Scottish Conservative Party (website). <www.conservatives.com/people/scotland.cfm>.

Scottish Green Party (website). <www.scottishgreens.org.uk>.

Scottish Labour Party (website). <www.scottishlabour.org.uk>.

Scottish Liberal Democrats (website). <www.scotlibdems.org.uk>.

Scottish National Party (website). <www.snp.org>.

Scottish Socialist Party (website). <www.scottishsocialistparty.org>.

Scottish Parliament Public Information Service. July 2002. *A Devolved Parliament*, 2d ed. (Factfile 1).

Scottish Water (website). <scottishwater.co.uk>.

Seel, G. E. 1999. *The English Wars and Republic, 1637-1660*. London: Routledge.

SerVaas, Cory. 2004. "Dr. Sohan Hayreh: World Authority on the Retina." *The Saturday Evening Post* (May/June): 40-44, 94

Sinn Féin (website). <www.sinnfein.ie>.

Slaughter, Anne-Marie. *A New World Order*. Princeton, NJ: Princeton University Press, 2004.

Social Democratic and Labour Party (website). <www.sdlp.ie>.

Stoessinger, John G. 1993. *The Might of Nations: World Politics in Our Time*, 10th ed. New York: McGraw-Hill.

St. Louis (Missouri) *Post-Dispatch*, April 7, 2006, p. A9.

The Times (London) Online, September 19, 2005 (www.timesonline.co.uk).

Ulster Unionist Party (website). <www.uup.org>.

Wallace, Gordan (with Sally Ann Wallace Jefferson), "John Wallace's Journey," *Aberdeen & North-East Scotland Family History Society Journal* 93(November 2004): 27.

Welsh Conservative Party (website). <www.conservatives.com/wales>.

Welsh Labour Party (website). <www.waleslabourparty.org.uk>.

Wikipedia.org (a community web-based encyclopedia with sources).

Wood, David M., and Birol A. Yeşilada. 1996. *The Emerging European Union*. White Plains, NY: Longman.

Glossary

Chapter One

Celtic Fringe: The peripheral region of the United Kingdom (UK) where the Celts are found today. This region includes Scotland, Wales, and Northern Ireland. Of course, the Republic of Ireland is a small Celtic island and an overwhelming majority of its inhabitants share ethnic, linguistic, and cultural ties to the Celts of the UK.

Political Systems: A conceptualization of a government and its operations as a number of variables in a series of dynamic, symbiotic interactions such as interest groups (pressure groups) interacting with government (either the executive or legislature) and certain outputs from the "system" occur as a result of those interactions (such as laws or rebuffs).

Comparative Politics: The study of politics via comparative method whereby nation-states are aligned side-by-side and literally compared for functional or structural purposes. It also utilizes a heavy theoretical component in assessing the validity of theories that apply to multiple countries either in one region or globally.

Scottish Saltire: The royal blue national flag of Scotland with its distinct "Cross of St. Andrew" (a large white "X") in the middle. It is one of the symbols of the Scottish nation, along with the gold flag with the red lion emblazoned on it known as the "Lion Rampant."

Model: A model is the same thing as a conceptual approach or theory in political science. It may not be a precise scientific theory as in the natural or physical sciences, but it helps the political scientist to know what facts to look for in his or her research in building generalizations about groups and institutions' behaviors.

Nation: A group of people with several shared characteristics such as a common religion, language, ethnicity, common economic patterns of work and development, cultural identity, and usually (but not always) territory.

Nationalism: The advocacy of the right of a nation to pursue its own interests and to promote its national identity, goals, and agenda at the expense of other nations, states, and global institutions. Nationalism can lead to extremism in some forms (Nazism in Germany from 1933–45) and it can also be applied in a softer bourgeois (and even leftwing) sense (as seen in Scotland with the Scottish National Party government after 2007).

National Socialism: The form of nationalism that was adopted by Adolph Hitler in Germany after 1923 in the form of the National Socialist German Workers Party (NSDAP), better known as "Nazis." The movement called for both extreme nationalist identity for ethnic Germans, the removal of Jews from Germany, and a corporatist economic program, and some elements of socialism to maintain German community, economic development, and identity. Some extremist groups still adhere to these principles today (even in Germany, although outlawed by the German government).

Fascism: An ideology that draws its name from the Roman "Fasci," or battle axe, which Mussolini used to impose his system of Italian nationalism on Italians from 1922–44. Mussolini and Hitler's fascism was a brand of nationalism that factored in the worst forms of race hatred, oppression of minorities, and extreme national chauvinism based on race. Both systems were defeated by Americans, Britons, and Soviets by the end of the Second World War in 1945.

Celts: A group of people who came from what is now the western part of the European continent in Germany and Switzerland and ended up in Ireland in 3000 BC. These people then branched out into what is today the British mainland (England, Wales, and Scotland) and they ended up in modern-day Scotland, Ireland, Wales, part of northern France (Bretagne) and southwestern England (Cornwall).

Hadrian's Wall: Built by the troops of Roman Emperor Hadrian beginning in 122 AD. It took eight years to build. It was used to keep invading Picts (Celts) out from the north and provide a northern boundary for the Romans in Britain stretching nearly 75 miles (just over 115 kilometers) across northern England. Its remains can still be visited today in England.

Picts: The *Picti* or "painted people" were the original Celtic inhabitants of the land that is today known as Scotland. They are believed to have existed from the time of the Roman conquest of Britain under Julius Caesar in 55 BC until the 10th century. Eventually, they were amalgamated into various invading groups including the Scots (who came from Ireland) and the Vikings.

Scots: The Scots or *pirates* in the ancient Gaelic were Celtic invaders from Ireland who took over the northern part of what is now the British mainland (known today as Scotland or *Alba* in the Scottish Gaelic). The Scots invaded the area of north Britain in the fifth century and eventually absorbed the Picts and then battled other groups most notably Vikings and Anglo-Saxons in subsequent centuries prior to the Norman Invasion of 1066.

Gaels: The Celtic peoples of Ireland who branch out into other areas of the British Isles. Some Gaels invaded Scotland in the fifth century and subdued the Picts, another Celtic tribe. Others went to Wales, the Isle of Man, and Cornwall in England. The Gaels produced the dominant Celtic language of Goidelic, better known as Gaelic which still exists in two major forms in Ireland and northern Scotland today.

Welsh: The Welsh are a Celtic people that appear to have emigrated from the Iberian Peninsula into what is now the British Isles several thousand years ago like the Gaels in Ireland. The Welsh were first subdued by the Romans and then the Anglo-Saxons. The Welsh speak a Brythonic language, a different Celtic tongue from the Irish and Scots. Like the Welsh, the Bretons in northern France speak a Brythonic language as well.

Éire: The Irish (Gaelic) name for the island of Ireland. The term was used along with "Ireland" in the Free State's Constitution of 1937. It was meant to give greater political and legal legitimacy to an eventual independent Republic and distance the Irish from their colonial overlords—the British. Still, today the term is used on Irish license plates with full European Union approval, but it still is avoided in connection with fostering closer ties between the northern Six Counties (under British rule) and the Republic, especially in some sporting events such as rugby.

Chapter Two

William Wallace: The medieval Scottish hero who represented the landed classes in numerous clashes against their English overlords for control of Scotland from the late 1290s until his death by execution at the Tower of London in 1305. Wallace can be seen as an early form of political nationalism and his stunning victory at Stirling Bridge in 1297 has been memorialized in "Braveheart," an Oscar-winning movie (1996) starring Mel Gibson as Wallace.

Longshanks: English King Edward I who stanched rebellion in Scotland with brutal methods and eventually caught William Wallace. However, his legacy was sullied as his son, Edward II, failed to hold onto Scotland.

Robert the Bruce: The Scottish nobleman who defeated Edward II of England in an epic battle at Bannockburn in 1314. Bruce helped consolidate control of Scotland by the Scottish landlords who were tired of taking orders from the English monarchy. He also attempted to help his brother stave off revolt in northern Ireland as well. His victory at Bannockburn is seen as very significant in the long struggle for Scottish independence vis-à-vis England.

Bannockburn: Battle of June 23, 1314 in which the Scots led by Robert the Bruce defeated the English under Edward II. The victory is seen as a seminal battle win in the medieval struggle for power in Scotland between the Scottish and the English. It allowed Bruce gain power as a unified king of the Scots.,

James VI of Scotland (James I of England): The Scottish king who took control of the Scottish throne in 1685 at the age of 19 and then in 1603 became king of England upon the death of Queen Elizabeth I. He was the son of Mary Queen of Scots and the merging of the two kingdoms was the reunification of two crowns that had never been formally unified despite periodic Scottish acquiescence to English interests in the region for nearly 600 years following the Norman invasion.

Roundheads: The Puritan supporters of Oliver Cromwell and his Parliamentary army that sought to rid England of a corrupt monarchy and landed aristocracy and to replace them with a republican form of government that would represent the people, make England a more godly nation, and make England a practicing Protestant state without rigid liturgical high church or Catholic elements. The "Roundheads" were known for their haircuts and for their austerity and convictions.

Cavaliers: The followers of King Charles I and supporters in the House of Commons and Lords who wanted the monarchy to remain the dominant power in England during the English revolution of 1640-60 and specifically, the English (or British) Civil War(s) of 1642–50.

Oliver Cromwell: A member of the landed gentry (a country squire) from Ely near Cambridge (north of London) who became the most dominant figure of the English Civil War as a military and political leader advocating the cause of the Roundheads in calling for a devout Christian England, removal of a corrupt king, and political power to be given to the people in the form of a republic. When the latter did not happen, he marched on parliament and took control of the English state via the army and ruled as a military leader.

Claim of Right: One of Scotland's most famous covenants which was passed by the Scottish parliament in 1689 and limited the power of the deposed Scottish monarch, James VII (James II of England). As a result, the new British monarch, William III, accepted the terms given to him by the Scottish parliament.

Treaties of Union: The treaties of Union were presented by the English government to the Scottish Parliament in 1706 and promulgated in 1707. This politically and legally legitimated the union of the two crowns (which had occurred in 1603) and parliaments (chief lawmaking bodies). The English did the same with the Irish in 1800 and the United Kingdom of Great Britain and Ireland was born in 1801.
Neither treaty sat well with all Celts (as subsequent events in Ireland, Scotland, Wales suggest, but many did accept the unions if even begrudgingly so after the fact).

Jacobites: The Scots who defended the Stewart claims to the English throne. They wanted to reestablish the heir to Scottish King James VII (James I of England). After 30 years of mischief in the Highlands, the Jacobites were finally defeated by the English at Culloden Moor in 1745 when "Bonnie Prince Charlie" Stewart, the son of the exiled Stewart monarchical heir, led an uprising in the Highlands to retake power in Scotland and Britain. The battle went miserably for the Stewarts and their supporters as some 1200 of the 5000-strong Jacobite army perished.

Vikings: The pagan people of Scandinavia (today's Norway, Sweden, and Denmark) who brutally invaded the British Isles in the late eighth and ninth centuries. They also invaded, traded, and inter-married along estuaries in northern, central, and eastern Europe. The Slavic people are descended from Vikings who made their way to Kiev (in modern-day Ukraine) to amalgamate with Slavs coming up from the Balkans. The Vikings also came from Norway and settled in northern France and produced the Normans who conquered England in 1066 under the leadership of William the Conqueror. Cities like Dublin, Ireland are ancient Viking towns with Viking names dating back over 1000 years.

Brian Boru: The famous Irish king of ancient history who ruled Ireland from 976 to 1014. He is credited with being the first Irish king to consolidate power over much of the land we know as the Emerald Isle today.

Henry II: The great Plantagenet and Norman King of England from 1154–89. He is credited with setting up the great administrative system in England that developed the English socio-political system by ensconcing common law and elements in it, such as trial by jury, further and deeper.

Strongbow: The Norman aristocrat and lord, the Earl of Pembroke (Richard Fitzgilbert de Clare) sailed to Ireland in 1167 and with Welsh supporters took the kingdom of Leinster and put the Normans in Ireland (100 years after the Normans had invaded England), and hence, the English in Ireland for the next 750 years.

Normans: The people who came from modern-day northern France on the English Channel who invaded England in 1066 and foisted a new system of socio-political development on the Anglo-Saxons, who had ruled most of Britain since 450. The Normans were descendants of Vikings from Norway and their leader William the Conqueror was crowned King of England on Christmas Day 1066 in Westminster Abbey in London. His grave is located at St. Eitienne Cathedral in Caen, France.

Tudors (Tewdrs): The Tudors (Tewdrs in Welsh) were the Welsh family that came to power in England in 1485 and ruled until 1603. The most famous Tudor king was Henry VIII who despite being a formidable intellect, athlete, and person of gargantuan tastes, was known for breaking the English church from Rome and divorcing several wives. He also completed the full legal annexation of his family's homeland, Wales, into the English ambit in 1536 when England's parliament passed legislation furthering what Edward I had done in 1284 as he forcefully absorbed Wales under English control.

New Model Army: The army of Parliament during the English (British) Civil War(s). It was led by men who were of both noble and gentrified background and its spirited training and zealously spiritual preparation led it to be an ideological army on a divine mission under its chief leader, Oliver Cromwell, as it fought Civil War battles in England (1642–47) and in Scotland and Ireland as well.

Drogheda and Wexford: The two Irish towns that were brutally laid siege to in September and October 1649 by the New Model Army under Cromwell during the English (British) Civil War(s) in order to force Irish supporters of the dauphin, the future King Charles II, to stop resisting England's parliament and its army.

Caernarfon: The town in northwest Wales where Longshanks (Edward I) built a fortress to control Wales and incorporate it into the English geo-political orbit. Its castle became famous as the site after 1911 for the investiture of the next in line to the British throne, the Prince of Wales.

Welsh Marches: The area overlapping between the English border areas and Welsh border areas in eastern Wales which were used by English monarchs to control land via "Marcher Lords," that is, lords who were English and Welsh who controlled the lands and paid homage to the English monarch. These areas gave rise to Anglo-Welsh identity which still persists today.

Henry VIII: The king of England, descended from the Welsh Tudors (Tewdwrs), who formally incorporated Wales into the English political orbit with the Acts of Union in 1536 which made Wales a formal region of England.

Acts of Union: The laws passed from 1536–42 that ensconced Wales into England as a part of the English monarchy's legal territory. Henry VIII was interested in making sure Marcher Lords would abide by his rule and the English Parliament in London passed several acts that were to be known several hundred years later as "Acts of Union."

David (Dafydd) Lloyd George: The only Welsh prime minister of the United Kingdom (1916–22). He spoke Welsh and left a major imprint on British government negotiating the First World War and Irish Home Rule during his important, yet rocky tenure. He was a Liberal Party leader and pushed the nonconformity bill through parliament in 1919.

Springtime of Nations: The advent of liberal nationalist revolts in Europe in 1848 in which nationalism came to the fore and challenged centuries of conservative monarchical dominance on the continent. It gave the impetus for nations and modern democracy to move forward in the face of hostile royalist-based governments (such as the Habsburgs in Austria and Hungary and the Hohenzollern system in Prussia).

Fenian Brotherhood: A cell-based, militant nationalist organization in Ireland that wanted complete removal of the British from Ireland. The organization had active cells in Ireland and the United States in the middle of the nineteenth century and some of its members were ex-American Civil War veterans from Irish units.

Home Rule: The transfer of power from a central government to a constituent or member government in which the central government still retains legal power over the constituent government. Usually, in the case of nation-states, localized powers such as taxation, education, and social welfare are given to the constituent government while high politics areas such as foreign and defense policies stay within the purview of the central government. Examples of Home Rule (or devolution as it is also called) are found in Northern Ireland from 1998-2003 and after March 2007 and Scotland and Wales after 1999. Home Rule occurs in the United States as well between states and counties and cities where the latter two get more legal and political authority to govern them and tax their citizens.

Charles Stewart Parnell: Irish nationalist leader of the late nineteenth century who was the first to lead the charge for Irish Home Rule. He bedeviled the governments of Gladstone in passionately advocating for the rights of the Irish who were being mistreated. Ironically, he was from a landed Protestant family who had been in Ireland for several generations. He was known for his parliamentary shenanigans in delaying legislative business in order to get his main cause (Irish Home Rule) across to the English MPs.

William Ewart Gladstone: The Scotsman, who was raised in England, was prime minister of Britain on four occasions from 1868-94. He was the leader of the Liberal Party and saw his tenure vexed with Irish home rule and colonial war in Africa fighting radical Muslims in Sudan.

Elizabeth I: The daughter of Henry VIII and Anne Boleyn (Henry's second wife). She ascended to the English throne in 1558 after replacing her sister, Queen Mary "Bloody Mary" Tudor (1553–58). Elizabeth was known for sending English landlords into Ireland to create plantations that helped consolidate English control of the island. This deepened the English hold on the land and drew England and Ireland closer together socially, economically, and politically creating a colonial context for future Irish discontent.

Battle of Boyne: The Battle of Boyne occurred on July 12, 1690 in what is now northeast part of the Republic of Ireland (just south of the Six Counties of Ulster). The battle saw the defeat of the dauphin to the English throne, James VII of Scotland (James II of England), by William of Orange, who became King William III of England. Today, this battle is significant since it represents the triumph of Protestant identity over Catholic identity (since James was Catholic) and it is used to stir up sectarian fervor during the Protestant "Orange" Marching season in Northern Ireland.

Terrence O'Neill: Ulster Unionist prime minister from 1963–69 who tried to engage in reformist politics and find a middle-ground with Catholics in Northern Ireland. The centrifugal forces of politics in Ulster pushed the discussion to the extremes and he was voted out of power in his own constituency and replaced by Rev. Ian Paisley who at the time advocated an extreme form of non-cooperation with Republican forces. O'Neill's moderation did pay off and even Paisley had adopted most of O'Neill's positions some 40 years later.

Cymru: Literally, "nation" in Welsh. Pronounced, "KEM-ree." *Cymru* is the title of the country of "Wales" in Welsh.

Methodism: The great Christian Protestant denomination which took root in Wales in the eighteenth and nineteenth century. Its founder, John Wesley, was an English Anglican who wanted to reform the religiosity and traditions of the Church of England from within. He and his brother Charles (the author of the Christmas hymn, "Hark the Herald Angels Sing") had no idea, when undergraduates at Oxford University's Lincoln College, that their small band of strange believers, known for their "methodical" ways, would go on to see an entire region of their country and even parts of the globe in the United States and Africa transformed by their passionate, evangelical message.

John Wesley: One of the world's most famous Christian theologians and evangelists. Born in 1703 into an English Anglican home, he founded one of the most important Protestant Christian sects in operation globally today, the Methodist church (which is now in numerous iterations with the largest, the United Methodist Church). Its rejection of Calvinism (found in the Scottish Kirk) and Catholicism and their theological claims, were tied to Wesley's insistence on free will (in the Lutheran sense) and salvation by grace through faith in Christ. The movement spread like wild fire through Wales and helped lead to the Chapel movement in the nineteenth century in Wales.

Chapter Three

The Strange Death of Liberal England (1935): A seminal work in the study of modern British history and politics written by George Dangerfield. He discusses the battle between the Liberal-led House of Commons under Asquith and Lloyd George and their attempts to reform Britain's conservative political settlement by ending the House of Lords absolute veto over legislation that came out of the Commons. Dangerfield also talks about the Irish Home Rule battle between Liberals and Tories in England which contributed to the end of the Lords dominance, but strangely cut short Liberal ascendancy in British politics and ushered in nearly 100 years of Tory domination in British politics in the twentieth century.

Easter Rising: The revolt of the Irish nationalists in 1916 in Dublin which was led by the Irish Republican Brotherhood during Easter week. It was a six-day battle between the British authorities and Irish nationalists and the nationalists were defeated and their leaders caught and executed. It was the seminal uprising in what was to become an active paramilitary rebellion by Sinn Féin and its Irish Republican Army by 1919.

*Michael Collins (*Micheál Seán Ó Coileáin*):* The founder of the Irish Republican Army in 1919 which sought to oust the British from Ireland by the gun rather than via parliamentary means. As a result, he was one of the negotiators for the Irish nationalists in London in 1920 with the British government in finalizing the Home Rule treaty. He had a falling out with the Sinn Féin leader, Éamon de Valera, and he was killed in the Irish Civil War in 1922.

Sir Winston L. S. Churchill: The British Conservative Party prime minister on two occasions (1940–45 and 1951–55) who started political life in the House of Commons as a Tory and then switched to the Liberal party in 1906 and held a Scottish seat (Dundee) until 1922. He then switched back to the Tories. However, as colonial secretary under Lloyd George in 1920 he was responsible for Ireland and helped negotiate the settlement that ended up partitioning Ireland.

Black and Tans: The British paramilitary force who assisted the Royal Irish Constabulary. "Black and Tans" were called in to quell the nationalist uprising in 1919–20 in Ireland. Their methods were brutal and some participated in the invasion of Croke Park (*Páirc an Chrócaigh*) during a Gaelic football game in Dublin on November 21, 1920 which led to 30 deaths and the infamous epithet, "Bloody Sunday." The Black and Tans were responding to the deaths of 14 British agents in Ireland at the hands of the IRA that day.

Government of Ireland Act: The law that was passed in 1920 that saw Ireland get home rule in the south with a parliament in Dublin, but the north refused and a separate assembly was formed in Belfast that kept the Six Counties tied to the United Kingdom. After the Irish Civil War of 1922, the Irish Free State operated as a Home Rule dominion (like Canada) under the British sovereign and Ulster operated as part of the United Kingdom.

Irish Free State: Created in 1921 as a result of the Government of Ireland Act. The Free State was born as 26 counties in the southern part of the island of Ireland and it was distinct from the Six Counties in the north (colloquially called "Ulster" by the British—although Ulster was historically nine counties in the north, three of which ended up in the southern Free State). The Free State's constitution was revised in 1937 to give it more autonomy vis-à-vis England and in 1949 all legal and political ties with the British were severed and the Republic of Ireland was born.

Devolution: The concept that power can be transferred politically from a central government to a constituent or local government in a unitary state such as happened in Ireland in 1921 or in Scotland and Wales in 1999. It is similar to the concept of Home Rule.

Scottish Office: Created in 1885, the Scottish Office was the administrative arm of the British government in Scotland. It was housed in Edinburgh after 1939 and represented a kind of administrative devolution to provide "Scottish" solutions to "Scottish" problems. Even after devolution in 1999, the Labour government in London kept the Scottish Office and the post of Secretary of State for Scotland, but both roles were greatly reduced. By 2003, the post had been placed in a new Department of Constitutional Affairs and its holder at the time, Scottish Labour MP Alistair Darling, the United Kingdom's transportation secretary, assumed the Scottish secretary portfolio as well.

Éamon de Valera: The prime minister and president of the Irish Free State and Republic of Ireland from the 1920s into the early 1970s. The George Washington of Irish politics, he led a guerrilla war and unconventional political struggle against the British in Ireland to bring about the end of over 700 years of British rule in Ireland. He was the founder of the Fianna Fáil (Soldiers of Destiny) party, a conservative nationalist party, which ruled Ireland during the first several years of the new millennium.

Scotch-Irish: The people who came from Ireland, mainly northern parts of Ireland (including Ulster) who were part of the English and Scottish families from the British mainland who settled in Ireland over several centuries and helped the British control the territory. American presidents Bill Clinton and Woodrow Wilson are descendants of this group of people who make up some 25 million in the United States today.

Downing Street Declaration: The 1993 agreement in which the British, under premier John Major, and the Irish, under Taoiseach Albert Reynolds, attempted to bring nationalists and unionists together in Northern Ireland and get paramilitary groups like the Irish Republican Army and the Ulster Volunteer Forces to lay down their arms. It was helped by the direct intervention of the United States under President Bill Clinton. But, it was not as successful as the 1998 Belfast agreement.

Court of St. James's: The official monarchical court (or place of authority) where the British sovereign sits when doing official business. It used to always be at St. James's palace, but that is an administrative center for the sovereign's business. However, the court may be at Buckingham Palace in London or the Palace of Holyrood in Edinburgh. The American ambassador to the Court of St. James's is the United States' top diplomat in the United Kingdom.

Official Secrets Acts: The legislative acts of the British government that govern conduct by intelligence services and other public servants dealing with security and intelligence matters. It was also applied in the United Kingdom after the 9-11 attacks on America and the 7-7-2005 attacks by militant Islamists on the London subway and bus system.

Mitchell Principles: These were the six principles put forth by a former American senator George Mitchell (a Maine Democrat) who helped broker peace in Northern Ireland prior to the Good Friday Agreement. The principles called for sectarian communities in Northern Ireland to seek peace, disarm, verify arms, oppose the use of force by various groups in Ulster, abide by the agreement once in place, renounce the use of force, and punish violators of the agreement.

Good Friday Agreement: The 1998 agreement (also known as the Belfast agreement) that allowed for the first significant devolution of power in Northern Ireland in 26 years. Under Tony Blair, the new Labour government brought forth multiparty elections and a new power-sharing legislature in which unionists and republicans shared power. The agreement also led to many other specific measures on policing, economic development, and socio-cultural elements to bring Protestants and Catholics together in Northern Ireland.

Confederation: A confederation or confederal form of government is one in which the member or constituent governments hold most power and give legal and political authority to the central government. What's more, the member governments may wish to withdraw their legal support of the central government which will cause the confederation to collapse. Examples of confederal government include the Confederate States of America during the American Civil War (1861–65), the first American government—the Articles of Confederation (1781–89), the European Union, the Commonwealth of Independent States (in the region of the former Soviet Union), and the United Nations.

Federal form of government: A federal form of government is one in which the member or constituent governments hold power and legal authority in their spheres of influence and the central government holds power and legal authority in its sphere of influence. The central government, however, may hold a preponderance of power due to high politics (foreign policy and defense) issues, as well as other issues related to constitutional obligations (rights of minorities, etc). However, in a federation, each government (both the central and subsidiary governments) has the right to exist and may have concurrent powers (such as the right to tax or make policy in education). Examples of a federal form of government include the United States, Germany, and Canada.

Unitary form of government: A unitary form of government is one in which the central government hold all legal and political power and authority and member or constituent governments are created and allowed to exist by virtue of the actions of the central government. If the central government wants to create or abolish subsidiary or constituent governments it may do so. Examples of unitary forms of government include the United Kingdom, Ireland, and France. A layer of unitary government exists in the United States between the state governments and counties and local governments.

Chapter Four

Thatcherism: The colloquial term for the political ideology and policies of Conservative British premier Margaret Thatcher (who was in power at No. 10 Downing Street from 1979 until 1990). Thatcher was known for her monetarist (neo-liberal) economic policies, tough-minded law and order views, and staunch unionist proclivities. She helped deliver the Anglo-Irish Agreement in 1985 with Éire's Taoiseach Garret FitzGerald.

Keir Hardie: An illegitimate Scottish coal miner who lost sympathy for the Liberal Party and founded the Scottish Socialist Party (the first Marxian socialist party in the United Kingdom) in 1888. As an MP, he brought various Labour groups together to found the Labour Representation Committee, which became the United Kingdom's Labour Party which governed the UK at the turn of the twenty-first century. He won one of Labour first two seats at Westminster in the 1900 general election. The seat was one from south Wales.

Labour Party: The Labour Party was founded in 1900 when Keir Hardie, the Scottish socialist MP, brought workers' groups together from all parts of the United Kingdom. He was one of two Labour MPs to win seats at the 1900 general election. By 1924, the Labour Party, a Marxian workers' party heavily influenced by trade unions and committed to democratic socialism, would be able to take power in a minority government in Britain. It was not until 1945 that it could rule as a majority party for the first time. The party ended the twentieth century in power in Britain with most of its power base in the Celtic parts of the country.

"Red Clydeside:" The area around Glasgow, Scotland, especially the shipyards and inner-city, where the Independent Labour Party (ILP), a radical off-shoot of the more mainstream Labour Party, did very well in the 1920s. It was led by Socialist firebrands Immanuel Shinwell, William Gallacher, James Maxton, David Kirkwood, and Mary Barbour.

Ramsay MacDonald: The first Labour prime minister in the United Kingdom's minority government led by Labour in 1924 and the Labour-led national coalition government with the Tories in 1929–31. He had been foreign secretary prior to the 1924 government and was a Scotsman who led Labour into political respectability.

Tony Blair: Half-Irish (on his mother's side) and half-Scottish (on his father's side) prime minister of the United Kingdom from 1997-2007. After attending grammar school in Edinburgh, settled into English life and attended Oxford and ran for parliament in 1983 winning a Labour Party seat in northern England. He will be remembered for devolution in Scotland and Wales in 1999 and the Belfast agreement of 1998 as well as supporting the United States in its Iraq 2003 war.

Gordon Brown: A Scotsman and son of a Kirk minister, Brown earned a doctorate in political science and taught before entering politics. He was the chancellor of the exchequer for the New Labour government under Tony Blair from 1997–2007 prior to taking the reins as British premier.

Donald Dewar: Longtime Scottish Labour MP who was the inaugural first minister of the Scottish Parliament in Edinburgh. He also served as Scottish secretary under Tony Blair after Labour came to power in 1997. He died in office (after just over one year as first minister) of heart-related problems in 2000 at the age of 63.

Scottish National Party (SNP): The *Pàrtaidh Nàiseanta na h-Alba* ("Scottish National Party" in Scottish Gaelic) was founded in 1934 when the National Party of Scotland merged with the Scottish Party. The party stood for an independent Scotland and a complete break from ties with England. It won its first seat in the House of Commons in 1945 and its second in 1967. In October 1974, it won just over 30% of the Scottish vote in the British general election and sent 11 MPs to the House of Commons. It is a moderately left-of-center party with a focus on independence for Scotland and social democratic and statist approaches to welfare and economy. Its leader, Alex Salmond, was elected first minister after the SNP formed a minority government in the late Spring of 2007 after winning a plurality (for the first time) of votes in the Scottish elections for Holyrood.

By-Election: An election in the British electoral system which takes place during an MP's term in office in which an MP stands down or dies in office. It is often seen as a measure of the safety of the constituency or the popularity of the party in power. In 1988, the Scottish National Party's Jim Sillars overturned a 19,500 Labour majority (from the 1987 general election) when he took the seat in a by-election in the Glasgow Govan constituency.

Winnie Ewing: The winner of the Scottish National Party's second ever seat at Westminster in a 1967 by-election in the Glasgow Hamilton constituency. She became the *grand dame* of SNP politics as she went on to represent a Highlands seat in the European Parliament and worked with other nationalist groups (including more conservative nationalists) at Strasbourg and she earned the nickname, *Madame Ecosse* (Mrs. Scotland)!

Alex Salmond: The mercurial leader of the Scottish National Party (SNP) who was a government and then Bank of Scotland economist. He led the SNP from 1990 until 2000 and then again after 2004 and won the first minister post at Holyrood to govern Scotland as its first nationalist leader in the post-1999 devolutionary era. He was a MP for Banff and

Buchan in the Highlands after 1987 and held the seat continuously while serving as an MSP after 1999. He put the party firmly on the "gradualist" path in seeking devolution prior to the party's (and his) stated goal of independence from the United Kingdom.

Sean Connery: The famous Scottish actor who played the quintessential English secret agent James Bond in seven films from 1962–83. He was the most famous Scottish National Party (SNP) activist allowing his image, voice, and name to be associated with the SNP (including SNP advertisements) during its move toward greater legitimacy and recognition in the 1990s and 2000s. Connery even gave the SNP a monthly grant of nearly £5000 by 2003.

Liberal Democrats: Once the party of Gladstone, Home Rule for Ireland and the Celtic regions, and the dominant party in Scotland and Wales, the party linked with a conservative offshoot of the Labour Party, the Social Democratic Party, in 1983 and 1987 for electoral purposes. After running as the "Alliance" in those elections, the Liberal Democratic Party formally merged as one party. Despite having consistently low electoral returns in both regional and Westminster elections, it was successful enough to become the junior partner in both Scottish and Welsh governments from 1999–2007.

Menzies Campbell: The Scotsman who was the United Kingdom Liberal Democratic Party leader from 2006-2007 (only 15 months) after fellow Scotsman Charles Kennedy resigned in early 2006. Menzies (Pronounced "Meeng-us") Campbell was a former Olympic sprinter for Britain in Tokyo in 1964 and a practicing attorney. He continued to follow Kennedy's role (which led to an upturn in Liberal Democrat support in England) in criticizing at the Blair government for its involvement in the United States-led Iraq conflict.

Shadow Cabinet: The main opposition party's front bench leaders in a legislature in the United Kingdom (as well as Scotland and Wales). In the eventuality that the opposition would take power, these individuals (all sitting MPs at Westminster, MSPs at Holyrood, AMs in Cardiff or MLAs at Stormont) would join the cabinet (government) and hold the portfolios (prime minister, minister of health, minister of finance, etc) they mirror (of the current government in power) in the shadow cabinet.

Tories: The king's men who supported the monarch and his agenda in the British parliament which was usually a conservative, status quo-oriented one. This nickname stuck as parties evolved in the early nineteenth century from informal caucuses of landed elites in the House of Commons. Eventually, the Tories became more formalized as the Conservative and Unionist Party and eventually the latter "Unionist" was dropped as the post-1921 settlement in Ulster that gave Home Rule to both parts of the partitioned Emerald Isle.
Scottish Socialist Party: Several iterations of the Scottish Socialists have taken place since Keir Hardie founded the Scottish Labour Party in 1888. The most recent formed in 1998 and took some seats in the 1999 Scottish parliamentary elections. Its leader was the flamboyant trade union radical Tommy Sheridan. However, Sheridan left the party in 2006 and started another one, Solidarity, and he failed to get re-elected to the Scottish Parliament in 2007. The SSP failed to re-elect anyone to its six seats (won in the 2003 election) in 2007.

Poll Tax: Also known as the "Community Charge, " was the invidious policy that was put into effect by the Conservative Thatcher government in 1989 in Scotland (and in

1990 in England and Wales) which sought to replace property taxes by taxing the number of people who resided in a dwelling place. It was a regressive tax that was difficult to bear for the average person (if the charge was made per person, many families had to pay a one-time—at year's end—charge of several thousand pounds, which most could not afford). After riots and campaigns by various socio-political groups against it, the tax was repealed.

Scottish Greens (Pårtaidh Uaine na h-Alba): The Scottish version of the founding Green Party, the German Greens (*die Grünen*), which was founded in 1990 as a separate entity from the United Kingdom (UK) Green Party. The UK party was founded as the ecology party in 1973 in Coventry, England. The Scottish Greens won one seat in the inaugural Holyrood elections of 1999, seven in 2003, and two in 2007. It is party known for its sustainable living approach, pluralistic conceptions of democracy and leadership, and anti-war agenda. It gave support to the Scottish Nationalists (but was not part of the government) once the SNP took power in Scotland's devolved political system in 2007.

"Single-Issue"-type Party: A political party that is seen as focusing on either one major issue (such as green parties with the environment) or just a small number of issues (such as women's parties in Europe or radical right-wing populist parties such as *Front National* in France). These parties are often defeated by larger, better established parties since the issues the "single-issue" parties espouse are swallowed up by the larger parties.

Giovanni Sartori: The Italian political scientist who authored the seminal work, *Parties and Party Systems* (1976) on classifying party systems. His work brought us the concepts and models of polarized pluralist party systems (as in Northern Ireland 1972–2007) or limited or moderate pluralism as seen today in Scotland, Ireland, and Wales.

Limited (or Moderate) Pluralism: According to political scientist Giovanni Sartori, this is a political party system in which three to four parties vie for power and centripetal forces end up forcing coalitions of both center left and right to form and party system stability will evolve. This is the type of party system found in Scotland, Ireland, and Wales today.

Cumann na nGaedheal (Society of the Gaels): Was originally part of the grouping of Irish nationalists after 1900 who were anti-English and became part of Sinn Féin, but after the 1922 Irish Civil War, the Society of the Gaels became the "pro-treaty" faction of Sinn Féin (led by the likes of Arthur Griffith and Michael Collins) who wanted gradualism to win out over Éamon de Valera's "anti-treaty" Fianna Fáil movement. The Society of the Gaels were the progenitors of today's Fine Gael right-of-center party (which was in opposition after 1997 in Ireland, although its election numbers in terms of votes and seats in the Dáil improved in the 2007 general election).

Fianna Fáil (Soldiers of Destiny): The right-of-center nationalist party that governed Ireland for much of the twentieth century and into the twenty-first century. It originated from the "anti-treaty" faction of the Irish Civil War of 1922 led by future prime minister and president Éamon de Valera. Its leader, Bertie Ahern, at the turn of the twenty-first century, held the Irish premiership longer than any individual in the modern Republic's history.

Catchall-type party: A term created by German political scientist Otto Kirchheimer. It is a broad umbrella grouping of tendencies and factions within one party that comes together for electoral purposes and may even splinter after an election. Many political parties in modern political systems can be conceptualized as "catchall" parties such as the British Labour Party, the American Republican or Democratic parties, or the Gaullist UMP (*Union pour un Mouvement Populaire*) under Jacques Chirac or Nicolas Sarkozy in France.

Predominant Party System: According to political scientist Giovanni Sartori, this is a political party system in which one major party dominates the political system for several years and legal limitations may be placed on minority voters and groups to keep them from challenging the dominant party's hegemony over the system. The Ulster system from 1921–72 is an example of this type of political system. The German Democratic Republic from 1948–90 may also be an example of this type of system under the Socialist Unity Party in which smaller parties were allowed to persist, but not control the party and political system.

Bertie Ahern: The Taoiseach from 1997 and his party Fianna Fáil was reelected in 2002 and 2007 to lead Éire. A native of Dublin, he was known for working with Britain's Tony Blair to bring about the Good Friday Agreement in 1998 spurring sectarian groups to work together for political settlement in Northern Ireland. He also helped drive the famous Irish "Celtic Tiger" economy of the 1990s which help further ensconce Ireland deeper into the European Union (which the Irish had joined in 1973).

Teachta Dálas (Deputies): Teachta Dálas (TDs) or "deputies" in the Irish are the members of the Irish lower house, the *Dáil Éireann* in Dublin (in which 166 TDs are found). The term is pronounced: CHOCK-taw dawlas.

Fine Gael: The modern Irish nationalist party that was formed as the "pro-treaty" (supporting the 1921 home rule settlement with England) faction after the 1922 Irish Civil War. It has been in government and ruled as a centrist party. It is generally characterized as a right-of-center nationalist party (like its main competitor Fianna Fáil). But, in the 1980s, it governed with the left-wing Irish Labour Party and attempted to usher in several liberal social reforms focusing on abortion and contraception.

"Rainbow" Coalitions: At times in Ireland's recent republican history, it has been necessary for Fine Gael to govern Ireland with several parties to counter its nationalist rival Fianna Fáil. Normally, Fine Gael's coalition partners are found on the left side of the spectrum (while the two major parties are center-right nationalist ones). Most recently, from 1994–97, Fine Gael governed with the Irish Labour Party and the party of the Democratic Left. A "Rainbow Coalition" was first used in Ireland from 1948-51.

Garret FitzGerald: FitzGerald was the Taoiseach on two occasions from mid-1981 to early 1982 and late 1982 until early 1987. Dr. FitzGerald became a Fine Gael TD in the Dáil in 1969 after working as an economist for *Aer Lingus* and teaching economics at University College Dublin. Under his leadership, Ireland liberalized socially and sought rapprochement with England on Northern Ireland via he and Margaret Thatcher's Anglo-Irish Agreement of 1985.

Irish Labour Party (Páirtí an Lucht Oibre): The oldest political party in the modern (post-colonial) Irish party system. It is a Marxist-oriented party and one that has been committed to social democracy. It has been a part of several "Rainbow Coalitions" first in 1948 and most recently from December 1994 until June 1997.

Mary Robinson (Máire Mhic Róibin): The first woman president of the Republic of Ireland from 1990–97. She was a member of the Irish Labour Party and long-time Irish senator. Robinson was popular, visited Queen Elizabeth II at Buckingham Palace and entertained the Prince of Wales (Charles Windsor) at the Irish president's official residence in Dublin. She also met with Gerry Adams, the renegade Sinn Féin MP. She was the second president (Éamon de Valera was the first in 1966) to address the Irish government (*Oireachtas*). She enacted laws liberalizing Irish policies on contraception and homosexuality. After the presidency, she went onto become the United Nation's High Commissioner for Human Rights, a post she held until 2002.

Progressive Democratic Party (An Páirti Daonlathach): A classically liberal, free-market political party founded in the Republic of Ireland in 1985, much like the German liberals (*Frei Demokrats* or Free Democrats), which advocate a libertarian approach to politics and economics. They are economically liberal (conservative or pro-market) and socially liberal (opposed to government control of personal freedoms and liberties). They were in government from 1997–2007 with the moderately center-right nationalist party, Fianna Fáil.

Mary Harney (Máire Ní Áime): Harney, a longtime leader in the Progressive Democrats and a government minister, was the *Tánaiste* (deputy prime minister) of the Republic of Ireland from 1997 until 2006 working with *Taoiseach* Bertie Ahern and his Fianna Fáil party. She was the first female deputy prime minister in the Republic's history. She was first elected to the Dáil in 1981 as a Fianna Fáil TD. She left the party to help found the Progressive Democrats in 1985. She resigned as party leader and *Tánaiste* in late 2006 only to take back the party leadership after the problematic 2007 elections which saw most of the Progressive Democrat seats lost.

Sinn Féinn: The party grew out of the Irish nationalist movement of the nineteenth century. It is the Irish word for "ourselves." It formed a break-away government in 1919 and then fought a guerrilla war with the British. It then got an agreement from Britain for devolution in 1921, but the party split into two factions ("pro-treaty" and "anti-treaty"). It then was tied largely to the Irish Republican Army operating clandestinely in Northern Ireland and the party resumed both parliamentary and extra-governmental activity (with its support of the reconstituted IRA) to inflict terror on Northern Ireland after 1970. It won seats in both the Stormont and Westminster legislatures in the United Kingdom and also began winning seats in the Dáil and the European Parliament. After foreswearing terrorism (and implicit acknowledgment of it and the IRA's activities), in 2003 and 2007, it entered historical governments with its arch enemy the Democratic Unionist Party in the assembly in Belfast.

Irish Green Party (Comhaontas Glas): The small party formed as the Ecology party of Ireland in 1981. After 1999, the party started gaining some strength in the European Parliament and in the Dáil. It got six TDs in the 2002 and 2007 elections. It even won a seat in the Northern Ireland assembly in 2007. It is a party that favors environmental politics, sustainable living, more education spending, and a focus on human rights.

Left-libertarian Party: The concept was coined by American political scientist Herbert Kitschelt and describes a party that is moderately left of center, favors libertarian approaches (liberal or individualistic) to social issues and statist approaches to economic issues. Groups like the green parties of Europe and some moderately left-wing nationalist parties like the Scottish National Party may be classified as such.

Karl Marx: The German Jew (1818–83) and radical revolutionary who founded the major school of socialism in the mid-nineteenth century with his writings on capitalism (*Das Kapital*) and the ideal Communist party (*The Communist Manifesto*). Most modern democratic socialist (now conceptualized as "social democratic") labor movements and most communist regimes drew part of their inspiration from his work.

Aneurin Bevin: The Welshman and socialist trade unionist who helped found Britain's modern-day National Health Service as minister for health in 1945.

Plaid Llafur Cymru (Welsh Labour Party): Prior to World War I, Welsh trade unionists and socialists tried to create an Independent Labour Party along Scottish lines. The Welsh Labour Party was not given autonomy within the general United Kingdom Labour Party federation until 1947. *Llafur* has controlled the Welsh assembly in coalition with the Liberal Democrats (1999–2003), by itself as a minority government (2003–07), and after the 2007 Welsh elections with Plaid Cymru in a "Red-Green" coalition. The party was been the dominant party in Wales since the early twentieth century when it supplanted the Liberals.

Penyberth: The site of the notorious 1937 nationalist attack on a Royal Air Force bombing school. Several Welsh nationalists were arrested and it became a political rallying marker for Welsh nationalists and others seeking Welsh separation from England.

Gwynfor Evans: Evans (1912–2005) was a lawyer and leader of *Plaid Cymru* from 1945-81. He was the first Welsh nationalist to win a seat at Westminster winning the Carmarthen by-election in July 1966 upon the death of the Labour incumbent, Megan Lloyd George (David Lloyd George's daughter). He lost the seat at the 1970 election and never won another seat at Westminster. He was the president (a post later abolished) of the Celtic League from 1961–71 and the Scottish National Party's first MP, Dr. Robert McIntyre was the vice president of the league at that time.

Welsh Liberal Democrats (Democratiaid Rhyddfrydol Cymru): The Welsh Liberal Democrats are part of the United Kingdom-wide Liberal Democratic Party. They are the followers of the Liberal Party which dominated Welsh politics into the early 1920s. The Liberal Democrats were in government in the Welsh National Assembly from 1999–2003 as the junior coalition party with *Llafur*.

Welsh Conservatives (Ceidwadwyr Cymreig): The Welsh Conservatives are the regional branch of the United Kingdom's Conservative party. The party's electoral fortunes were not great after devolution in 1999, but they were the third party ahead of the Welsh Liberal Democrats. During the 2007 elections, the Tories began sounding a more moderate tone on social and environmental issues in Britain and even had a fully bilingual party website (in both English and Welsh) in Wales to compete with the Welsh Nationalists.

Ulster Unionist Party: The Ulster Unionist Party was the party of government in Northern Ireland from 1921–72. It was a staunch defender of the Protestant and unionist status quo. It was also the dominant party in Ulster's regional government at Stormont after 1998. But, after the assembly was suspended in 2002, the party's fortunes plummeted and it was not able to become the dominant party at Stormont. Also, in 2005, its leader, MP and Nobel laureate David Trimble, was ousted from Westminster.

Orange Order: The fraternal Protestant organization in Ulster that celebrates the controversial and divisive Battle of Boyne (1690) every July with "marching season." Its actions have been subject to bans and control by authorities in Northern Ireland after 1998 given the inflammatory nature of relations over the Order's activities in relation to Catholic feelings in Northern Ireland. The marches project a measure of Protestant and British nationalism in the face of Catholic reaction and republican sympathy.

David Trimble: The Ulster Unionist first minister (1998–2001) who won the Nobel peace prize (shared with John Hume) for bringing post-Belfast Agreement (1998) democratic government to Northern Ireland. He lost his seat at Westminster in 2005 as the Democratic Unionist Party replaced the more moderate Ulster Unionist Party (UUP) as the dominant unionist party in Northern Ireland. In 2006, he was made a lord and as "Lord Trimble" took a seat in the British House of Lords and in 2007 he left the UUP and joined the Conservatives.

Provisional Irish Republican Army: The Provisional Irish Republican Army (IRA), also known as the "Provos" or "PIRA," was the arm of the IRA that wanted to use unconventional methods and terrorism to achieve its ends fighting for Ireland's unification and an end to British control of the northern Six Counties. It was the paramilitary arm of Sinn Féin. The Provos broke with the "Official" IRA in 1969.

"Official" Irish Republican Army: The "Official" Irish Republican Army (IRA) manifested when the IRA split into two factions in 1969. The larger was the "Provos" who went on to fight the British for control of Northern Ireland and the smaller faction, the Official IRA, were more committed to Marxism and socialism than the Provos. Although, Sinn Féin continued to espouse socialism, the Official IRA and its parliamentary wing, Sinn Féin Workers Party, were notably more leftwing than the Provos and Sinn Féin.

Gerry Adams (Gearóid Mac Ádhaimh): The leader of Sinn Féin after 1983 and an MP from West Belfast. Adams joined the nationalist movement in the late 1960s and served time in jail for his activities. He has denied ties to the Irish Republican Army, although Sinn Féin is the organization's parliamentary arm. He helped engineer peace among unionist and republican factions in Northern Ireland and by the early twenty-first century helped to guide his party toward respectability at Stormont, the Dáil, and in the European Parliament in Strasbourg.

"Bloody Sunday:" Two specific events affiliated with modern Irish politics are referred to as "Bloody Sunday." The first occurred on November 20, 1920 in Dublin at Croke Park when the British paramilitary forces retaliated for the assassinations of its agents by the Irish Republican Army. Some 14 people (including children and athletes) were killed in the middle of a Gaelic football match when the British opened fire. The second "Bloody Sunday" (known in Irish as *Domhnach na Fola)* event occurred on January 30, 1972 during a civil rights march in Derry (Londonderry), Northern Ireland. Fourteen protestors were killed and 26 injured when British troops fired on the crowd. The 1972 event is immortalized in the U2 (a popular modern Irish rock group) song of the same name.

Democratic Unionist Party: The rightwing unionist party in Ulster founded by Reverend Ian Paisley in the 1960s. It rose to prominence after 2003 when it won a plurality of seats in the Northern Ireland Assembly elections. It then went into a power-sharing democratic government in 2007 with its arch nemesis, the republican Sinn Féin with Paisley serving as first minister.

Ian Paisley: The Calvinist firebrand who refused for decades to brook republican opposition in Ulster. He supported maintaining the Protestant and unionist status quo in Ulster. However, in 2006, with the chance of becoming first minister clear and the Irish Republican Army putting its weapons out of commission, he agreed to move his party, the Democratic Unionist Party (DUP), toward power-sharing with Sinn Féin. The historic moment occurred in March 2007 when the DUP and Sinn Féin ended winning the most seats at Stormont and the two polarized opposite parties went into a government together beginning to end decades of animosity between extreme republicans and unionists.

Social Democratic and Labour Party: The moderate left-of-center republican party that held power with the Ulster Unionist Party after the historical 1998 Good Friday Agreement. Its leader and most high profile member was John Hume who shared the Nobel Peace Prize in 1998 with Ulster Unionist MP and Ulster first minister David Trimble.

John Hume: The school teacher who was elected to Ulster's parliament in the late 1960s as a Catholic republican. He went on to lead the Social Democratic and Labour Party (SDLP). As SDLP leader he won a seat at Westminster and was an European MEP. In 1998, he was awarded the Nobel Peace prize (with David Trimble) for his work in bringing about the Belfast Agreement.

Republicans: The individuals who supported seeing the Six Counties in the north of Ireland join with the other 26 counties in the south to form a united Ireland. These individuals were usually, but not always, Catholic. They were also conceptualized as "nationalists" as well.

Nobel Peace Prize: The award given each year to the individual, individuals or groups which empirically advance the cause of peace globally. The award is named after the Swedish scientist Alfred Nobel and it is one of several Nobel prizes given in other areas (science, literature, etc). It is awarded in Oslo, Norway each year.

Unionists: The individuals who supported maintaining the "union" between Britain and the Six Counties in Ulster (Northern Ireland). Unionists were oftentimes referred to as "loyalists" since they were "loyal" to the United Kingdom, its monarchy, and its parliament. Unionists were usually, but not always, Protestants.

Chapter Five

Behavioralism: The school of thought in American political science that came to dominate the discipline in the 1960s. It focuses on the empirical study of politics using conceptual approaches (models or theories) and quantitative methodologies that scientifically verify political behavior and generalize and make scientific hypotheses about individual, group, and institutional political behavior.

Institutionalism: An approach to the study of politics that allows the political scientist to look at how legislatures affect government and society. It also analyzes how political institutions (legislatures, judicial branches, and executives) are affected by outside variables. It is an extension of behavioralism.

Scottish Parliament: A parliament in Scotland existed from the mid-thirteenth century (as a kind of Scottish King's Council) until 1707 and the Treaty of Union with the English. After nearly 300 years of union, the United Kingdom government under Tony Blair's Labour Party devolved most domestic powers back to Scotland in 1999 in the form of a 129-seat parliament. Elections are held every four years (at a minimum) and its seats are assigned based on two electoral systems: proportional representation (a form of PR known as the additional member system) and single member district voting. Members of the Scottish Parliament (MSP) are elected as "constituency" (73 seats) MSPs. The remaining 56 are assigned based on the PR system and are known as "regional" MSPs. Currently, the average constituency seat represents about 55,000 people.

Additional Member System (AMS): A form of proportional representation that allows for members of a legislature to be elected by both PR and the single member district (SMD) systems. In the AMS system voters (or electors as they are called in Britain) will have two votes one for a candidate in their constituency (which will be elected via SMD) and a vote for a party (based on a list system). Seats are then assigned based on the constituency (SMD) vote and the party list (PR) vote. This system is used in Scotland and Wales.

MSP: A Member of the Scottish Parliament (MSP) is an elected legislator of the Scottish Parliament. MSPs are similar to MPs in the Westminster parliament in London or Assembly Members (AMs) in Wales.

First Minister: The highest elected official in the Scottish Parliament, Welsh Assembly or Northern Irish Assembly. This individual is the de facto premier of the devolved governments in Scotland, Wales, and Northern Ireland. They are elected like any other legislator via constituency or regional party list votes, but are selected by their parties to be the top leader in the legislature and then voted in by a majority vote of the legislature. In 2007, the first minister in Scotland was Alex Salmond of the Scottish National Party; in Wales the post was held by Rhodri Morgan of *Llafur*, and in Ulster it was held by the Democratic Unionist Party's Ian Paisley.

Proportional Representation (PR): An electoral system where seats are allocated based on the percentage of votes attained from electors voting for specific parties and then seats are assigned based on a party list. If a political party gets 35% of the votes in a PR election it will get 35% of the seats in the legislature. An example of a pure PR electoral system is the Israeli *Knesset* where all 120 seats are allocated by PR. There are hybrid PR systems such as the Additional Member Systems in Scotland and Wales and the Single Transferrable Vote systems in Ireland and Northern Ireland.

Single Member District (SMD): The electoral system used exclusively in the United States and in United Kingdom parliamentary elections in which legislators run for office representing parties and electors select one individual candidate in a constituency and the winner will be the person who wins a plurality (the most) of the vote if more than two candidates contest the seat or 50% + 1 if only two candidates contest the seat. It is also known colloquially as the "first-past-the-post" system. The SMD system is used in part in several electoral systems such as the Additional Member System in Scotland and Wales and in the SMD-Proportional Representation (PR) hybrid system in Germany's *Bundes-*

republik where half the seats in the 662-seat *Bundestag* are selected by PR and the other half by SMD.

Oireachtas (Irish Parliament): The Irish Parliament in Dublin which consists of two houses: the lower house, the 166-seat *Dáil Éireann* (Chamber of Deputies) and the upper house, the 60-seat *Seanad Éireann* (Senate).

Dáil Éireann (House of Representatives): The Irish legislature which was recognized as the devolved home rule legislature of Ireland in 1922. It had been a revolutionary assembly after 1919 under Sinn Féin leadership and was only recognized by one other world government (the Communist government in Moscow). After 1937, and the creation of the Irish Free State, the Dáil, became the legislature that contained the de facto and de jure government of the south of Ireland, becoming a full republic in 1949.

Seanad Éireann (Senate): The upper house of the Irish legislature that ratifies legislation passed by the Dáil. It is elected based on an indirect democratic method like the French Senate. It is known for more free-wheeling debate than its more constrained and stage-managed junior partner (the Dáil).

House of Commons: The ancient seat of Anglo-Saxon democracy in England. The House of Commons (Westminster) in London is the lower house of the British Parliament and it has 659 members representing constituencies in the four regions of the United Kingdom.

Single Transferable Vote (STV) System: An electoral system which is a form of proportional representation (PR) that is complex, but it allows for electors to rank order candidates and vote for them and then used left over votes for other candidates selected on the ballot. It tries to keep from wasting votes and allows votes to be transferred once a candidate has won one of the constituency's seats. A voter in an STV system would rank order candidates in terms of preference based on candidates and not party. This system is used in Ireland, Northern Ireland, and New Zealand.

House of Lords: The upper house of the British legislature which until 1999 was a body of appointed and inherited life peers. The House of Lords after 1949 served mainly as a body to scrutinize legislation and delay its implementation if need be for two years. Prior to 1949, the Lords could kill legislation passed by the House of Commons. It is also the court of last resort in England under the Common Law system (but not Scotland).

Taoiseach (Head of Government): The term means "chief" in the Irish and Scottish Gaelic. It is the formal term for the prime minister (chief executive) in the Irish government. The Taoiseach from 1997–2007 who was reelected by the Dáil in 2007 was Fianna Fáil's Bertie Ahern.

Tánaiste (Deputy Prime Minister): The number two leader in the government in the Dáil in the Republic of Ireland. It has been held by members of the dominant coalition partner and the junior partner in the Irish government. The first woman to hold the post was the Progressive Democrats' Mary Harney from 1997–2006.

Presidency: The President of Éire is the chief of state post in the Republic and was created by the 1937 constitution. Like the American and French president it carries out formal duties of state (including recognizing foreign ambassadors and other heads of state).

But, unlike those posts, it does not have chief executive responsibilities like the *Taoiseach*. Its occupant can hold the post for up to two seven-year terms. Its first occupant was Douglas Hyde. The first female Irish president was Irish Labour's Mary Robinson from 1990-1997. She was replaced by another woman, Fianna Fáil's Mary McAleese.

Mary McAleese (Máire Pádraigín Bean Mhic Ghiolla Íosa): The second woman to hold the post of Irish president. A member of Fianna Fáil, she was elected in 1997 and re-elected in 2004. She is the first person to be born in Northern Ireland to become president of the Republic. She is a lawyer and law professor by training.

Cynulliad Cenedlaethol Cymru (National Assembly of Wales): The Welsh legislature established in 1999. It consists of 60 members and is known for its "administrative" devolution versus more robust parliamentary devolution (as seen in Scotland).

Executive Devolution: The official designation of the Welsh devolved political system and the Welsh Assembly. It was allowed by law to have minimal powers that affected some aspects of the domestic political scene in Wales and the assembly was given the purview over some issues such as education, culture, tourism, and sport among several. However, it did not have the taxing powers of the Scottish Parliament.

EU's Commission: Known as the European Commission, it is the main executive arm of the European Union (EU) in Brussels, Belgium that carries out the 27-member country international organization's agenda and enforces EU law. The Commission has 27 commissioners who oversee various portfolios (environment, tourism, etc). It is headed by a president who is ratified by the European Parliament.

Stormont Legislature: The Stormont legislature is an historical assembly that operated as a devolved legislature in Belfast from 1921–72. It was then stopped off and on as Britain ruled the province directly from London and it resumed as a home rule power-sharing legislature from 1998-2002 and after 2007. Today's Northern Ireland Assembly has 108 members (known as Members of the Legislative Assembly or MLAs).

Terrorism: The use of organized and premeditated violence for political ends. It was used during the 1919 Irish Republican Army (IRA) campaign against the British in Ireland and after 1969 by the Provisional IRA in Northern Ireland to get the British to leave the province. It has taken on new meaning for Britons since 7-7-2005 when Islamic radicals blew up London Underground trains and double-decker buses and killed many innocent citizens in propagating Islamist extremist terrorism.

Consociationalism: A concept in the study of democratization created by American political scientist Arend Lijphart which looks at democratic legislative and executive development in terms of power-sharing between groups. It is a system in which (by law) both majority and minority groups are given power in government and a certain amount of "interest intermediation" occurs. This interest intermediation is due to the high level of "segmentation" (or factionalism) in the party system among polarized opposites either based on ethnicity or confessional status. The term is both a descriptive label for government and an heuristic one for learning more about how these systems evolve and stabilize. Some examples of consociational governments include Iraq after 2003, Lebanon, Belgium, and Northern Ireland after 1998.

Decommissioning: The act of giving up one group's armaments and weapons in order to advance peace and stability. This was the case in Northern Ireland after the Good Friday Agreement and eventually both the republican and unionist groups moved toward decommissioning with the Provisional Irish Republican Army and the Ulster Volunteer Force giving up weapons in order to move toward an apparent political settlement in Northern Ireland by 2007.

Chapter Six

The Civic Culture *(1963):* The seminal work by political scientists Gabriel A. Almond and Sidney Verba that brought the study of political culture to the fore in political science. Political culture is the attitudes, values, and orientations of individuals toward their government. The study was a cross-national study of political culture in several advanced industrial democracies. It helped bring greater behavioral and theoretical sophistication to the study of comparative politics.

Celtic Political Cultures: Were narrowly defined along parochial (ethnic) lines for much of the mid-to-late twentieth century. They have given way to a broader definition that includes general social democratic political culture, post-industrial economic development, and improved education and increased immigration (as opposed to time-honored emigration) into Celtic lands.

Political Culture: The attitudes, values, and orientations of individuals toward their government. According to political scientists Gabriel A. Almond and Sidney Verba, parochialism may be seen in most political cultures (even in political subcultures in states), yet increased democratization in many states may see an increase in participant identification (as opposed to subject identification) in many political cultures (an example of this transformation is Germany since the 1960s).

The Kirk: The Kirk is the Church of Scotland. It is an historically Calvinist church with a focus on Protestant values and political and spiritual independence. The Kirk gave rise to much of the focus on education of Scots and freedom for the people from English control from the founding of the Kirk via the Scottish Reformation during the mid-sixteenth century. It is the historical state church in Scotland and its equivalent is the Presbyterian Church in its various forms in the United States.

Scottish Reformation: The era of the mid-sixteenth century when the Scottish Church, under the leadership of John Knox, broke from the Church of England and its hierarchical leadership. The Scottish Parliament sanctioned the Presbyterian organization of Scottish churches and a rupture between the Anglican Church and the Kirk began and the long-standing political divide between the Scots and the English continued.

John Knox: The Calvinist minister who helped lead the Scottish Reformation preaching an austere brand of theology and condemning the Scottish monarchy for its papal loyalties. He helped lead the Scots toward national identification away from Anglicanism and embracing a distinctly Scottish Christianity—Presbyterianism with its strictness and egalitarian, as opposed to hierarchical, order.

"Wee Wee Frees:" The members of the Free Presbyterian Church of Scotland broke from Free Church of Scotland in 1893. The former, the "Wee Wee Frees," were not happy with the proposed union of the Free Church with another Presbyterian sect. The Free Church was made up of members which had broken from the Kirk in 1843 during the "Great Disruption." The Wee Wee Frees still make up a majority in some Highland islands. They are austere and forbid links with Roman Catholics. In the early 1990s, the Lord Chancellor of the United Kingdom (Lord MacKay of Clashfern) was sanctioned by the church (of which he was a member) for attending a colleague's requiem mass and belonging to a club that allowed golf to be played on Sundays. He later left the Free Presbyterian Church for a newer amalgamated Presbyterian church.

Scots Law: The brand of civil or code law used in Scotland that is akin to code law in France or in the American state of Louisiana. It is fundamentally different from the common law in the south in England. Yet, it borrows some from the common law tradition. Today, some of Scots law is based on an amalgamation of indigenous civil law, common law, and European Union law.

Sir Walter Scott: The famous Scottish novelist of the early nineteenth century who helped popularize Scottish patriotism and identity while embracing the pastoral nature of the land, as well as espousing a passionate liberal (individualistic) culture which gave rise to the party of Gladstone (the Liberals) in the nineteenth century as the party of Scotland.

Liberalism: The political ideology that calls for individualism, economic freedom, and social responsibility as carried out by private individuals or enterprise and at times regulated by the state. This is the philosophy that brought the globe capitalist democracy that is in over 50% of the world's states today. It was the dominant philosophy politically in Scotland and Wales in the mid-to-late nineteenth century.

Kailyard Culture: The conservative meritocratic culture of the rural areas of Scotland (including the Highlands) that saw education produce professionals (from peasant youth) who left the farm (feudal manor) and went into education, law, and ministry. It was a romanticized culture and did not apply as much to the industrial belt in the central lowlands where much of the Scottish populace lived.

Communalism: The egalitarian instinct in Scottish, Welsh, and Irish political culture that seeks to bring about equality of opportunity and outcome for all. It is found in heavily working class areas where socialism and labor activism took root by the late nineteenth century and early twentieth century. It has had a healthy tension with liberalism in the twentieth and twenty-first century among political groups and the tension is best seen in political parties like the Liberal Democrats in Scotland and Wales and the nationalist parties (Scottish National Party in Scotland and *Plaid Cymru* in Wales). These parties try to be liberal and communalistic simultaneously.

Irish Roman Catholicism: Historically, the Irish Church was much less interested in taking orders from Rome than most continental churches or even the English church prior to the Reformation era. The modern Irish Catholic Church has had a nationalist tinge and a conservative hold on various institutions in Irish society including the educational establishment. Secularism in Ireland has slowly taken root and undermined the Church's long held authority in the social arena. Conservatives and traditionalists frown on this and liberals, radicals, and secularists welcome this development.

Irish Gaelic (Gaeilge): The Irish language, also known as Irish Gaelic or *Gaeilge*, has been taught in many of Ireland's sectarian schools. Just over 1 ½ million Irish speak *Gaeilge*. It is the official language of the Republic of Ireland, yet due to the history of British control of Ireland, English has continued to dominate as the language of society in Éire.

Agrarian Society: A society that patterns its social and economic development on agriculture and its concomitant economic and social benefits. Most Celtic areas were once agrarian societies. These societies gave way to industrial development and then after 1945 the service economy. Ireland continued (in both the south and north) to be the dominant agrarian society in both the Celtic world and British Isles until the 1960s when industry and services began changing the shape of Irish society.

Irish Civil War: The internecine struggle between Irish partisans (pro and anti-treaty factions) after the devolved political settlement with Britain in 1921. The war was fought in 1922 and some 4000 Irish were killed.

Chapel Culture: The nineteenth century development in Wales that saw some 8000 nonconformist Protestant chapels erected that led to a flowering of Christianity, Welsh all-male choirs, and the rise of Welsh cultural identity and nationalism.

Evangelical Christianity: Characterized by individuals who take the Bible literally and practice its teachings. A heavy emphasis is placed on Christ as personal savior. This was the norm in Wales in the late eighteenth and into the nineteenth century as Methodism advanced and religious and national revival swept the land.

Anglo-Welsh Identity: Individuals who see themselves as Welsh, but have either lived their entire lives in England or immigrated to England from Wales. They may speak no Welsh and have rarely traveled to Wales, but still consider themselves more Welsh than English. The absorption of Wales by the English politically after 1284 led to this amorphous development. Today, thousands of Anglo-Welsh live in large English cities and intermarriage among Welsh and English natives have led to greater amalgamation of the two nations.

Welsh Diaspora: The thousands of Welsh (both indigenous and non-indigenous) persons who live in large English cities and continue to identify with the Welsh nation and its culture.

Ulster: In Irish history, Ulster was the nine counties of the north of the island of Ireland. Six are now in the British statelet of Northern Ireland; they are Antrim, Armagh, Down, Fermanagh, Londonderry, and Tyrone. The other three are in the southern Republic; they are Cavan (*an Cabhán*), Donegal (*Dún na nGall*), and Monaghan (*Muineachán*). In recent British history, the six counties in Britain's Northern Ireland province have been called "Ulster." Thus, southern Irish Catholic sentiment prefers the nine county definition and the northern Irish Protestant sentiment prefers the six county label.

Republicans: Irish people that prefer Northern Ireland to be part of the Republic of Ireland in the South. The term "republican" refers to the Republic.

Nationalists: Irish people in either the north or south of Ireland that favor the Irish nation as found in the southern Republic in Dublin. He or she would want the island united as one Ireland.

Unionists: Irish people that prefer Northern Ireland to continue to be part of the United Kingdom and maintain the "union" with Britain.

Loyalists: Irish people that favor the continued alignment of Northern Ireland with Britain politically. He or she would remain "loyal" to the United Kingdom and its monarch.

Britishness: A kind of national identity that is in the minority in the United Kingdom (UK). It is found in the form of British nationalism or patriotism in Northern Ireland among unionist groups. It has also been espoused by British prime minister Gordon Brown. Brown has called for a regionally distinct UK (where Celtic and English national identity flower), but an emboldened British national identity to strengthen the unitary state.

Ulster Protestants: The dominant majority in Northern Ireland making up some 53% of the population in the statelet. These are individuals who are Protestant (usually Scottish Presbyterian or Anglican). They are in the minority overall on the Emerald Isle.

Scotch-Irish: The dominant majority of Protestants in Northern Ireland who are descended from Scottish settlers sent to Ulster in the seventeenth century to continue British colonization of the area. Today, some 26 million Americans are descendants of Scotch-Irish including former American presidents Woodrow Wilson, Ronald Reagan and Bill Clinton.

Northern Irish Catholics: They make up a minority of the six counties in the Northern Irish statelet, but are the largest Christian denomination in the region. Catholics make up some 44% of citizens in Northern Ireland.

Gaelic Sports: The two dominant Gaelic sports are hurling (*iománaíocht*) and Gaelic football (*caid*). These sports are played in Ireland (both parts of the south and north), but are predominantly found in the Republic. They are governed by the Gaelic Athletic Association (*Cumann Lúthchleas Gael*) which is the predominant governing body of Gaelic sports in Ireland. Gaelic sports are found in Scotland as well. Shinty (*camanachd*) is similar to hurling, but played on a smaller field with a different stick. Shinty is found mainly in the Scottish Highlands and islands.

Sectarian Division: The historical (and at times seemingly irreparable) divide between religious confessions in a society. This has been seen in Ireland between Christians—Catholics and Protestants in the north. This is seen in other contexts globally such as the social and political rifts between Christians and Muslims in Lebanon or in intra-faith struggles between Sunni and Shia Muslims in Iraq today.

Direct Rule: The governing of Northern Ireland from London by fiat from 1972–98. The home rule assembly in Belfast was suspended and the British government under Harold Wilson took over direct rule of the province. Attempts were made at jump starting the suspended legislative process, but none took root until 1998 and even then Stormont was suspended in 2002 and finally elections were held and a power-sharing assembly reconvened in 2007.

Power-sharing Assembly: The attempt to start a democratic legislature with fixed representation from all sectarian communities in Northern Ireland after 1998. Legislative elections were held in 1998, 2003, and 2007. The power-sharing assembly (which allowed the majority Protestants and unionists to control most portfolios in the statetlet's cabinet while sharing power with the Catholics and nationalists) was suspended in 2002 but jump-started again in 2007.

Crofting: The system of small landholder farming in the Highlands and islands of Scotland. It has largely ended, but some small crofters are still there today.

Oil: Oil was found by British Petroleum in the North Sea off Scotland's coast in 1970. It has been a major component of Britain's and the globe's energy economy ever since. Some 10-15,000 people live and work for oil firms on 130 oil rigs off Scotland's coast in the North Sea today.

Scottish Financial Services Sector: Home to famous banks like the Royal Bank of Scotland, Scotland has become one of the United Kingdom's and Europe's important financial services centers. By 2005, 51% of jobs in Scotland's finance economy were in Edinburgh (the Scottish capital) and 26% in Glasgow (Scotland's biggest city).

European Economic Community: The forerunner of today's European Union (EU). The international organization was created in 1958 with the implementation of the Rome treaty and it created a movement toward a common market for goods, people, and capital among its nine members (Belgium, the Netherlands, Luxembourg, West Germany, France, and Italy) at the time. Today, the EU has 27 members and over 495 million citizens in its purview.

Light Manufacturing: The development of electronics and other types of manufacturing that still employs production line methods, but may not require the back-breaking labor (like heavy manufacturing—steel and coal production) of other eras. The Celtic areas have seen an upswing in the production of computers, microprocessors, electronics, and other light manufacturing since the late 1980s.

Aer Lingus: The national air carrier of Ireland. It was created by the Irish government in 1936 and by the early twenty-first century was a owned by the Irish government, its employees, and private companies in a true mixed economic model not unlike other European conglomerates like Volkswagen, the German automobile.

Eircom: The Irish state telecommunications company. It started under the post office in 1893 in Ireland and then became a separate telephone company owned by the government. Under broadening globalization, it was privatized in 1999. A multi-billion dollar business, globalization led to it becoming entwined with a private companies from outside Ireland and closer ties to other European states. Thus, forging closer EU cooperation in the marketplace in a functional sense.

Celtic Tiger Economies: Éire was the leader of the Celtic economies as it grew at unprecedented levels from 1995-2000. The Irish economy grew at 10% annually during those years. Fueled largely by the growth of tourism, light manufacturing in the electronics sector, and an increase in services, the Irish economy began to see its labor pool increase as fewer Irish sought to emigrate (a problem with a 150- year history). Scotland's economy grew due to growth in similar sectors and both Ireland and Scotland's rich entrepreneurial leaders started to keep their resources in indigenous ventures. The lone exception to economic fortune in the late 1990s and early twenty-first century appeared to be Wales who had stagnation as historical industries such as slate and coal were completely dried up and tourism, although growing, was not enough to give the economy the kind of boost seen in Scotland and Ireland.

Mining: The great engine of the nineteenth century British Empire. It was found in Wales and Scotland. The Welsh coal mining industry was all but dried up by the 1960s. By 1989, only 11 coalmines operated in Wales. Five years later, only one was left.

Slate: A staple of the northern Wales economy. It was here that the globe's slate industry found its prowess in the nineteenth and early twentieth century. It was used to construct roads and for roof shingles. Today, most slate is mined in Spain, although some of it is still gleaned from Wales.

Coal: Coal was the king of the modern world economy in the nineteenth century as industrialization occurred in Britain. It was mined for great wealth in Scotland and Wales. Despite its decline, it was still a powerful economic and political tool in Britain and Europe as Britain was kept out of the European Coal and Steel Community in 1952. In 1945, Wales had 212 coal mines. By 1994, it had one left. "King Coal" had been replaced by oil as the engine of the late twentieth century global economy.

Unconventional Politics: The use of methods of getting one's point across that are not conventional in the political arena, such as protest or even political intimidation (or even terrorism). Some nationalist groups like *Meibion Glyndŵr* (Sons of Glyndŵr) burned English summer homes in northern Wales and the Provisional Irish Republican Army attacked British military installations in Northern Ireland to make political points via "unconventional" political means.

Tourism: A key staple in the modern global economy is tourism. This is the promotion of the community, region, and state as an attractive place for visitors from out of the area to holiday, visit temporarily, and spend time in so as to learn more about the area and to spend money to bring capital into the area. It has become a purposeful economic sector in the modern global service economy. Many areas of the Celtic fringe, such as south Wales and the central lowlands of Scotland have adapted formerly heavy manufacturing areas to service economy-based regions were tourism is one of the top economic sectors today.

Harold Wilson: The Labour premier in Britain from 1964–76. He was known for attempting to bring the United Kingdom's economy forward via planned economic growth. Along with Tory premier Ted Heath (1970-74), he was also responsible for guiding direct rule after the start of the Troubles in Northern Ireland.

"White Heat of Technology:" The phrase attributed to the Wilson government's economic development policies in Britain in the 1960s. Prime Minister Harold Wilson hoped that new technological advancements would help Britain jump start its economy and allow for regional prosperity and growth.

Economic Discrimination: The use of discriminatory tactics in assigning jobs based on class and religious background. This was a problem in Northern Ireland after the division of the island in 1921, but became a bone of contention for civil rights activists (mainly Catholics) in the 1960s in Northern Ireland.

MacBride Principles: The United States government's attempt to tie fairness in investment policies to free trade with Britain in Northern Ireland. It tried to use the work of Seán MacBride, an Irish republican and peace activist and United Nations official, who wanted to help Catholics who were dislocated by economic discrimination. MacBride won the 1974 Nobel Peace Prize.

Convergence and Harmonization: The goal of the European Union in converging economies via European monetary and political union and harmonizing member states' laws so as to make the free movement of people, goods, and capital easier. The Celtic areas are watching this process affect them both at the national levels (in Dublin and London) and at the sub-national levels in Edinburgh, Cardiff, and Belfast.

Statism and Protectionism: "Statism" is the concept of the state playing a guiding, if not leading role, in the economy. The state may be the dominant player in several economic sectors controlling various industrious (wholly or in part). "Protectionaism" is a form of economic nationalism in which the state attempts to "protect" its companies and industries from outside pressure via setting high tariffs on goods (imports) coming in from other states.

"Disruption:" The event where the split occurred in the Church of Scotland in 1843 when evangelicals left and formed the Free Church of Scotland. Later subsequent splits in the Free Church led to the formation of an off-shoot denomination called "the Free Church of Scotland" after the original Free Church had unified with another church. The new small Free Church (after 1900) was called the "Wee Frees." They are different from the more conservative and austere "Wee Wee Frees," or the Free Presbyterian Church of Scotland (found largely in the Highlands).

Gàidhlig (Scottish Gaelic): The Gaelic language found in Scotland and spoken mainly in the Highlands and islands. It is spoken by roughly 60,000 people in Scotland.

Gaeilge (Irish or Irish Gaelic): The Irish Gaelic or Irish language is found in Ireland and spoken by 1.5 million people (1/4 of all Irish).

Gaeltacht (Gaelic-speaking Region): An area where large parts of the Irish population speaks Irish Gaelic. These are found mainly in the western and southern parts of the Republic of Ireland.

Ulster-Scots Language: A language which is a combination of Scots and English that is spoken in Northern Ireland by two percent of the population (around 20,000 people).

Scots Language: An ancient language spoken in Scotland which is a derivative of English which was found in Scotland by the fourth century AD. Around 1.5 million speak the language in Scotland. Many English words have evolved from Scots words such as "cuddle."

Cymraeg (Welsh): Cymraeg, the Welsh language, is the word for "Welsh." The Welsh language is spoken by 20.5% of the Welsh population. Due to cultural and political nationalism in the twentieth century, *Cymraeg* once an all but dead language has revived and, under the sponsorship of the British and Welsh governments, *Cymraeg* has flourished in schools, television, culture, and arts.

Football (Soccer): The English game invented in the late nineteenth century and sent around the world by British merchants, missionaries, traders, and educators. It is the world's most popular sport and is relatively easy to play—all you need is a ball and few accoutrements.

George Best (1946–2005): The Northern Irish football star who was European player of the year in 1968 and led Manchester United to a European Cup (now UEFA Champions League) title in the same year. He was capped (played in international matches for his country, Northern Ireland) 37 times scoring nine goals. Like English star David Beckham, he played part of his latter career in the United States in the 1970s. Some called him the greatest forward (striker) of his generation. Off the field, he had a turbulent personal life and died of kidney failure in 2005.

"The Old Firm:" The two Scottish Premier League clubs, Glasgow Rangers and Glasgow Celtic. The two are called "the Old Firm" because they have dominated Scottish soccer since its inception in the late nineteenth century and some argue that the two have colluded like monopolistic companies (hence "the Old Firm" moniker) to keep a lock on Scottish football, its glory, and revenues. It is reminiscent of the Americans' National Basketball Association in the 1980s with the Los Angeles Lakers and the Boston Celtics dominating the league for over a decade. Of course, "the Old Firm" has its historical downside of sectarianism and division which helped stoke passions not only between Catholics and Protestants in Scotland, but in Northern Ireland during "the Troubles" as well.

Gaelic Football (Caid): This is a game similar to soccer and rugby played in Ireland. It is played with 15 on each side and games last 60 minutes. Points are scored by kicking a round ball over goalposts (like American football) or in the goal under the goal posts (like global football/soccer). It is one of the two signpost Gaelic sports (along with hurling).

Hurling (Iománaíocht): This is one of the two major Gaelic sports and it is played with a stick (somewhat like a hockey stick) and a small ball. Its pitch and scoring are exactly like Gaelic Football. It is a mixture of field hockey and la crosse.

Shinty (Camanachd): This is the Scottish game that evolved from hurling in the 1300s. It is played with a stick (*caman*) and a small ball largely in the Scottish Gaelic-speaking areas of the Highlands and Islands of Scotland. Its rules are a bit different from hurling, but the game is roughly the same in the main. A similar game is played on the Isle of Man; it is called *Cammag*.

Chapter 7

Regionalism: In comparative politics or history, regionalism is the study of areas where common regional linkages occur such as economics, language, religion, and culture are found. In the study of international relations regionalism refers to a grouping of states to form a regional bloc based on geo-political or economic considerations, such as the European Union or the North Atlantic Treaty Organization.

Intergovernmentalism: When nation-states join international organizations to work on common problems and issues, but give up some sovereignty and retain the majority of their sovereignty in their national governments so as not to allow the international organization to have complete say in all matters of politics, economics, and security. The European Union today is an example of intergovernmentalism in most areas.

Supranationalism: The voluntary pooling of sovereignty by states in the form of an international organization (IO) that allows the IO to gain sovereignty and power over its members states and the move from an intergovernmental IO to a supranational (above and beyond the nation-state) begins to occur. The European Union is today is moving in a greater supranational direction today.

EU's Committee of Regions: The European Union (EU) body that represents sub-national interests at Brussels. It is a key component in the growing area of EU-sub-state/regional relations.

Functionalism: The international relations theory that argues that prior to international political integration that "functionalist" approaches to international harmony and integration must (and do empirically) occur first, especially in the areas of economics, social (culture, sports, etc), and technical relations since all countries can agree on the need for these things. The most famous functionalism theorists in the sub-discipline of international relations in the field of political science were Ernst B. Haas and David Mitrany.

Global Governance: The increasing movement toward global (as opposed to state-centric or even regional) approaches to problem-solving and governance of political issues. It is issue-focused and produces a global level of analysis for problems (such as environment, health concerns, and global economic convergence). International organizations like the United Nations and various regional IOs play a major role in working with nation-states in the global governance movement.

Political Systems Analysis: The dominant behavioral paradigm created by American political scientist David Easton in 1958 which conceptualizes political processes and government action as a system (like a series of symbiotic organisms and functions in a scientific system in studying the human body). The "political system" allows for parts to be broken down and studied in more precise and scientific rigor empirically and methodologically.

Multi-level Governance (MLG): Multi-level governance (MLG) is a political science theory that applies to the study of international organizations (IOs) like the European Union and its relationship with nation-states. MLG is based on the idea that governance occurs not just between the nation-state and its government and IOs, but a varying levels such as the sub-state level and even at the trans-national level. Certainly, MLG is seen in the Celtic regions of Britain and Ireland as Scotland and Wales have access channels in Brussels (as well as representation from the United Kingdom in Brussels as well). The theory has been posited by political scientist Gary Marks and others.

Index